ALL·NEW

GHOST RIDER

LEGEND

ALL-NEW GHOST RIDER VOL. 2: LEGEND. Contains material originally published in magazine form as ALL-NEW GHOST RIDER #6-12. First printing 2015. ISBN# 978-0-7851-5456-3. Published by MARVEL WORLDWIDE, INC., a subsidiary of MARVEL ENTERTAINMENT, LLC. OFFICE OF PUBLICATION: 135 West 50th Street, New York, NY 10020. Copyright © 2015 MARVEL No similarity between any of the names, characters, persons, and/or institutions in this magazine with those of any living or dead person or institution is intended, and any such similarity which may exist is purely coincidental. **Printed in the U.S.A.** ALAN FINE, President, Marvel Entertainment; DAN BUCKLEY, President, TV, Publishing and Brand Management; JOE QUESADA, Chief Creative Officer; TOM BREVOORT, SVP of Publishing; DAVID BOGART, SVP of Operations & Procurement, Publishing; B. CEBULSKI, VP of International Development & Brand Management; DAVID GABRIEL, SVP Print, Sales & Marketing; JIM O'KEEFE, VP of Operations & Logistics; DAN CARR, Executive Director of Publishing Technology; SUSAN CRESPI, Editorial Operations Manager; ALEX MORALES, Publishing Operations Manager; STAN LEE, Chairman Emeritus. For information regarding advertising in Marvel Comics or on Marvel.com, please contact Jonathan Rheingold, VP of Custom Solutions & Ad Sales, at jrheingold@marvel.com. For Marvel subscription inquiries, please call 800-217-9158. **Manufactured between 3/27/2015 and 5/4/2015 by R.R. DONNELLEY, INC., SALEM, VA, USA.**

10 9 8 7 6 5 4 3 2 1

ALL-NEW

GHOST RIDER

LEGEND

WRITER FELIPE SMITH

#6-10
PENCILER DAMION SCOTT
INKERS ROBERT CAMPANELLA (#6-7)
& CORY HAMSCHER (#8-10)
WITH VICTOR OLAZABA (#9) & DON HO (#9)

#11-12
ARTISTS FELIPE SMITH (#11-12) **& KRIS ANKA** (#12)

COLORISTS **VAL STAPLES** WITH **NELSON DANIEL** (#6) **& ESTHER SANZ** (#8)
LETTERER **VC'S JOE CARAMAGNA**

COVER ARTISTS **TRADD MOORE & FELIPE SOBREIRO** (#6);
DAMION SCOTT, ROB CAMPANELLA & GURU-EFX (#7);
DAMION SCOTT & VAL STAPLES (#8-9); **DAMION SCOTT &**
BRAD ANDERSON (#10); **FIONA STAPLES** (#11); **AND FELIPE SMITH** (#12)

ASSISTANT EDITOR **EMILY SHAW**
EDITOR **MARK PANICCIA**

THE GHOST RIDER.

DEAD OR ALIVE?

GOOD OR EVIL?

ANGEL OR DEMON?

FOR YEARS, A DARK VIGILANTE HAS
WALKED THE LINE BETWEEN TWO WORLDS,
HAUNTING THE DREAMS OF BAD GUYS
EVERYWHERE, STARING INTO THEIR SOULS
WITH FLAMING EYES OF *VENGEANCE*.

BUT THIS IS NOT
THE GHOST RIDER YOU KNOW.

THIS IS THE TALE OF AN ORDINARY KID
NAMED *ROBBIE REYES*,
WHOSE LIFE IS ABOUT TO BECOME
A *HELL* OF A LOT LESS ORDINARY.

GET IN.

LET'S RIDE.

COLLECTION EDITOR: ALEX STARBUCK
ASSISTANT EDITOR: SARAH BRUNSTAD
EDITORS, SPECIAL PROJECTS: JENNIFER GRÜNWALD & MARK D. BEAZLEY
SENIOR EDITOR, SPECIAL PROJECTS: JEFF YOUNGQUIST
SVP PRINT, SALES & MARKETING: DAVID GABRIEL

EDITOR IN CHIEF: AXEL ALONSO
CHIEF CREATIVE OFFICER: JOE QUESADA
PUBLISHER: DAN BUCKLEY
EXECUTIVE PRODUCER: ALAN FINE

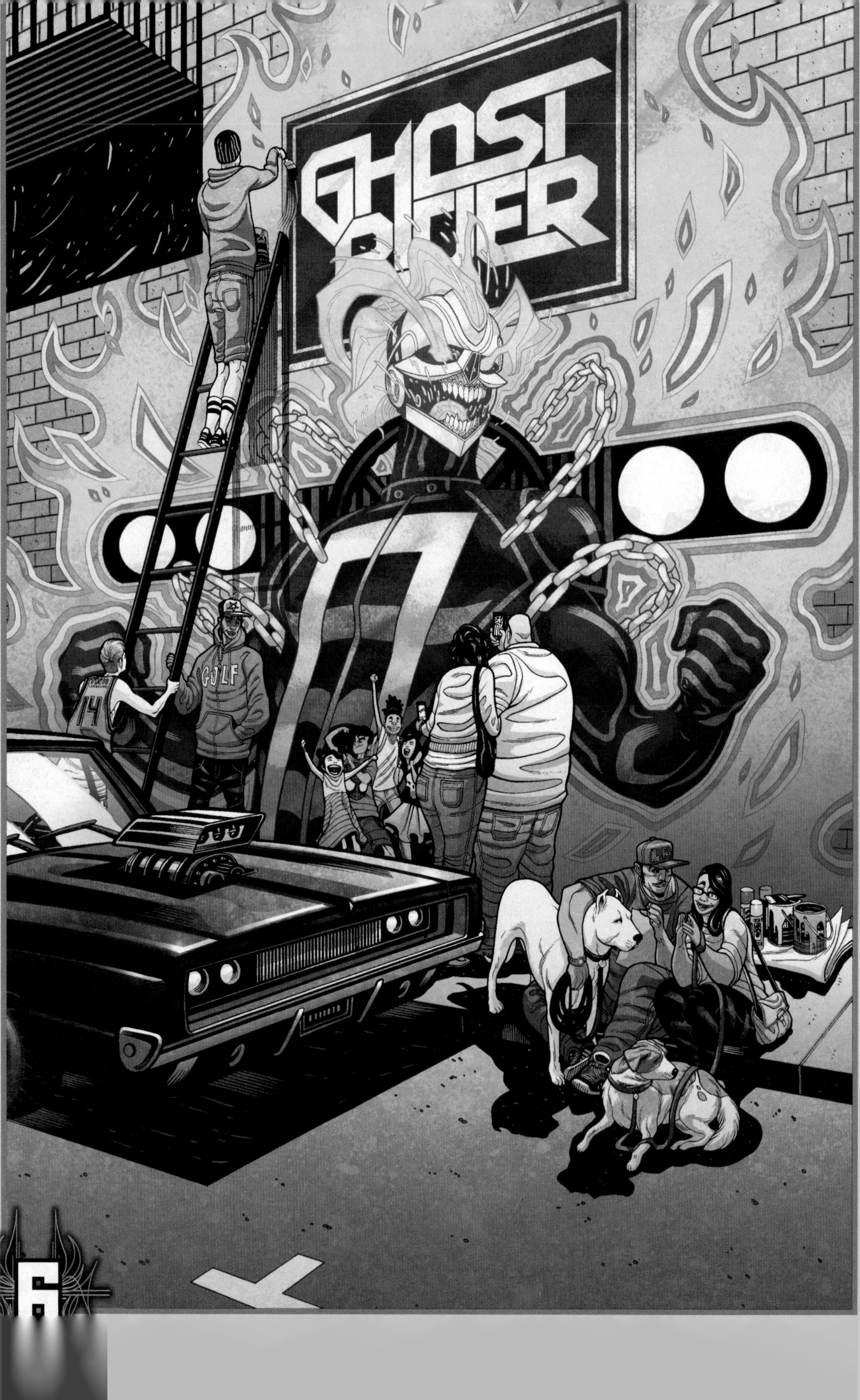
GHOST RIDER
GOLF
14
6

« SMALL-BLOCK V8 CRATE ENGINE : 900-HP
« 5.7-LITER OHV « 2600 RPM STALL TORQUE CONVERTER
« TURBOHYDRAMATIC 400 THREE-SPEED AUTOMATIC TRANSMISSION
« 0-60MPH 4.5 SEC
« MOPAR MADNESS

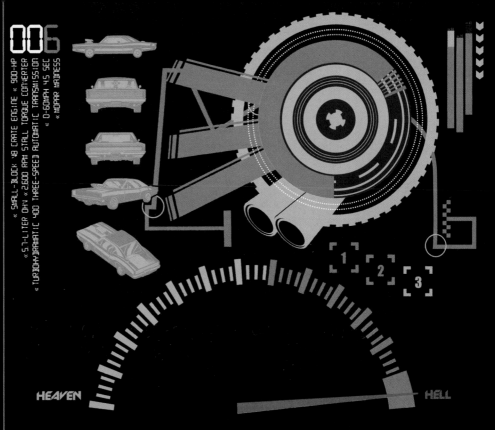

HEAVEN   HELL

GO. GO. GO.

ALL ROBBIE REYES WANTS IS TO PROTECT HIS DISABLED BROTHER, GABE.
GABE IS BULLIED BY ROBBIE'S CLASSMATES, GUERO AND HIS FRIENDS. THEY
EVEN STOLE GABE'S WHEELCHAIR.

ONE NIGHT, ROBBIE ENTERED A STREET RACE TO EARN SOME MONEY SO HE
AND GABE COULD MOVE TO A NEW NEIGHBORHOOD.

THE CAR ROBBIE BORROWED HAD STOLEN CONTRABAND IN ITS TRUNK
- PINK PILLS CREATED BY CARTEL LEADER, DR. ZABO. THE CARTEL SHOT
ROBBIE DEAD AND SET THE CAR ON FIRE.

THE CAR WAS ALSO HAUNTED BY A SPIRIT NAMED ELI MORROW.
MORROW BROUGHT ROBBIE BACK TO LIFE AND EMBEDDED HIMSELF IN
ROBBIE'S PSYCHE, GIVING ROBBIE THE POWER TO TRANSFORM INTO A
SUPERNATURAL BEING WITH INCREDIBLE STRENGTH AND SPEED.

AFTER AN ALL-OUT WAR BROKE OUT IN ROBBIE'S NEIGHBORHOOD
BETWEEN LOCAL GANGS AND ZABO'S CARTEL, ROBBIE WAS ABLE
TO USE HIS NEW POWERS TO FIGHT OFF ZABO'S MEN AND SAVE THE
NEIGHBORHOOD.

AFTERWARD, STILL DISGUISED AS THE SUPERNATURAL RACER, ROBBIE BEAT
UP GUERO AND HIS CREW AND TOOK BACK GABE'S WHEELCHAIR.

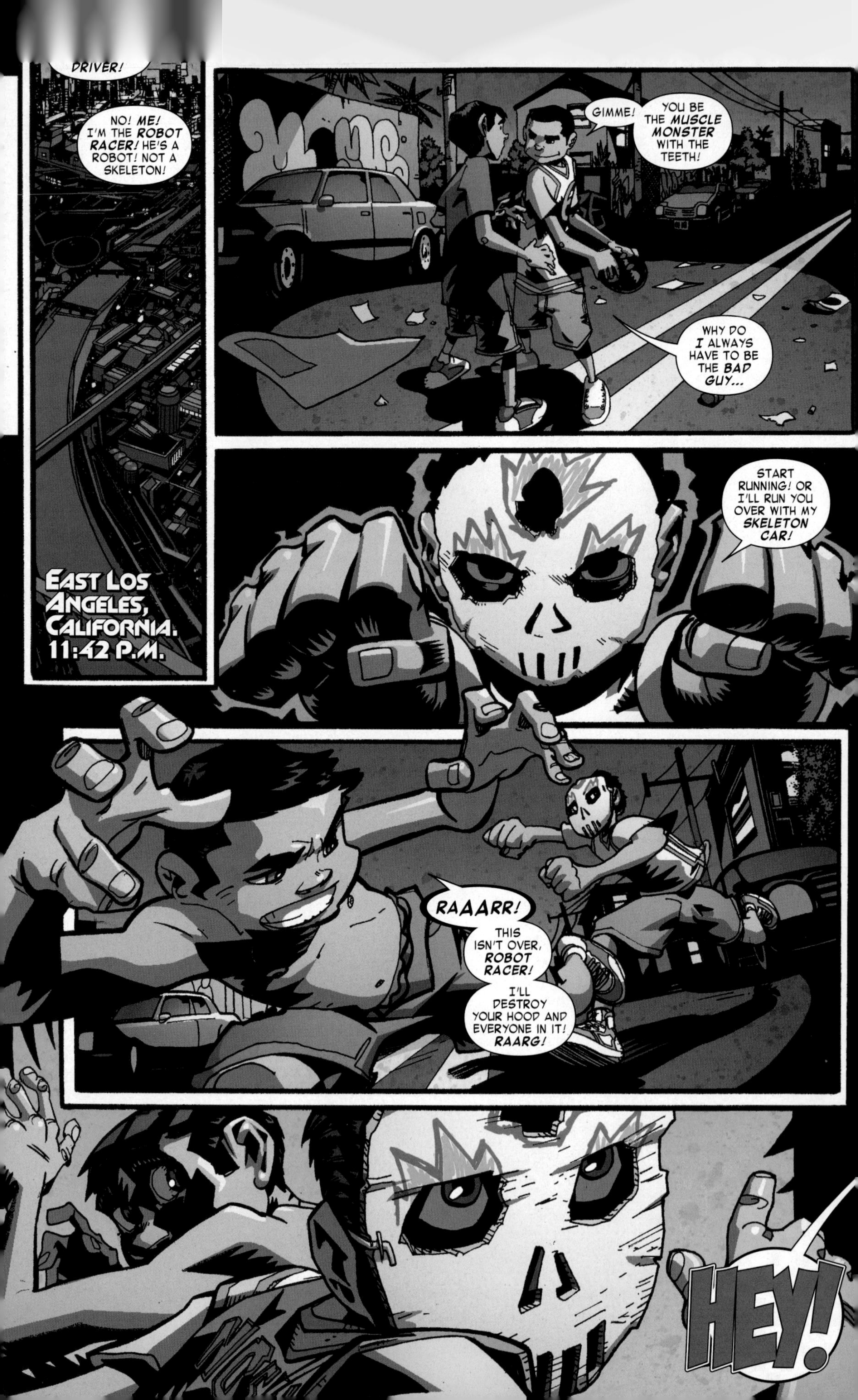
DRIVER!
NO! ME! I'M THE ROBOT RACER! HE'S A ROBOT! NOT A SKELETON!
GIMME!
YOU BE THE MUSCLE MONSTER WITH THE TEETH!
WHY DO I ALWAYS HAVE TO BE THE BAD GUY...
East Los Angeles, California. 11:42 P.M.
START RUNNING! OR I'LL RUN YOU OVER WITH MY SKELETON CAR!
RAAARR!
THIS ISN'T OVER, ROBOT RACER!
I'LL DESTROY YOUR HOOD AND EVERYONE IN IT! RAARG!
HEY!

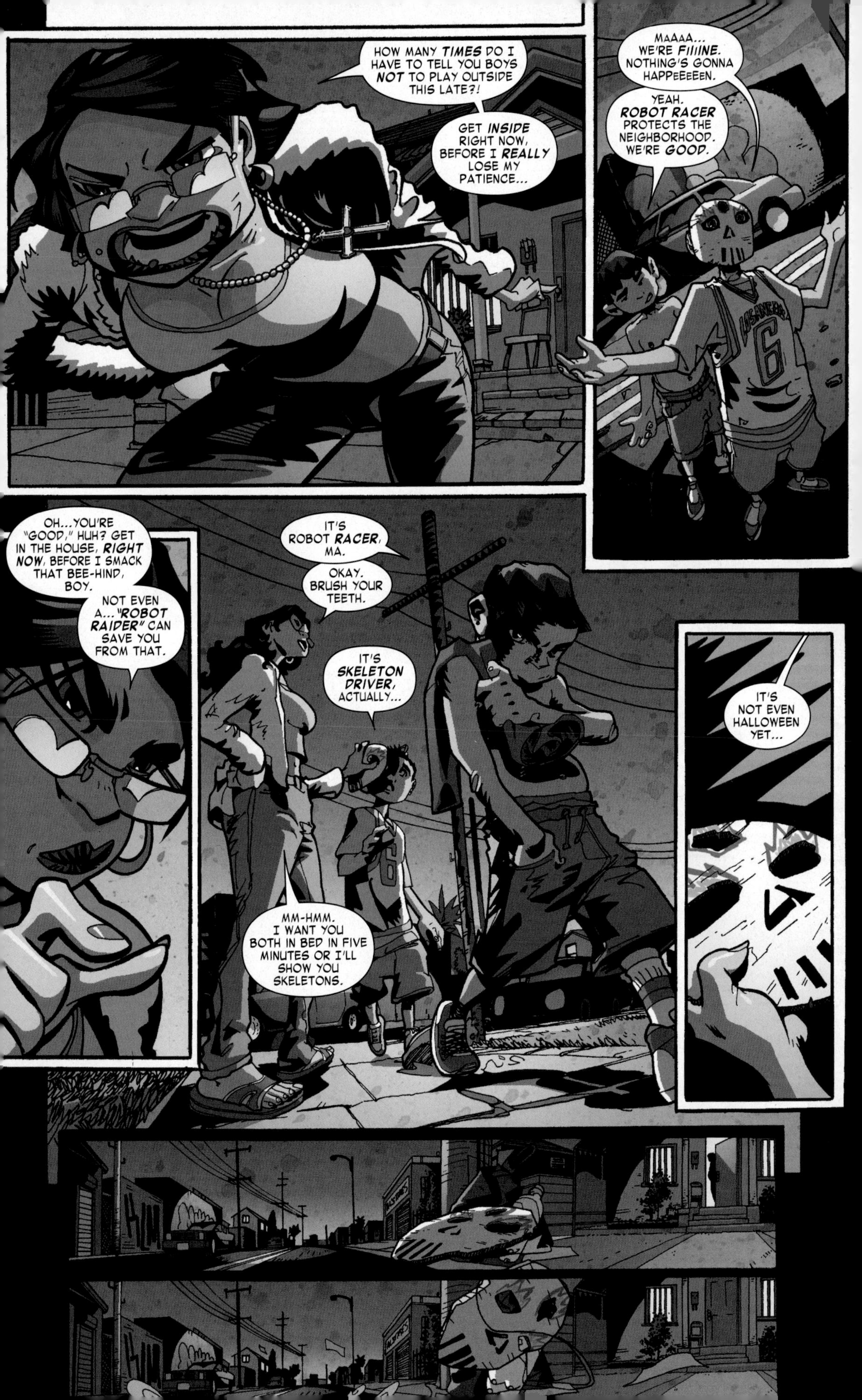
HOW MANY *TIMES* DO I HAVE TO TELL YOU BOYS *NOT* TO PLAY OUTSIDE THIS LATE?!
GET *INSIDE* RIGHT NOW, BEFORE I *REALLY* LOSE MY PATIENCE...
MAAAA... WE'RE *FIIIINE.* NOTHING'S GONNA HAPPEEEEEN.
YEAH. *ROBOT RACER* PROTECTS THE NEIGHBORHOOD. WE'RE *GOOD.*
OH...YOU'RE "GOOD," HUH? GET IN THE HOUSE, *RIGHT NOW*, BEFORE I SMACK THAT BEE-HIND, BOY.
NOT EVEN A..."*ROBOT RAIDER*" CAN SAVE YOU FROM THAT.
IT'S ROBOT *RACER*, MA.
OKAY. BRUSH YOUR TEETH.
IT'S *SKELETON DRIVER,* ACTUALLY...
MM-HMM. I WANT YOU BOTH IN BED IN FIVE MINUTES OR I'LL SHOW YOU SKELETONS.
IT'S NOT EVEN HALLOWEEN YET...

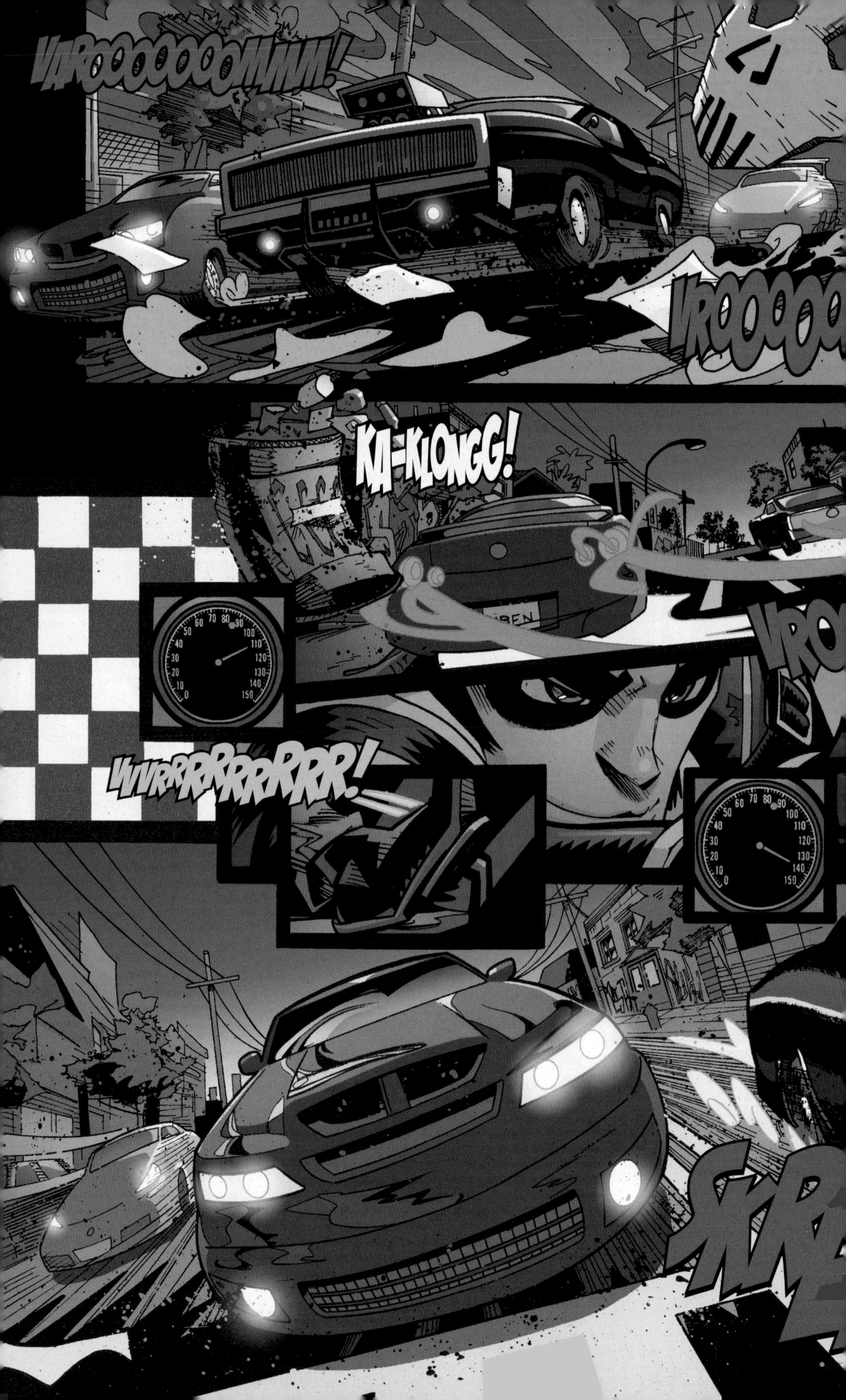
VAROOOOOOOMMMM!
VROOOOO
KA-KLONGG!
VRO
WVRRRRRRRRR!
SKR

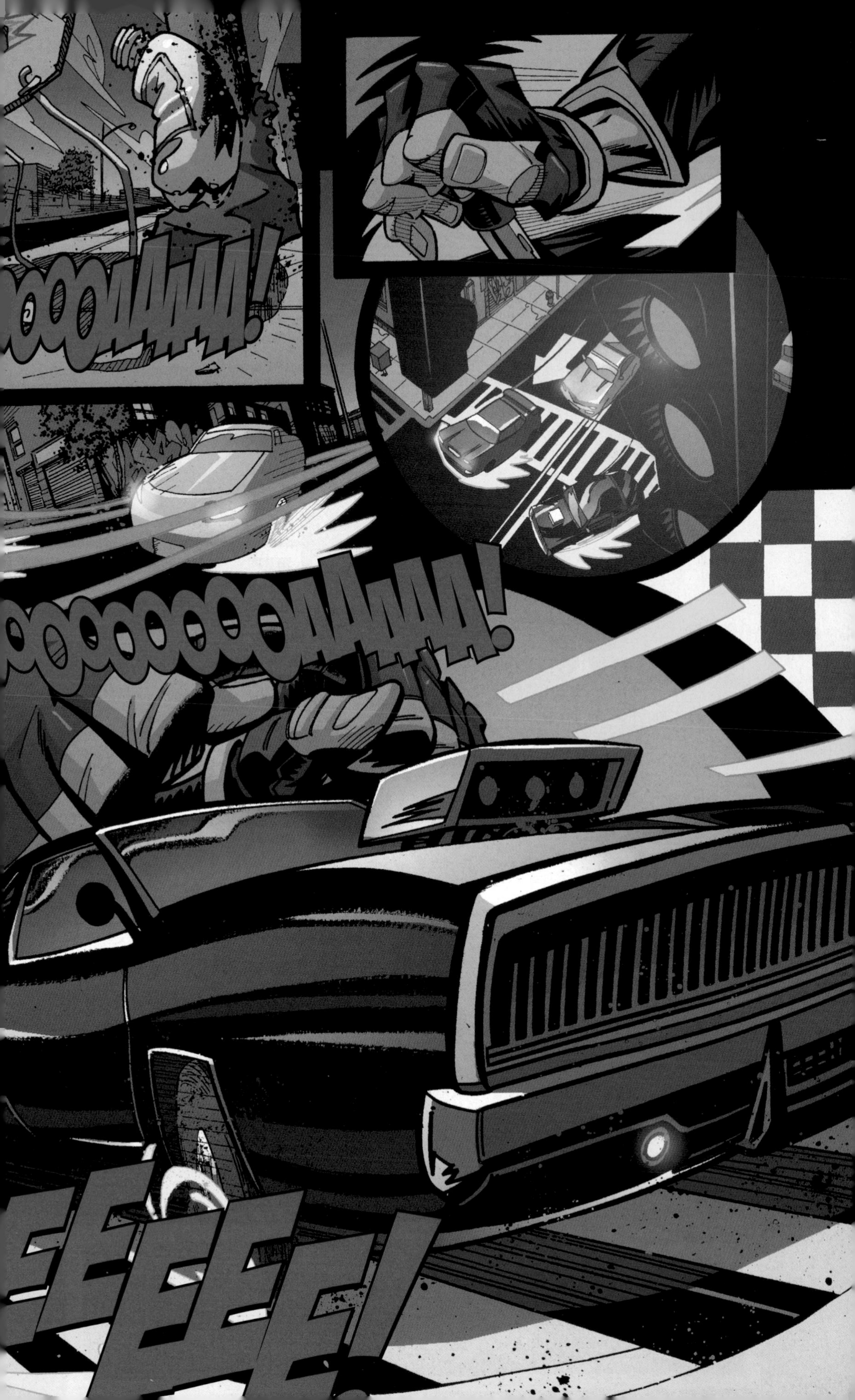

OOOOAAAAA!
OOOOOOOOOAAAAA!
EEEEEE!

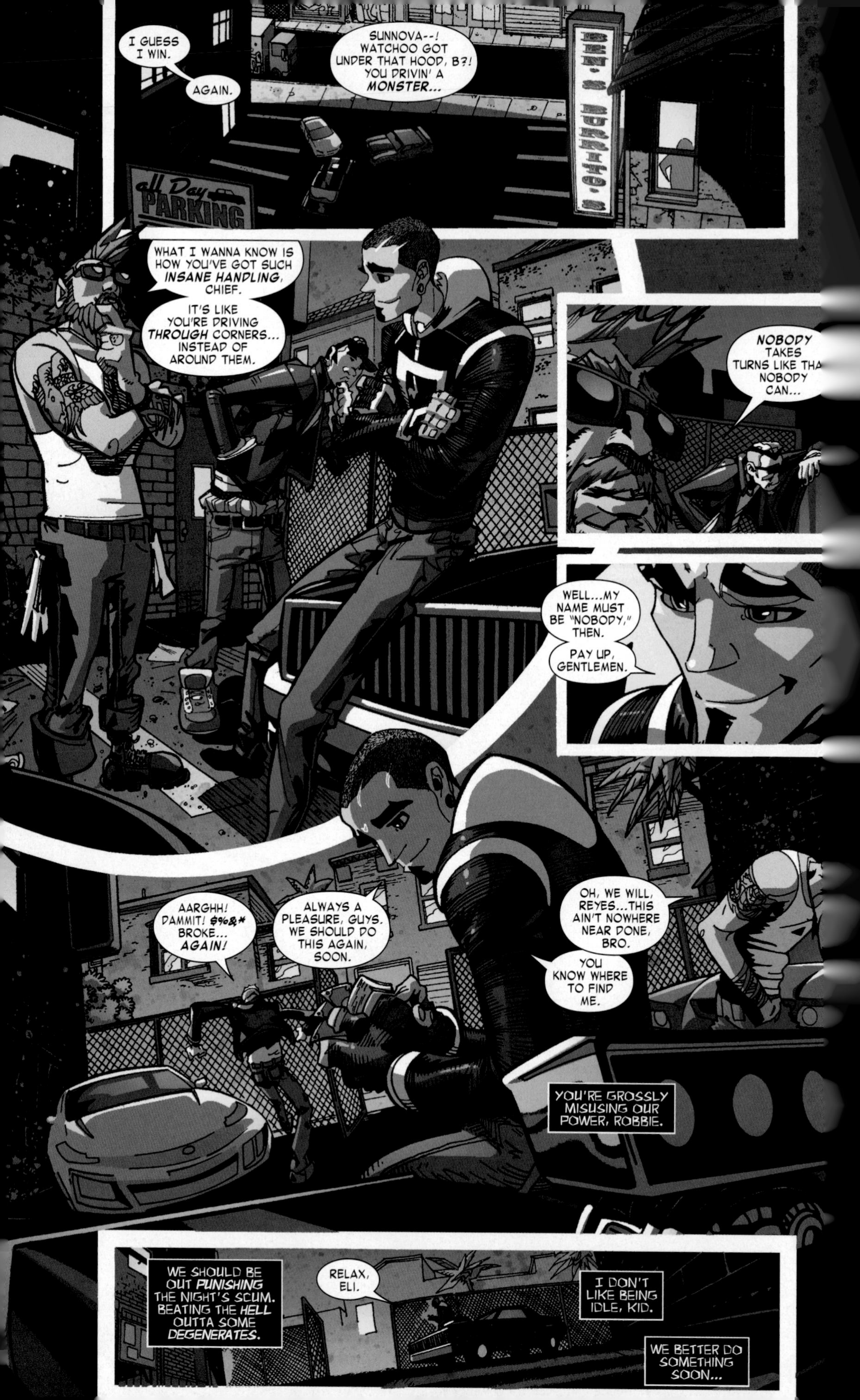
I GUESS I WIN.
AGAIN.
SUNNOVA--! WATCHOO GOT UNDER THAT HOOD, B?! YOU DRIVIN' A MONSTER...
BEN'S BURRITO'S
all Day PARKING
WHAT I WANNA KNOW IS HOW YOU'VE GOT SUCH INSANE HANDLING, CHIEF.
IT'S LIKE YOU'RE DRIVING THROUGH CORNERS... INSTEAD OF AROUND THEM.
NOBODY TAKES TURNS LIKE THA NOBODY CAN...
WELL...MY NAME MUST BE "NOBODY," THEN.
PAY UP, GENTLEMEN.
AARGHH! DAMMIT! $%&* BROKE... AGAIN!
ALWAYS A PLEASURE, GUYS. WE SHOULD DO THIS AGAIN, SOON.
OH, WE WILL, REYES...THIS AIN'T NOWHERE NEAR DONE, BRO.
YOU KNOW WHERE TO FIND ME.
YOU'RE GROSSLY MISUSING OUR POWER, ROBBIE.
WE SHOULD BE OUT PUNISHING THE NIGHT'S SCUM. BEATING THE HELL OUTTA SOME DEGENERATES.
RELAX, ELI.
I DON'T LIKE BEING IDLE, KID.
WE BETTER DO SOMETHING SOON...

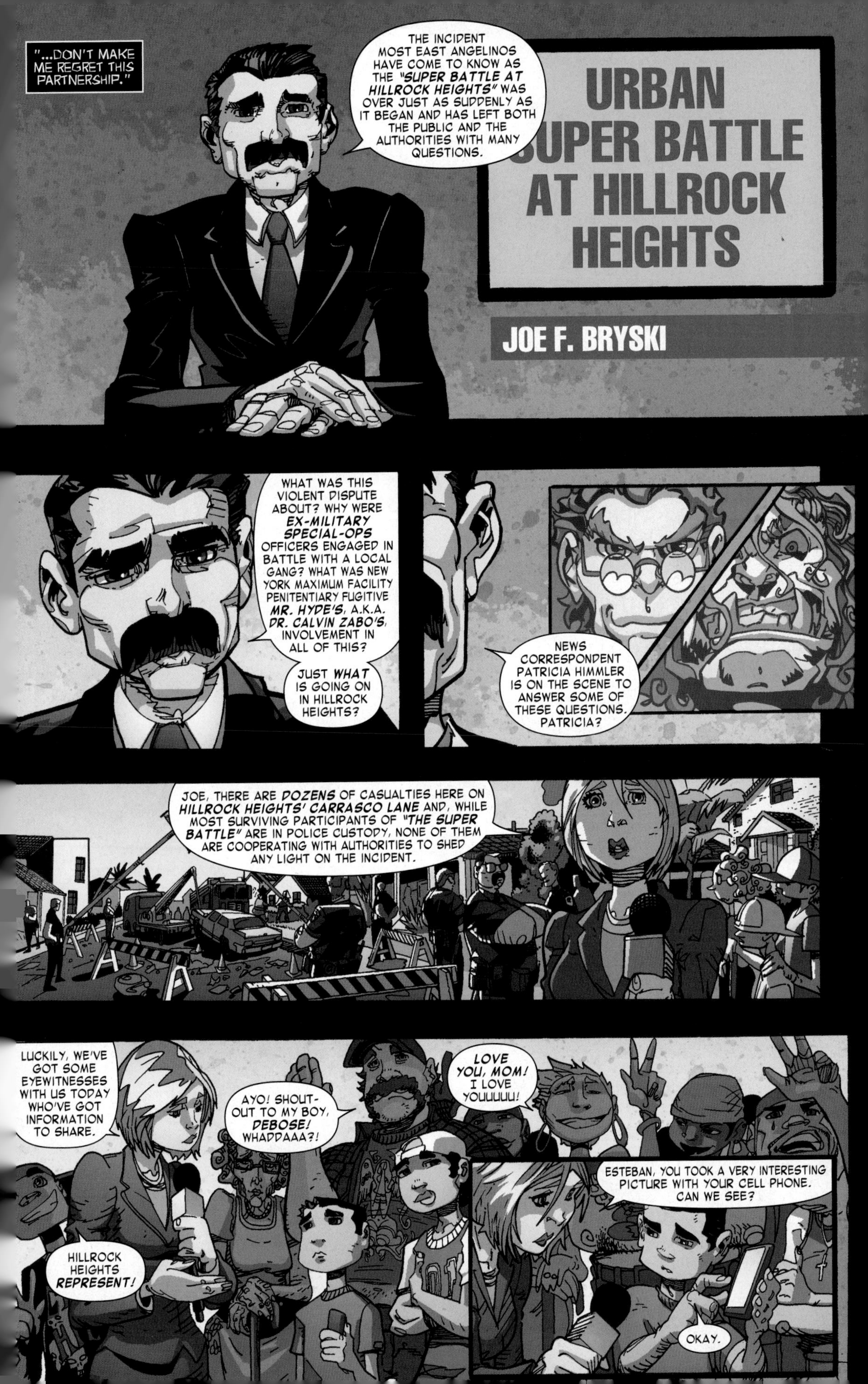
"...DON'T MAKE ME REGRET THIS PARTNERSHIP."
THE INCIDENT MOST EAST ANGELINOS HAVE COME TO KNOW AS THE "SUPER BATTLE AT HILLROCK HEIGHTS" WAS OVER JUST AS SUDDENLY AS IT BEGAN AND HAS LEFT BOTH THE PUBLIC AND THE AUTHORITIES WITH MANY QUESTIONS.
URBAN SUPER BATTLE AT HILLROCK HEIGHTS
JOE F. BRYSKI
WHAT WAS THIS VIOLENT DISPUTE ABOUT? WHY WERE EX-MILITARY SPECIAL-OPS OFFICERS ENGAGED IN BATTLE WITH A LOCAL GANG? WHAT WAS NEW YORK MAXIMUM FACILITY PENITENTIARY FUGITIVE MR. HYDE'S, A.K.A. DR. CALVIN ZABO'S, INVOLVEMENT IN ALL OF THIS?
JUST WHAT IS GOING ON IN HILLROCK HEIGHTS?
NEWS CORRESPONDENT PATRICIA HIMMLER IS ON THE SCENE TO ANSWER SOME OF THESE QUESTIONS. PATRICIA?
JOE, THERE ARE DOZENS OF CASUALTIES HERE ON HILLROCK HEIGHTS' CARRASCO LANE AND, WHILE MOST SURVIVING PARTICIPANTS OF "THE SUPER BATTLE" ARE IN POLICE CUSTODY, NONE OF THEM ARE COOPERATING WITH AUTHORITIES TO SHED ANY LIGHT ON THE INCIDENT.
LUCKILY, WE'VE GOT SOME EYEWITNESSES WITH US TODAY WHO'VE GOT INFORMATION TO SHARE.
AYO! SHOUT-OUT TO MY BOY, DEBOSE! WHADDAAA?!
LOVE YOU, MOM! I LOVE YOUUUUU!
HILLROCK HEIGHTS REPRESENT!
ESTEBAN, YOU TOOK A VERY INTERESTING PICTURE WITH YOUR CELL PHONE. CAN WE SEE?
OKAY.

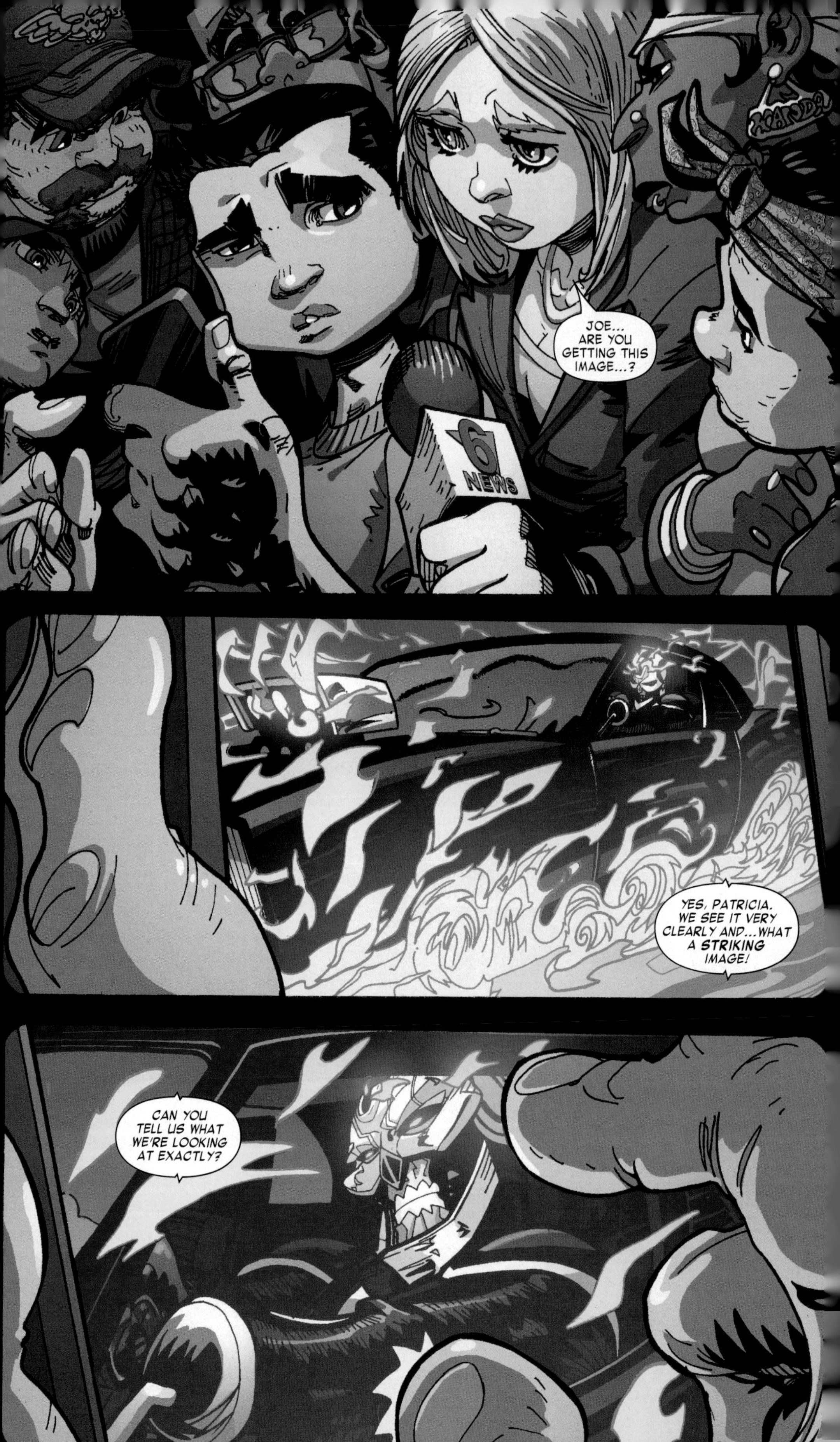
JOE... ARE YOU GETTING THIS IMAGE...?
6 NEWS
YES, PATRICIA. WE SEE IT VERY CLEARLY AND...WHAT A **STRIKING** IMAGE!
CAN YOU TELL US WHAT WE'RE LOOKING AT EXACTLY?

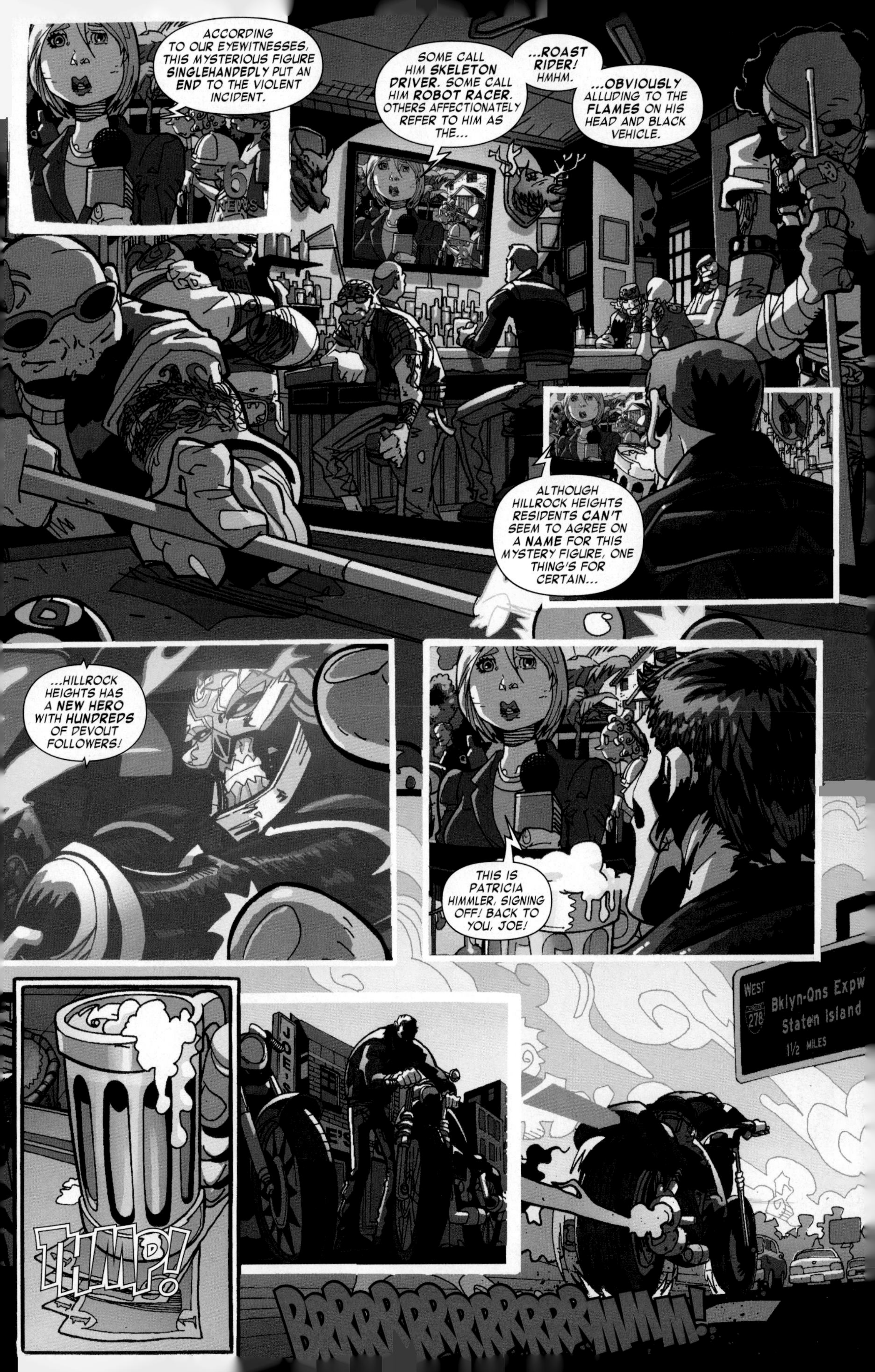
ACCORDING TO OUR EYEWITNESSES, THIS MYSTERIOUS FIGURE SINGLEHANDEDLY PUT AN END TO THE VIOLENT INCIDENT.
6 NEWS
SOME CALL HIM SKELETON DRIVER. SOME CALL HIM ROBOT RACER. OTHERS AFFECTIONATELY REFER TO HIM AS THE...
...ROAST RIDER! HMHM.
...OBVIOUSLY ALLUDING TO THE FLAMES ON HIS HEAD AND BLACK VEHICLE.
ALTHOUGH HILLROCK HEIGHTS RESIDENTS CAN'T SEEM TO AGREE ON A NAME FOR THIS MYSTERY FIGURE, ONE THING'S FOR CERTAIN...
...HILLROCK HEIGHTS HAS A NEW HERO WITH HUNDREDS OF DEVOUT FOLLOWERS!
THIS IS PATRICIA HIMMLER, SIGNING OFF! BACK TO YOU, JOE!
THMP!
WEST 278 Bklyn-Qns Expwy Staten Island 1½ MILES
BRRRRRRRRRRRRRMMM!

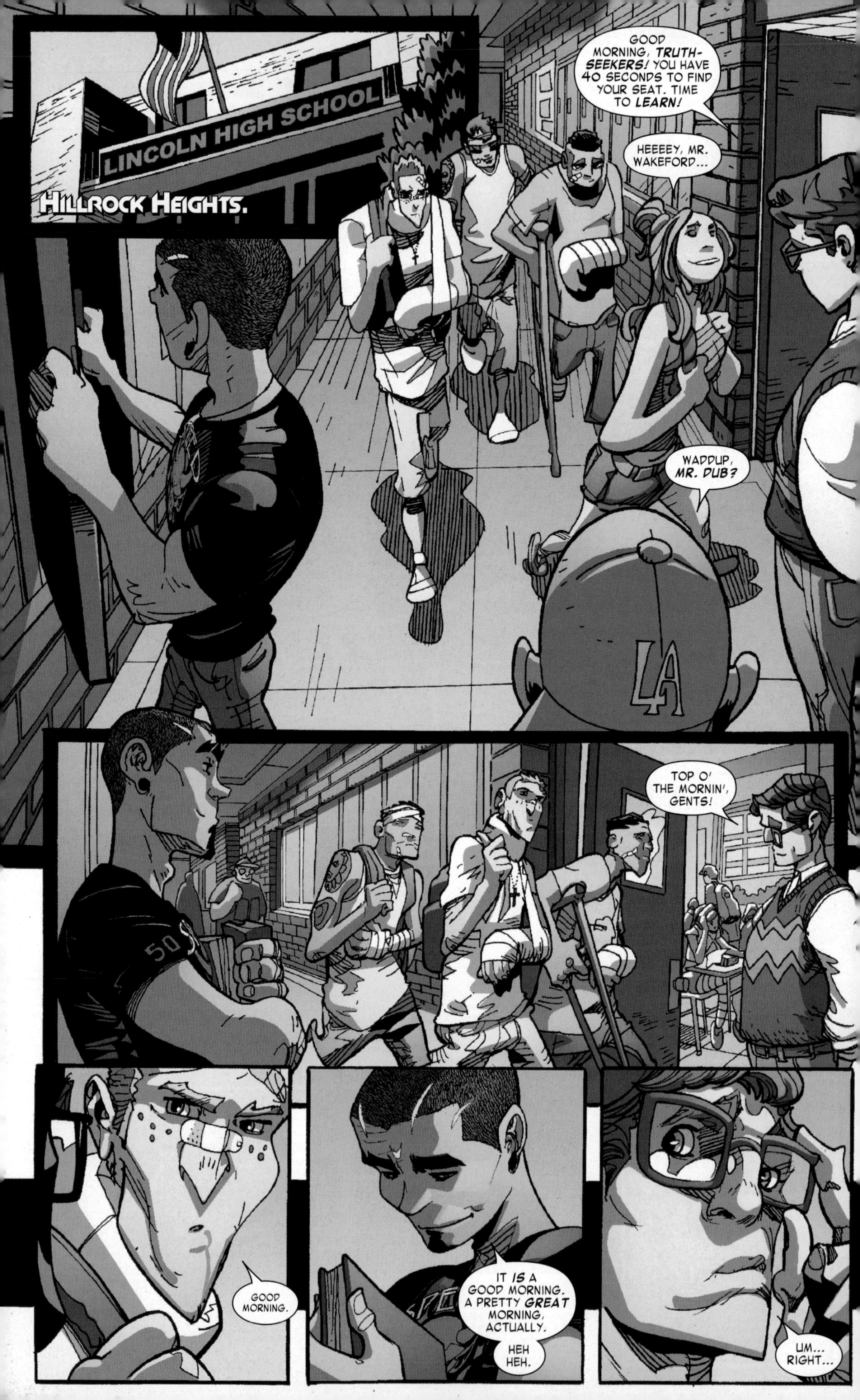
LINCOLN HIGH SCHOOL
HILLROCK HEIGHTS.
GOOD MORNING, TRUTH-SEEKERS! YOU HAVE 40 SECONDS TO FIND YOUR SEAT. TIME TO LEARN!
HEEEEY, MR. WAKEFORD...
WADDUP, MR. DUB?
LA
TOP O' THE MORNIN', GENTS!
50
GOOD MORNING.
IT IS A GOOD MORNING. A PRETTY GREAT MORNING, ACTUALLY.
HEH HEH.
UM... RIGHT...

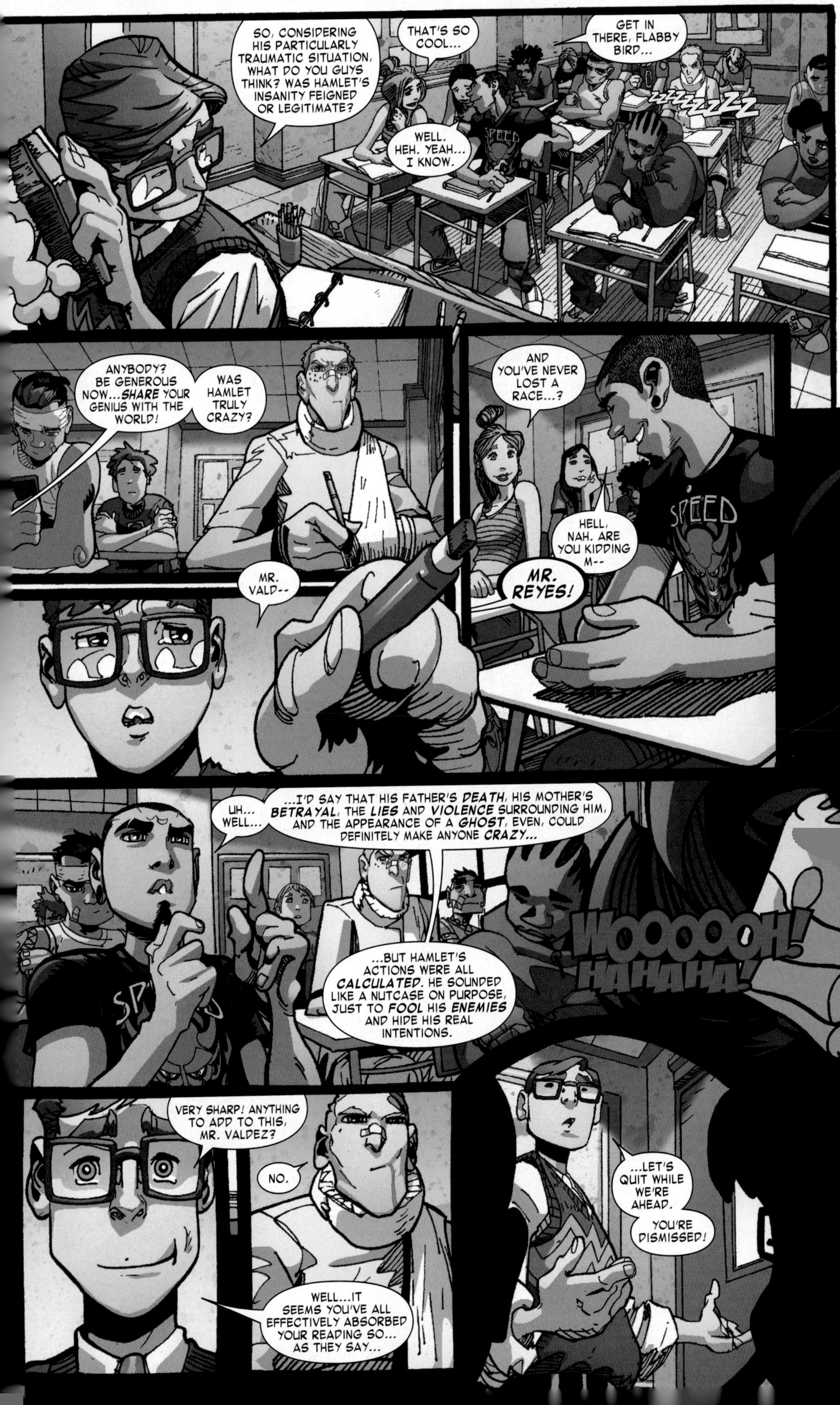
SO, CONSIDERING HIS PARTICULARLY TRAUMATIC SITUATION, WHAT DO YOU GUYS THINK? WAS HAMLET'S INSANITY FEIGNED OR LEGITIMATE?
THAT'S SO COOL...
GET IN THERE, FLABBY BIRD...
WELL. HEH. YEAH... I KNOW.
ZZZZZZZZZ
ANYBODY? BE GENEROUS NOW...SHARE YOUR GENIUS WITH THE WORLD!
WAS HAMLET TRULY CRAZY?
AND YOU'VE NEVER LOST A RACE...?
HELL, NAH. ARE YOU KIDDING M--
MR. VALD--
MR. REYES!
UH... WELL...
...I'D SAY THAT HIS FATHER'S DEATH, HIS MOTHER'S BETRAYAL, THE LIES AND VIOLENCE SURROUNDING HIM, AND THE APPEARANCE OF A GHOST, EVEN, COULD DEFINITELY MAKE ANYONE CRAZY...
...BUT HAMLET'S ACTIONS WERE ALL CALCULATED. HE SOUNDED LIKE A NUTCASE ON PURPOSE, JUST TO FOOL HIS ENEMIES AND HIDE HIS REAL INTENTIONS.
WOOOOOH! HAHAHA!
VERY SHARP! ANYTHING TO ADD TO THIS, MR. VALDEZ?
NO.
WELL...IT SEEMS YOU'VE ALL EFFECTIVELY ABSORBED YOUR READING SO... AS THEY SAY...
...LET'S QUIT WHILE WE'RE AHEAD.
YOU'RE DISMISSED!

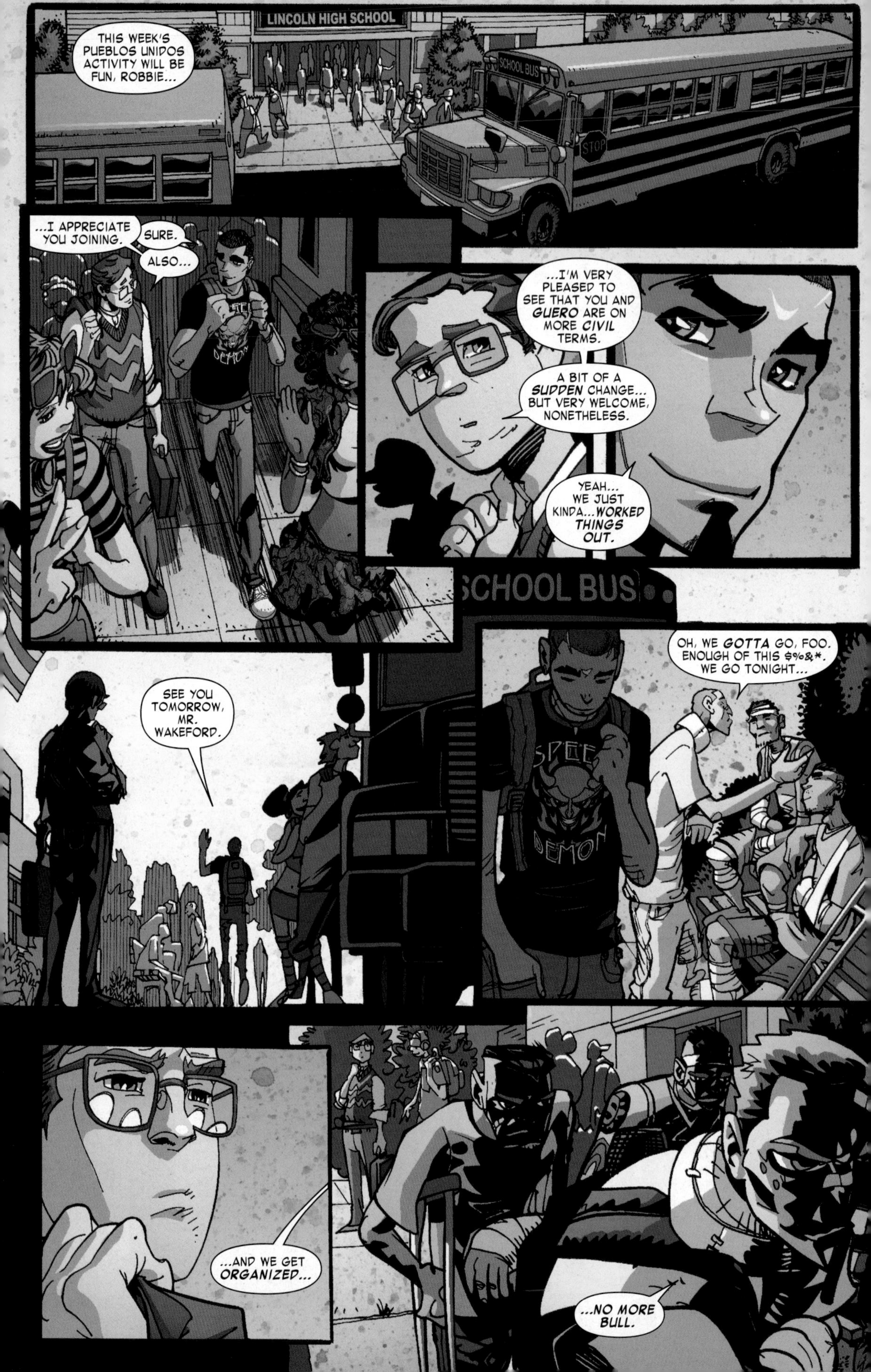
LINCOLN HIGH SCHOOL
THIS WEEK'S PUEBLOS UNIDOS ACTIVITY WILL BE FUN, ROBBIE...
SCHOOL BUS
STOP
...I APPRECIATE YOU JOINING.
SURE.
ALSO...
...I'M VERY PLEASED TO SEE THAT YOU AND GUERO ARE ON MORE CIVIL TERMS.
A BIT OF A SUDDEN CHANGE... BUT VERY WELCOME, NONETHELESS.
YEAH... WE JUST KINDA...WORKED THINGS OUT.
SCHOOL BUS
SEE YOU TOMORROW, MR. WAKEFORD.
OH, WE GOTTA GO, FOO. ENOUGH OF THIS $%&*. WE GO TONIGHT...
...AND WE GET ORGANIZED...
...NO MORE BULL.

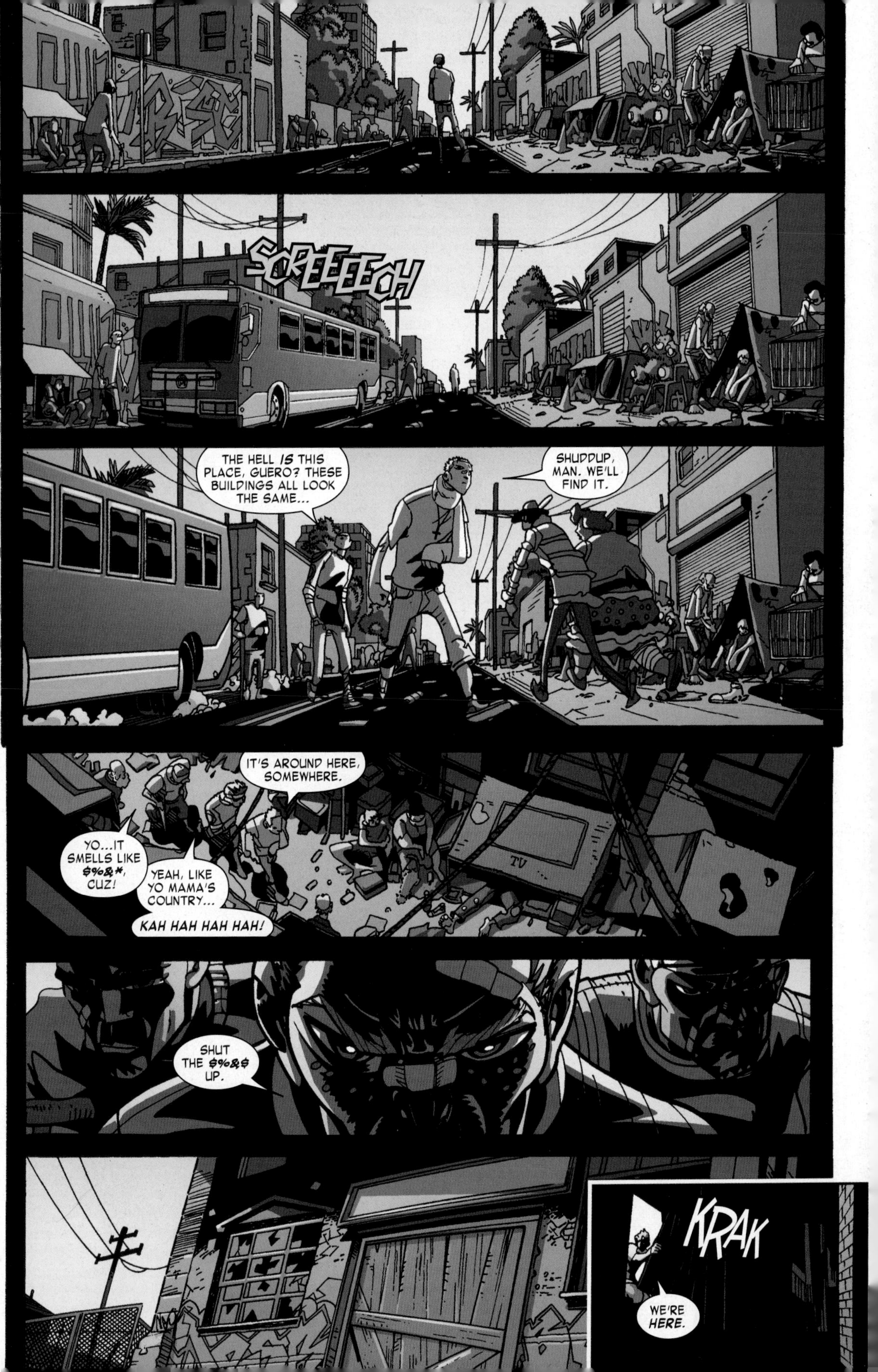

SCREEEEECH
THE HELL *IS* THIS PLACE, GUERO? THESE BUILDINGS ALL LOOK THE SAME...
SHUDDUP, MAN. WE'LL FIND IT.
IT'S AROUND HERE, SOMEWHERE.
YO...IT SMELLS LIKE $%&*, CUZ!
YEAH, LIKE YO MAMA'S COUNTRY...
KAH HAH HAH HAH!
SHUT THE $%&$ UP.
KRAK
WE'RE HERE.

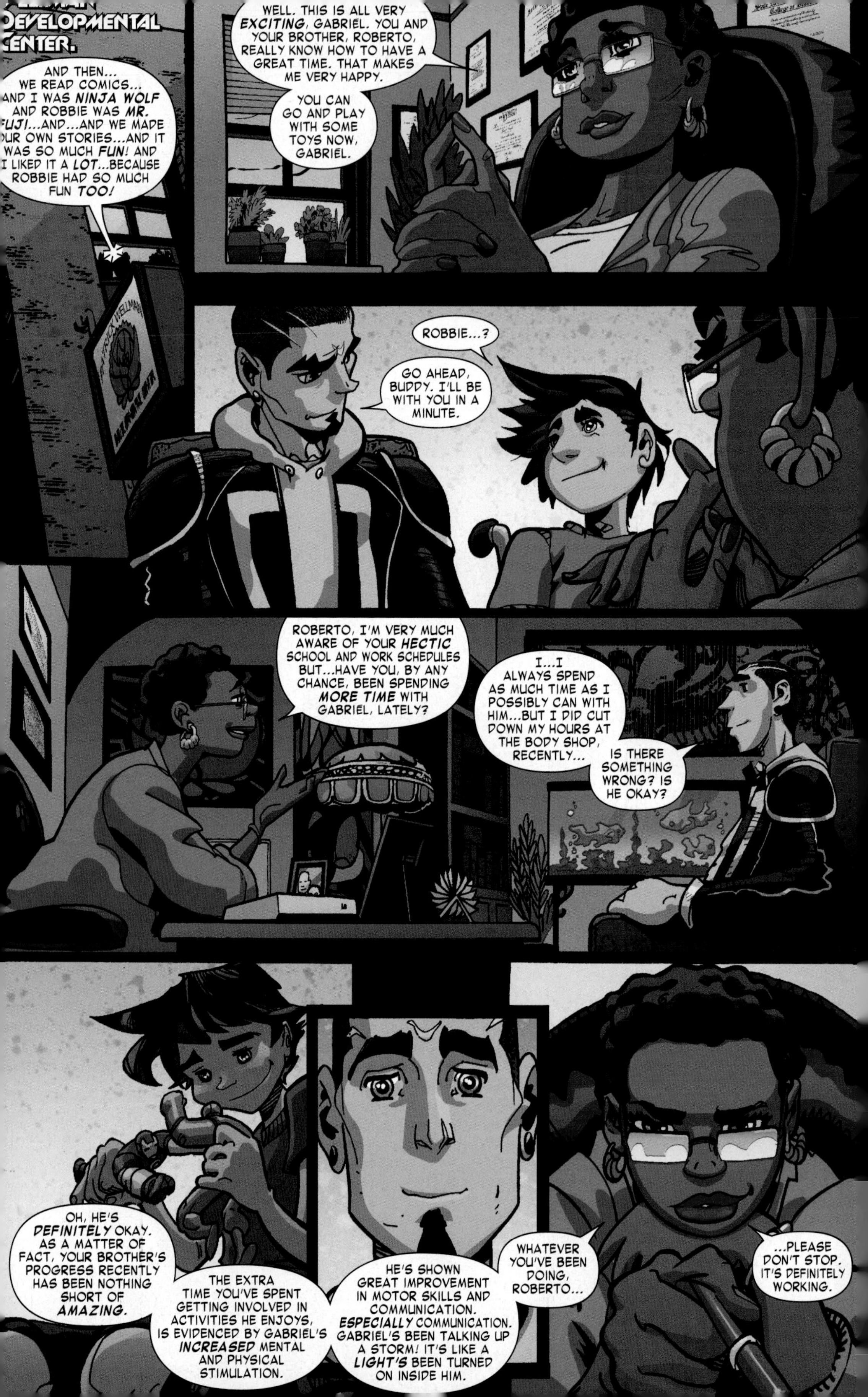

DEVELOPMENTAL CENTER.
AND THEN... WE READ COMICS... AND I WAS NINJA WOLF AND ROBBIE WAS MR. FUJI!...AND...AND WE MADE OUR OWN STORIES...AND IT WAS SO MUCH FUN! AND I LIKED IT A LOT...BECAUSE ROBBIE HAD SO MUCH FUN TOO!
WELL. THIS IS ALL VERY EXCITING, GABRIEL. YOU AND YOUR BROTHER, ROBERTO, REALLY KNOW HOW TO HAVE A GREAT TIME. THAT MAKES ME VERY HAPPY.
YOU CAN GO AND PLAY WITH SOME TOYS NOW, GABRIEL.
ROBBIE...?
GO AHEAD, BUDDY. I'LL BE WITH YOU IN A MINUTE.
ROBERTO, I'M VERY MUCH AWARE OF YOUR HECTIC SCHOOL AND WORK SCHEDULES BUT...HAVE YOU, BY ANY CHANCE, BEEN SPENDING MORE TIME WITH GABRIEL, LATELY?
I...I ALWAYS SPEND AS MUCH TIME AS I POSSIBLY CAN WITH HIM...BUT I DID CUT DOWN MY HOURS AT THE BODY SHOP, RECENTLY...
IS THERE SOMETHING WRONG? IS HE OKAY?
OH, HE'S DEFINITELY OKAY. AS A MATTER OF FACT, YOUR BROTHER'S PROGRESS RECENTLY HAS BEEN NOTHING SHORT OF AMAZING.
THE EXTRA TIME YOU'VE SPENT GETTING INVOLVED IN ACTIVITIES HE ENJOYS, IS EVIDENCED BY GABRIEL'S INCREASED MENTAL AND PHYSICAL STIMULATION.
HE'S SHOWN GREAT IMPROVEMENT IN MOTOR SKILLS AND COMMUNICATION. ESPECIALLY COMMUNICATION. GABRIEL'S BEEN TALKING UP A STORM! IT'S LIKE A LIGHT'S BEEN TURNED ON INSIDE HIM.
WHATEVER YOU'VE BEEN DOING, ROBERTO...
...PLEASE DON'T STOP. IT'S DEFINITELY WORKING.

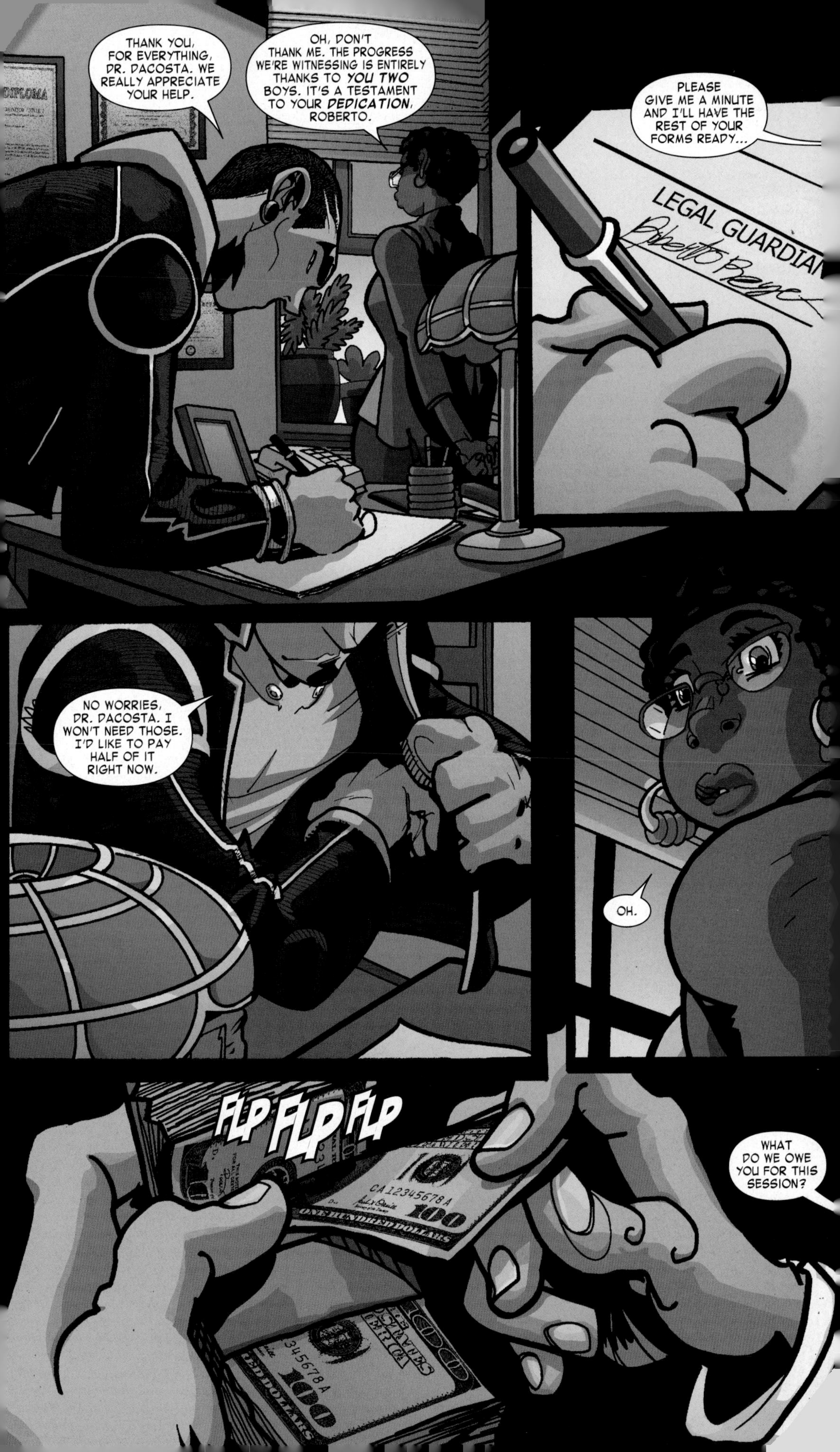
THANK YOU, FOR EVERYTHING, DR. DACOSTA. WE REALLY APPRECIATE YOUR HELP.
OH, DON'T THANK ME. THE PROGRESS WE'RE WITNESSING IS ENTIRELY THANKS TO YOU TWO BOYS. IT'S A TESTAMENT TO YOUR DEDICATION, ROBERTO.
DIPLOMA
PLEASE GIVE ME A MINUTE AND I'LL HAVE THE REST OF YOUR FORMS READY...
LEGAL GUARDIAN
NO WORRIES, DR. DACOSTA. I WON'T NEED THOSE. I'D LIKE TO PAY HALF OF IT RIGHT NOW.
OH.
FLP FLP FLP
WHAT DO WE OWE YOU FOR THIS SESSION?

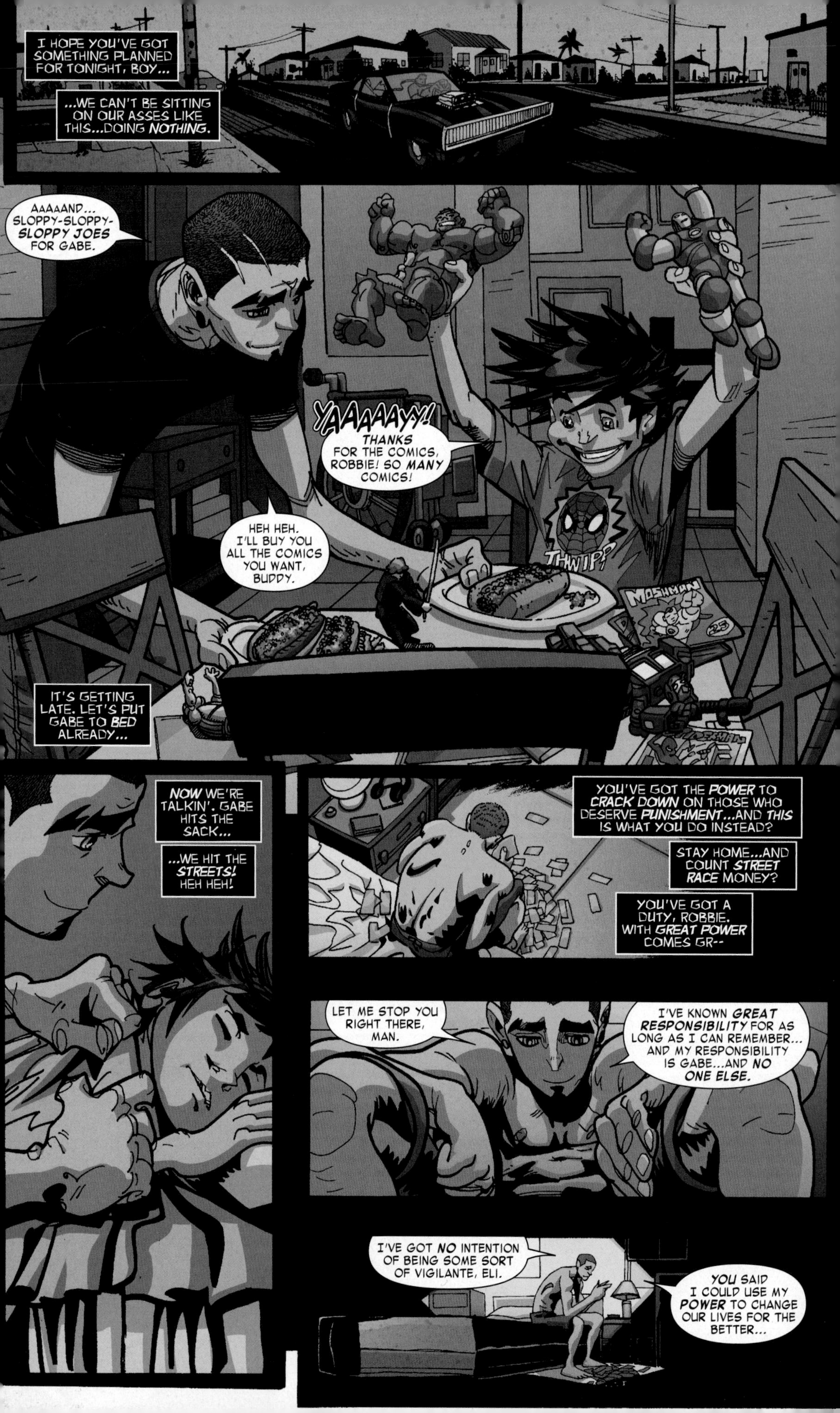

I HOPE YOU'VE GOT SOMETHING PLANNED FOR TONIGHT, BOY...
...WE CAN'T BE SITTING ON OUR ASSES LIKE THIS...DOING NOTHING.
AAAAAND... SLOPPY-SLOPPY-SLOPPY JOES FOR GABE.
YAAAAAYY!
THANKS FOR THE COMICS, ROBBIE! SO MANY COMICS!
HEH HEH. I'LL BUY YOU ALL THE COMICS YOU WANT, BUDDY.
THWIP
MOSHMAN
IT'S GETTING LATE. LET'S PUT GABE TO BED ALREADY...
NOW WE'RE TALKIN'. GABE HITS THE SACK...
...WE HIT THE STREETS! HEH HEH!
YOU'VE GOT THE POWER TO CRACK DOWN ON THOSE WHO DESERVE PUNISHMENT...AND THIS IS WHAT YOU DO INSTEAD?
STAY HOME...AND COUNT STREET RACE MONEY?
YOU'VE GOT A DUTY, ROBBIE. WITH GREAT POWER COMES GR--
LET ME STOP YOU RIGHT THERE, MAN.
I'VE KNOWN GREAT RESPONSIBILITY FOR AS LONG AS I CAN REMEMBER... AND MY RESPONSIBILITY IS GABE...AND NO ONE ELSE.
I'VE GOT NO INTENTION OF BEING SOME SORT OF VIGILANTE, ELI.
YOU SAID I COULD USE MY POWER TO CHANGE OUR LIVES FOR THE BETTER...

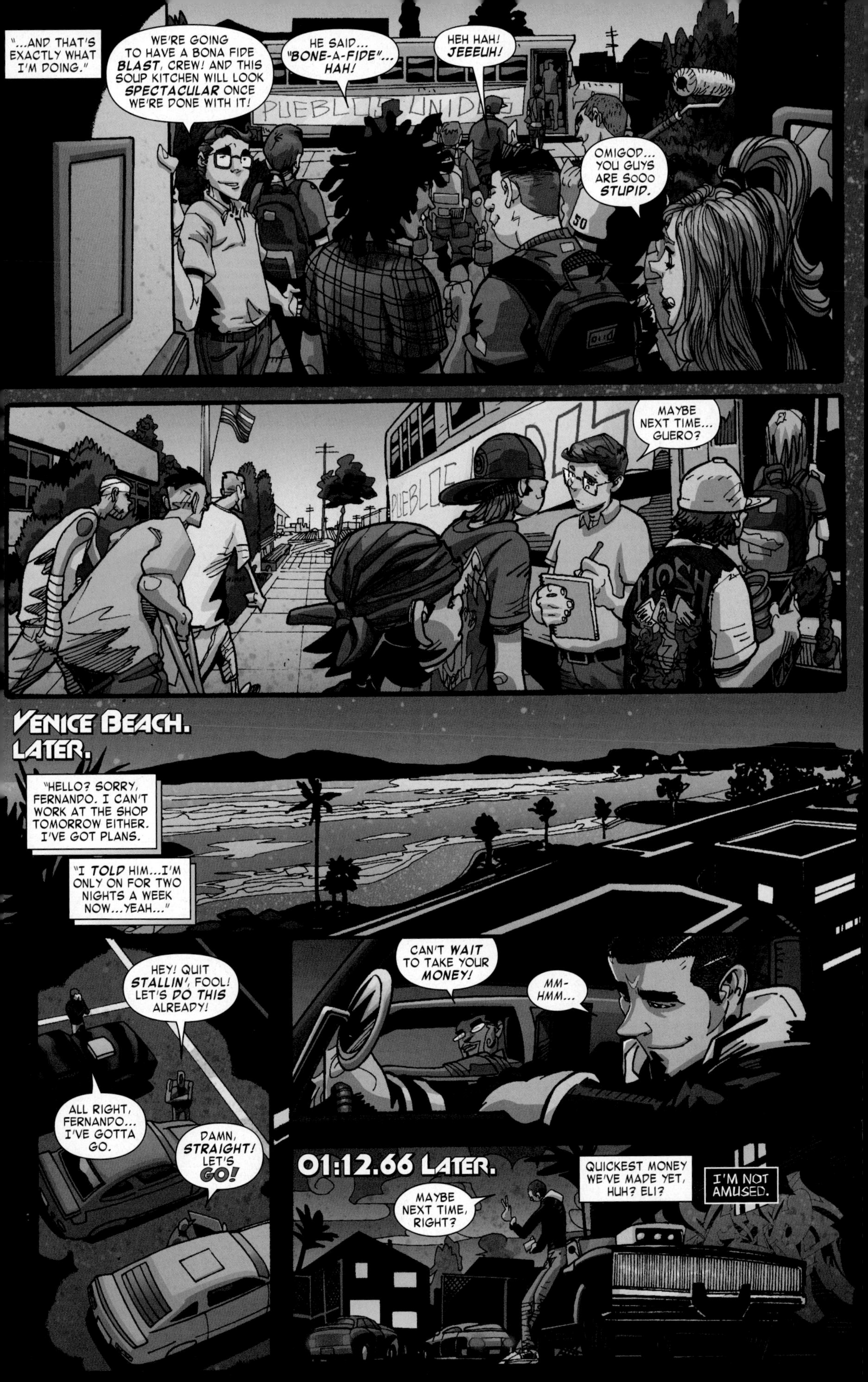
"...AND THAT'S EXACTLY WHAT I'M DOING."
WE'RE GOING TO HAVE A BONA FIDE BLAST, CREW! AND THIS SOUP KITCHEN WILL LOOK SPECTACULAR ONCE WE'RE DONE WITH IT!
HE SAID... "BONE-A-FIDE"... HAH!
HEH HAH! JEEEUH!
PUEBLOS UNIDOS
OMIGOD... YOU GUYS ARE SOOO STUPID.
MAYBE NEXT TIME... GUERO?
PUEBLOS
VENICE BEACH. LATER.
"HELLO? SORRY, FERNANDO. I CAN'T WORK AT THE SHOP TOMORROW EITHER. I'VE GOT PLANS.
"I TOLD HIM...I'M ONLY ON FOR TWO NIGHTS A WEEK NOW...YEAH..."
HEY! QUIT STALLIN', FOOL! LET'S DO THIS ALREADY!
CAN'T WAIT TO TAKE YOUR MONEY!
MM-HMM...
ALL RIGHT, FERNANDO... I'VE GOTTA GO.
DAMN, STRAIGHT! LET'S GO!
01:12.66 LATER.
MAYBE NEXT TIME, RIGHT?
QUICKEST MONEY WE'VE MADE YET, HUH? ELI?
I'M NOT AMUSED.

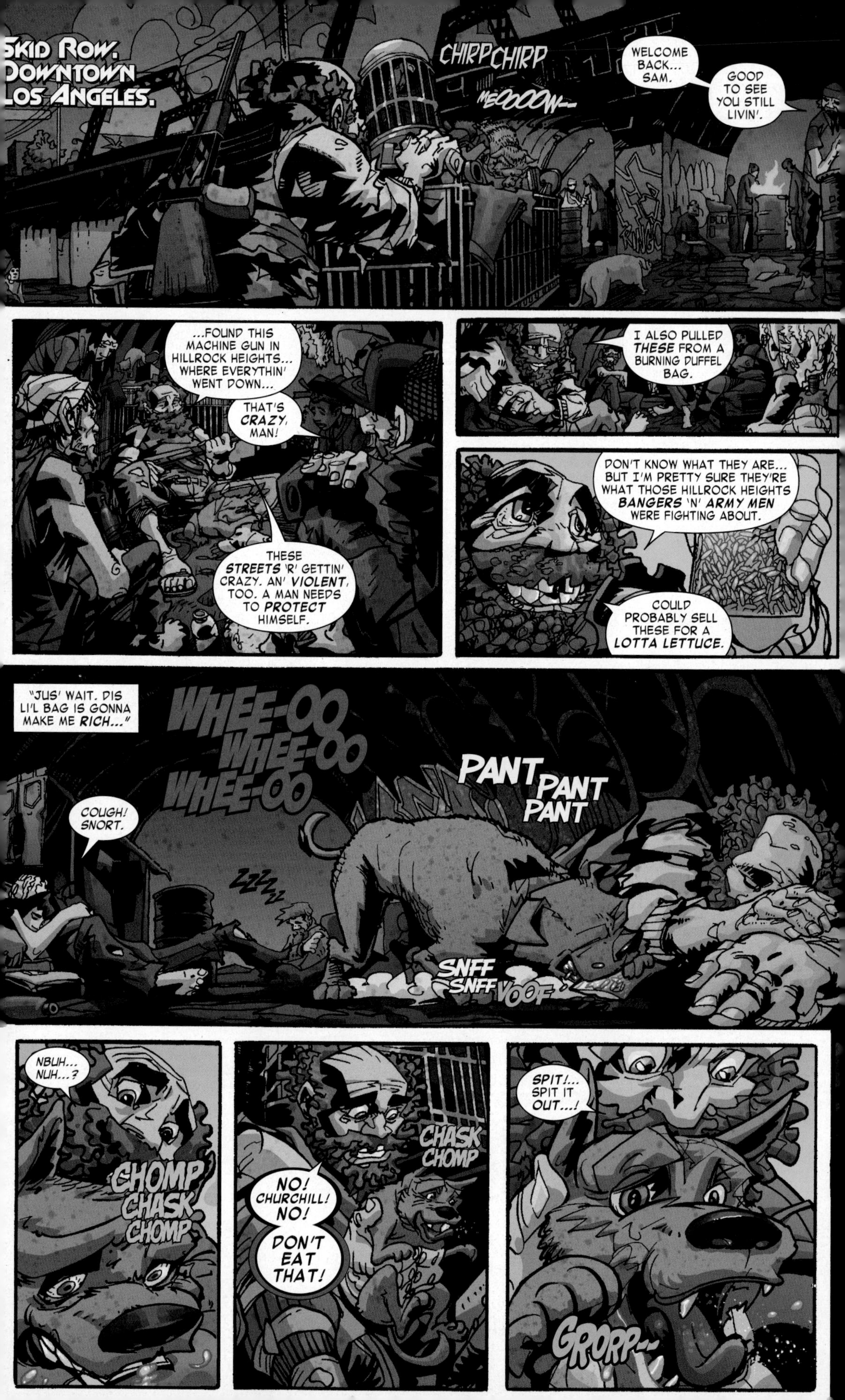
SKID ROW. DOWNTOWN LOS ANGELES.
CHIRP CHIRP
MEOOOOW--
WELCOME BACK... SAM.
GOOD TO SEE YOU STILL LIVIN'.
...FOUND THIS MACHINE GUN IN HILLROCK HEIGHTS... WHERE EVERYTHIN' WENT DOWN...
THAT'S CRAZY, MAN!
THESE STREETS 'R' GETTIN' CRAZY. AN' VIOLENT, TOO. A MAN NEEDS TO PROTECT HIMSELF.
I ALSO PULLED THESE FROM A BURNING DUFFEL BAG.
DON'T KNOW WHAT THEY ARE... BUT I'M PRETTY SURE THEY'RE WHAT THOSE HILLROCK HEIGHTS BANGERS 'N' ARMY MEN WERE FIGHTING ABOUT.
COULD PROBABLY SELL THESE FOR A LOTTA LETTUCE.
"JUS' WAIT. DIS LI'L BAG IS GONNA MAKE ME RICH..."
WHEE-OO WHEE-OO WHEE-OO
PANT PANT PANT
COUGH! SNORT.
ZZZZZ
SNFF SNFF VOOF
NBUH... NUH...?
CHOMP CHASK CHOMP
CHASK CHOMP
NO! CHURCHILL! NO!
DON'T EAT THAT!
SPIT!... SPIT IT OUT...!
GRORP--

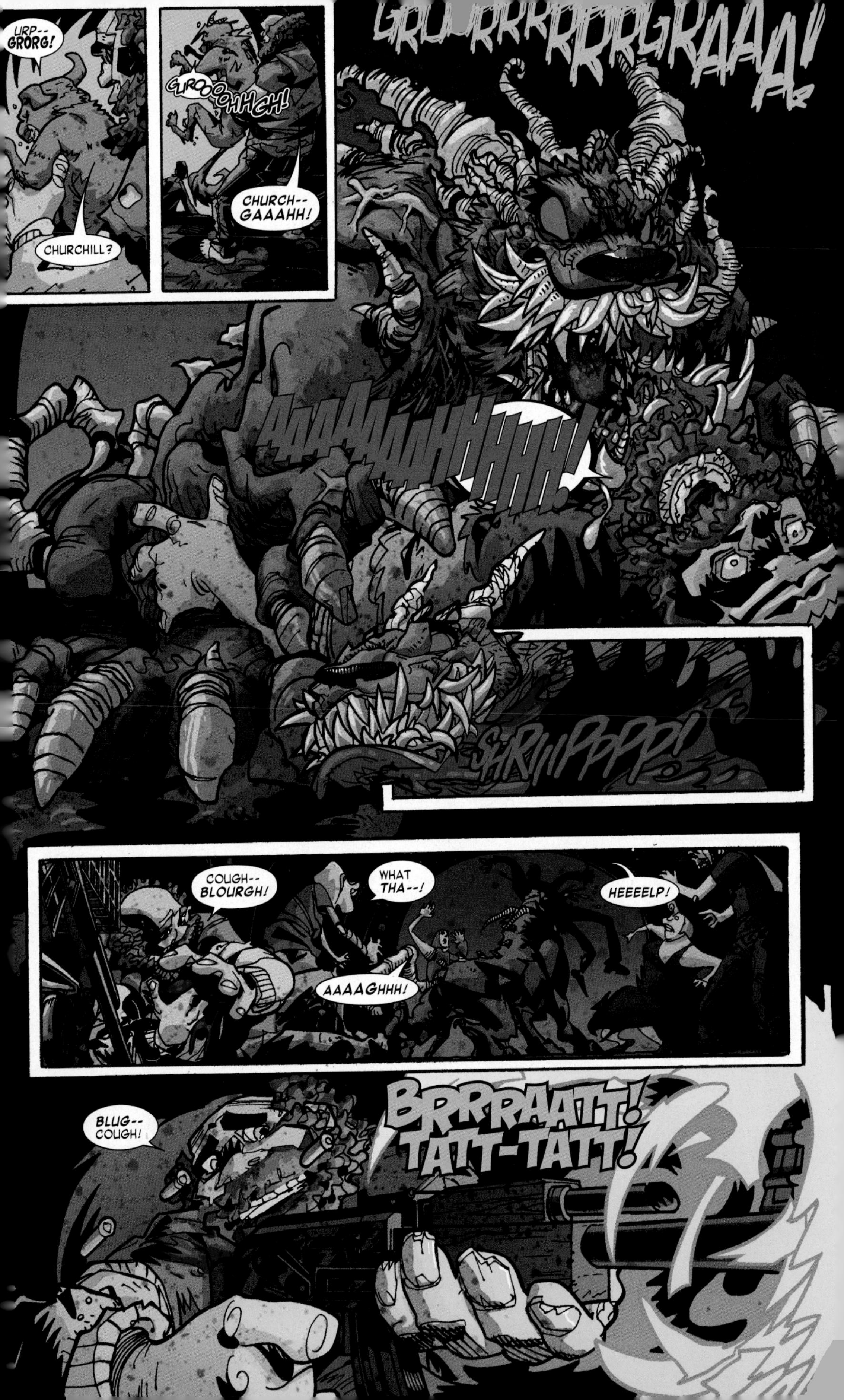
URP--
GRORG!
CHURCHILL?
GUROOOOHHGH!
CHURCH--
GAAAHH!
GROORRRRRRGRAAA!
AAAAAAAHHHHH!
SHRIIPPPP!
COUGH--
BLOURGH!
WHAT
THA--!
HEEEELP!
AAAAGHHH!
BLUG--
COUGH!
BRRRAATT!
TATT-TATT!

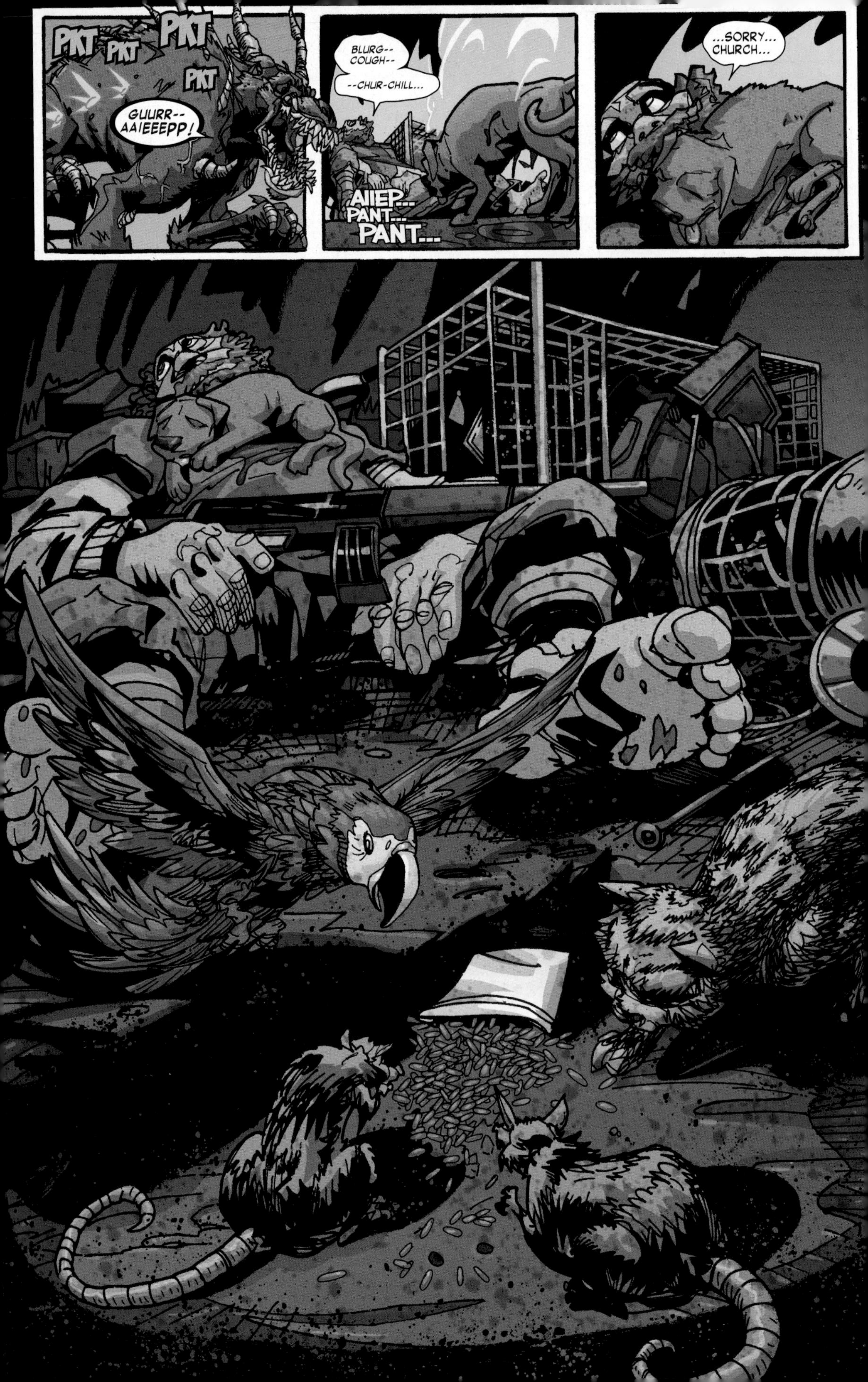
PKT PKT PKT
PKT
GUURR--AAIEEEPP!
BLURG--COUGH--
--CHUR-CHILL...
AIIEP... PANT... PANT...
...SORRY... CHURCH...

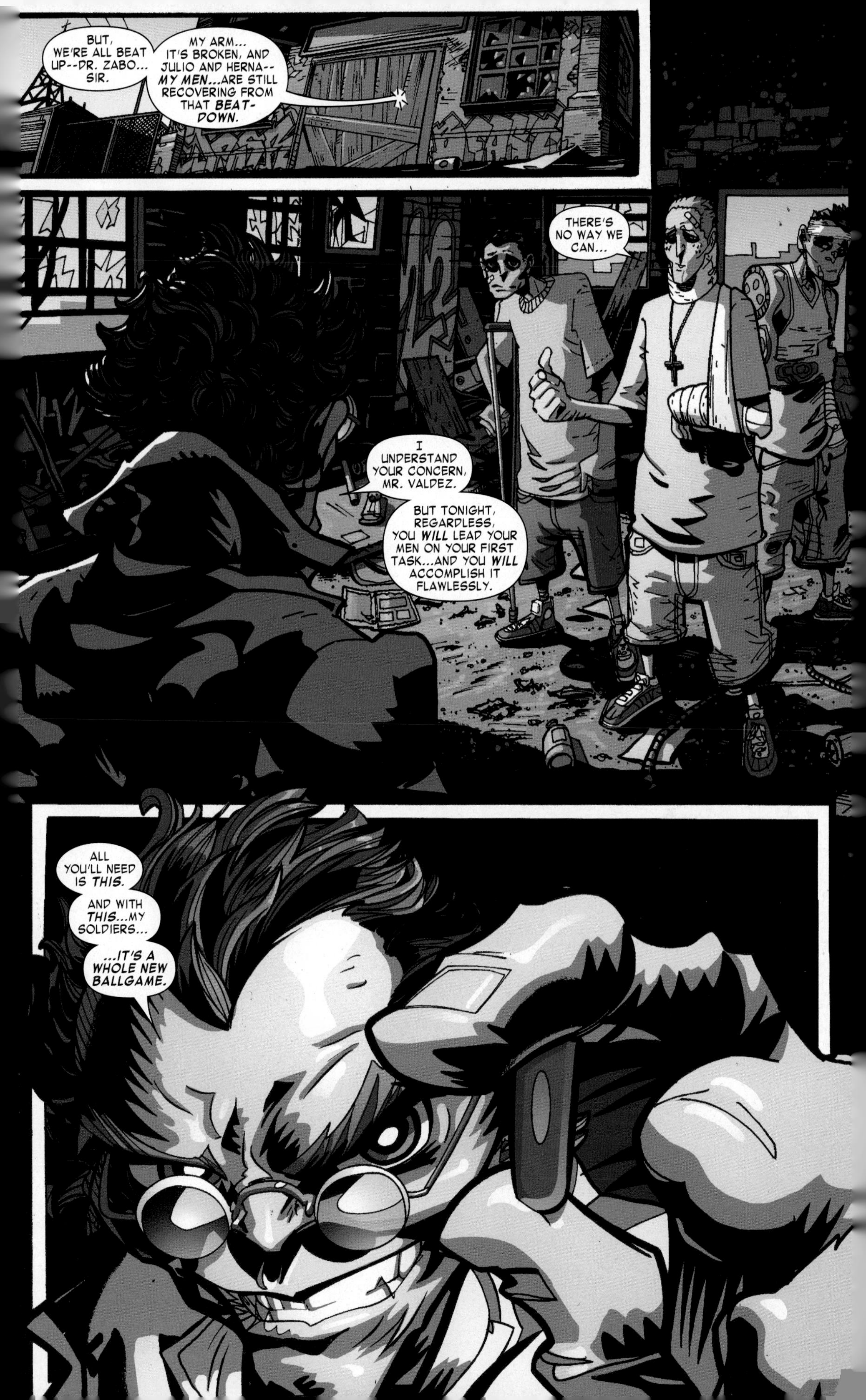

BUT, WE'RE ALL BEAT UP--DR. ZABO... SIR.
MY ARM... IT'S BROKEN, AND JULIO AND HERNA-- MY MEN...ARE STILL RECOVERING FROM THAT BEAT-DOWN.
THERE'S NO WAY WE CAN...
I UNDERSTAND YOUR CONCERN, MR. VALDEZ.
BUT TONIGHT, REGARDLESS, YOU WILL LEAD YOUR MEN ON YOUR FIRST TASK...AND YOU WILL ACCOMPLISH IT FLAWLESSLY.
ALL YOU'LL NEED IS THIS.
AND WITH THIS...MY SOLDIERS...
...IT'S A WHOLE NEW BALLGAME.

« SMALL-BLOCK «
« 5.7-LITER OH! « 2600 RPM
« TURBO-HYDRAMATIC 400 THREE-SPEED AUTO

GO. GO. GO.

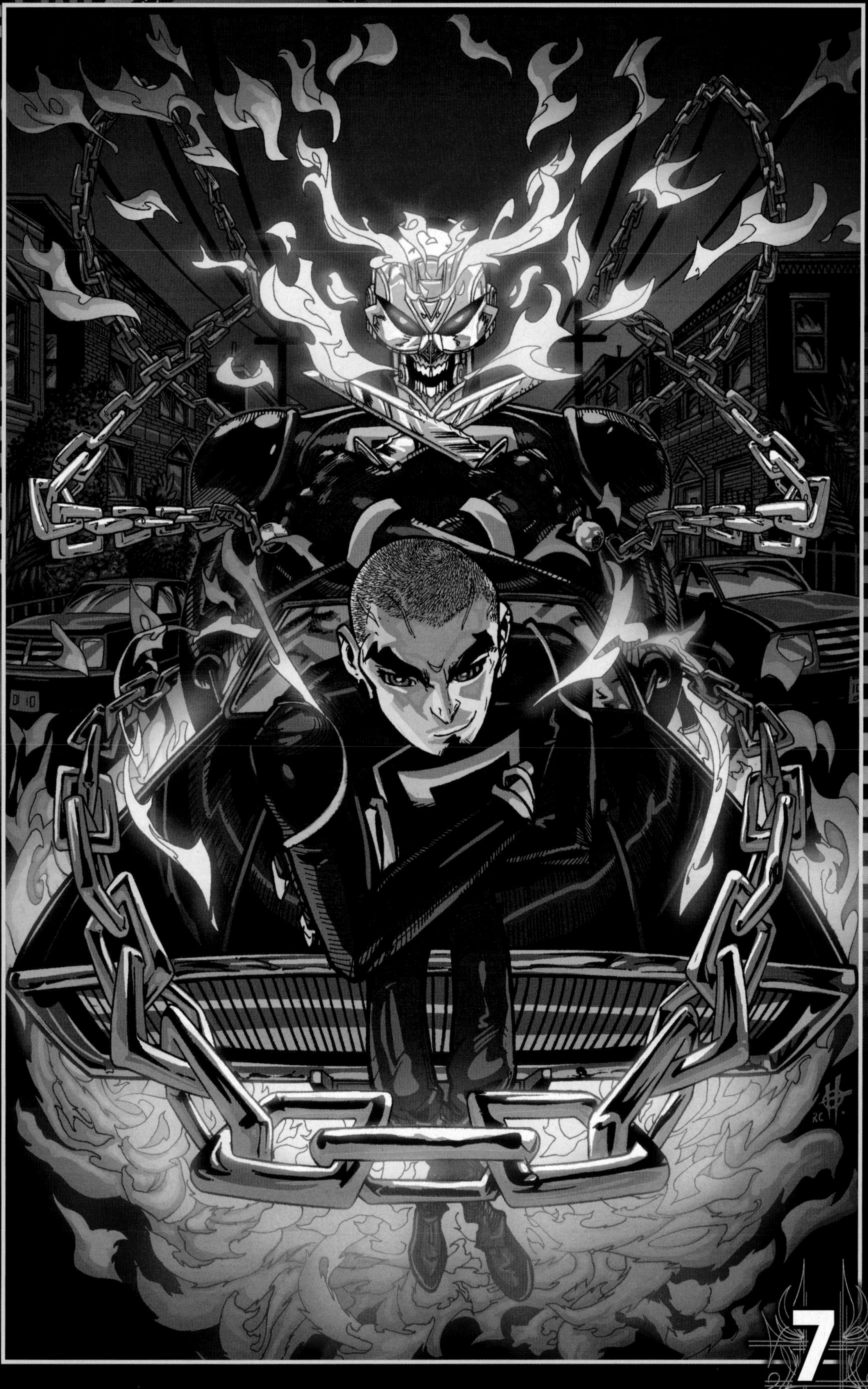

7

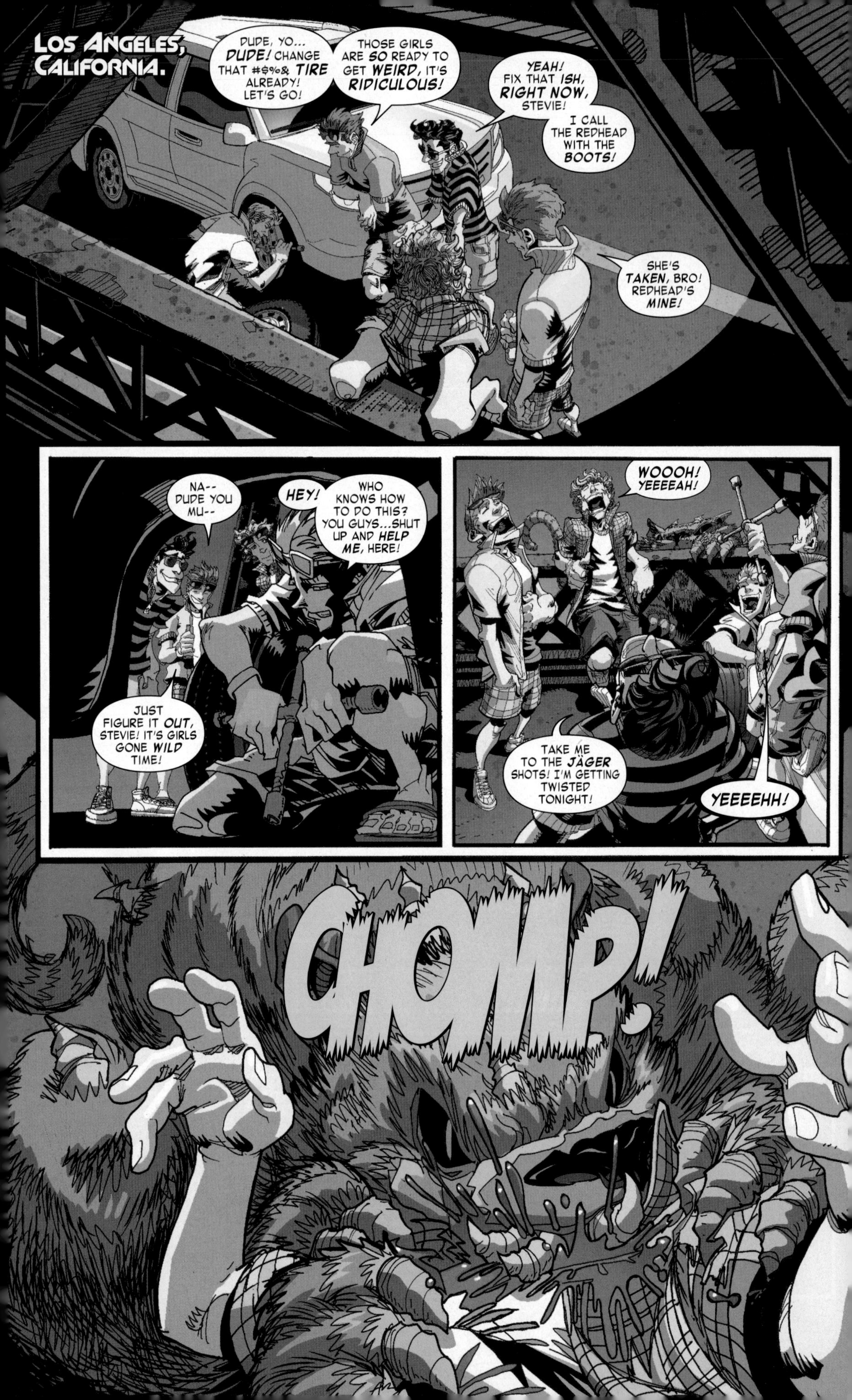
LOS ANGELES, CALIFORNIA.
DUDE, YO... DUDE! CHANGE THAT #$%& TIRE ALREADY! LET'S GO!
THOSE GIRLS ARE SO READY TO GET WEIRD, IT'S RIDICULOUS!
YEAH! FIX THAT ISH, RIGHT NOW, STEVIE!
I CALL THE REDHEAD WITH THE BOOTS!
SHE'S TAKEN, BRO! REDHEAD'S MINE!
NA-- DUDE YOU MU--
HEY!
WHO KNOWS HOW TO DO THIS? YOU GUYS...SHUT UP AND HELP ME, HERE!
JUST FIGURE IT OUT, STEVIE! IT'S GIRLS GONE WILD TIME!
WOOOH! YEEEEAH!
TAKE ME TO THE JÄGER SHOTS! I'M GETTING TWISTED TONIGHT!
YEEEEHH!
CHOMP!

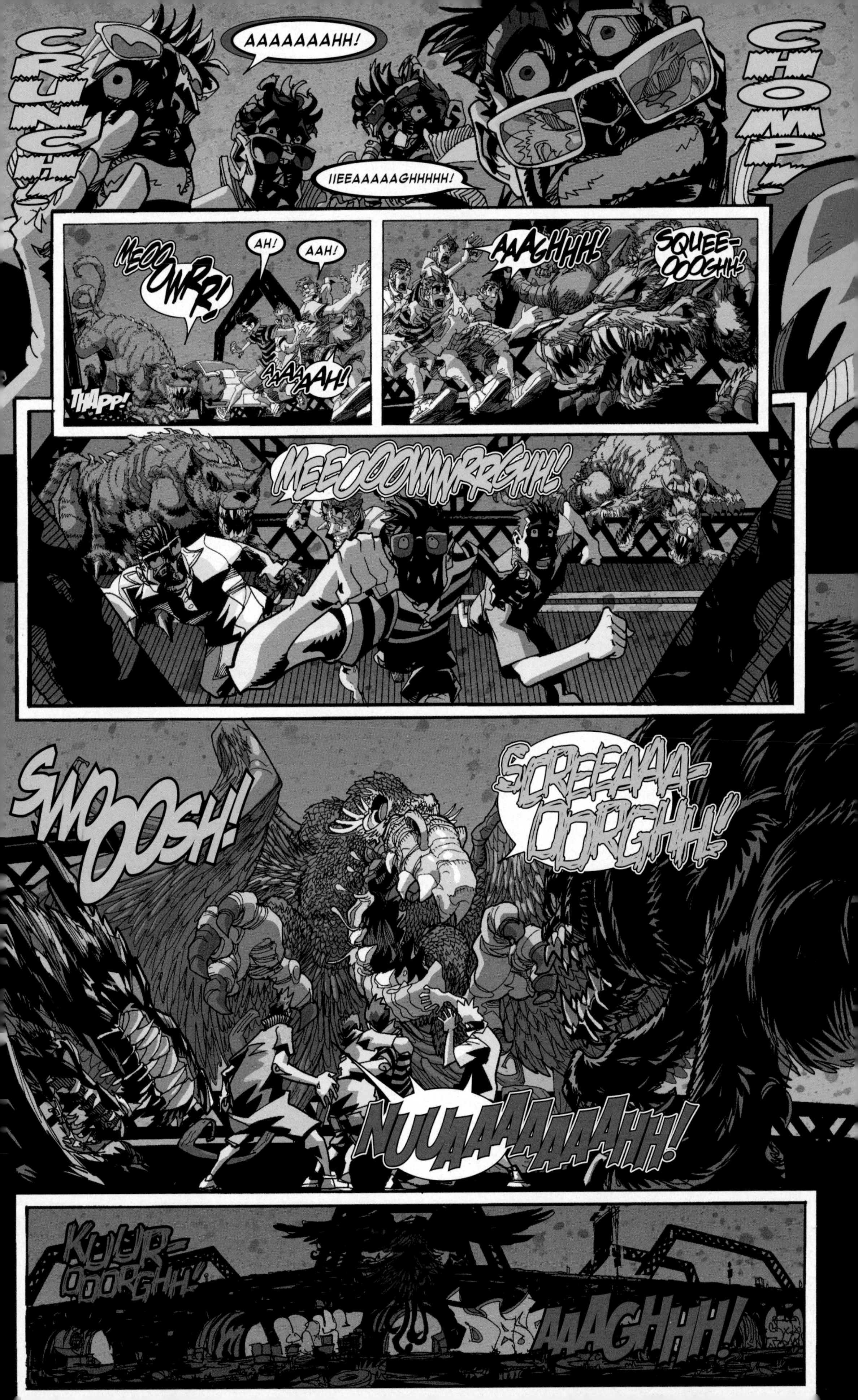
CRUNCH!
AAAAAAAHH!
IIEEAAAAAGHHHHH!
CHOMP!
MEOOOWRR!
AH!
AAH!
AAAAAH!
THAPP!
AAAGHHH!
SQUEE-OOOGHH!
MEEOOOOWWRRGHH!
SWOOOSH!
SCREEAAA-OOORGHH!
NUUAAAAAAAAHH!
KULUR-OOORGHH!
AAAGHHH!

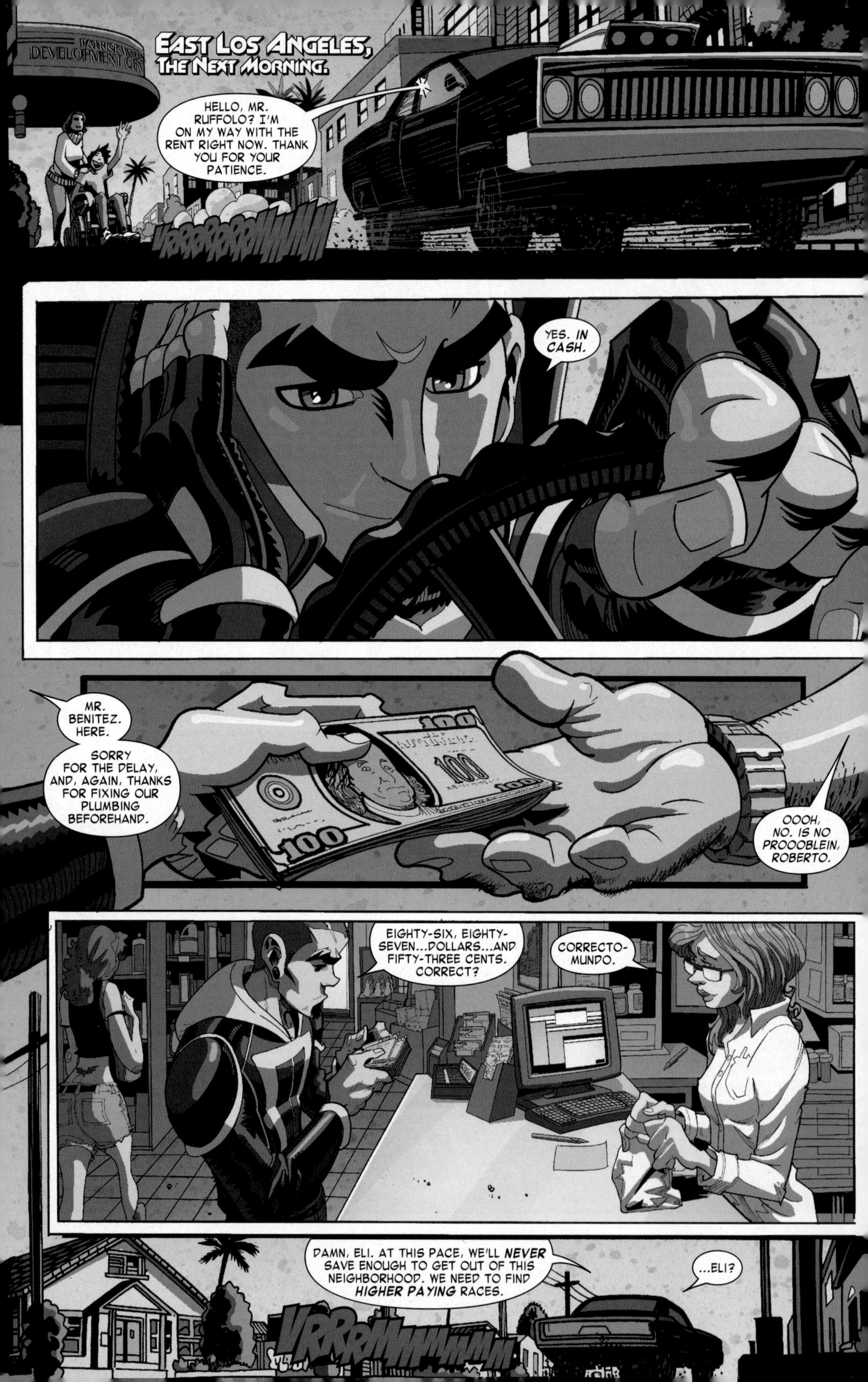
EAST LOS ANGELES, THE NEXT MORNING.
DEVELOPMENT CEN
HELLO, MR. RUFFOLO? I'M ON MY WAY WITH THE RENT RIGHT NOW. THANK YOU FOR YOUR PATIENCE.
VRRRRRRRMMMM
YES. IN CASH.
MR. BENITEZ. HERE.
SORRY FOR THE DELAY, AND, AGAIN, THANKS FOR FIXING OUR PLUMBING BEFOREHAND.
100
OOOH, NO. IS NO PROOOBLEIN, ROBERTO.
EIGHTY-SIX, EIGHTY-SEVEN...DOLLARS...AND FIFTY-THREE CENTS. CORRECT?
CORRECTO-MUNDO.
DAMN, ELI. AT THIS PACE, WE'LL NEVER SAVE ENOUGH TO GET OUT OF THIS NEIGHBORHOOD. WE NEED TO FIND HIGHER PAYING RACES.
...ELI?
VRRRMMMMMMM

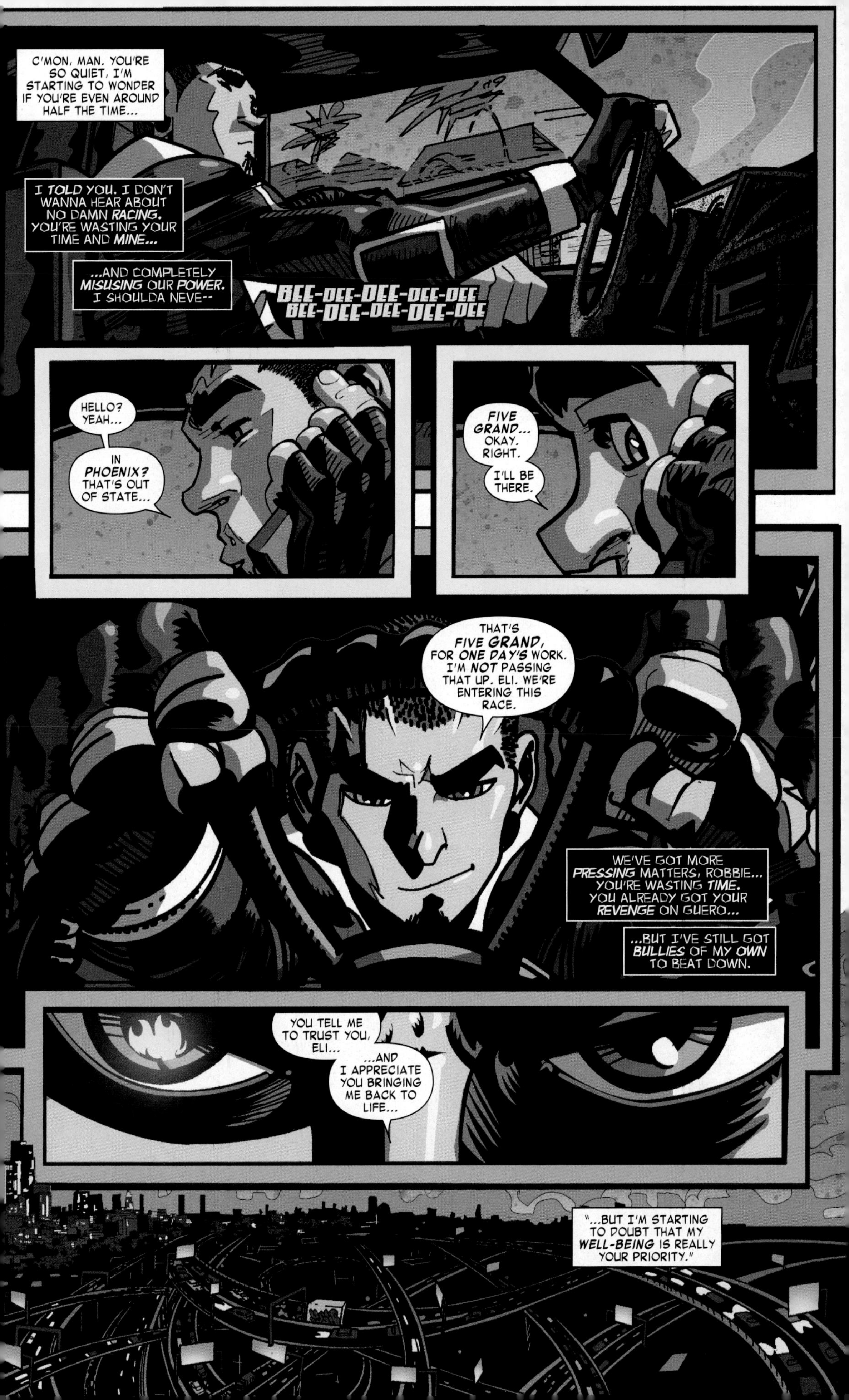
C'MON, MAN. YOU'RE SO QUIET, I'M STARTING TO WONDER IF YOU'RE EVEN AROUND HALF THE TIME...
I TOLD YOU. I DON'T WANNA HEAR ABOUT NO DAMN RACING. YOU'RE WASTING YOUR TIME AND MINE...
...AND COMPLETELY MISUSING OUR POWER. I SHOULDA NEVE--
BEE-DEE-DEE-DEE-DEE BEE-DEE-DEE-DEE-DEE
HELLO? YEAH...
IN PHOENIX? THAT'S OUT OF STATE...
FIVE GRAND... OKAY. RIGHT.
I'LL BE THERE.
THAT'S FIVE GRAND, FOR ONE DAY'S WORK. I'M NOT PASSING THAT UP. ELI. WE'RE ENTERING THIS RACE.
WE'VE GOT MORE PRESSING MATTERS, ROBBIE... YOU'RE WASTING TIME. YOU ALREADY GOT YOUR REVENGE ON GUERO...
...BUT I'VE STILL GOT BULLIES OF MY OWN TO BEAT DOWN.
YOU TELL ME TO TRUST YOU, ELI...
...AND I APPRECIATE YOU BRINGING ME BACK TO LIFE...
"...BUT I'M STARTING TO DOUBT THAT MY WELL-BEING IS REALLY YOUR PRIORITY."

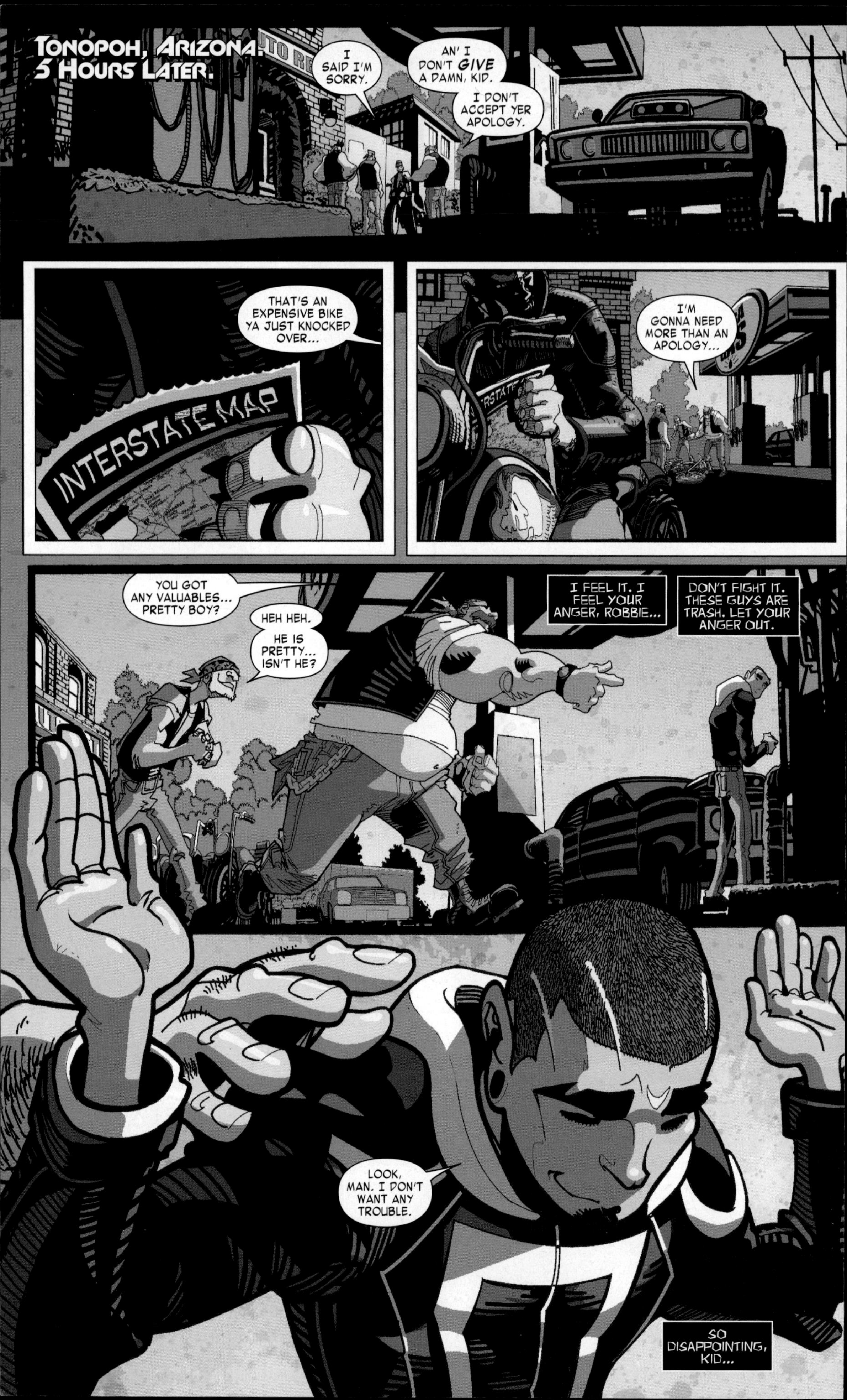

TONOPOH, ARIZONA. 5 HOURS LATER.
I SAID I'M SORRY.
AN' I DON'T GIVE A DAMN, KID.
I DON'T ACCEPT YER APOLOGY.
AUTO RE
THAT'S AN EXPENSIVE BIKE YA JUST KNOCKED OVER...
INTERSTATE MAP
I'M GONNA NEED MORE THAN AN APOLOGY...
YOU GOT ANY VALUABLES... PRETTY BOY?
HEH HEH.
HE IS PRETTY... ISN'T HE?
I FEEL IT. I FEEL YOUR ANGER, ROBBIE...
DON'T FIGHT IT. THESE GUYS ARE TRASH. LET YOUR ANGER OUT.
LOOK, MAN. I DON'T WANT ANY TROUBLE.
SO DISAPPOINTING, KID...

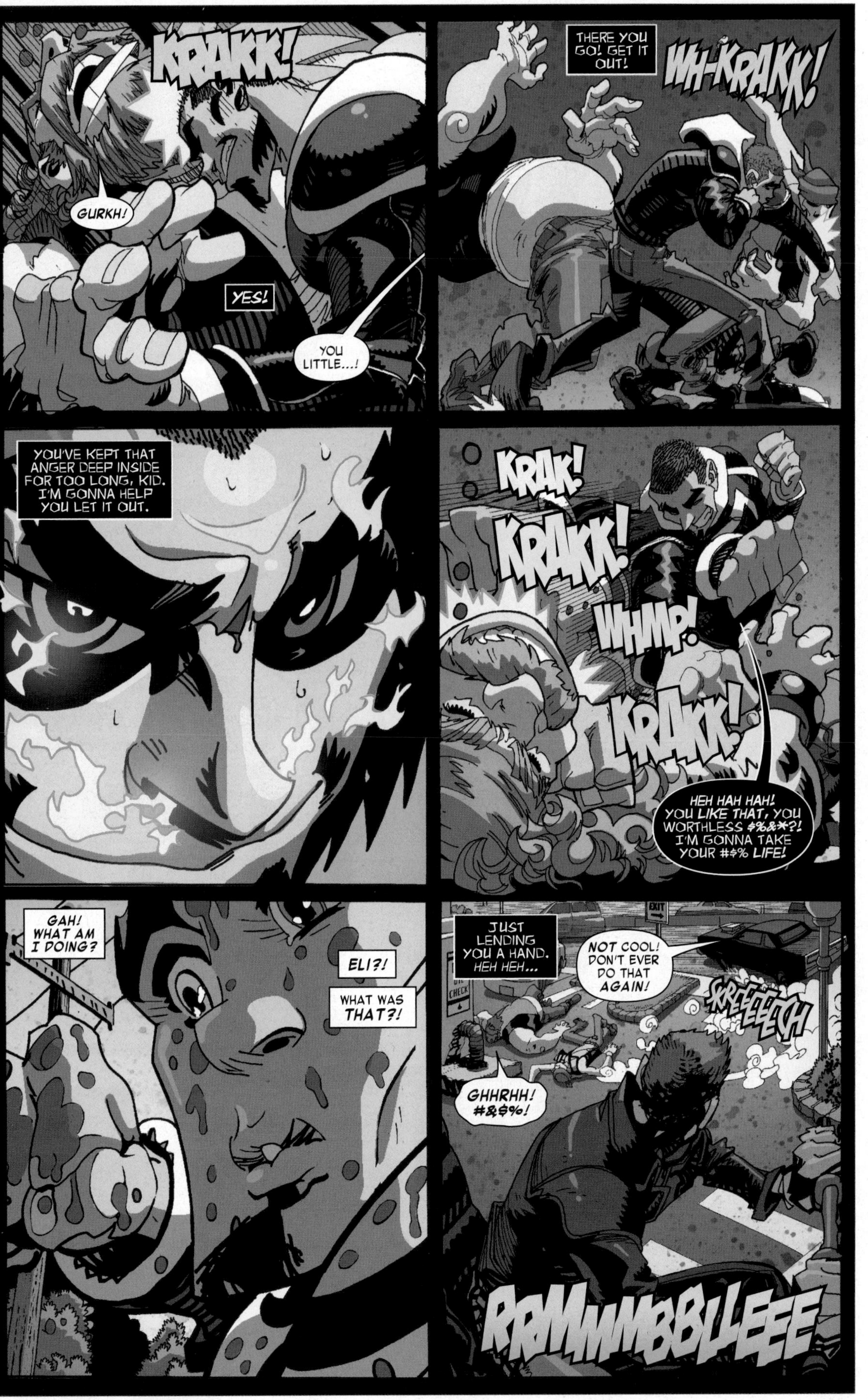
KRAKK!
GURKH!
YES!
YOU LITTLE...!
THERE YOU GO! GET IT OUT!
WH-KRAKK!
YOU'VE KEPT THAT ANGER DEEP INSIDE FOR TOO LONG, KID. I'M GONNA HELP YOU LET IT OUT.
KRAK!
KRAKK!
WHMP!
KRAKK!
HEH HAH HAH! YOU LIKE THAT, YOU WORTHLESS $%&*?! I'M GONNA TAKE YOUR #$% LIFE!
GAH! WHAT AM I DOING?
ELI?!
WHAT WAS THAT?!
JUST LENDING YOU A HAND. HEH HEH...
NOT COOL! DON'T EVER DO THAT AGAIN!
EXIT
SKREEEEECH
GHHRHH! #&$%!
RRMMMMBBLLEEE

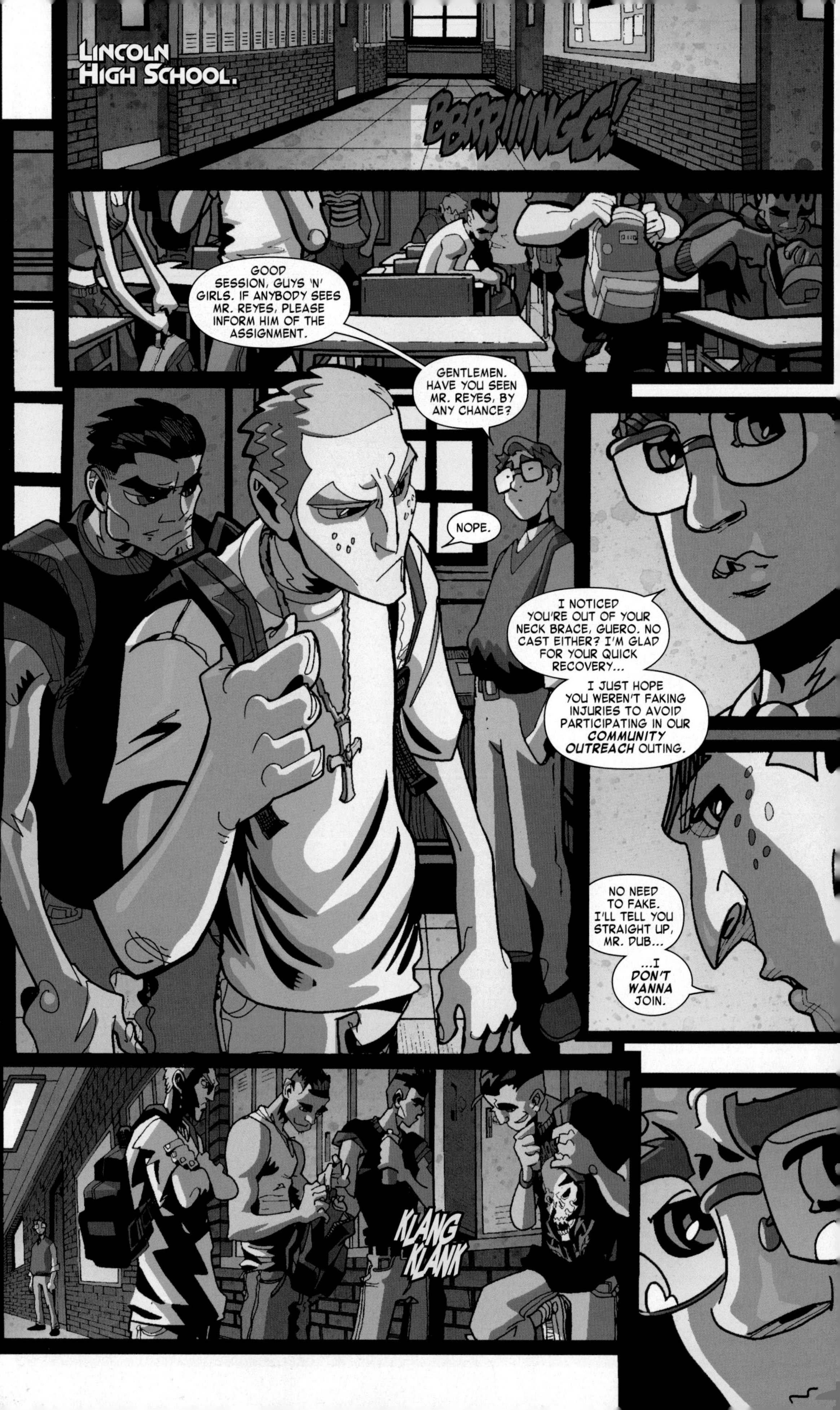
LINCOLN HIGH SCHOOL.
BBRRIIINGG!
GOOD SESSION, GUYS 'N' GIRLS. IF ANYBODY SEES MR. REYES, PLEASE INFORM HIM OF THE ASSIGNMENT.
GENTLEMEN. HAVE YOU SEEN MR. REYES, BY ANY CHANCE?
NOPE.
I NOTICED YOU'RE OUT OF YOUR NECK BRACE, GUERO. NO CAST EITHER? I'M GLAD FOR YOUR QUICK RECOVERY...
I JUST HOPE YOU WEREN'T FAKING INJURIES TO AVOID PARTICIPATING IN OUR COMMUNITY OUTREACH OUTING.
NO NEED TO FAKE. I'LL TELL YOU STRAIGHT UP, MR. DUB...
...I DON'T WANNA JOIN.
KLANG KLANK

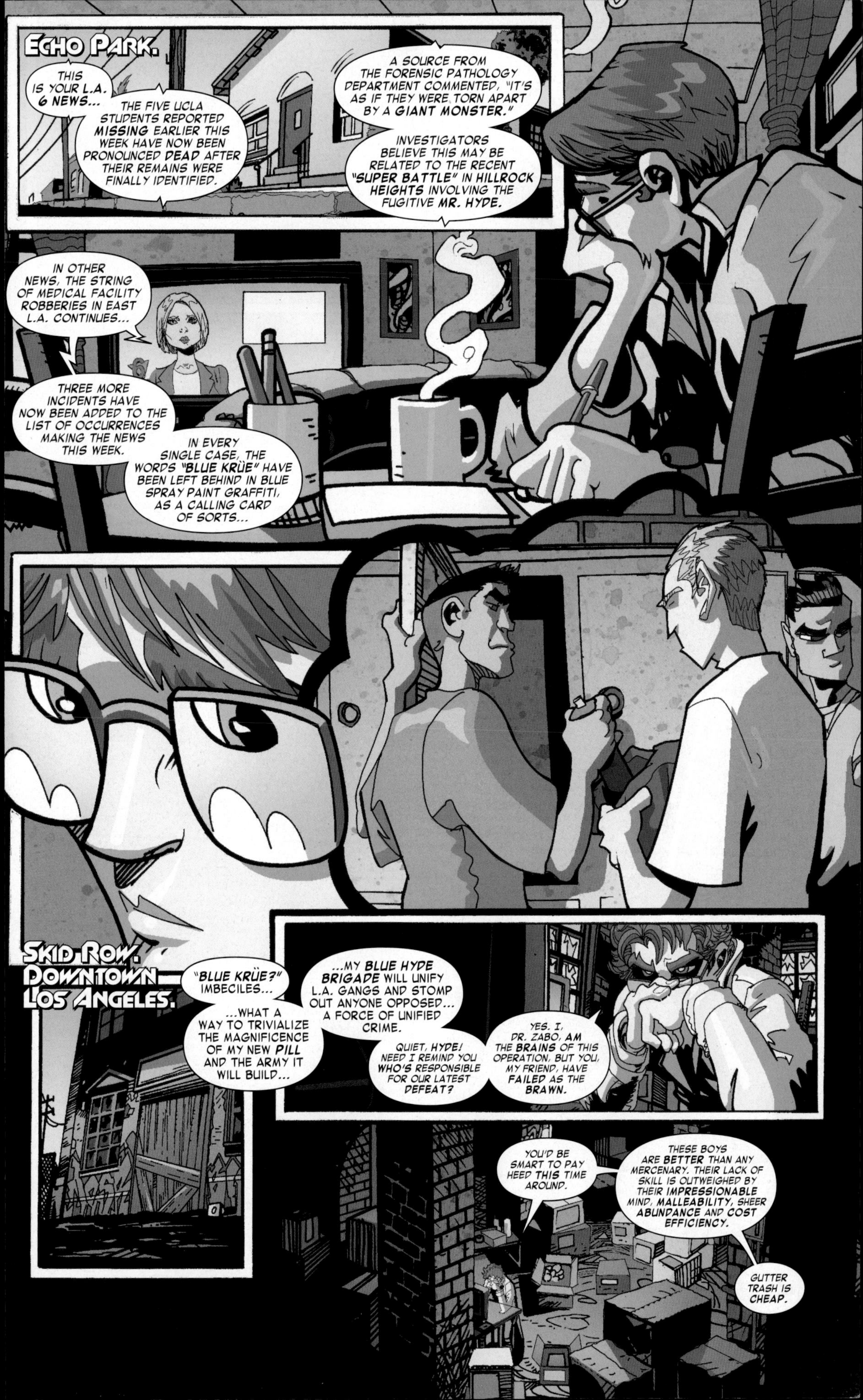
ECHO PARK.
THIS IS YOUR L.A. 6 NEWS...
THE FIVE UCLA STUDENTS REPORTED MISSING EARLIER THIS WEEK HAVE NOW BEEN PRONOUNCED DEAD AFTER THEIR REMAINS WERE FINALLY IDENTIFIED.
A SOURCE FROM THE FORENSIC PATHOLOGY DEPARTMENT COMMENTED, "IT'S AS IF THEY WERE TORN APART BY A GIANT MONSTER."
INVESTIGATORS BELIEVE THIS MAY BE RELATED TO THE RECENT "SUPER BATTLE" IN HILLROCK HEIGHTS INVOLVING THE FUGITIVE MR. HYDE.
IN OTHER NEWS, THE STRING OF MEDICAL FACILITY ROBBERIES IN EAST L.A. CONTINUES...
THREE MORE INCIDENTS HAVE NOW BEEN ADDED TO THE LIST OF OCCURRENCES MAKING THE NEWS THIS WEEK.
IN EVERY SINGLE CASE, THE WORDS "BLUE KRÜE" HAVE BEEN LEFT BEHIND IN BLUE SPRAY PAINT GRAFFITI, AS A CALLING CARD OF SORTS...
SKID ROW. DOWNTOWN LOS ANGELES.
"BLUE KRÜE?" IMBECILES...
...WHAT A WAY TO TRIVIALIZE THE MAGNIFICENCE OF MY NEW PILL AND THE ARMY IT WILL BUILD...
...MY BLUE HYDE BRIGADE WILL UNIFY L.A. GANGS AND STOMP OUT ANYONE OPPOSED... A FORCE OF UNIFIED CRIME.
QUIET, HYDE! NEED I REMIND YOU WHO'S RESPONSIBLE FOR OUR LATEST DEFEAT?
YES. I, DR. ZABO, AM THE BRAINS OF THIS OPERATION, BUT YOU, MY FRIEND, HAVE FAILED AS THE BRAWN.
YOU'D BE SMART TO PAY HEED THIS TIME AROUND.
THESE BOYS ARE BETTER THAN ANY MERCENARY. THEIR LACK OF SKILL IS OUTWEIGHED BY THEIR IMPRESSIONABLE MIND, MALLEABILITY, SHEER ABUNDANCE AND COST EFFICIENCY.
GUTTER TRASH IS CHEAP.

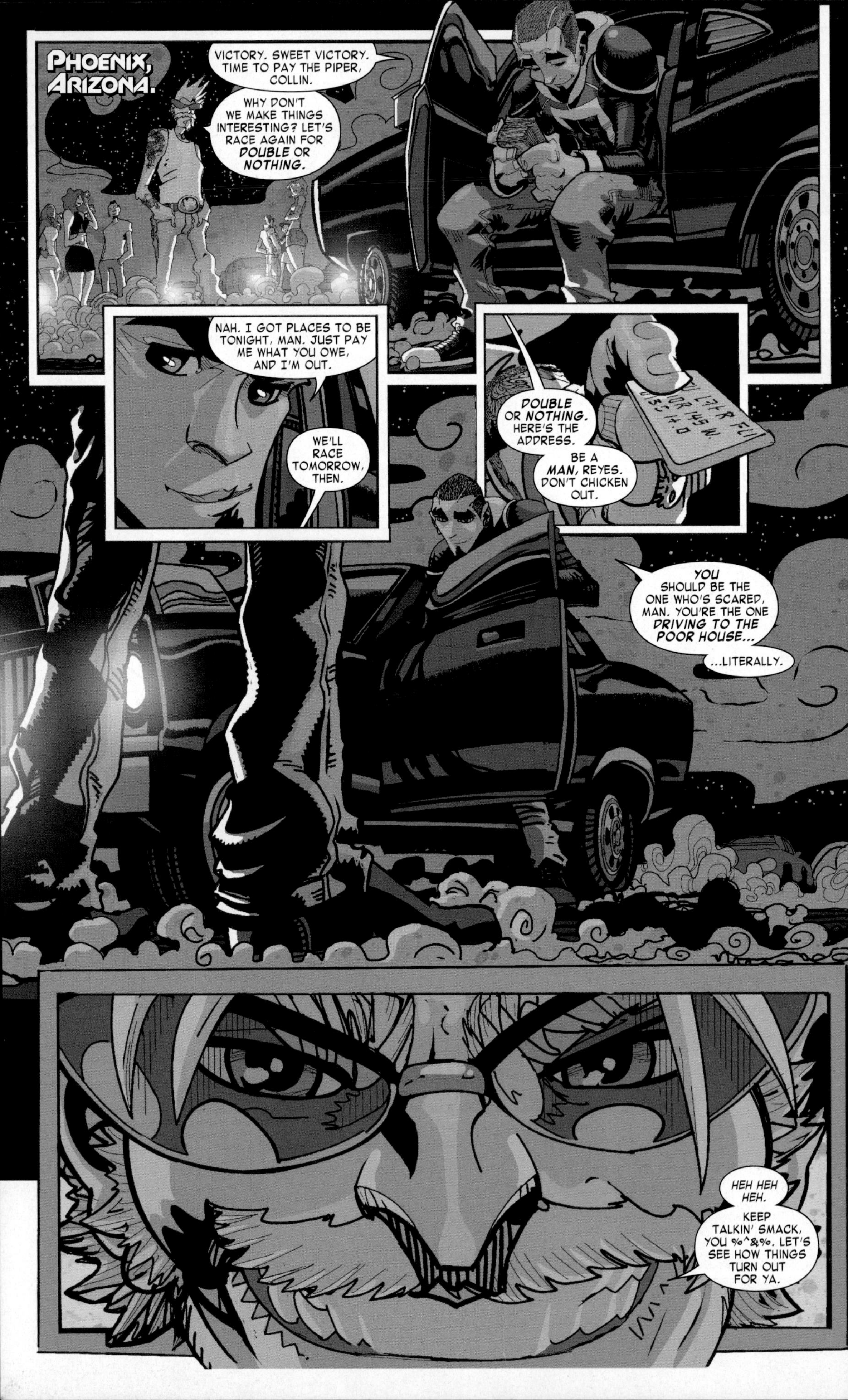

PHOENIX, ARIZONA.
VICTORY. SWEET VICTORY. TIME TO PAY THE PIPER, COLLIN.
WHY DON'T WE MAKE THINGS INTERESTING? LET'S RACE AGAIN FOR DOUBLE OR NOTHING.
NAH. I GOT PLACES TO BE TONIGHT, MAN. JUST PAY ME WHAT YOU OWE, AND I'M OUT.
WE'LL RACE TOMORROW, THEN.
DOUBLE OR NOTHING. HERE'S THE ADDRESS.
BE A MAN, REYES. DON'T CHICKEN OUT.
YOU SHOULD BE THE ONE WHO'S SCARED, MAN. YOU'RE THE ONE DRIVING TO THE POOR HOUSE...
...LITERALLY.
HEH HEH HEH.
KEEP TALKIN' SMACK, YOU %^&%. LET'S SEE HOW THINGS TURN OUT FOR YA.

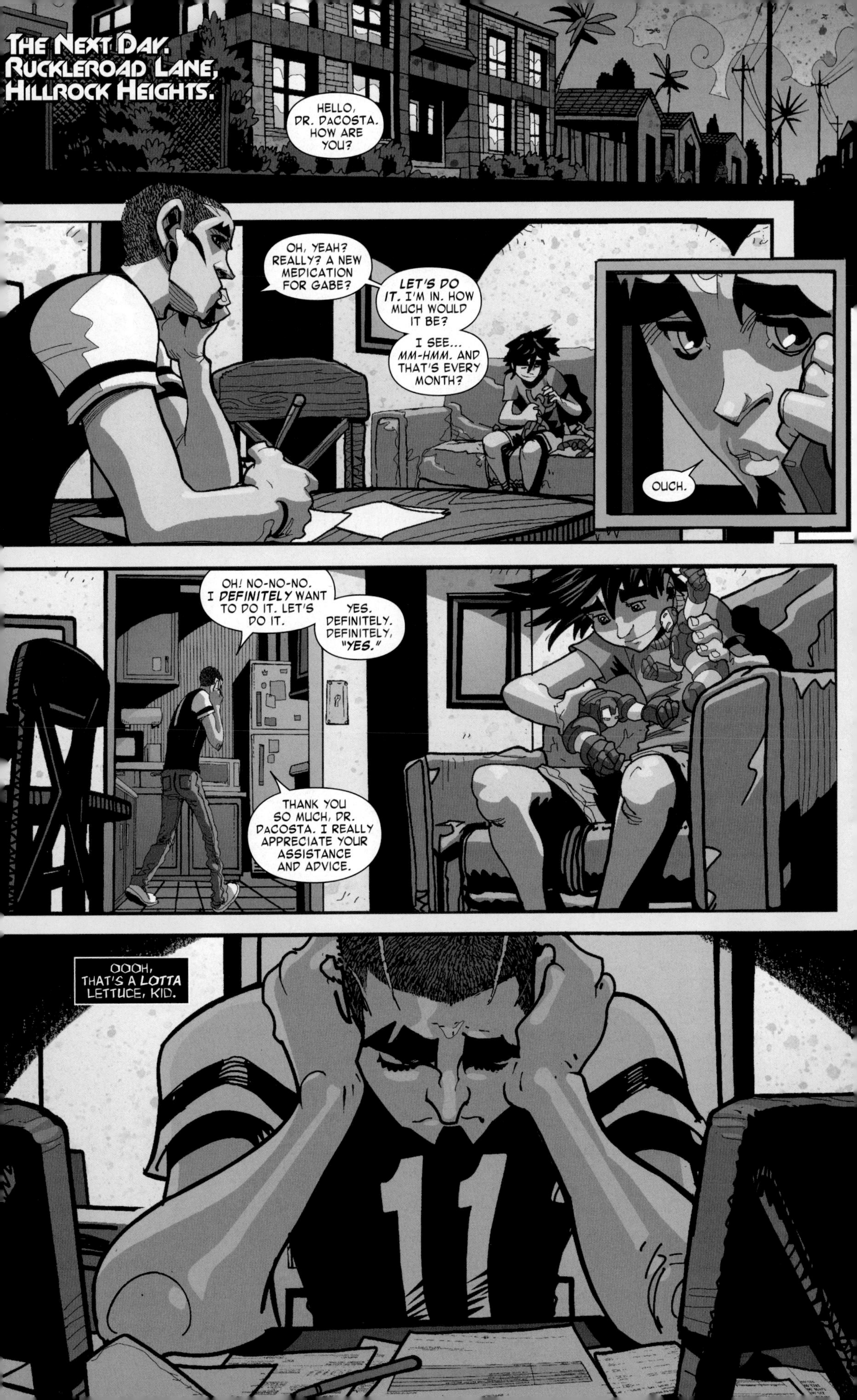
THE NEXT DAY. RUCKLEROAD LANE, HILLROCK HEIGHTS.
HELLO, DR. DACOSTA. HOW ARE YOU?
OH, YEAH? REALLY? A NEW MEDICATION FOR GABE?
LET'S DO IT. I'M IN. HOW MUCH WOULD IT BE?
I SEE... MM-HMM. AND THAT'S EVERY MONTH?
OUCH.
OH! NO-NO-NO. I DEFINITELY WANT TO DO IT. LET'S DO IT.
YES. DEFINITELY. DEFINITELY, "YES."
THANK YOU SO MUCH, DR. DACOSTA. I REALLY APPRECIATE YOUR ASSISTANCE AND ADVICE.
OOOH, THAT'S A LOTTA LETTUCE, KID.
11

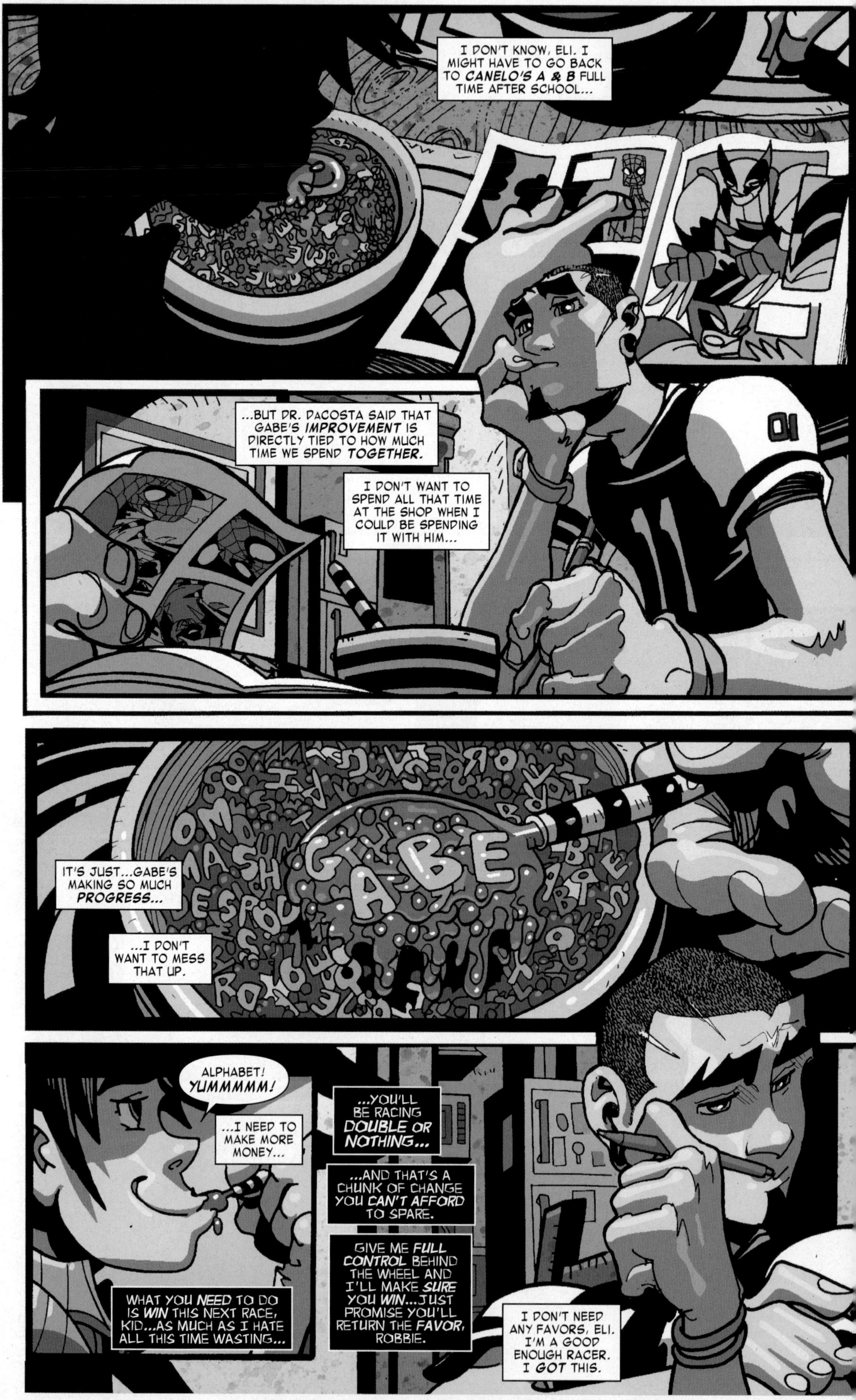

I DON'T KNOW, ELI. I MIGHT HAVE TO GO BACK TO CANELO'S A & B FULL TIME AFTER SCHOOL...
...BUT DR. DACOSTA SAID THAT GABE'S IMPROVEMENT IS DIRECTLY TIED TO HOW MUCH TIME WE SPEND TOGETHER.
I DON'T WANT TO SPEND ALL THAT TIME AT THE SHOP WHEN I COULD BE SPENDING IT WITH HIM...
IT'S JUST...GABE'S MAKING SO MUCH PROGRESS...
...I DON'T WANT TO MESS THAT UP.
ALPHABET! YUMMMMM!
...I NEED TO MAKE MORE MONEY...
WHAT YOU NEED TO DO IS WIN THIS NEXT RACE, KID...AS MUCH AS I HATE ALL THIS TIME WASTING...
...YOU'LL BE RACING DOUBLE OR NOTHING...
...AND THAT'S A CHUNK OF CHANGE YOU CAN'T AFFORD TO SPARE.
GIVE ME FULL CONTROL BEHIND THE WHEEL AND I'LL MAKE SURE YOU WIN...JUST PROMISE YOU'LL RETURN THE FAVOR, ROBBIE.
I DON'T NEED ANY FAVORS, ELI. I'M A GOOD ENOUGH RACER. I GOT THIS.

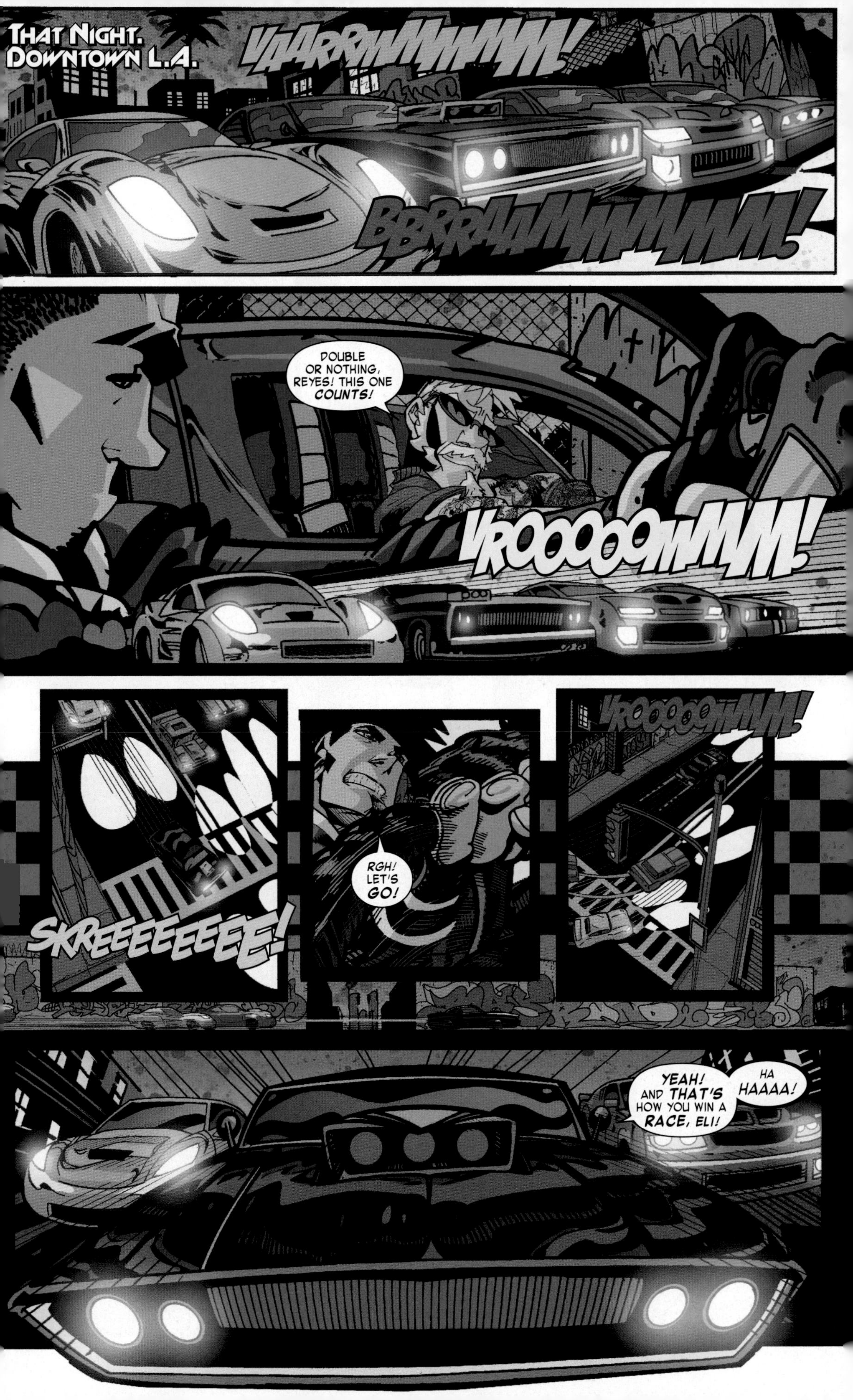
THAT NIGHT. DOWNTOWN L.A.
VAARRRMMMMM!
BBRRAAMMMMMM!
DOUBLE OR NOTHING, REYES! THIS ONE COUNTS!
VROOOOOOMMM!
SKREEEEEEEEE!
RGH! LET'S GO!
VROOOOOMMM!
YEAH! AND THAT'S HOW YOU WIN A RACE, ELI!
HA HAAAA!

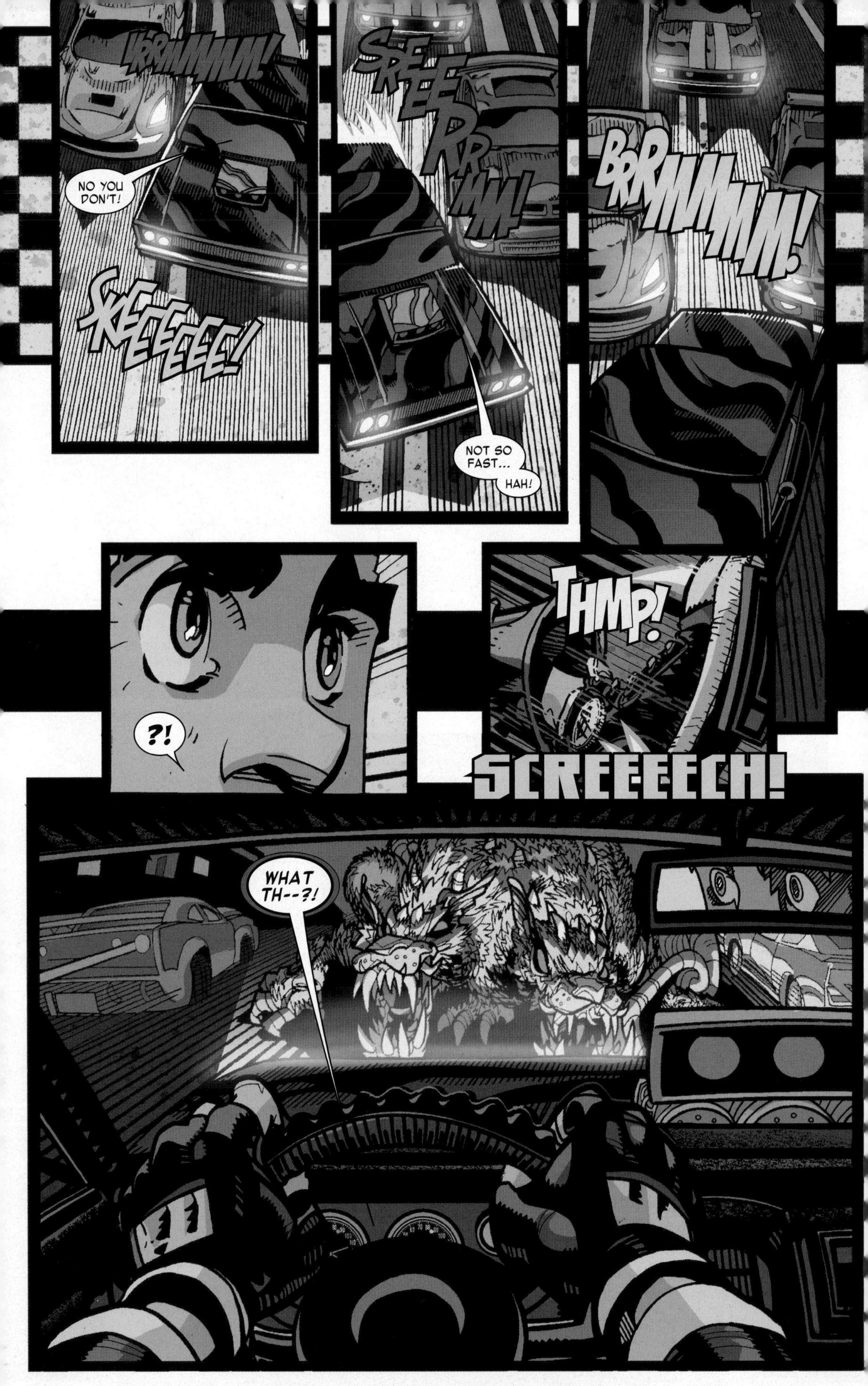
VRRMMMMM!
NO YOU DON'T!
SKEEEEEE!
SREEERRMM!
NOT SO FAST...
HAH!
BRRMMMMM!
?!
THMP!
SCREEEECH!
WHAT TH--?!

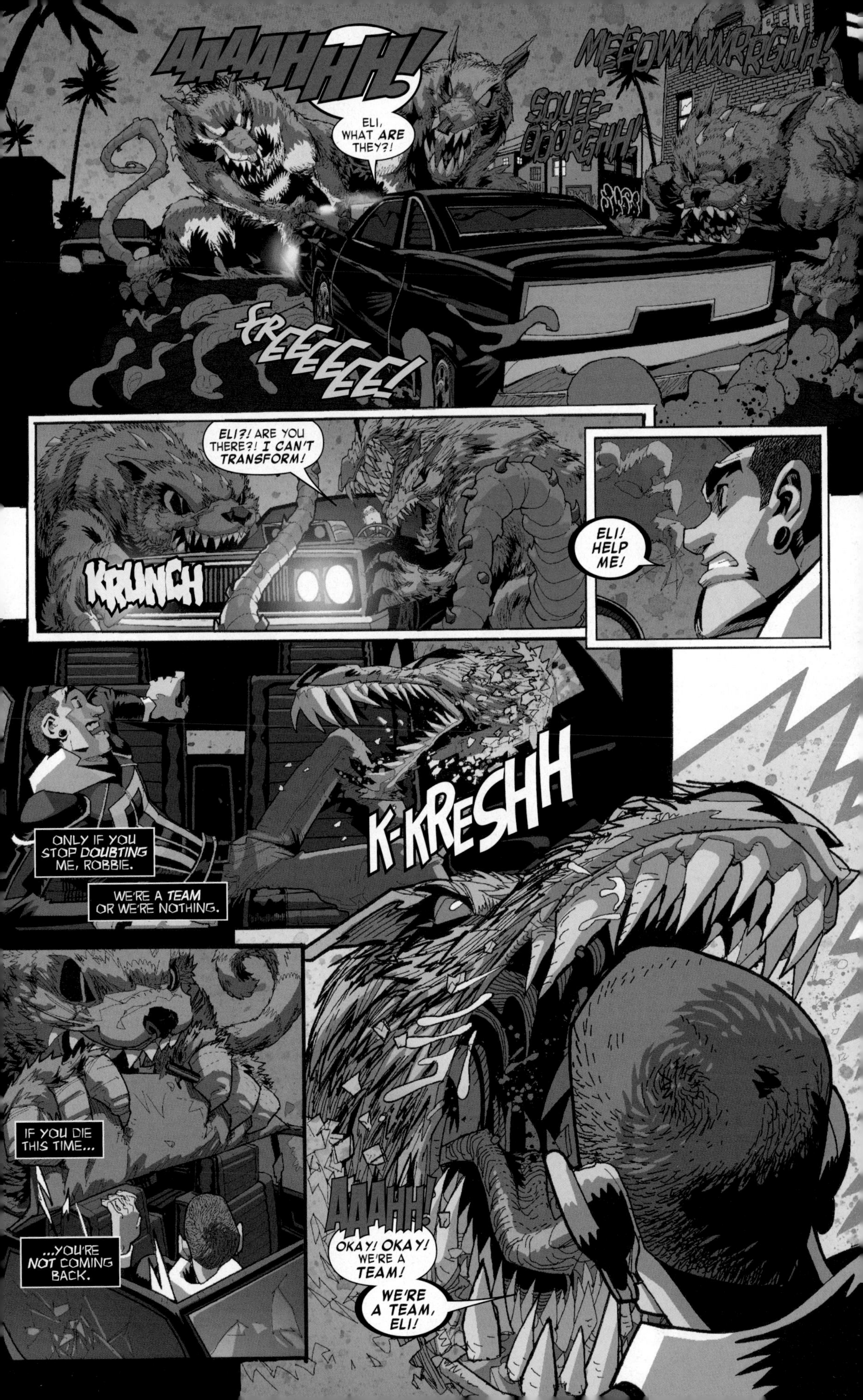
AAAAHHHH!
ELI, WHAT ARE THEY?!
MEEOWWWRRGHH!
SQUEE-OOORGHH!
EREEEEEE!
ELI?! ARE YOU THERE?! I CAN'T TRANSFORM!
KRUNCH
ELI! HELP ME!
K-KRESHH
ONLY IF YOU STOP DOUBTING ME, ROBBIE.
WE'RE A TEAM OR WE'RE NOTHING.
IF YOU DIE THIS TIME...
...YOU'RE NOT COMING BACK.
AAAHH!
OKAY! OKAY! WE'RE A TEAM!
WE'RE A TEAM, ELI!

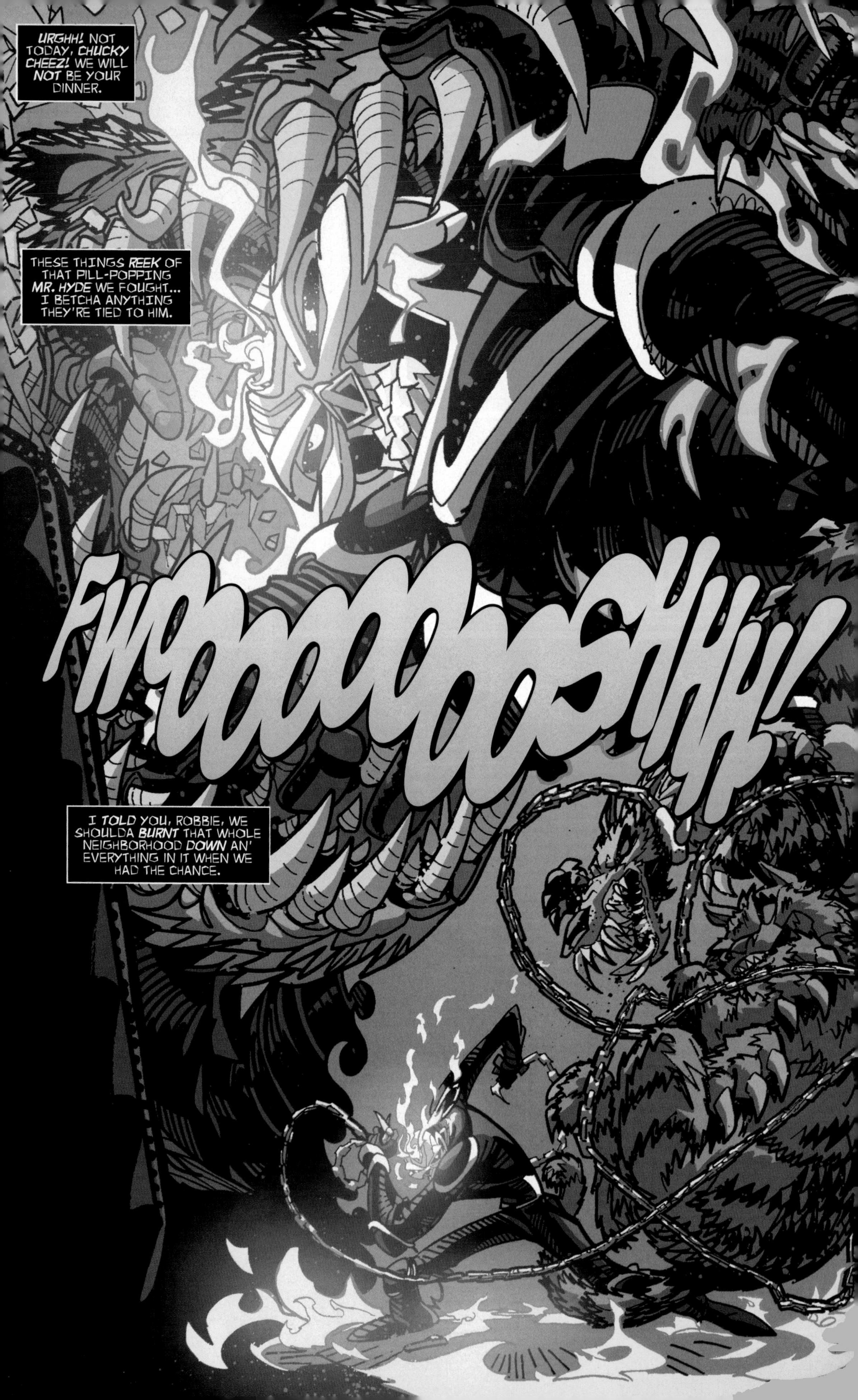
URGHH! NOT TODAY, CHUCKY CHEEZ! WE WILL NOT BE YOUR DINNER.
THESE THINGS REEK OF THAT PILL-POPPING MR. HYDE WE FOUGHT... I BETCHA ANYTHING THEY'RE TIED TO HIM.
FWOOOOOOSHH!
I TOLD YOU, ROBBIE, WE SHOULDA BURNT THAT WHOLE NEIGHBORHOOD DOWN AN' EVERYTHING IN IT WHEN WE HAD THE CHANCE.

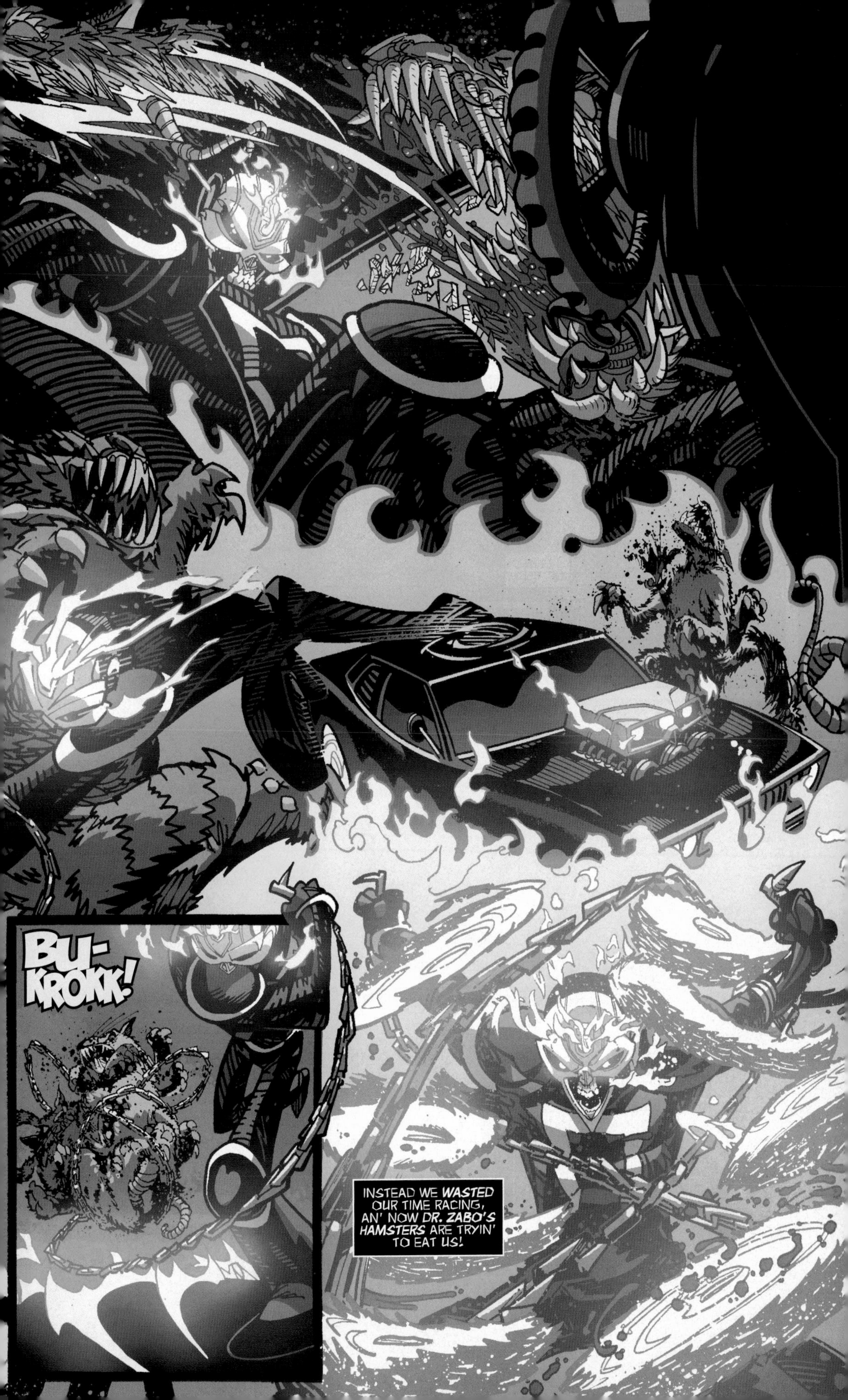
BU-KROKK!
INSTEAD WE WASTED OUR TIME RACING, AN' NOW DR. ZABO'S HAMSTERS ARE TRYIN' TO EAT US!

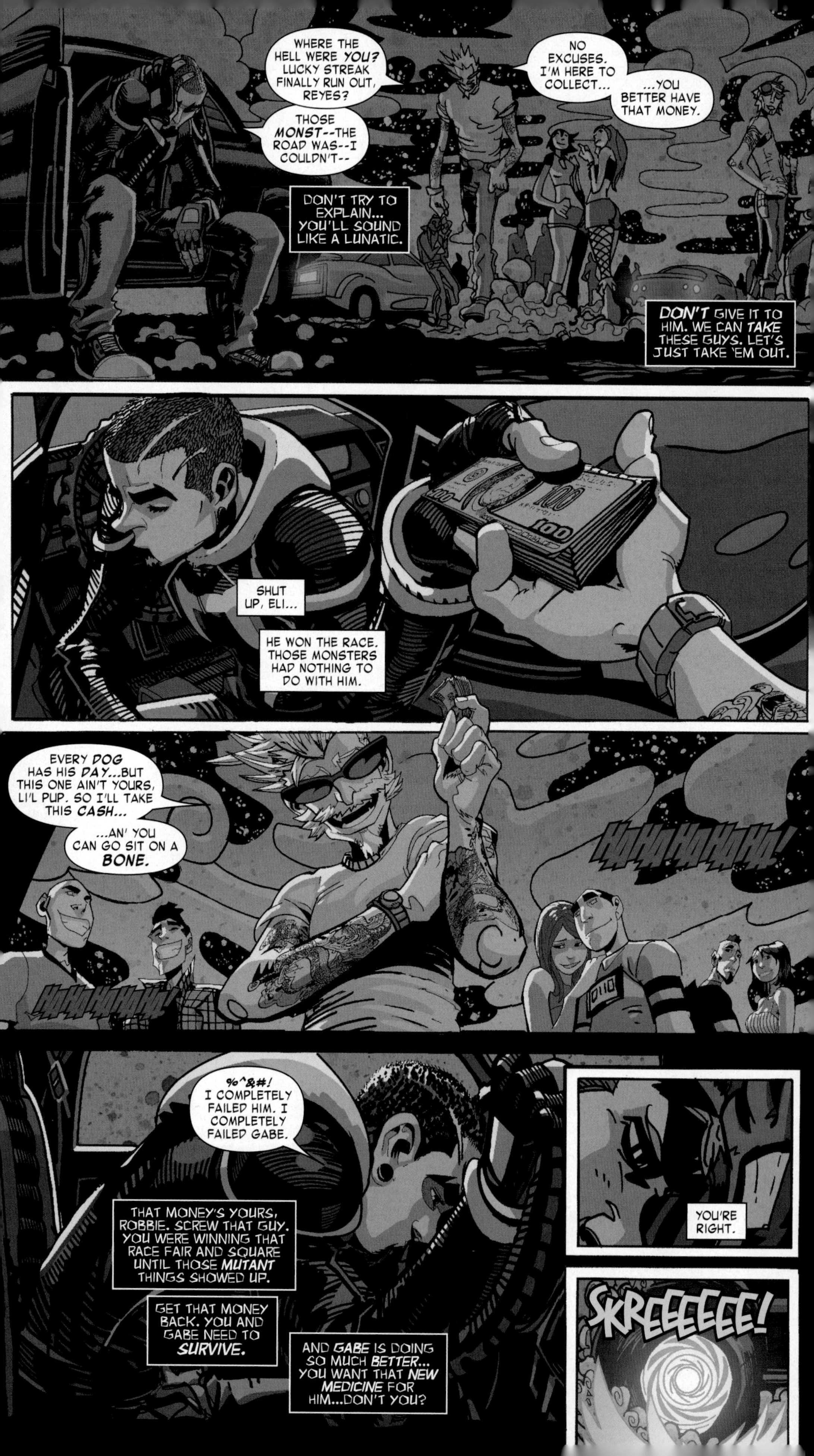
WHERE THE HELL WERE YOU? LUCKY STREAK FINALLY RUN OUT, REYES?
THOSE MONST--THE ROAD WAS--I COULDN'T--
NO EXCUSES. I'M HERE TO COLLECT...
...YOU BETTER HAVE THAT MONEY.
DON'T TRY TO EXPLAIN... YOU'LL SOUND LIKE A LUNATIC.
DON'T GIVE IT TO HIM. WE CAN TAKE THESE GUYS. LET'S JUST TAKE 'EM OUT.
SHUT UP, ELI...
HE WON THE RACE. THOSE MONSTERS HAD NOTHING TO DO WITH HIM.
EVERY DOG HAS HIS DAY...BUT THIS ONE AIN'T YOURS, LI'L PUP. SO I'LL TAKE THIS CASH...
...AN' YOU CAN GO SIT ON A BONE.
HAHAHAHAHA!
HAHAHAHAHA!
%^&#! I COMPLETELY FAILED HIM. I COMPLETELY FAILED GABE.
THAT MONEY'S YOURS, ROBBIE. SCREW THAT GUY. YOU WERE WINNING THAT RACE FAIR AND SQUARE UNTIL THOSE MUTANT THINGS SHOWED UP.
GET THAT MONEY BACK. YOU AND GABE NEED TO SURVIVE.
AND GABE IS DOING SO MUCH BETTER... YOU WANT THAT NEW MEDICINE FOR HIM...DON'T YOU?
YOU'RE RIGHT.
SKREEEEEEE!

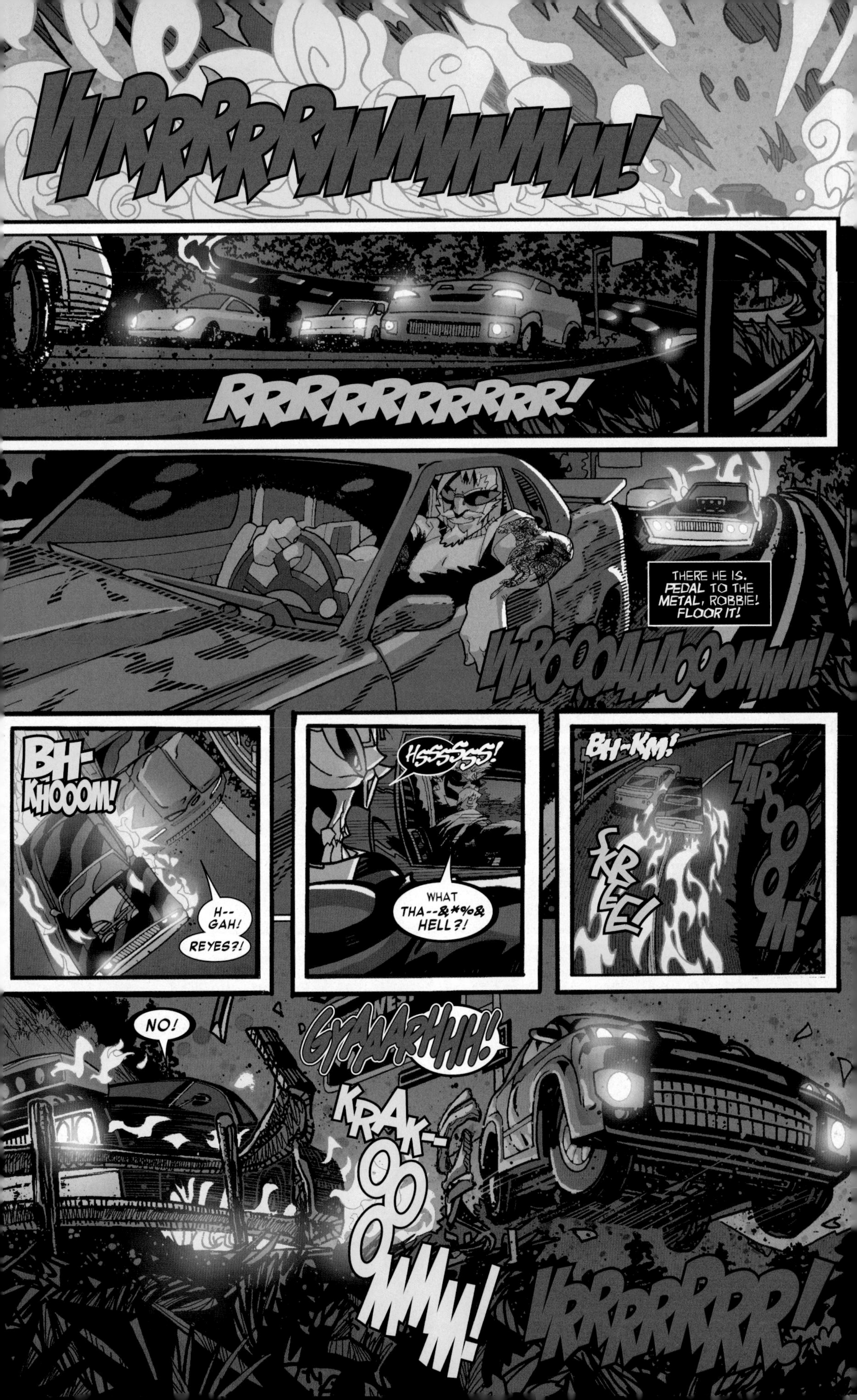
VVRRRRRRMMMMMM!
RRRRRRRRRRRR!
THERE HE IS. PEDAL TO THE METAL, ROBBIE! FLOOR IT!
VVROOOAAAOOOMMM!
BH-KHOOOM!
H--GAH! REYES?!
HSSSSSS!
WHAT THA--&*%& HELL?!
BH-KM!
VAROOOOM!
KREE!
NO!
GYAAARHHH!
KRAK--OOOMMM!
VRRRRRRRR!

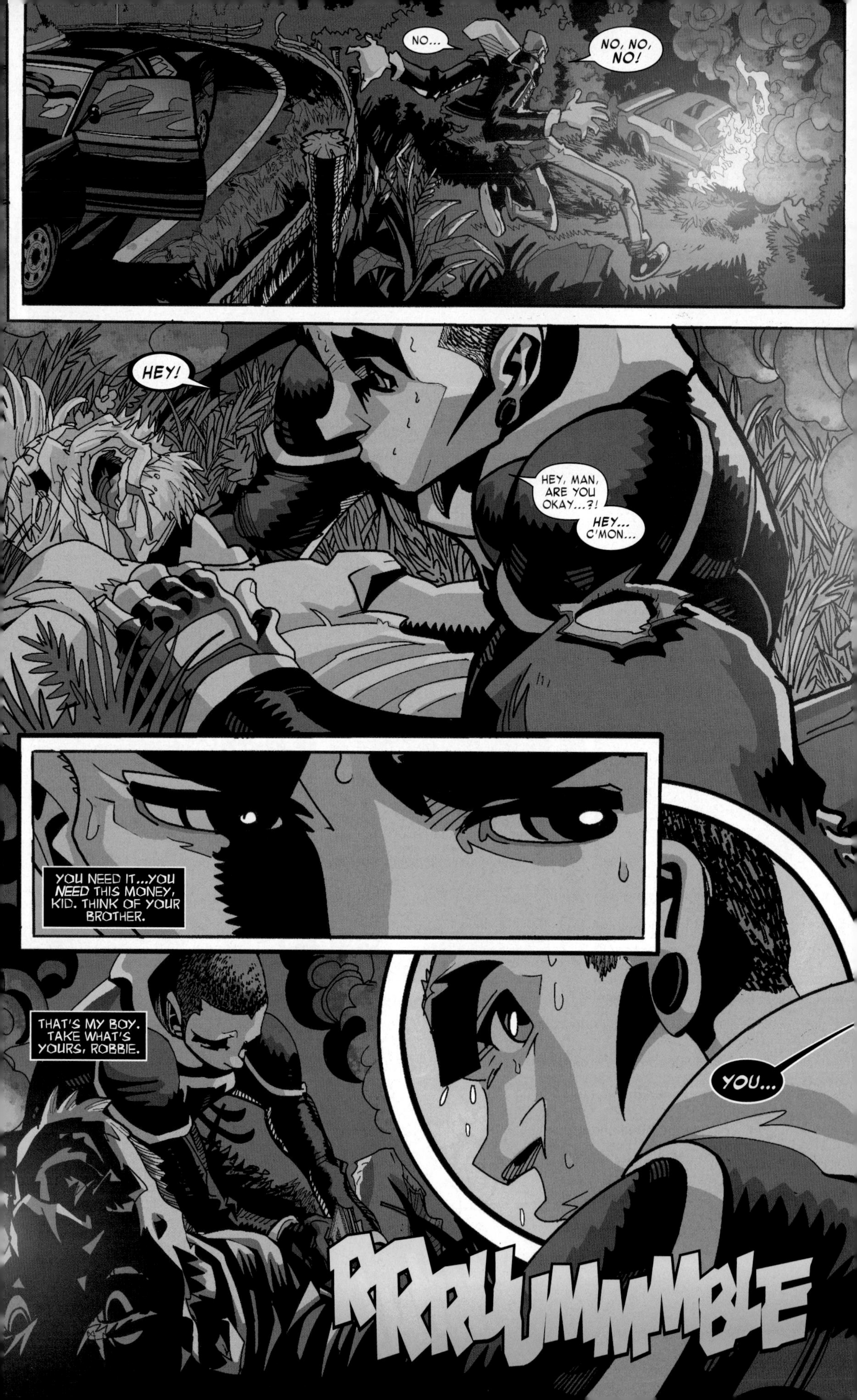
NO...
NO, NO, NO!
HEY!
HEY, MAN, ARE YOU OKAY...?!
HEY... C'MON...
YOU NEED IT...YOU NEED THIS MONEY, KID. THINK OF YOUR BROTHER.
THAT'S MY BOY. TAKE WHAT'S YOURS, ROBBIE.
YOU...
RRRRUUMMMMBLE

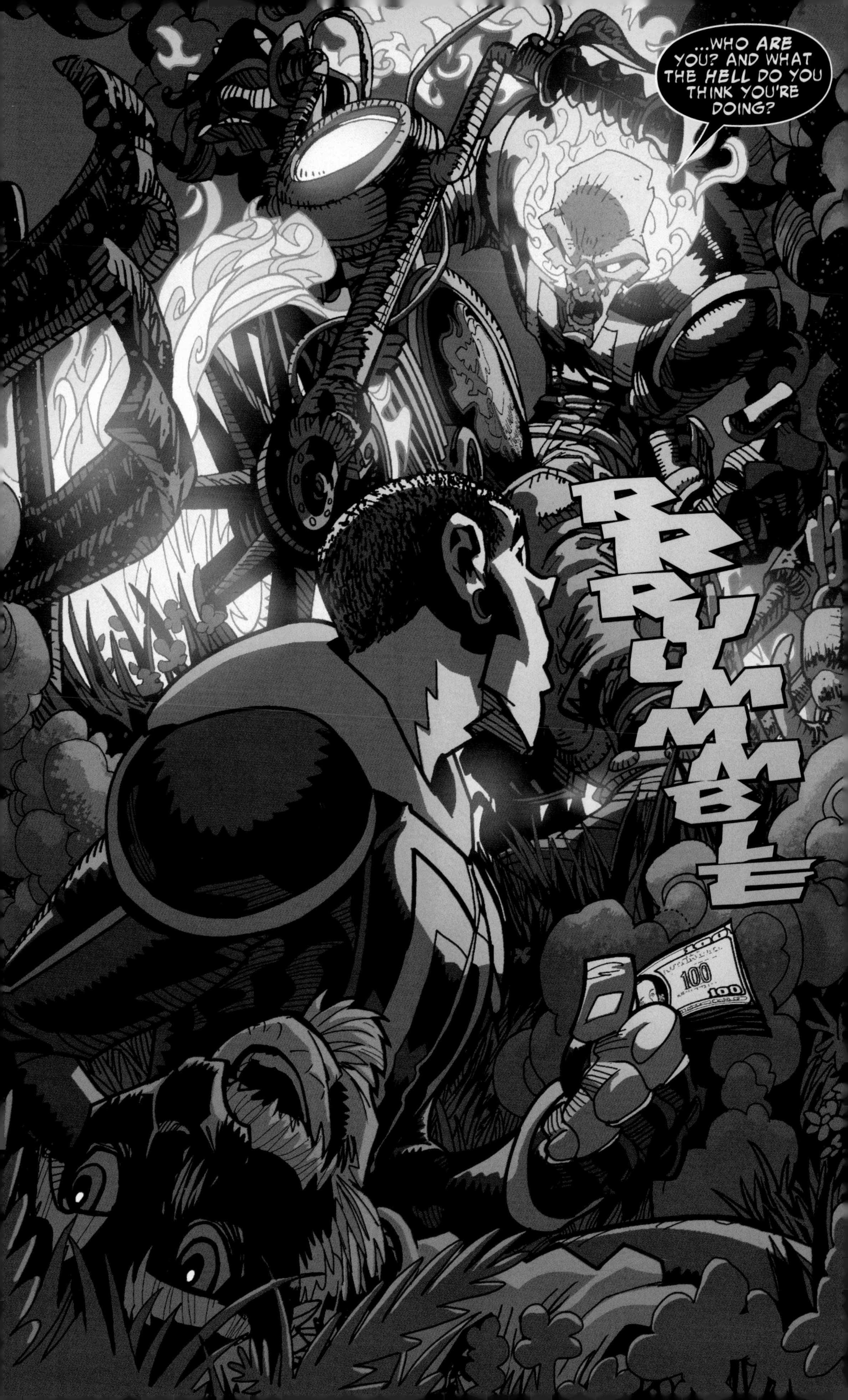
...WHO ARE YOU? AND WHAT THE HELL DO YOU THINK YOU'RE DOING?
RRRUMMMBLE
100

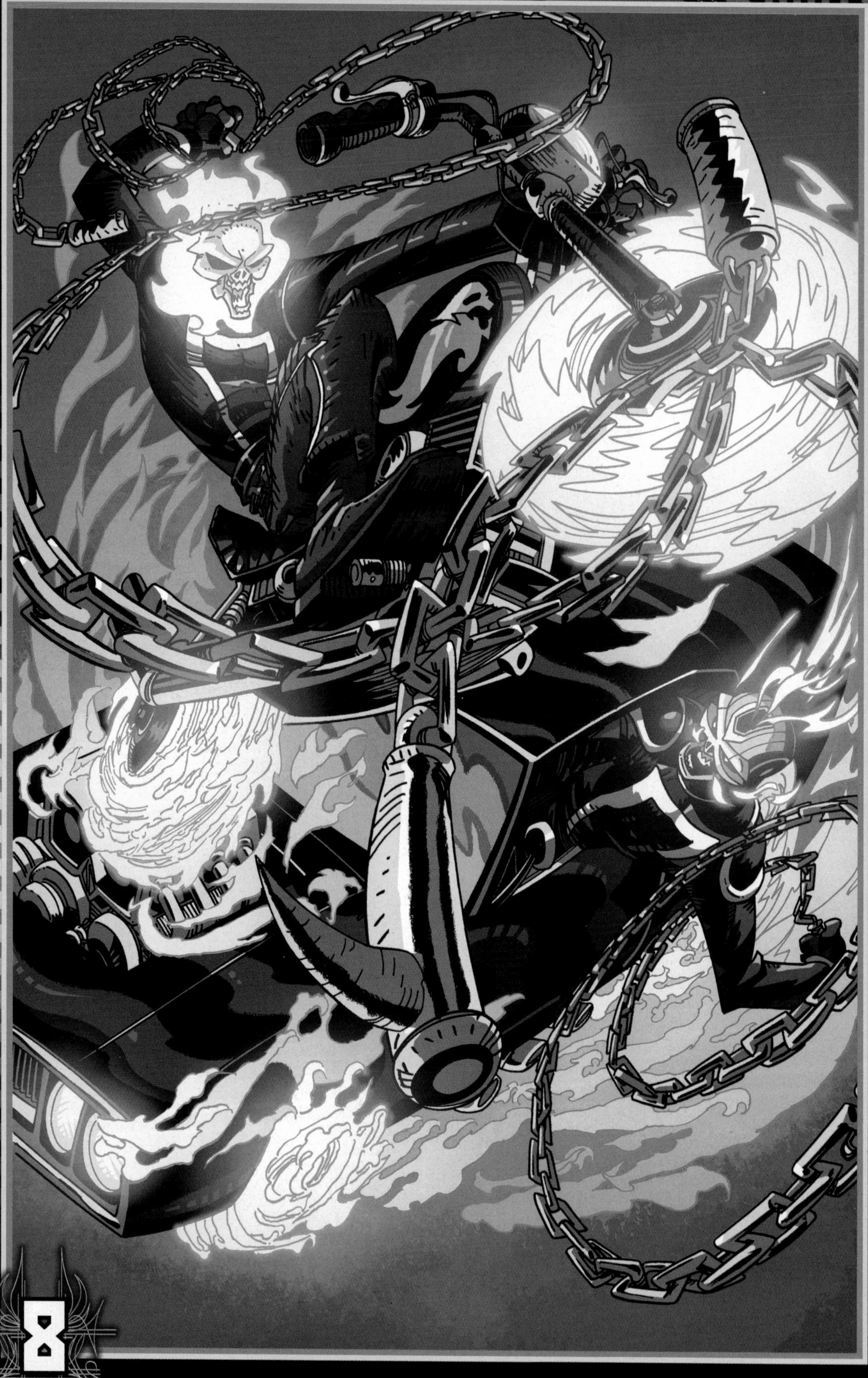

8

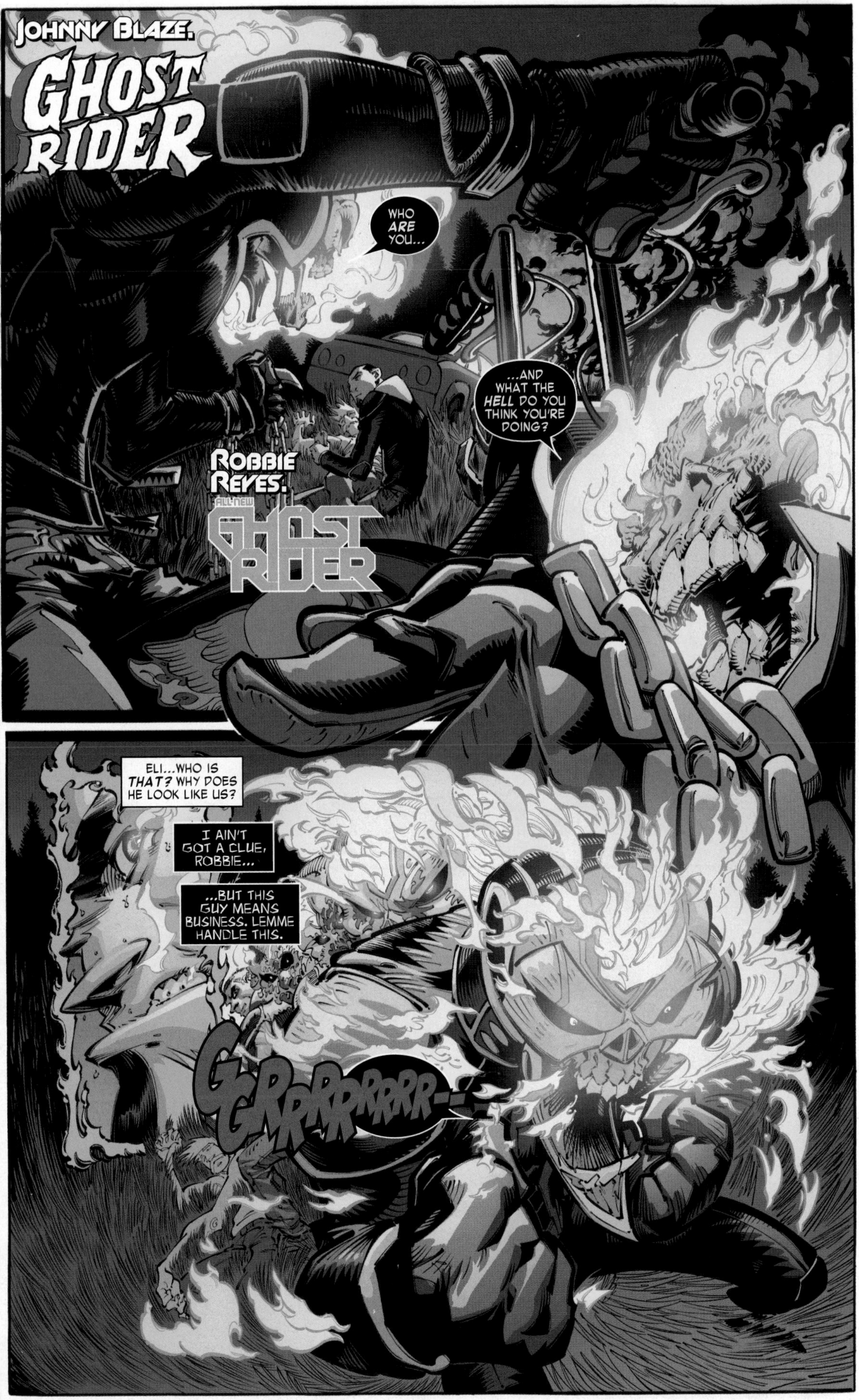
JOHNNY BLAZE.
GHOST RIDER
WHO ARE YOU...
...AND WHAT THE HELL DO YOU THINK YOU'RE DOING?
ROBBIE REYES.
ALL-NEW GHOST RIDER
ELI...WHO IS THAT? WHY DOES HE LOOK LIKE US?
I AIN'T GOT A CLUE, ROBBIE...
...BUT THIS GUY MEANS BUSINESS. LEMME HANDLE THIS.
GGRRRRRRRR--!

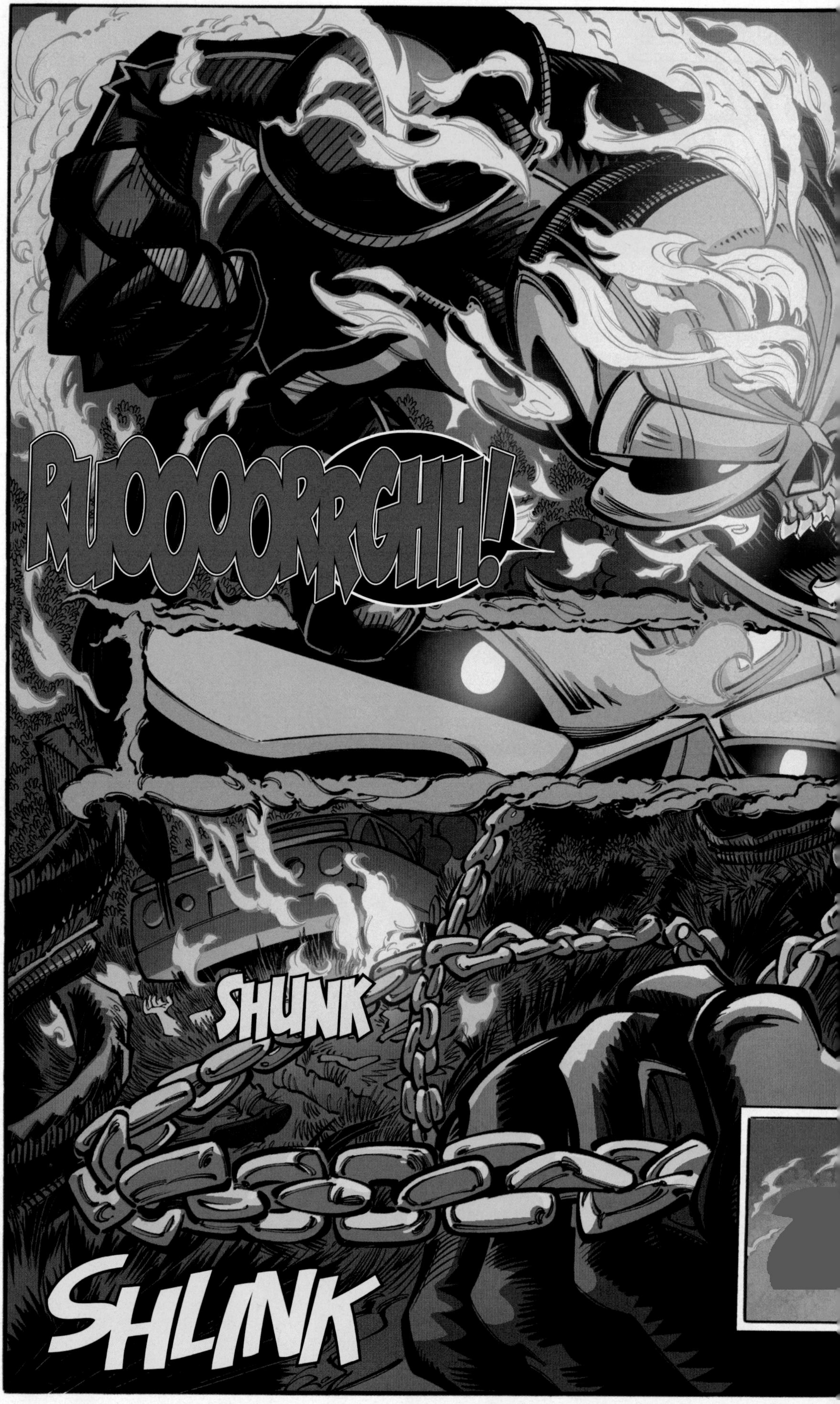
RUOOOORRGHH!
SHUNK
SHLINK

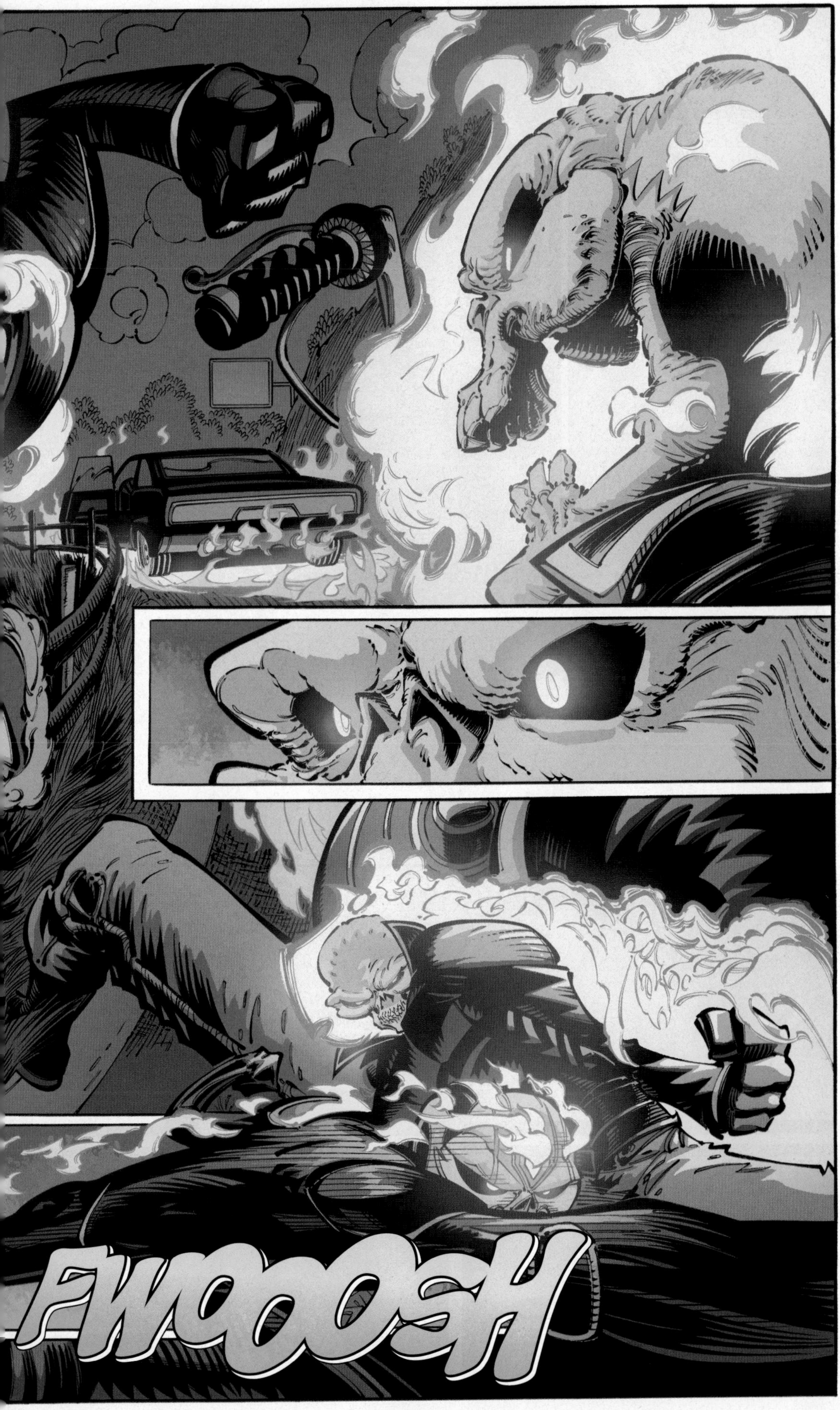
FWOOOSH

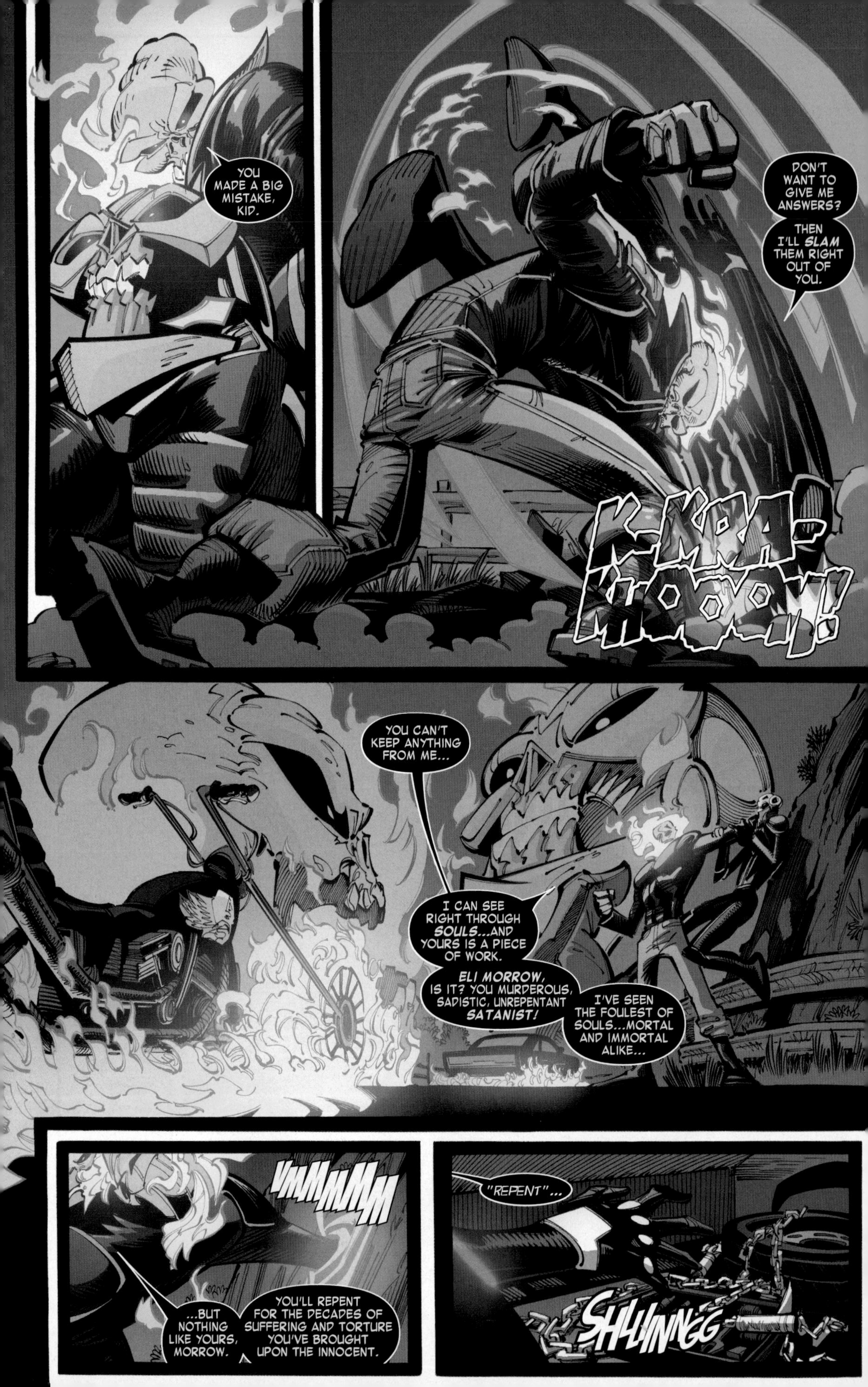

YOU MADE A BIG MISTAKE, KID.
DON'T WANT TO GIVE ME ANSWERS?
THEN I'LL SLAM THEM RIGHT OUT OF YOU.
K-KRA-KHOOOOM!
YOU CAN'T KEEP ANYTHING FROM ME...
I CAN SEE RIGHT THROUGH SOULS...AND YOURS IS A PIECE OF WORK.
ELI MORROW, IS IT? YOU MURDEROUS, SADISTIC, UNREPENTANT SATANIST!
I'VE SEEN THE FOULEST OF SOULS...MORTAL AND IMMORTAL ALIKE...
...BUT NOTHING LIKE YOURS, MORROW.
YOU'LL REPENT FOR THE DECADES OF SUFFERING AND TORTURE YOU'VE BROUGHT UPON THE INNOCENT.
UMMMMMM
"REPENT"...
SHUUNNGG

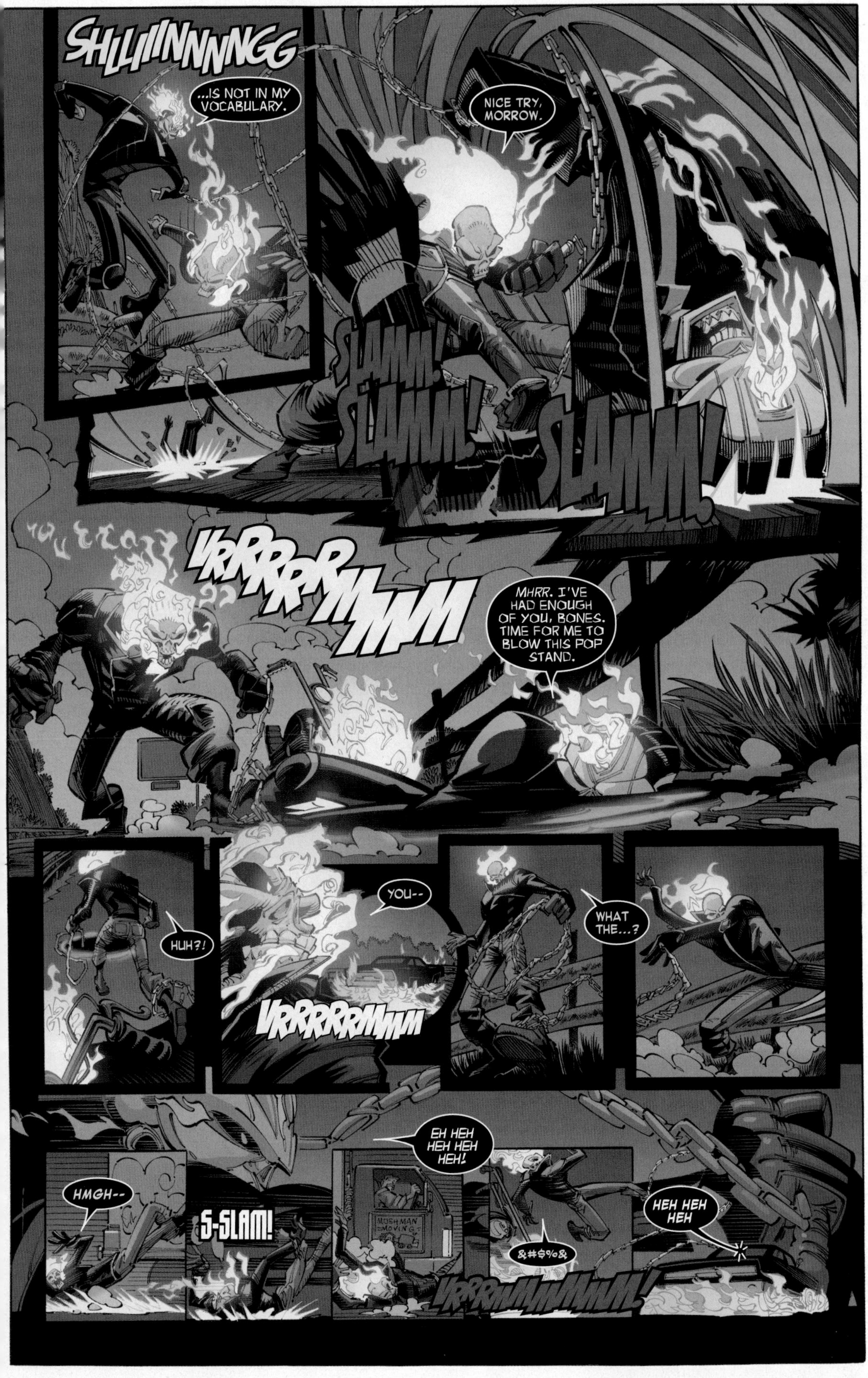
SHLLIIIINNNNGG
...IS NOT IN MY VOCABULARY.
NICE TRY, MORROW.
SLAMM! SLAMM! SLAMM!
VRRRRRMMMM
MHRR. I'VE HAD ENOUGH OF YOU, BONES. TIME FOR ME TO BLOW THIS POP STAND.
HUH?!
YOU--
VRRRRRMMM
WHAT THE...?
HMGH--
S-SLAM!
EH HEH HEH HEH HEH!
MOSHMAN MOVING
&#$%&
HEH HEH HEH
VRRRMMMMMMM!

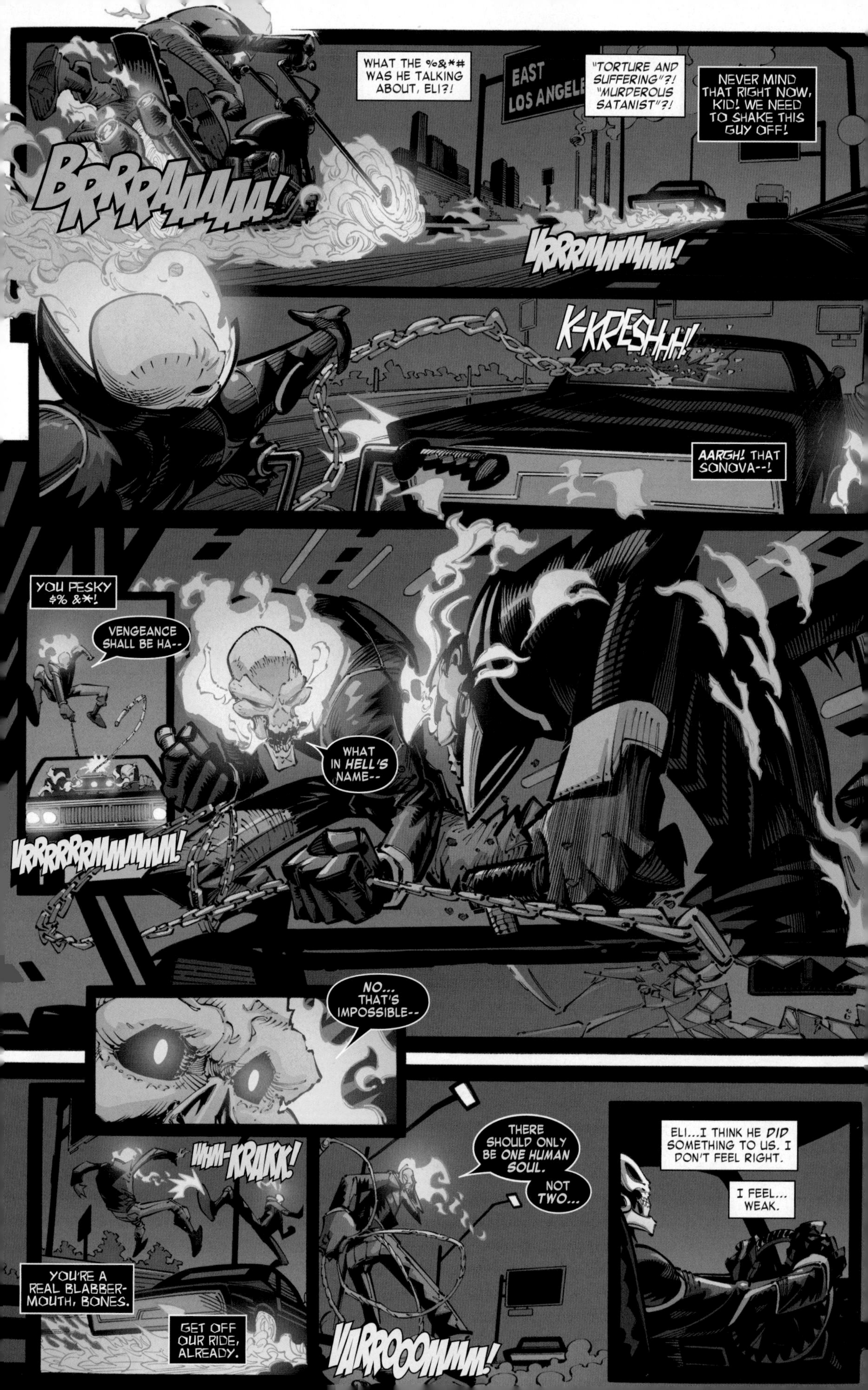

WHAT THE %&*# WAS HE TALKING ABOUT, ELI?!
EAST LOS ANGELE
"TORTURE AND SUFFERING"?! "MURDEROUS SATANIST"?!
NEVER MIND THAT RIGHT NOW, KID! WE NEED TO SHAKE THIS GUY OFF!
BRRRAAAAAA!
VRRRMMMMMM!
K-KRESHHH!
AARGH! THAT SONOVA--!
YOU PESKY $% &*!
VENGEANCE SHALL BE HA--
WHAT IN HELL'S NAME--
VRRRRRRMMMMM!
NO... THAT'S IMPOSSIBLE--
WHM-KRAKK!
YOU'RE A REAL BLABBERMOUTH, BONES.
GET OFF OUR RIDE, ALREADY.
THERE SHOULD ONLY BE ONE HUMAN SOUL.
NOT TWO...
VARROOOMMM!
ELI...I THINK HE DID SOMETHING TO US. I DON'T FEEL RIGHT.
I FEEL... WEAK.

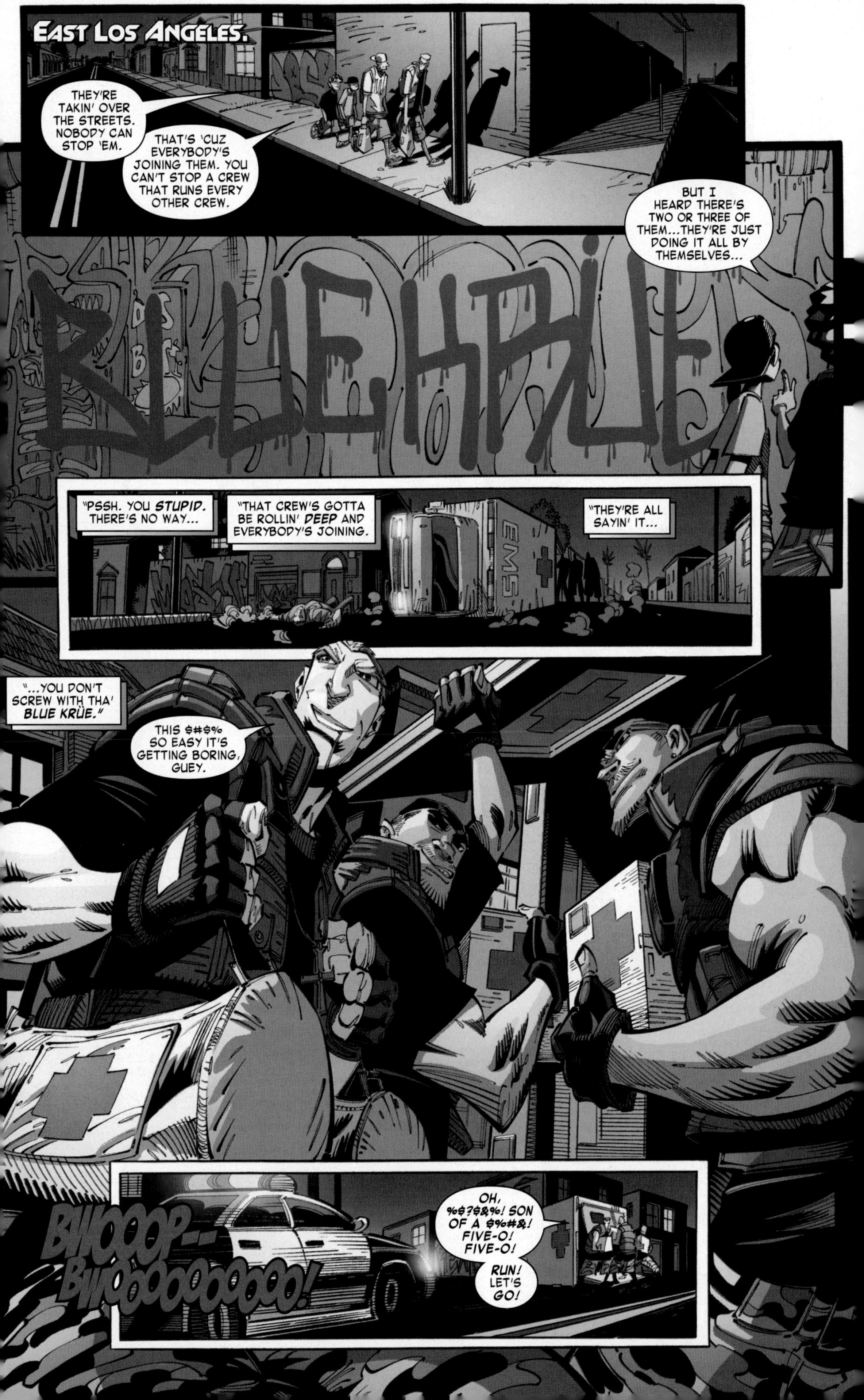
East Los Angeles.
THEY'RE TAKIN' OVER THE STREETS. NOBODY CAN STOP 'EM.
THAT'S 'CUZ EVERYBODY'S JOINING THEM. YOU CAN'T STOP A CREW THAT RUNS EVERY OTHER CREW.
BUT I HEARD THERE'S TWO OR THREE OF THEM...THEY'RE JUST DOING IT ALL BY THEMSELVES...
"PSSH. YOU STUPID. THERE'S NO WAY...
"THAT CREW'S GOTTA BE ROLLIN' DEEP AND EVERYBODY'S JOINING.
"THEY'RE ALL SAYIN' IT...
EMS
"...YOU DON'T SCREW WITH THA' BLUE KRÜE."
THIS $#$% SO EASY IT'S GETTING BORING, GUEY.
BWOOOP--BWOOOOOOOOOOO!
OH, %$?$&%! SON OF A $%#&! FIVE-O! FIVE-O!
RUN! LET'S GO!

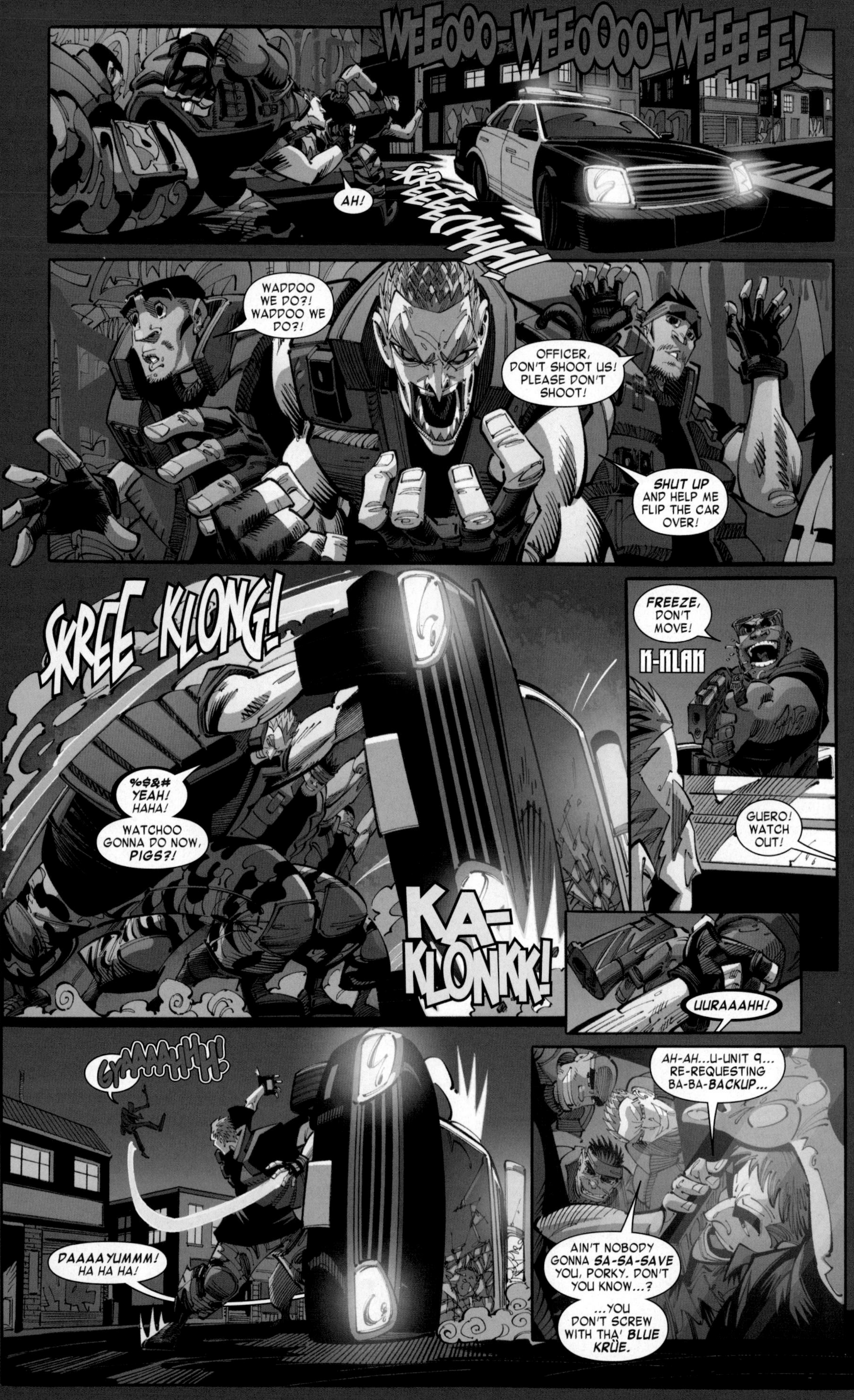
WEEOOO-WEEOOOO-WEEEEE!
AH!
SKREEECHHH!
WADDOO WE DO?! WADDOO WE DO?!
OFFICER, DON'T SHOOT US! PLEASE DON'T SHOOT!
SHUT UP AND HELP ME FLIP THE CAR OVER!
SKREE KLONG!
%$&# YEAH! HAHA!
WATCHOO GONNA DO NOW, PIGS?!
FREEZE, DON'T MOVE!
K-KLAK
GUERO! WATCH OUT!
KA-KLONKK!
UURAAAHH!
GYAAAHH!
DAAAAYUMMM! HA HA HA!
AH-AH...U-UNIT 9... RE-REQUESTING BA-BA-BACKUP...
AIN'T NOBODY GONNA SA-SA-SAVE YOU, PORKY. DON'T YOU KNOW...?
...YOU DON'T SCREW WITH THA' BLUE KRÜE.

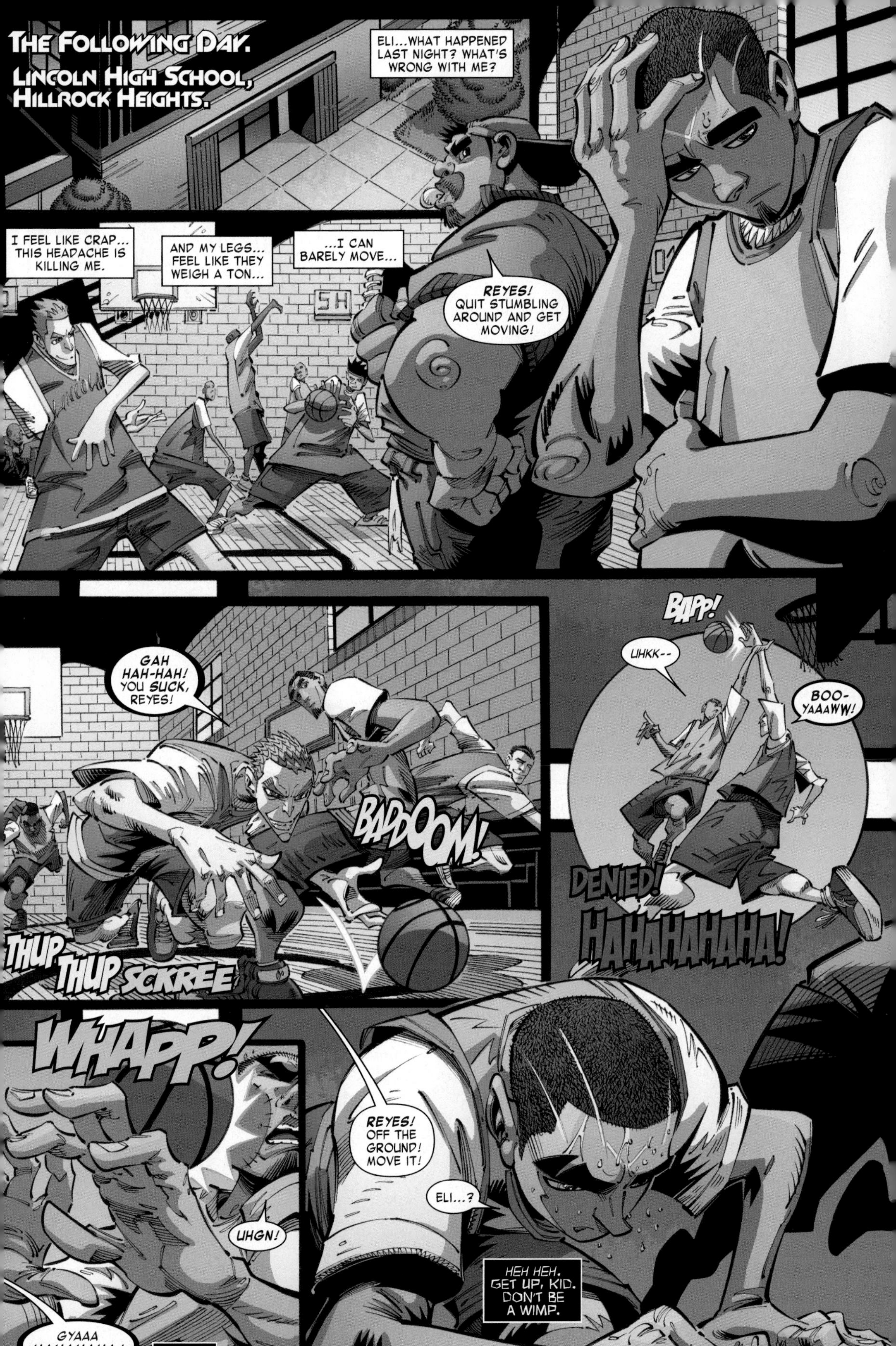
THE FOLLOWING DAY.
LINCOLN HIGH SCHOOL, HILLROCK HEIGHTS.
ELI...WHAT HAPPENED LAST NIGHT? WHAT'S WRONG WITH ME?
I FEEL LIKE CRAP... THIS HEADACHE IS KILLING ME.
AND MY LEGS... FEEL LIKE THEY WEIGH A TON...
...I CAN BARELY MOVE...
REYES! QUIT STUMBLING AROUND AND GET MOVING!
GAH HAH-HAH! YOU SUCK, REYES!
BADDOOM!
THUP THUP SCKREE
BAPP!
UHKK--
BOO-YAAAWW!
DENIED!
HAHAHAHAHA!
WHAPP!
UHGN!
GYAAA HAHAHAHA!
HEH HEH HEH.
REYES! OFF THE GROUND! MOVE IT!
ELI...?
HEH HEH. GET UP, KID. DON'T BE A WIMP.

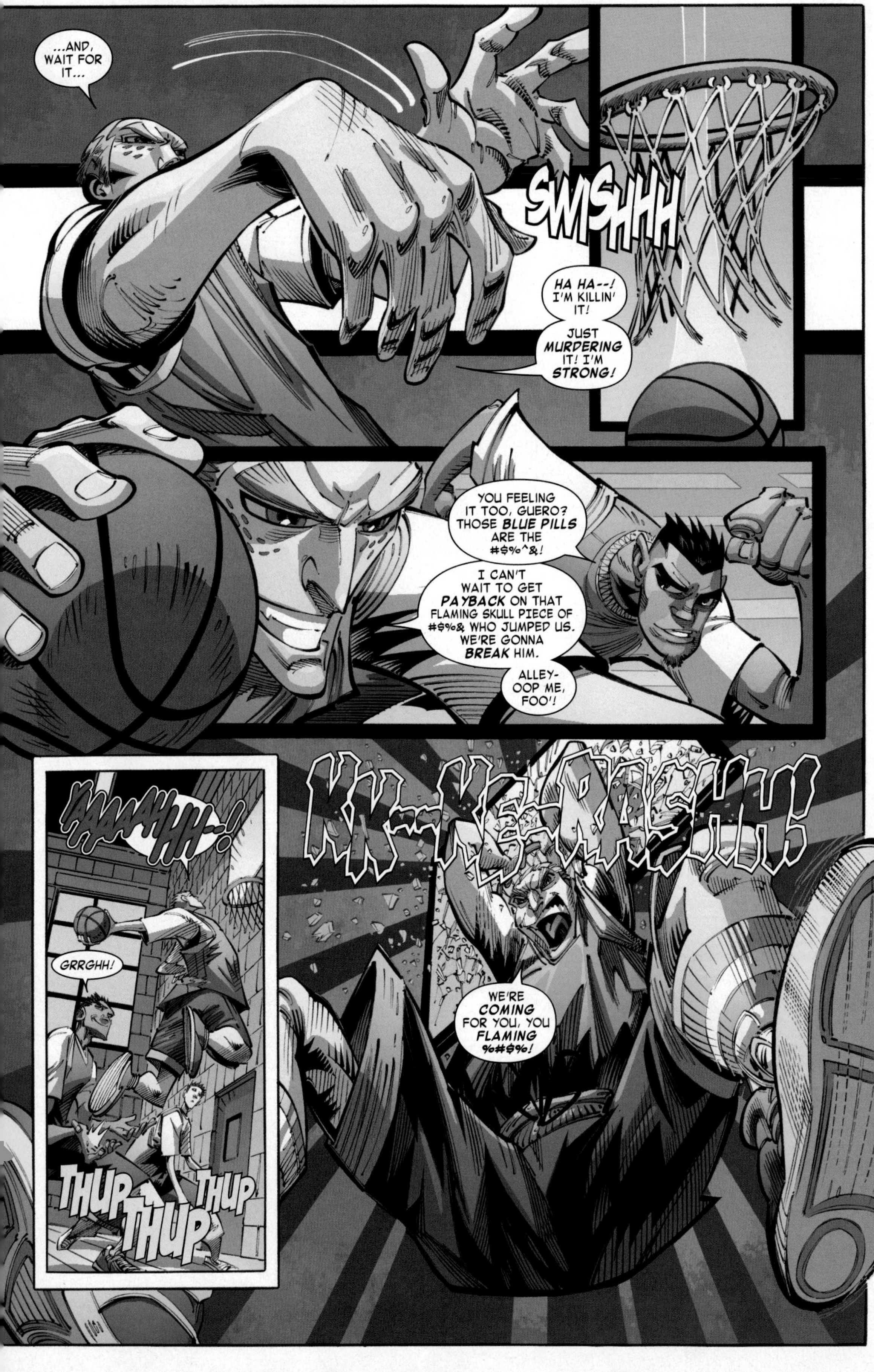
...AND, WAIT FOR IT...
SWISHHH
HA HA--! I'M KILLIN' IT!
JUST MURDERING IT! I'M STRONG!
YOU FEELING IT TOO, GUERO? THOSE BLUE PILLS ARE THE #$%^&!
I CAN'T WAIT TO GET PAYBACK ON THAT FLAMING SKULL PIECE OF #$%& WHO JUMPED US. WE'RE GONNA BREAK HIM.
ALLEY-OOP ME, FOO'!
YAAAAAHHH--!
GRRGHH!
THUP THUP THUP
WE'RE COMING FOR YOU, YOU FLAMING %#$%!

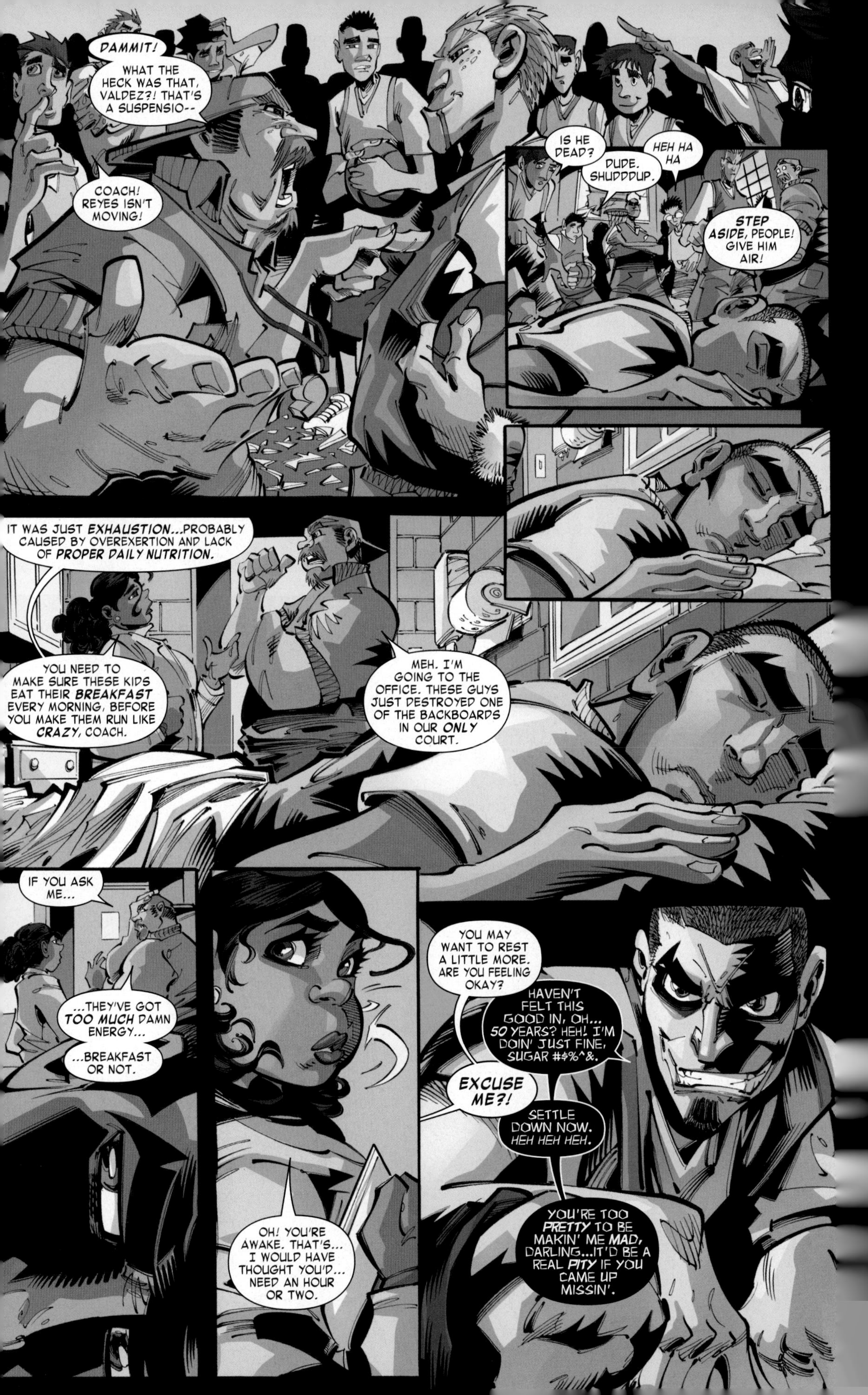
DAMMIT!
WHAT THE HECK WAS THAT, VALDEZ?! THAT'S A SUSPENSIO--
COACH! REYES ISN'T MOVING!
IS HE DEAD?
DUDE. SHUDDDUP.
HEH HA HA
STEP ASIDE, PEOPLE! GIVE HIM AIR!
IT WAS JUST EXHAUSTION...PROBABLY CAUSED BY OVEREXERTION AND LACK OF PROPER DAILY NUTRITION.
YOU NEED TO MAKE SURE THESE KIDS EAT THEIR BREAKFAST EVERY MORNING, BEFORE YOU MAKE THEM RUN LIKE CRAZY, COACH.
MEH. I'M GOING TO THE OFFICE. THESE GUYS JUST DESTROYED ONE OF THE BACKBOARDS IN OUR ONLY COURT.
IF YOU ASK ME...
...THEY'VE GOT TOO MUCH DAMN ENERGY...
...BREAKFAST OR NOT.
OH! YOU'RE AWAKE. THAT'S... I WOULD HAVE THOUGHT YOU'D... NEED AN HOUR OR TWO.
YOU MAY WANT TO REST A LITTLE MORE. ARE YOU FEELING OKAY?
HAVEN'T FELT THIS GOOD IN, OH... 50 YEARS? HEH! I'M DOIN' JUST FINE, SUGAR #$%^&.
EXCUSE ME?!
SETTLE DOWN NOW. HEH HEH HEH.
YOU'RE TOO PRETTY TO BE MAKIN' ME MAD, DARLING...IT'D BE A REAL PITY IF YOU CAME UP MISSIN'.

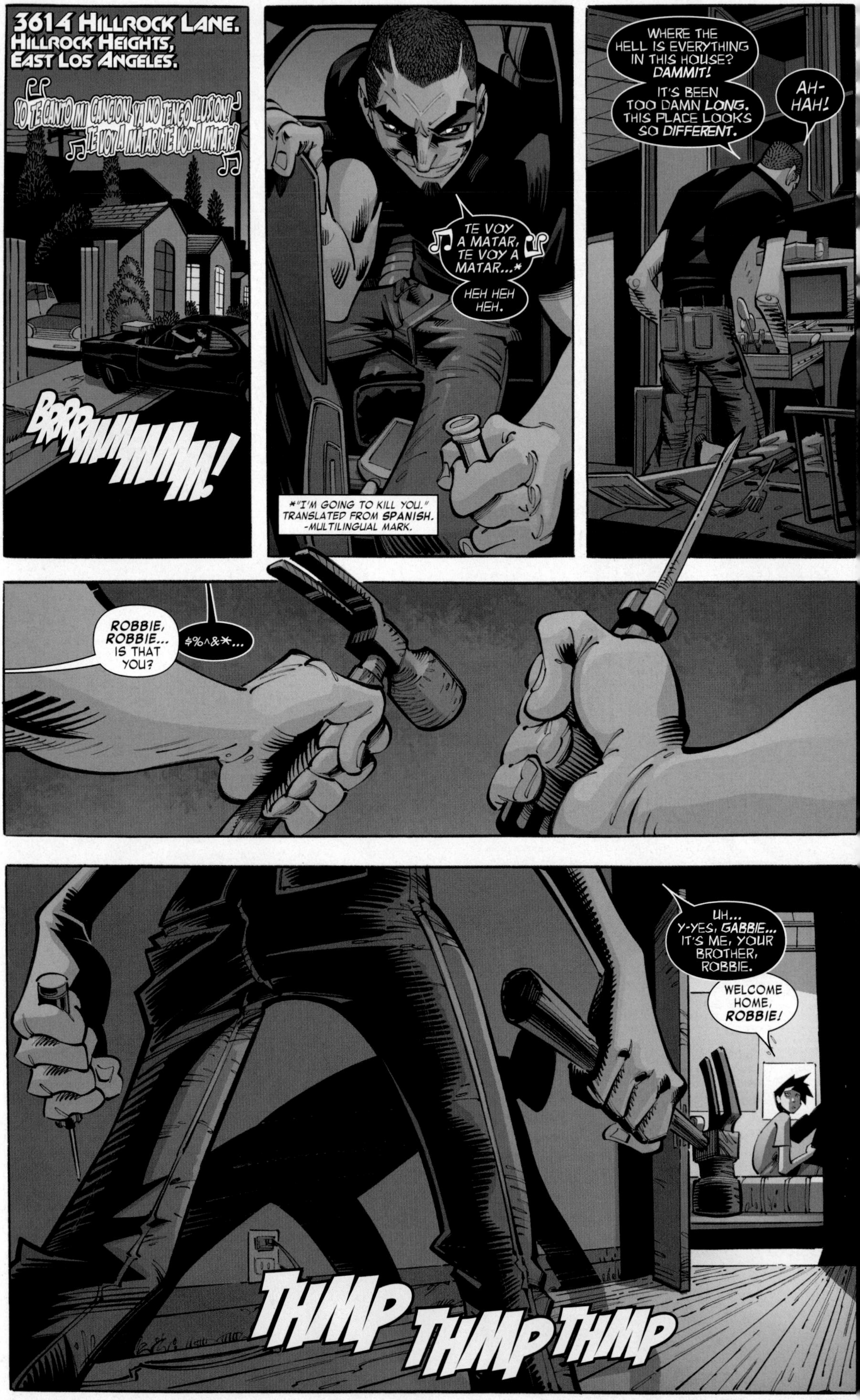
3614 Hillrock Lane. Hillrock Heights, East Los Angeles.
Yo te canto mi cancion, ya no tengo ilusion! Te voy a matar, te voy a matar!
BRRRMMMMMM!
TE VOY A MATAR, TE VOY A MATAR...*
HEH HEH HEH.
*"I'M GOING TO KILL YOU." TRANSLATED FROM SPANISH. -MULTILINGUAL MARK.
WHERE THE HELL IS EVERYTHING IN THIS HOUSE? DAMMIT!
IT'S BEEN TOO DAMN LONG. THIS PLACE LOOKS SO DIFFERENT.
AH-HAH!
ROBBIE, ROBBIE... IS THAT YOU?
$%^&*...
UH... Y-YES, GABBIE... IT'S ME, YOUR BROTHER, ROBBIE.
WELCOME HOME, ROBBIE!
THMP THMP THMP

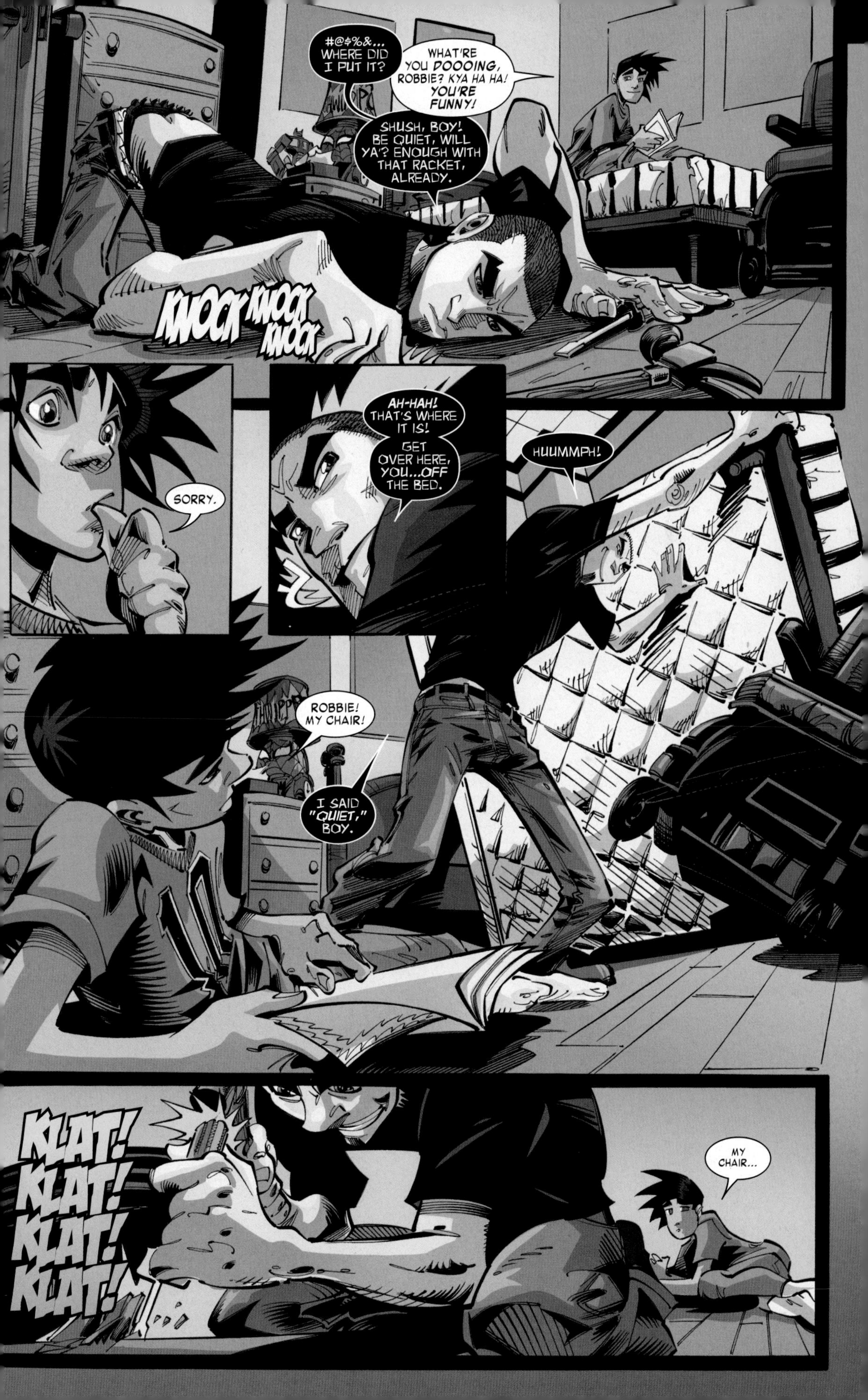
#@$%&... WHERE DID I PUT IT?
WHAT'RE YOU DOOOING, ROBBIE? KYA HA HA! YOU'RE FUNNY!
SHUSH, BOY! BE QUIET, WILL YA'? ENOUGH WITH THAT RACKET, ALREADY.
KNOCK KNOCK KNOCK
SORRY.
AH-HAH! THAT'S WHERE IT IS!
GET OVER HERE, YOU...OFF THE BED.
HUUMMPH!
ROBBIE! MY CHAIR!
I SAID "QUIET," BOY.
KLAT! KLAT! KLAT! KLAT!
MY CHAIR...

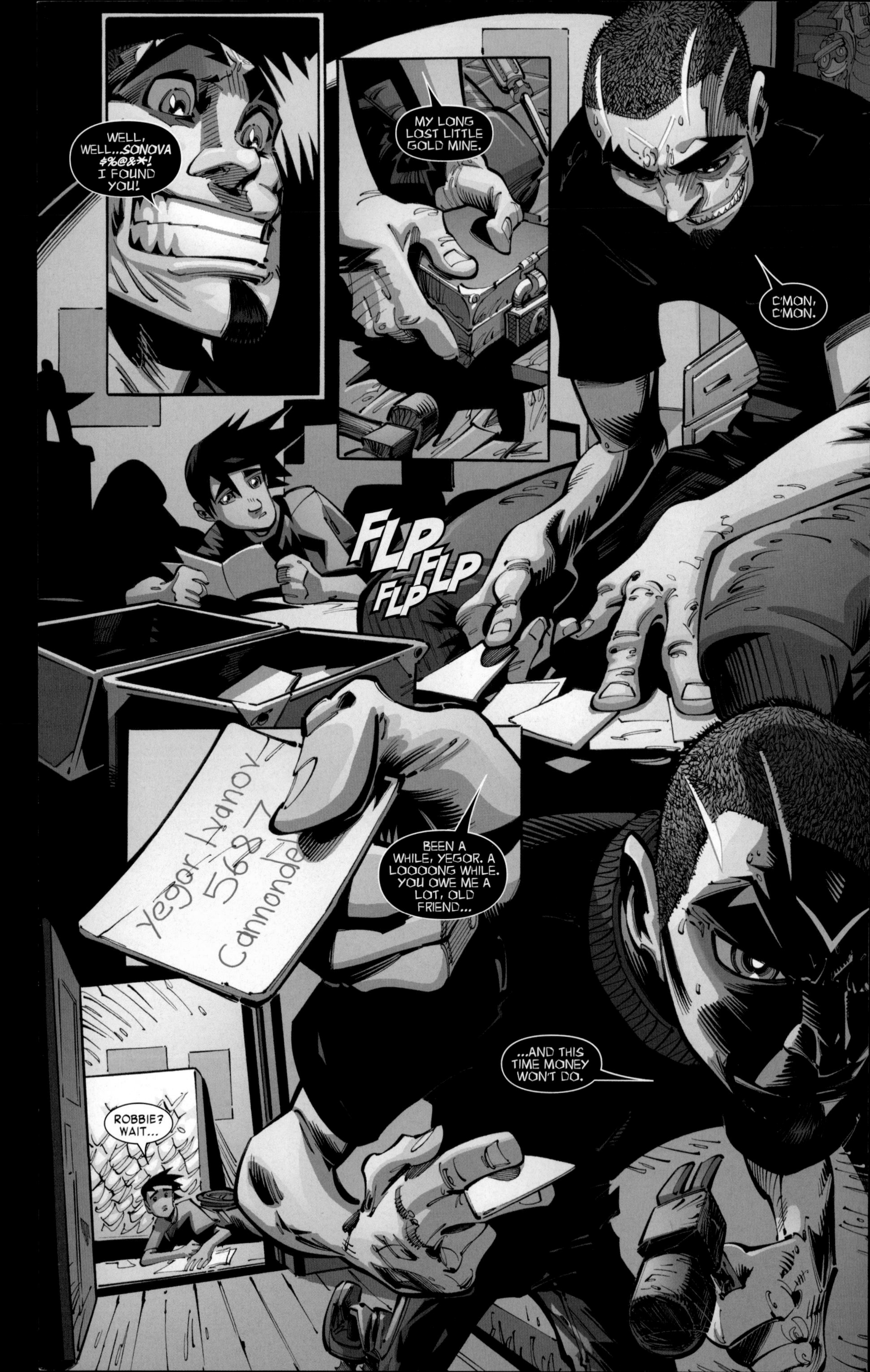
WELL, WELL...SONOVA $%@&*! I FOUND YOU!
MY LONG LOST LITTLE GOLD MINE.
C'MON, C'MON.
FLP FLP FLP
Yegor Ivanov
5687
Cannondel
BEEN A WHILE, YEGOR. A LOOOOONG WHILE. YOU OWE ME A LOT, OLD FRIEND...
...AND THIS TIME MONEY WON'T DO.
ROBBIE? WAIT...

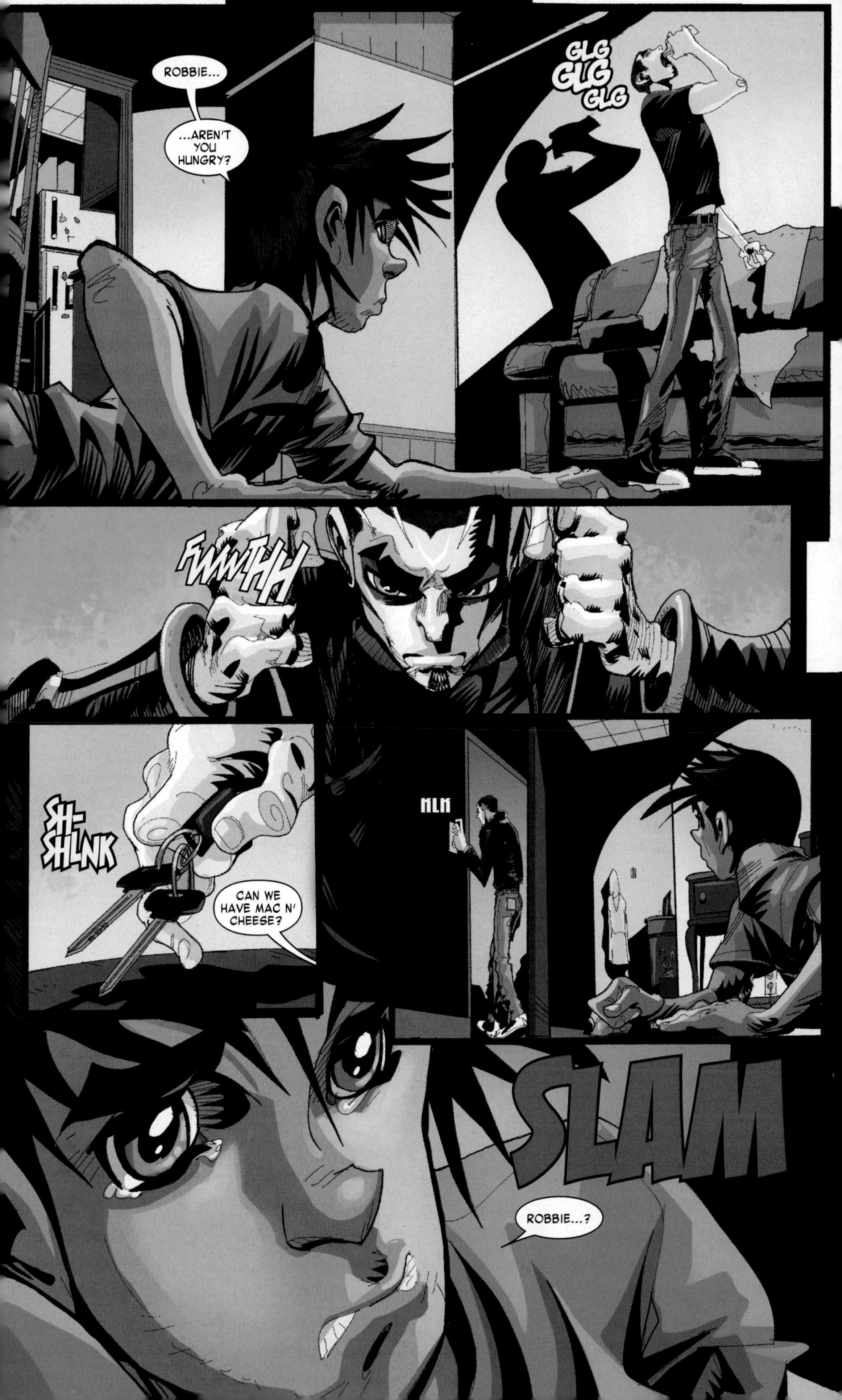
ROBBIE...
...AREN'T YOU HUNGRY?
GLG GLG GLG
FWWTHH
SH-SHLNK
CAN WE HAVE MAC N' CHEESE?
KLK
SLAM
ROBBIE...?

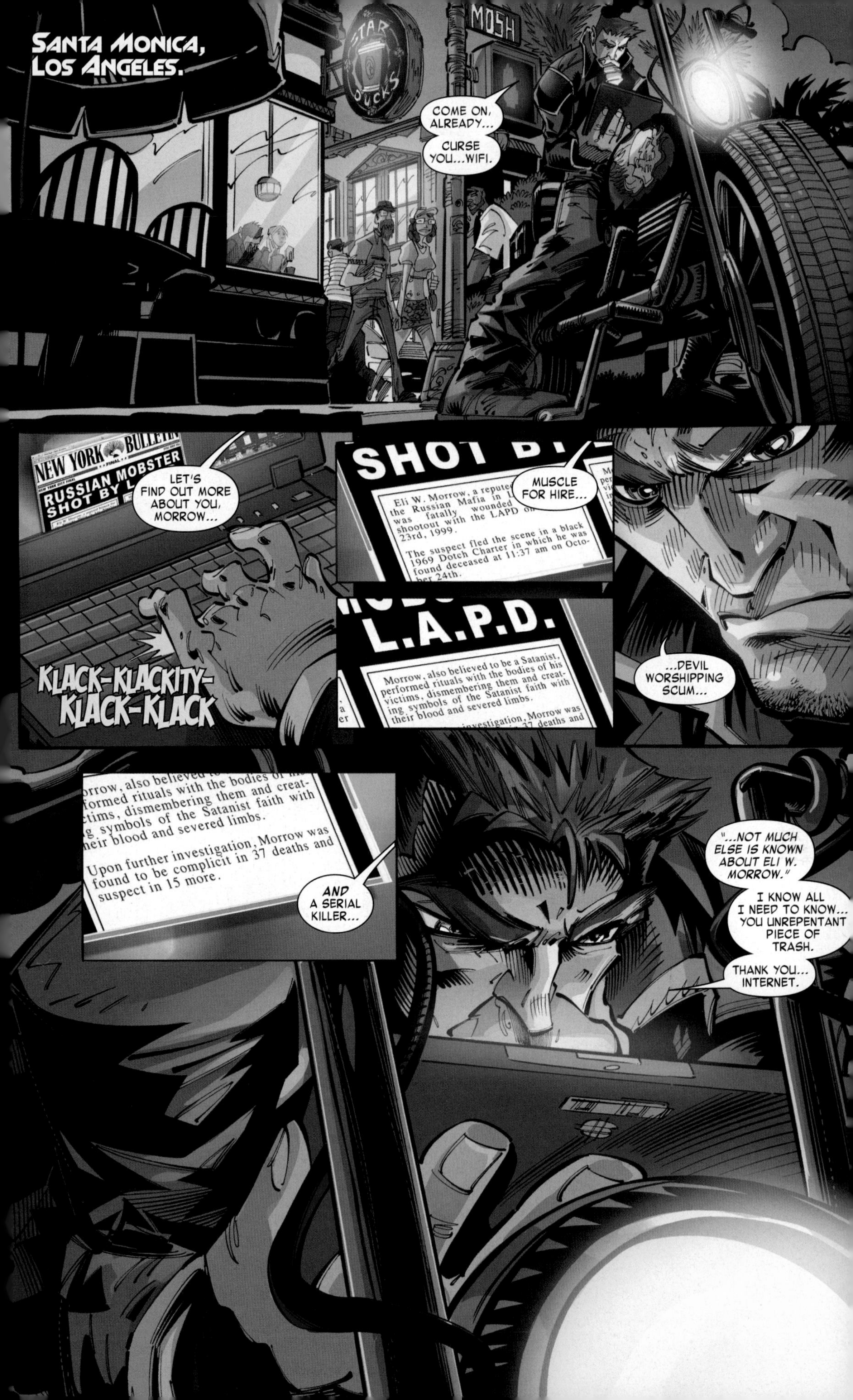
SANTA MONICA, LOS ANGELES.
STAR DUCKS
MOSH
COME ON, ALREADY...
CURSE YOU...WIFI.
NEW YORK BULLETIN
RUSSIAN MOBSTER
LET'S FIND OUT MORE ABOUT YOU, MORROW...
KLACK-KLACKITY-KLACK-KLACK
MUSCLE FOR HIRE...
The suspect fled the scene in a black 1969 Dotch Charter in which he was found deceased at 11:37 am on Octo-
L.A.P.D.
Morrow, also believed to be a Satanist,
performed rituals with the bodies of his
victims, dismembering them and creat-
ing symbols of the Satanist faith with
their blood and severed limbs.
...DEVIL WORSHIPPING SCUM...
Upon further investigation, Morrow was found to be complicit in 37 deaths and suspect in 15 more.
AND A SERIAL KILLER...
"...NOT MUCH ELSE IS KNOWN ABOUT ELI W. MORROW."
I KNOW ALL I NEED TO KNOW... YOU UNREPENTANT PIECE OF TRASH.
THANK YOU... INTERNET.

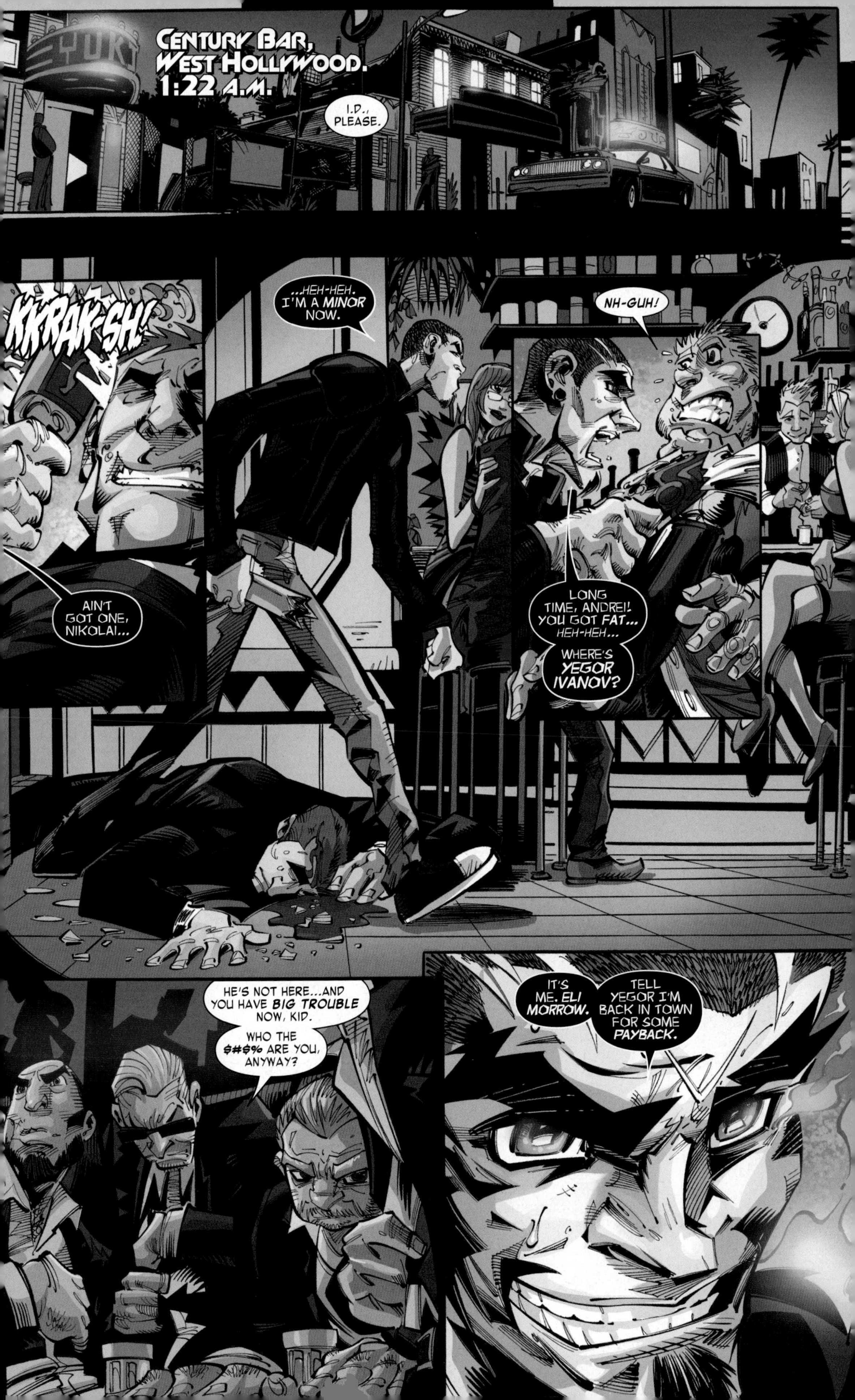
CENTURY BAR, WEST HOLLYWOOD. 1:22 A.M.
I.D., PLEASE.
KKRAK-SH!
AIN'T GOT ONE, NIKOLAI...
...HEH-HEH. I'M A MINOR NOW.
NH-GUH!
LONG TIME, ANDREI! YOU GOT FAT... HEH-HEH...
WHERE'S YEGOR IVANOV?
HE'S NOT HERE...AND YOU HAVE BIG TROUBLE NOW, KID.
WHO THE $#$% ARE YOU, ANYWAY?
IT'S ME. ELI MORROW.
TELL YEGOR I'M BACK IN TOWN FOR SOME PAYBACK.

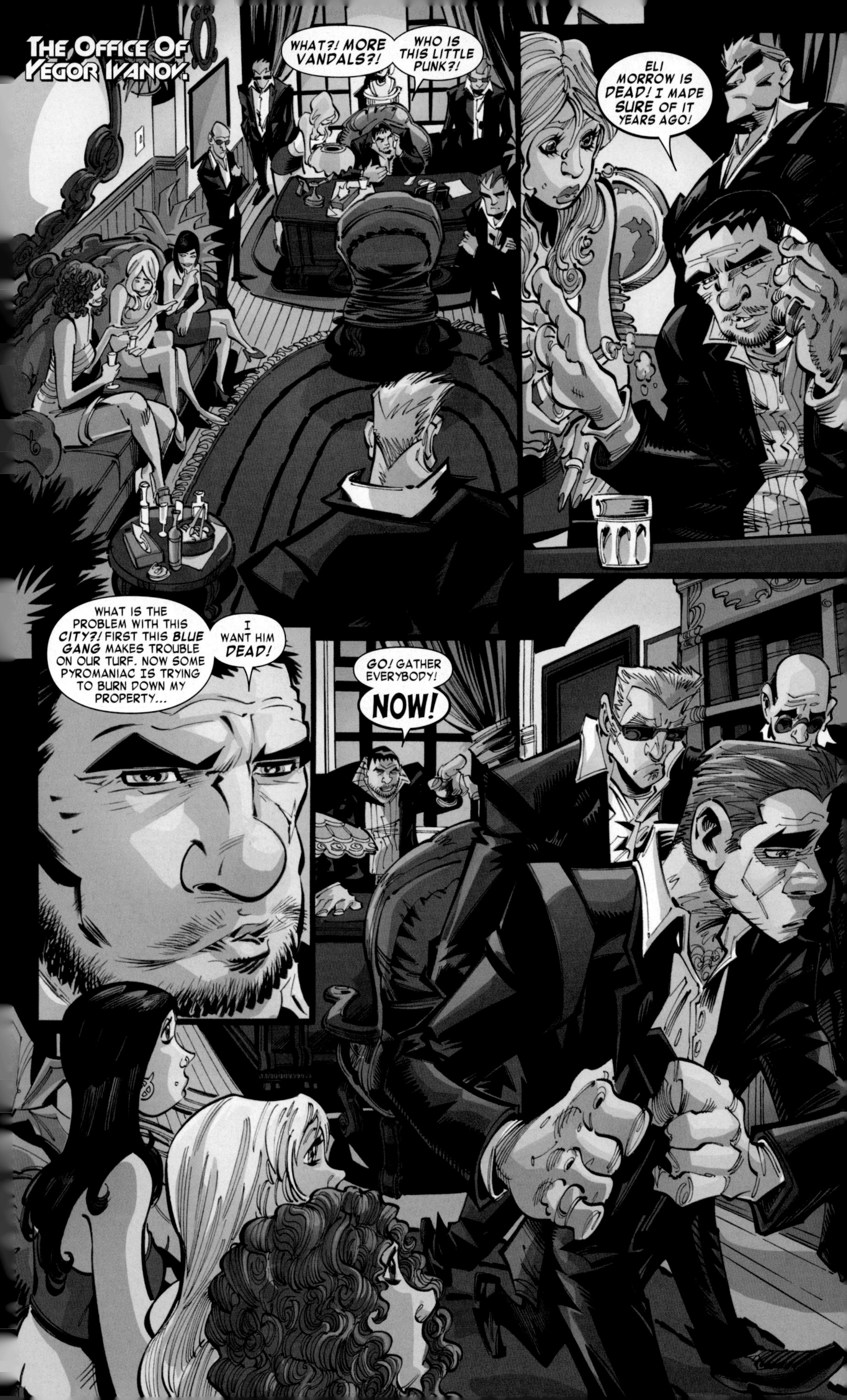
THE OFFICE OF YEGOR IVANOV.
WHAT?! MORE VANDALS?!
WHO IS THIS LITTLE PUNK?!
ELI MORROW IS DEAD! I MADE SURE OF IT YEARS AGO!
WHAT IS THE PROBLEM WITH THIS CITY?! FIRST THIS BLUE GANG MAKES TROUBLE ON OUR TURF. NOW SOME PYROMANIAC IS TRYING TO BURN DOWN MY PROPERTY...
I WANT HIM DEAD!
GO! GATHER EVERYBODY!
NOW!

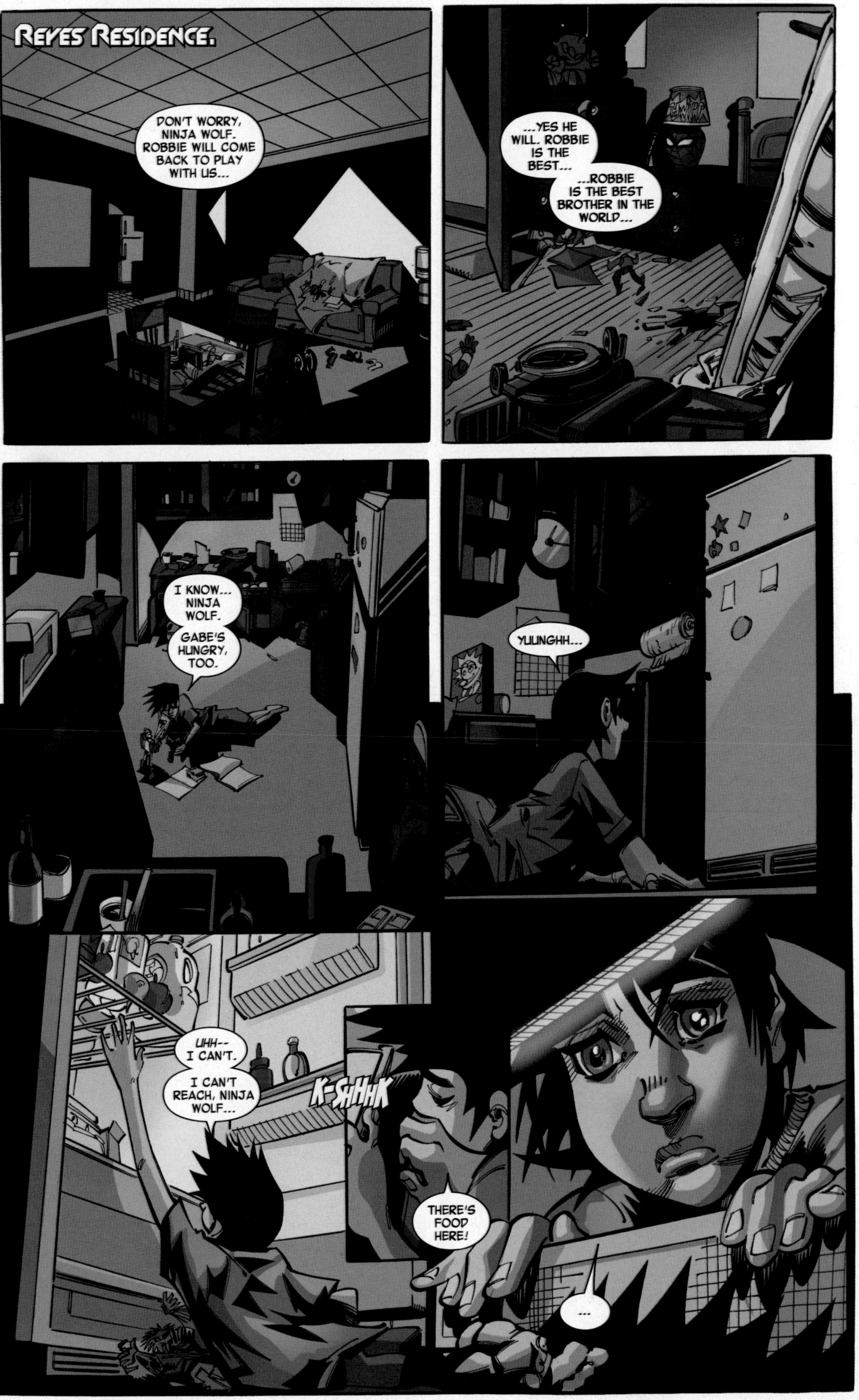
REYES RESIDENCE.
DON'T WORRY, NINJA WOLF. ROBBIE WILL COME BACK TO PLAY WITH US...
...YES HE WILL. ROBBIE IS THE BEST...
...ROBBIE IS THE BEST BROTHER IN THE WORLD...
I KNOW... NINJA WOLF.
GABE'S HUNGRY, TOO.
YUUNGHH...
UHH-- I CAN'T.
I CAN'T REACH, NINJA WOLF...
K-SHHHK
THERE'S FOOD HERE!
...

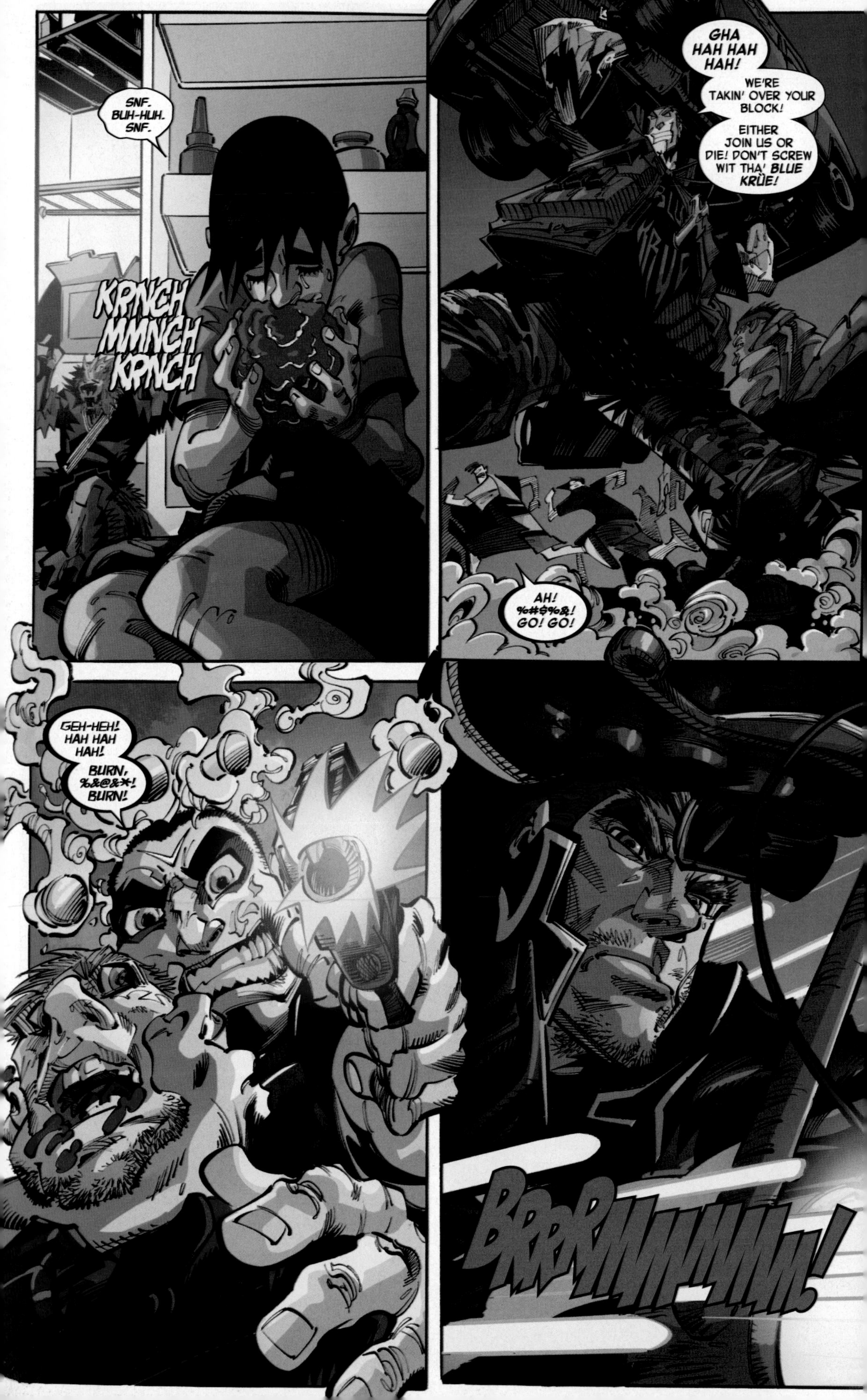
SNF. BUH-HUH. SNF.
KRNCH MMNCH KRNCH
GHA HAH HAH HAH!
WE'RE TAKIN' OVER YOUR BLOCK!
EITHER JOIN US OR DIE! DON'T SCREW WIT THA' BLUE KRÜE!
AH! %#$%&! GO! GO!
GEH-HEH! HAH HAH HAH!
BURN, %&@&*! BURN!
BRRRMMMMMM!

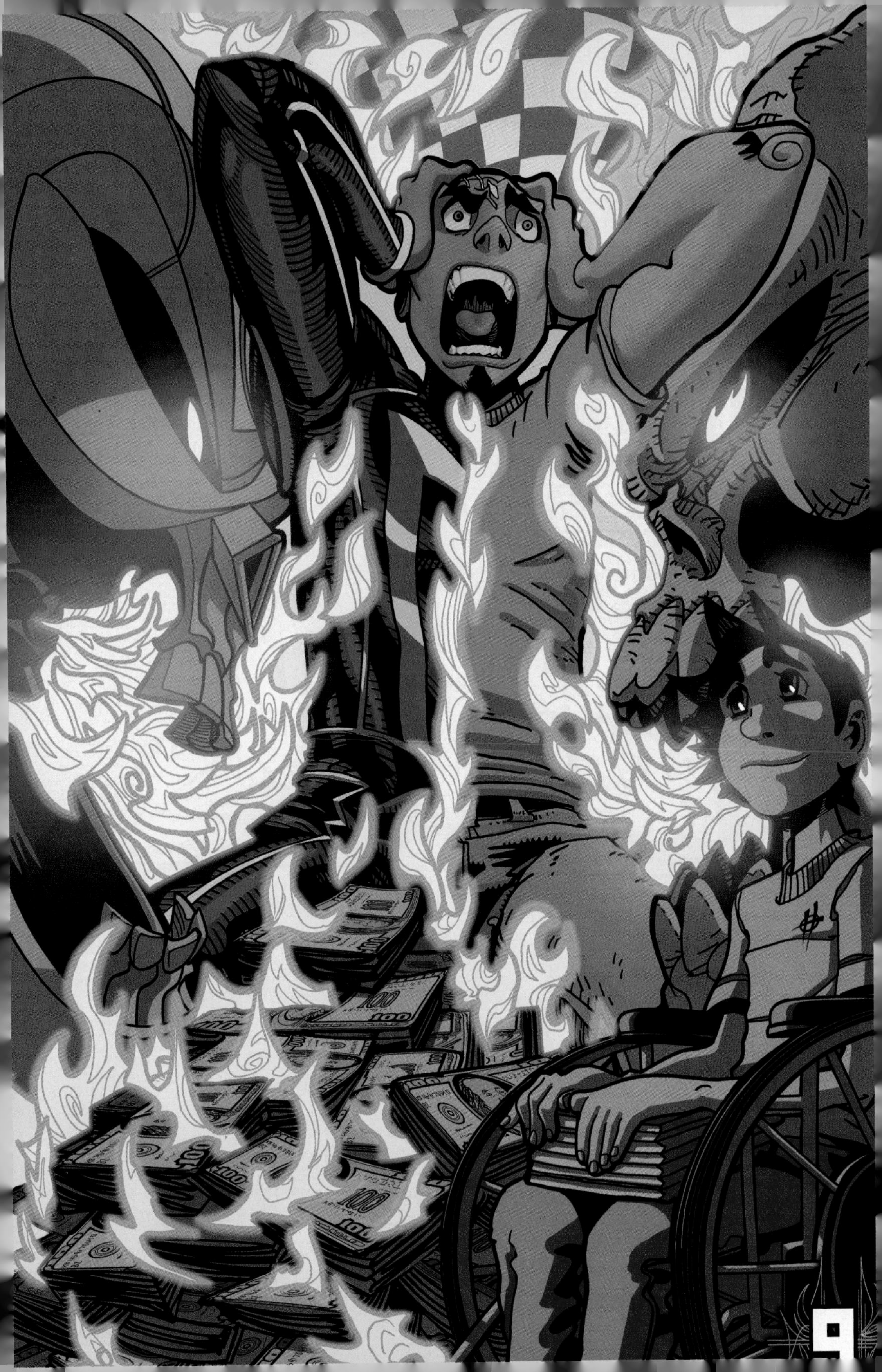

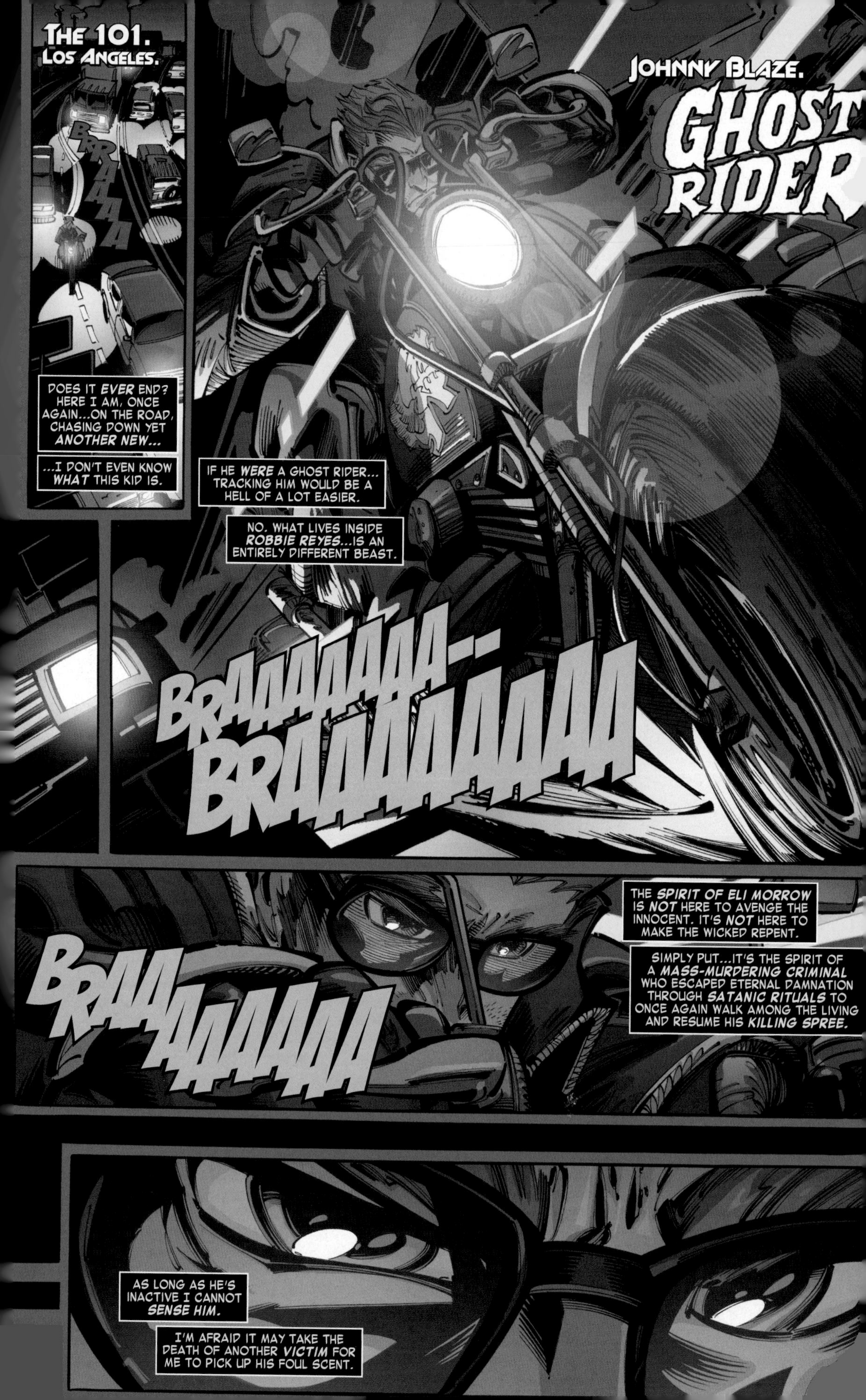
THE 101.
LOS ANGELES.
BRRAAAAA
DOES IT EVER END? HERE I AM, ONCE AGAIN...ON THE ROAD, CHASING DOWN YET ANOTHER NEW...
...I DON'T EVEN KNOW WHAT THIS KID IS.
JOHNNY BLAZE.
GHOST RIDER
IF HE WERE A GHOST RIDER... TRACKING HIM WOULD BE A HELL OF A LOT EASIER.
NO. WHAT LIVES INSIDE ROBBIE REYES...IS AN ENTIRELY DIFFERENT BEAST.
BRAAAAAAA--
BRAAAAAAAAA
BRAAAAAAAAAA
THE SPIRIT OF ELI MORROW IS NOT HERE TO AVENGE THE INNOCENT. IT'S NOT HERE TO MAKE THE WICKED REPENT.
SIMPLY PUT...IT'S THE SPIRIT OF A MASS-MURDERING CRIMINAL WHO ESCAPED ETERNAL DAMNATION THROUGH SATANIC RITUALS TO ONCE AGAIN WALK AMONG THE LIVING AND RESUME HIS KILLING SPREE.
AS LONG AS HE'S INACTIVE I CANNOT SENSE HIM.
I'M AFRAID IT MAY TAKE THE DEATH OF ANOTHER VICTIM FOR ME TO PICK UP HIS FOUL SCENT.

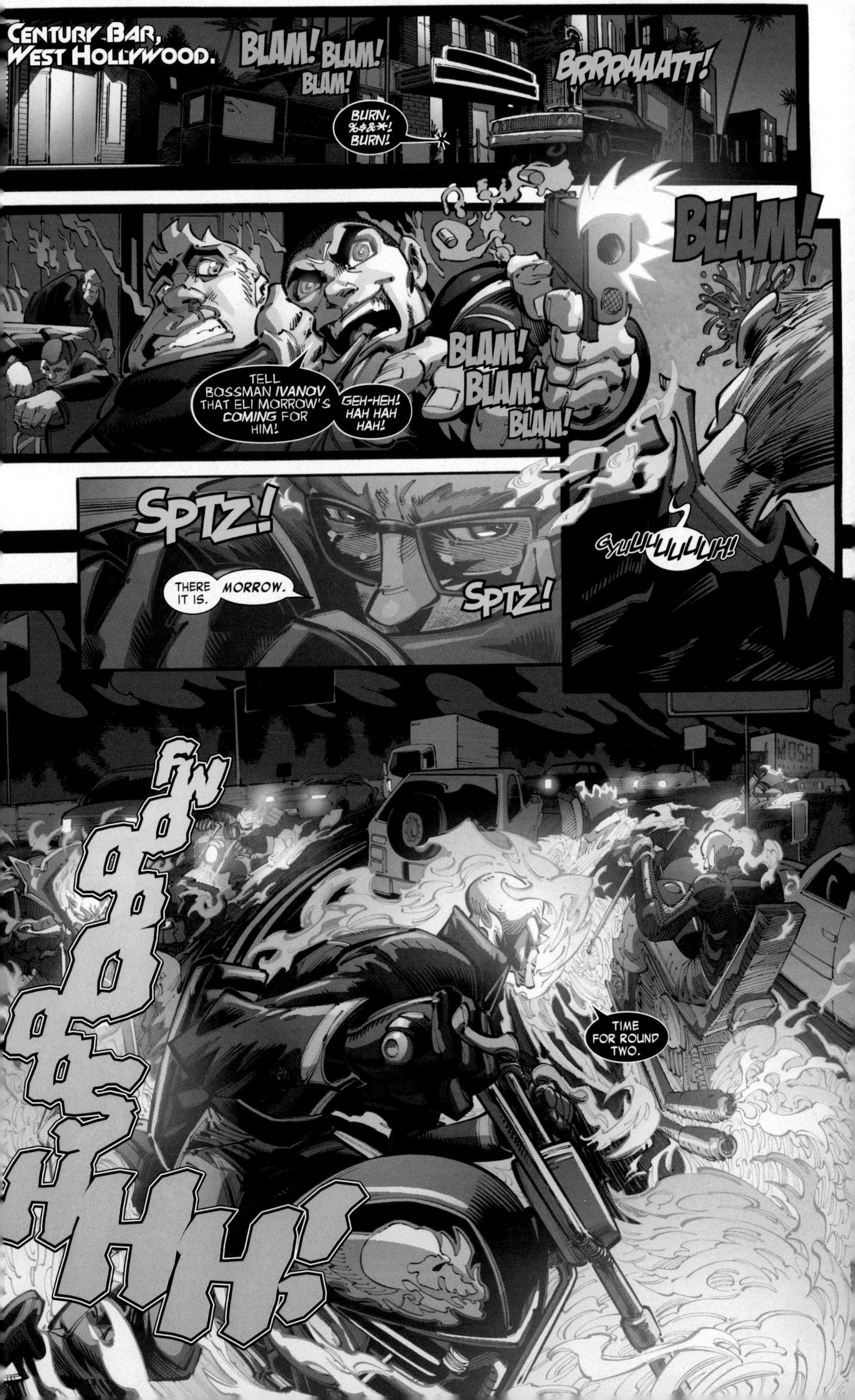

Century Bar, West Hollywood.
BLAM! BLAM! BLAM!
BURN, %$&*! BURN!
BRRRAAATT!
BLAM!
TELL BOSSMAN IVANOV THAT ELI MORROW'S COMING FOR HIM!
GEH-HEH! HAH HAH HAH!
BLAM! BLAM! BLAM!
SPTZ!
THERE IT IS.
MORROW.
SPTZ!
GYUUUUUUUH!
TIME FOR ROUND TWO.

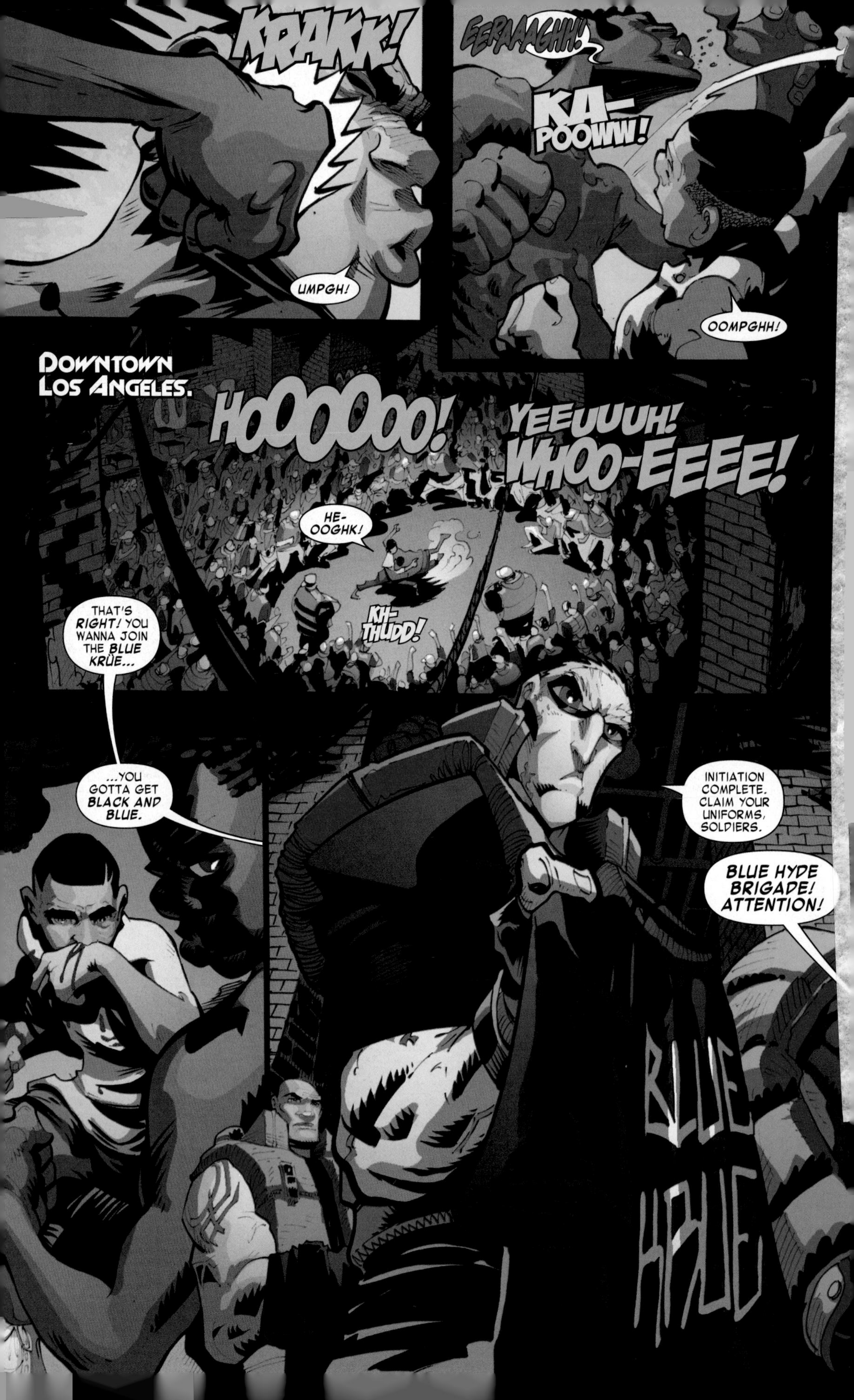
KRAKK!
UMPGH!
EERAAAGHH!
KA-POOWW!
OOMPGHH!
DOWNTOWN LOS ANGELES.
HOOOOOO!
YEEUUUH!
WHOO-EEEE!
HE-OOGHK!
KH-THUDD!
THAT'S RIGHT! YOU WANNA JOIN THE BLUE KRÜE...
...YOU GOTTA GET BLACK AND BLUE.
INITIATION COMPLETE. CLAIM YOUR UNIFORMS, SOLDIERS.
BLUE HYDE BRIGADE! ATTENTION!
BLUE HYDE

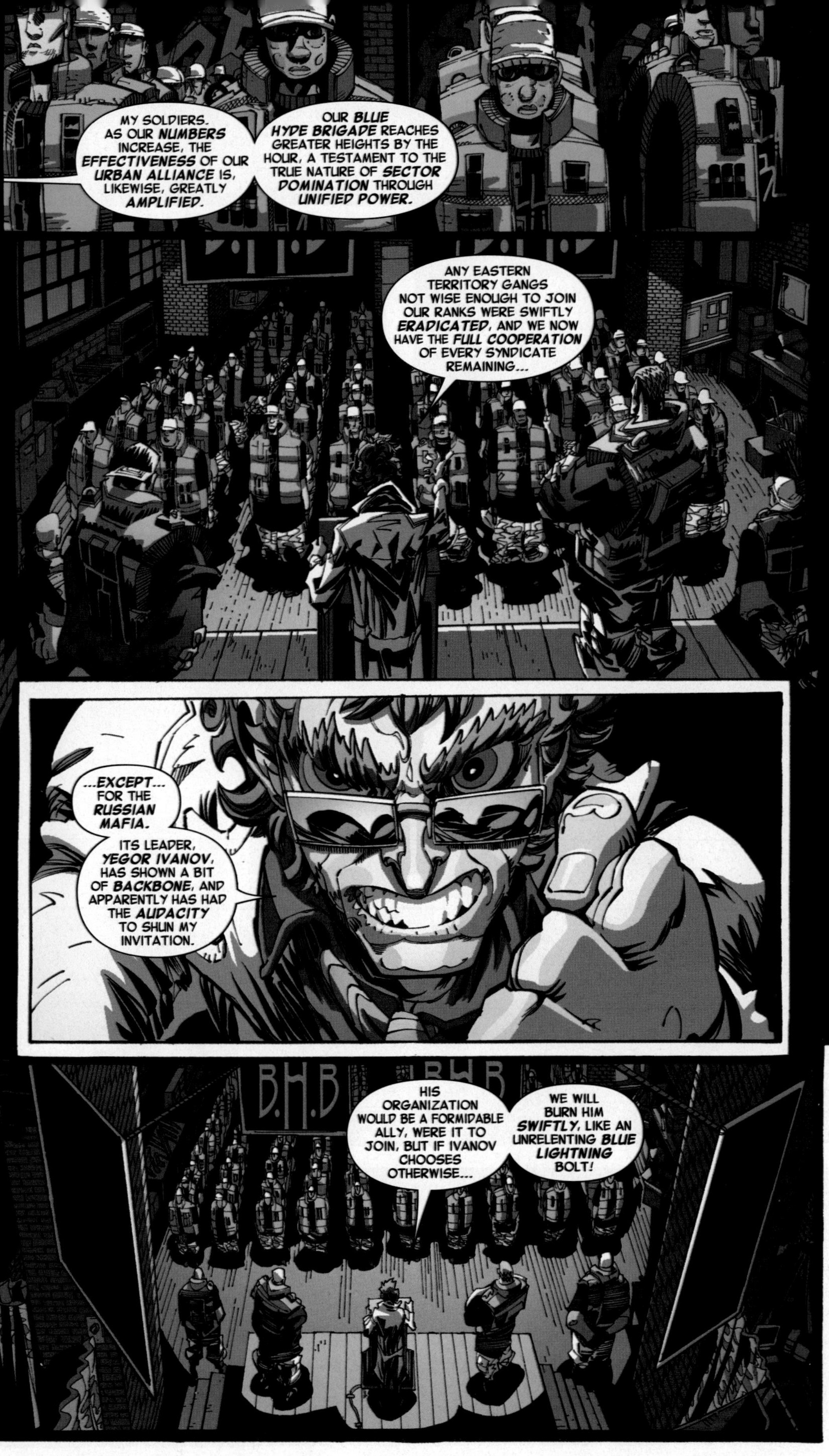
MY SOLDIERS. AS OUR NUMBERS INCREASE, THE EFFECTIVENESS OF OUR URBAN ALLIANCE IS, LIKEWISE, GREATLY AMPLIFIED.
OUR BLUE HYDE BRIGADE REACHES GREATER HEIGHTS BY THE HOUR, A TESTAMENT TO THE TRUE NATURE OF SECTOR DOMINATION THROUGH UNIFIED POWER.
ANY EASTERN TERRITORY GANGS NOT WISE ENOUGH TO JOIN OUR RANKS WERE SWIFTLY ERADICATED, AND WE NOW HAVE THE FULL COOPERATION OF EVERY SYNDICATE REMAINING...
...EXCEPT... FOR THE RUSSIAN MAFIA.
ITS LEADER, YEGOR IVANOV, HAS SHOWN A BIT OF BACKBONE, AND APPARENTLY HAS HAD THE AUDACITY TO SHUN MY INVITATION.
B.H.B
HIS ORGANIZATION WOULD BE A FORMIDABLE ALLY, WERE IT TO JOIN, BUT IF IVANOV CHOOSES OTHERWISE...
WE WILL BURN HIM SWIFTLY, LIKE AN UNRELENTING BLUE LIGHTNING BOLT!

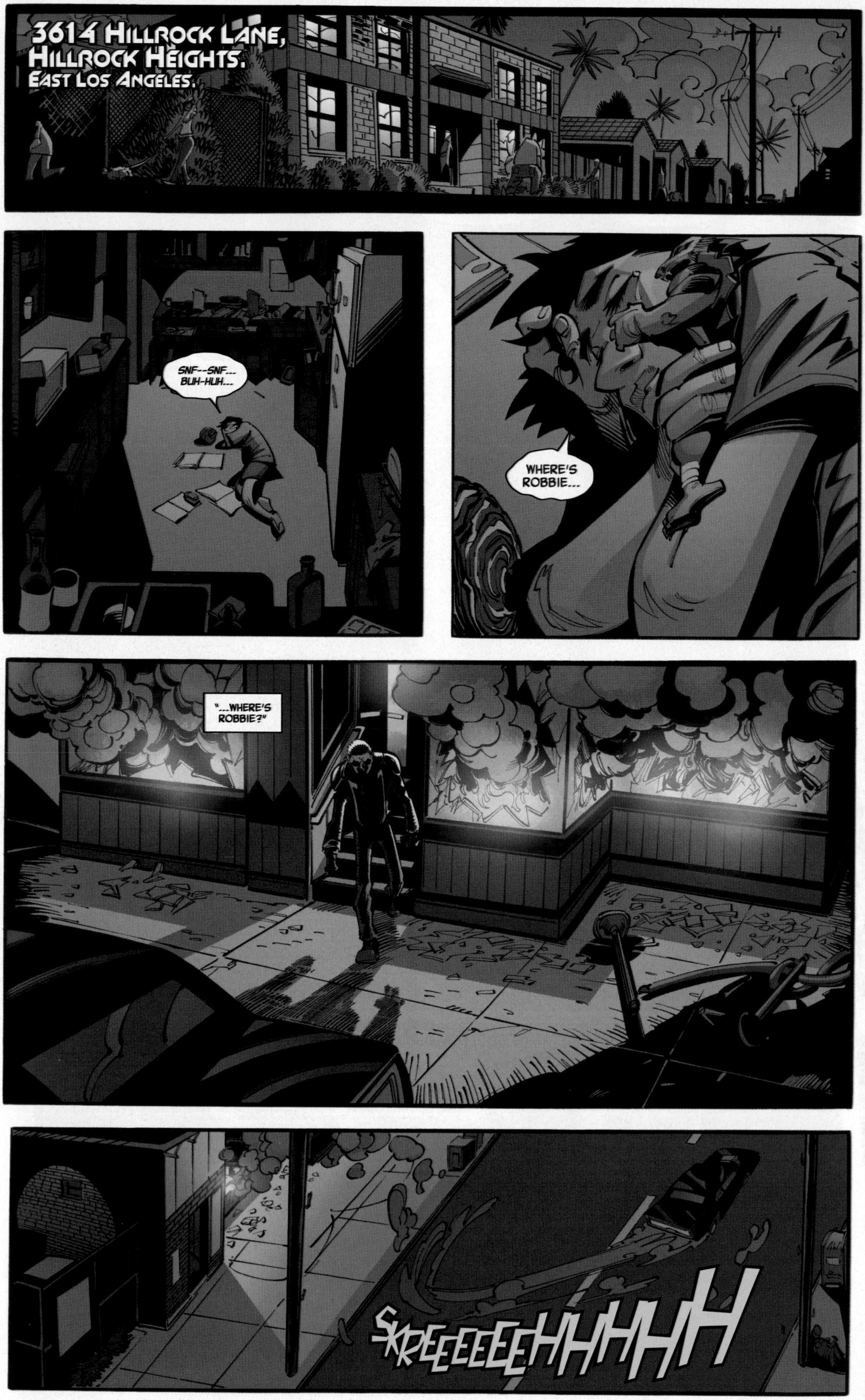
3614 Hillrock Lane,
Hillrock Heights.
East Los Angeles.
SNF--SNF...
BUH-HUH...
WHERE'S
ROBBIE...
"...WHERE'S
ROBBIE?"
SKREEEEEEEHHHHHH

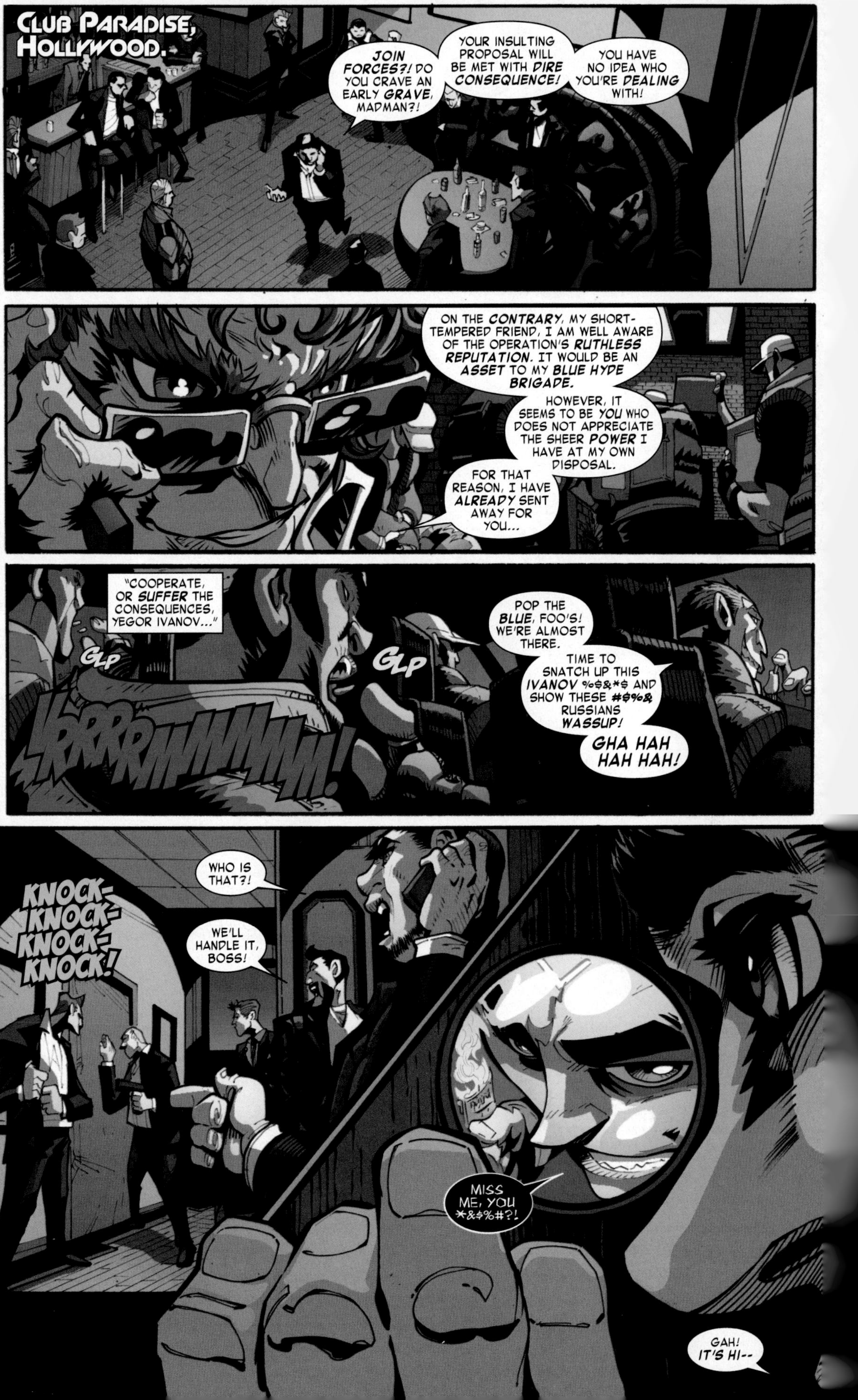
CLUB PARADISE, HOLLYWOOD.
JOIN FORCES?! DO YOU CRAVE AN EARLY GRAVE, MADMAN?!
YOUR INSULTING PROPOSAL WILL BE MET WITH DIRE CONSEQUENCE!
YOU HAVE NO IDEA WHO YOU'RE DEALING WITH!
ON THE CONTRARY, MY SHORT-TEMPERED FRIEND, I AM WELL AWARE OF THE OPERATION'S RUTHLESS REPUTATION. IT WOULD BE AN ASSET TO MY BLUE HYDE BRIGADE.
HOWEVER, IT SEEMS TO BE YOU WHO DOES NOT APPRECIATE THE SHEER POWER I HAVE AT MY OWN DISPOSAL.
FOR THAT REASON, I HAVE ALREADY SENT AWAY FOR YOU...
"COOPERATE, OR SUFFER THE CONSEQUENCES, YEGOR IVANOV..."
GLP
GLP
VRRRRMMMMMM!
POP THE BLUE, FOO'S! WE'RE ALMOST THERE.
TIME TO SNATCH UP THIS IVANOV %$&*$ AND SHOW THESE #$%& RUSSIANS WASSUP!
GHA HAH HAH HAH!
KNOCK-KNOCK-KNOCK-KNOCK!
WHO IS THAT?!
WE'LL HANDLE IT, BOSS!
MISS ME, YOU *&$%#?!
GAH! IT'S HI--

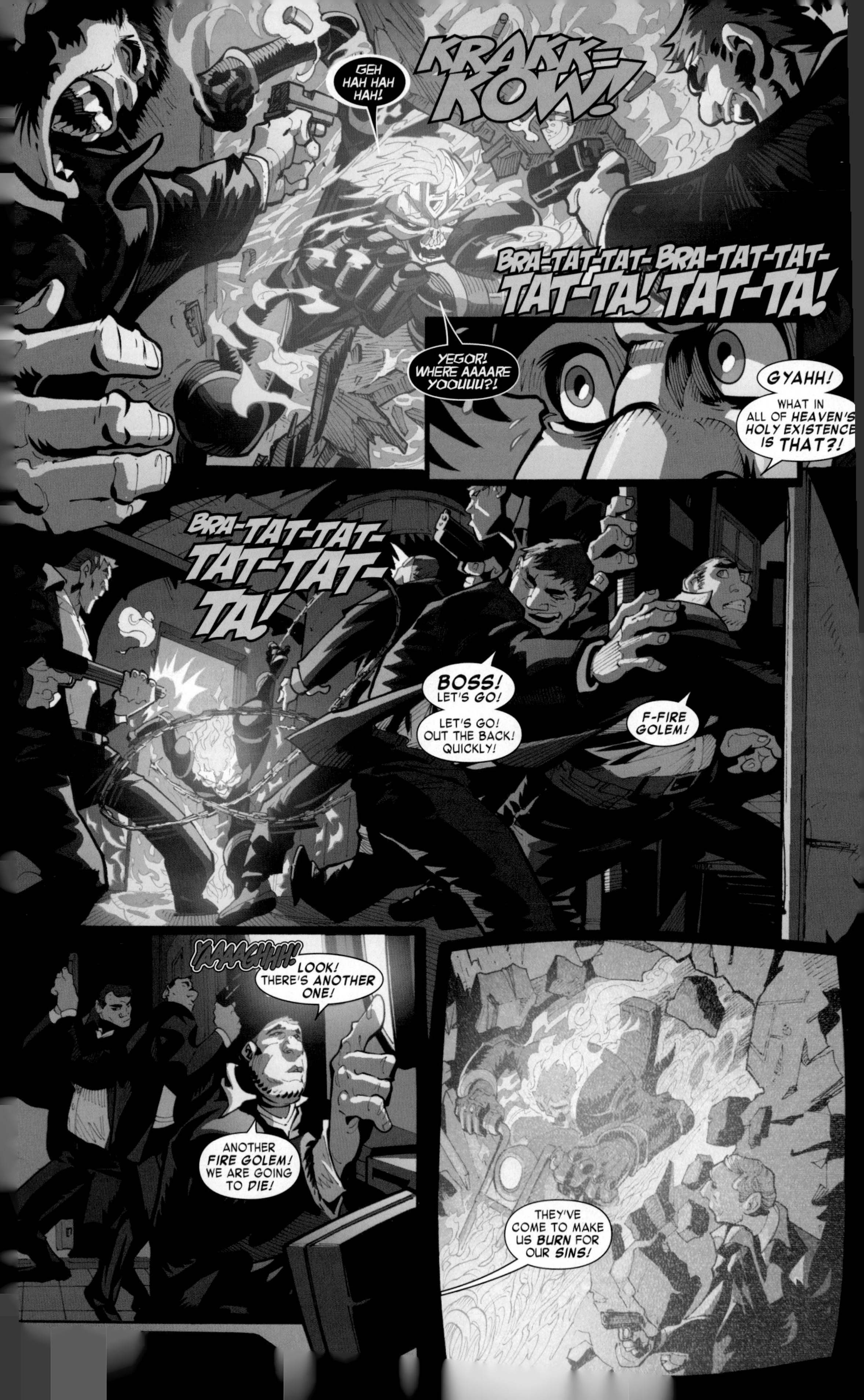
KRAKK-KOW!
GEH HAH HAH HAH!
BRA-TAT-TAT- BRA-TAT-TAT-
TAT-TA! TAT-TA!
YEGOR! WHERE AAAARE YOOUUU?!
GYAHH!
WHAT IN ALL OF HEAVEN'S HOLY EXISTENCE IS THAT?!
BRA-TAT-TAT-TAT-TAT-TA!
BOSS! LET'S GO!
LET'S GO! OUT THE BACK! QUICKLY!
F-FIRE GOLEM!
YAAAGHHH!
LOOK! THERE'S ANOTHER ONE!
ANOTHER FIRE GOLEM! WE ARE GOING TO DIE!
THEY'VE COME TO MAKE US BURN FOR OUR SINS!

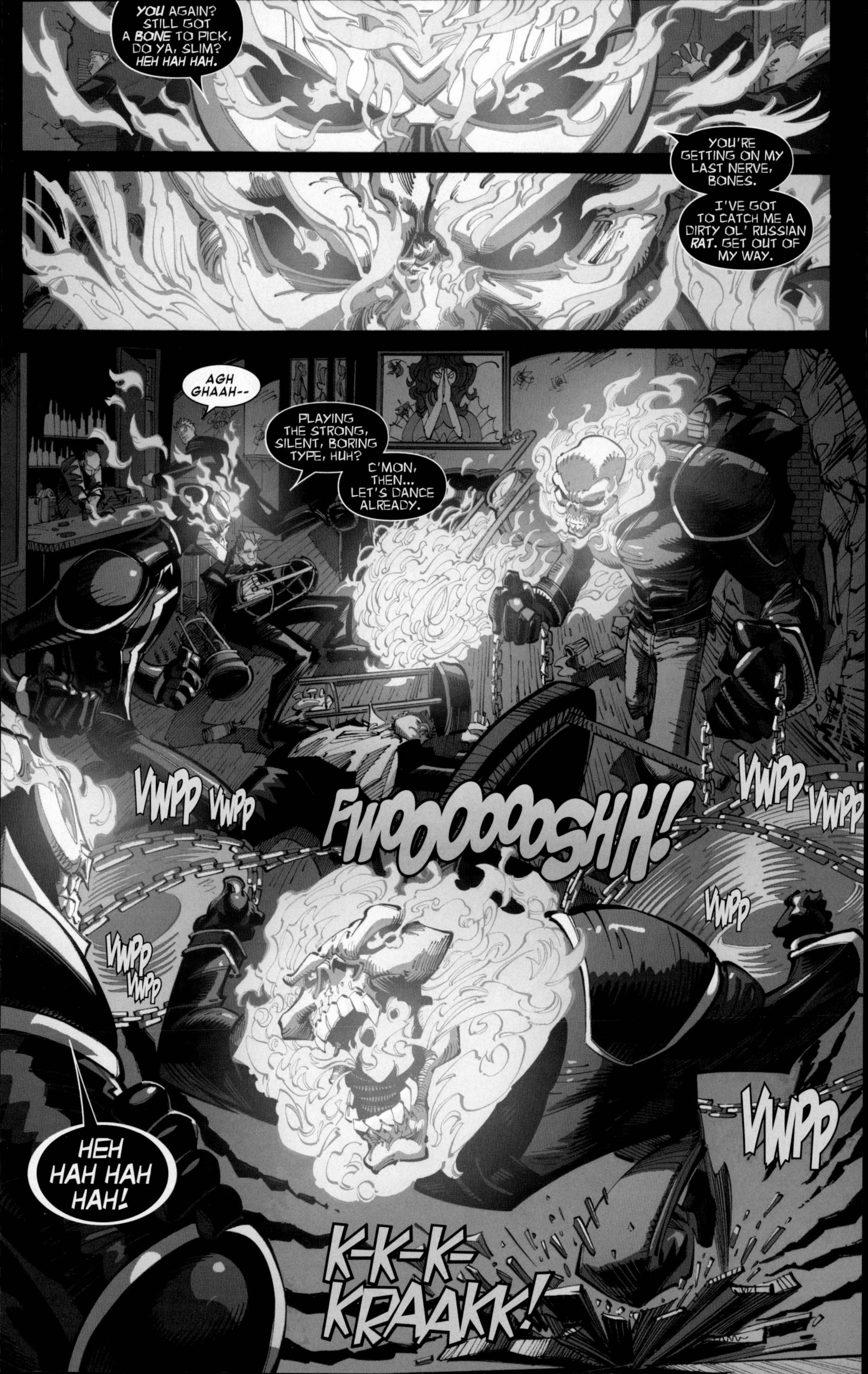
YOU AGAIN? STILL GOT A BONE TO PICK, DO YA, SLIM? HEH HAH HAH.
YOU'RE GETTING ON MY LAST NERVE, BONES.
I'VE GOT TO CATCH ME A DIRTY OL' RUSSIAN RAT. GET OUT OF MY WAY.
AGH GHAAH--
PLAYING THE STRONG, SILENT, BORING TYPE, HUH?
C'MON, THEN... LET'S DANCE ALREADY.
VWPP VWPP
FWOOOOOOOSHH!
VWPP VWPP
VWPP
VWPP VWPP
HEH HAH HAH HAH!
VWPP
K-K-K-KRAAKK!

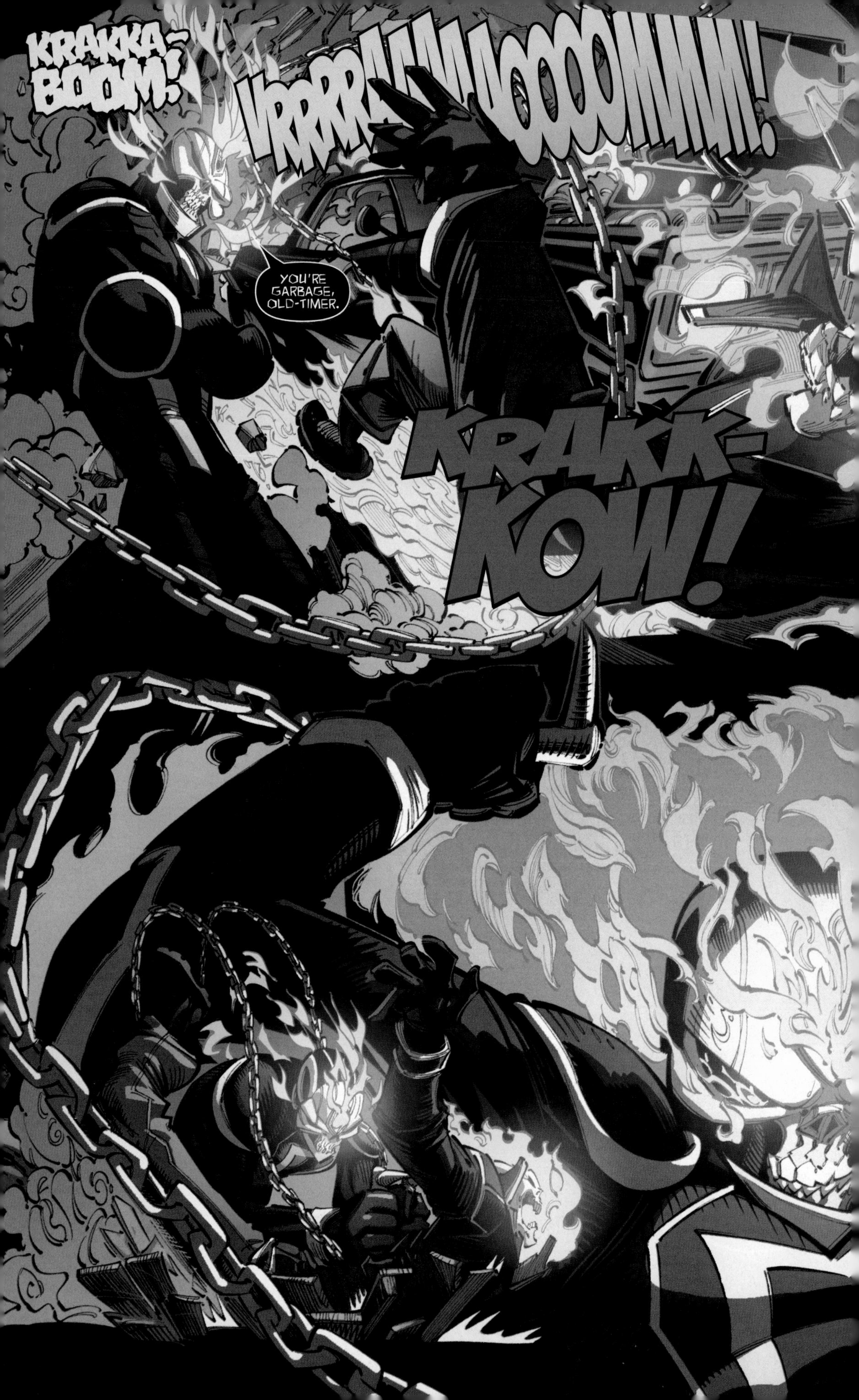
KRAKKA-BOOM!
VRRRRAAAAAOOOOMMMM!
YOU'RE GARBAGE, OLD-TIMER.
KRAKK-KOW!

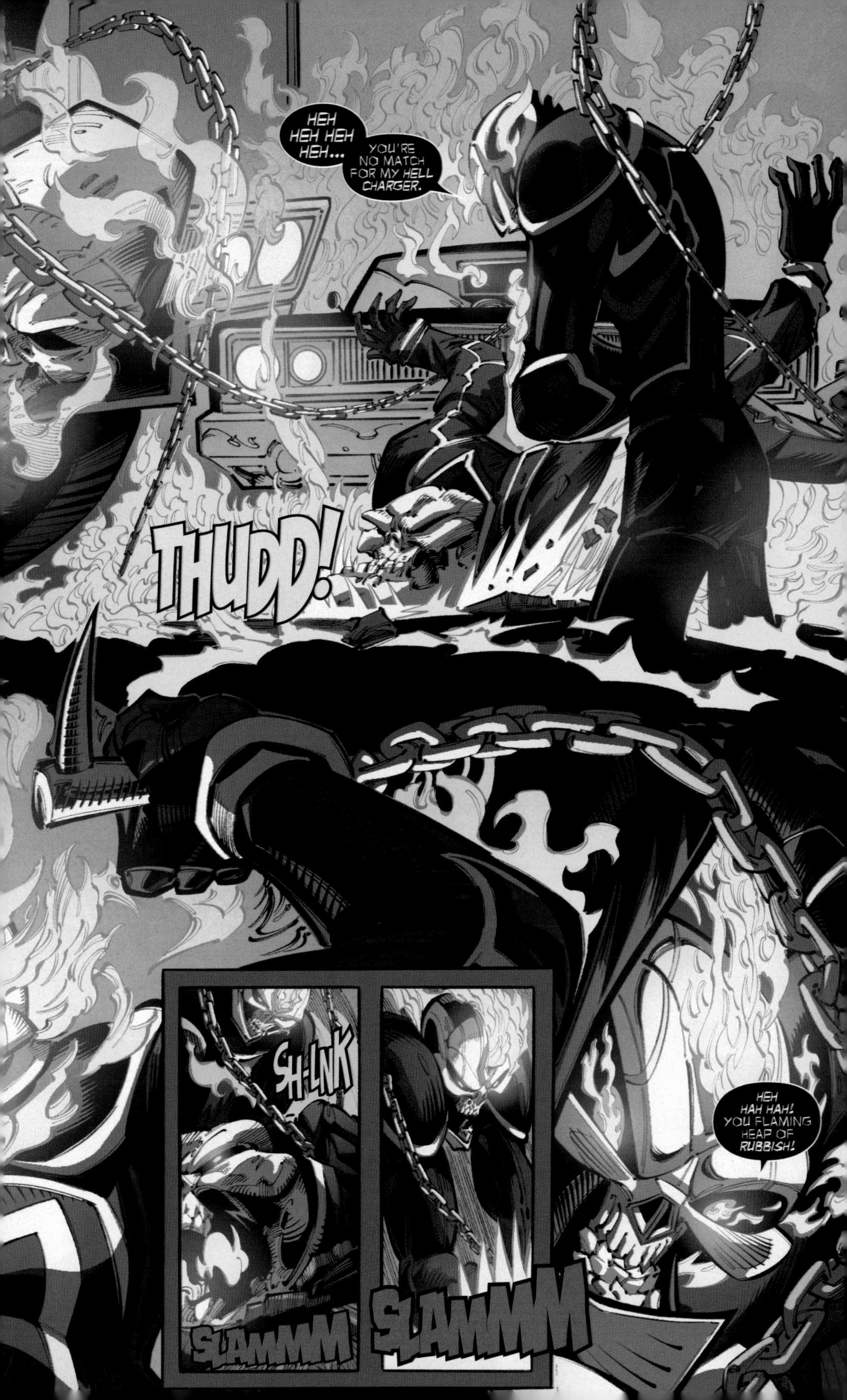
HEH HEH HEH HEH...
YOU'RE NO MATCH FOR MY HELL CHARGER.
THUDD!
SH-LNK
SLAMMM
SLAMMMM
HEH HAH HAH! YOU FLAMING HEAP OF RUBBISH!

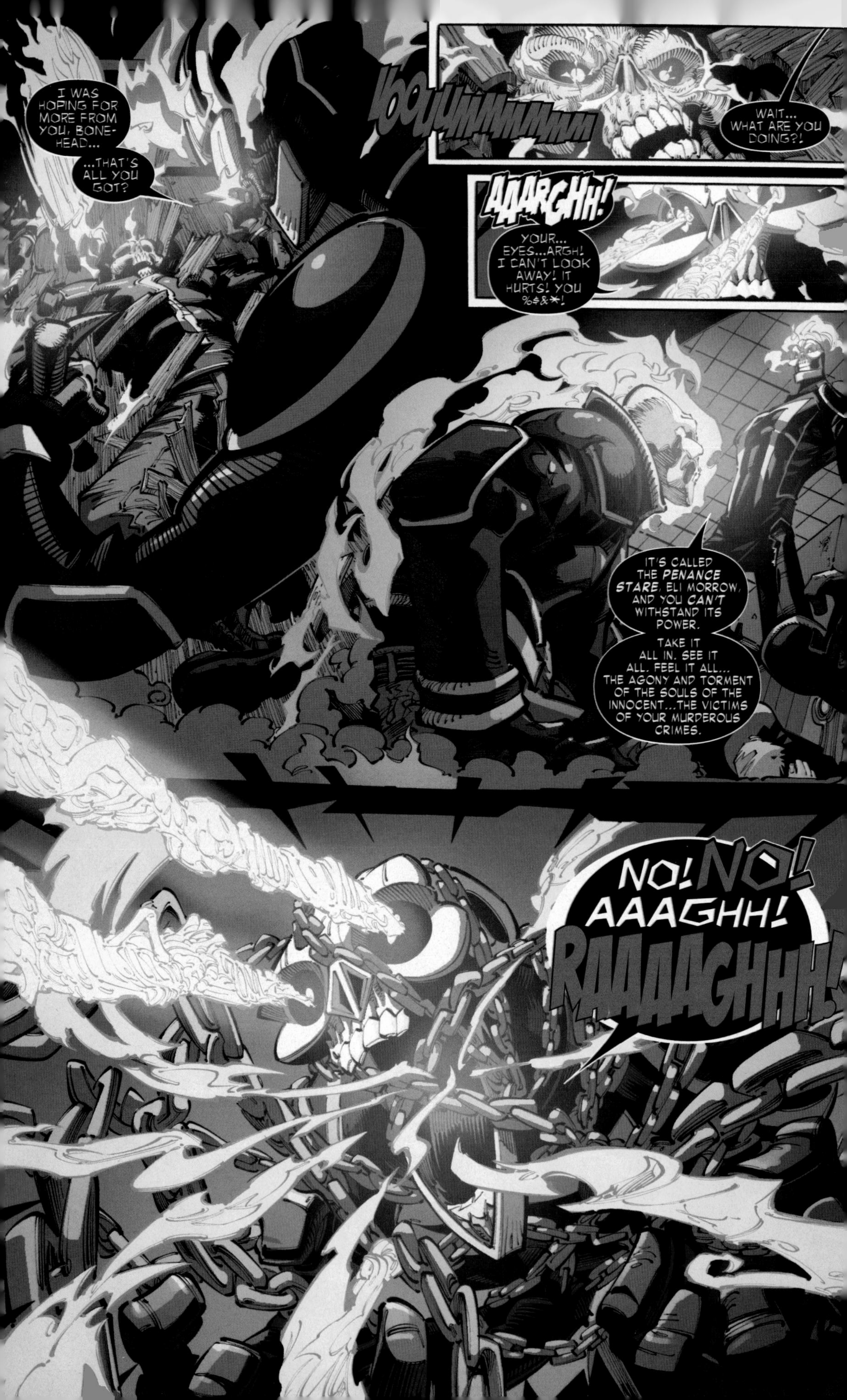
I WAS HOPING FOR MORE FROM YOU, BONE-HEAD...
...THAT'S ALL YOU GOT?
VOOUUMMMMMMM
WAIT... WHAT ARE YOU DOING?!
AAARGHH!
YOUR... EYES...ARGH! I CAN'T LOOK AWAY! IT HURTS! YOU %$&*!
IT'S CALLED THE PENANCE STARE, ELI MORROW, AND YOU CAN'T WITHSTAND ITS POWER.
TAKE IT ALL IN. SEE IT ALL. FEEL IT ALL... THE AGONY AND TORMENT OF THE SOULS OF THE INNOCENT...THE VICTIMS OF YOUR MURDEROUS CRIMES.
NO! NO! AAAGHH! RAAAAGHHH!

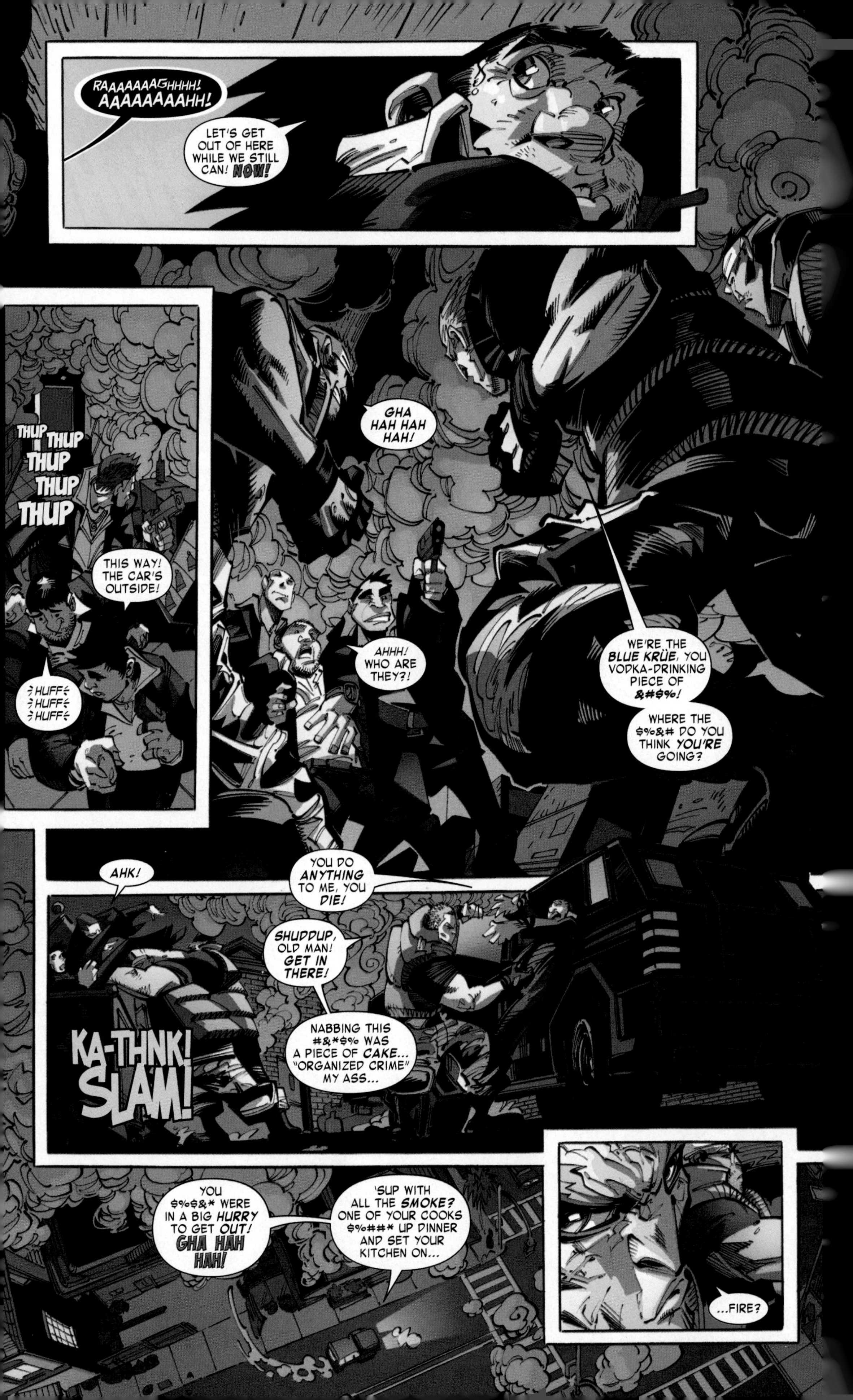
RAAAAAAAGHHHH! AAAAAAAAHH!
LET'S GET OUT OF HERE WHILE WE STILL CAN! NOW!
THUP THUP THUP THUP THUP
THIS WAY! THE CAR'S OUTSIDE!
HUFF HUFF HUFF
GHA HAH HAH HAH!
AHHH! WHO ARE THEY?!
WE'RE THE BLUE KRÜE, YOU VODKA-DRINKING PIECE OF &#$%!
WHERE THE $%&# DO YOU THINK YOU'RE GOING?
AHK!
YOU DO ANYTHING TO ME, YOU DIE!
SHUDDUP, OLD MAN! GET IN THERE!
NABBING THIS #&*$% WAS A PIECE OF CAKE... "ORGANIZED CRIME" MY ASS...
KA-THNK! SLAM!
YOU $%$&* WERE IN A BIG HURRY TO GET OUT! GHA HAH HAH!
'SUP WITH ALL THE SMOKE? ONE OF YOUR COOKS $%##* UP DINNER AND SET YOUR KITCHEN ON...
...FIRE?

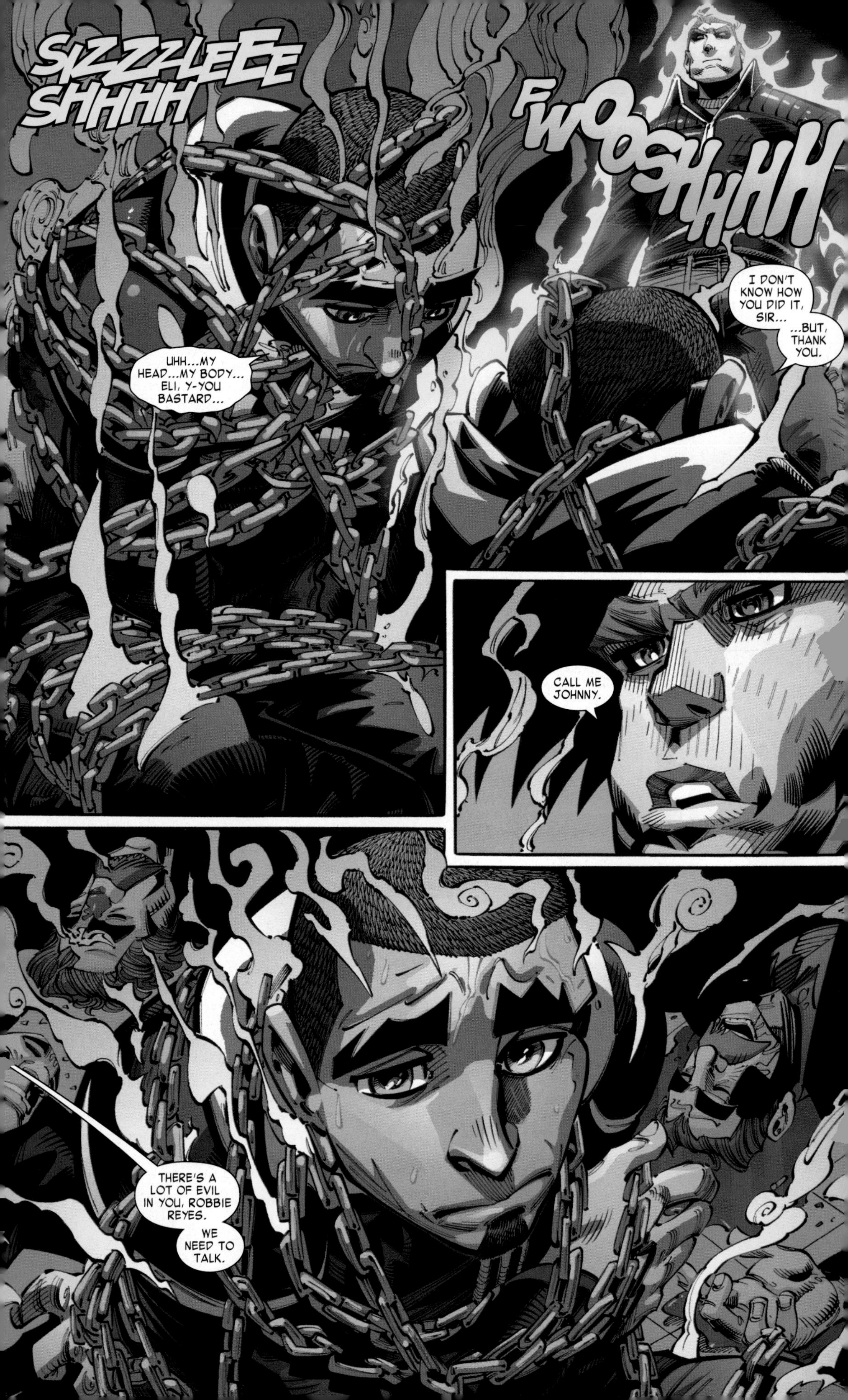
SIZZZLEEEE SHHHH
FWOOSHHHHH
UHH...MY HEAD...MY BODY... ELI, Y-YOU BASTARD...
I DON'T KNOW HOW YOU DID IT, SIR...
...BUT, THANK YOU.
CALL ME JOHNNY.
THERE'S A LOT OF EVIL IN YOU, ROBBIE REYES.
WE NEED TO TALK.

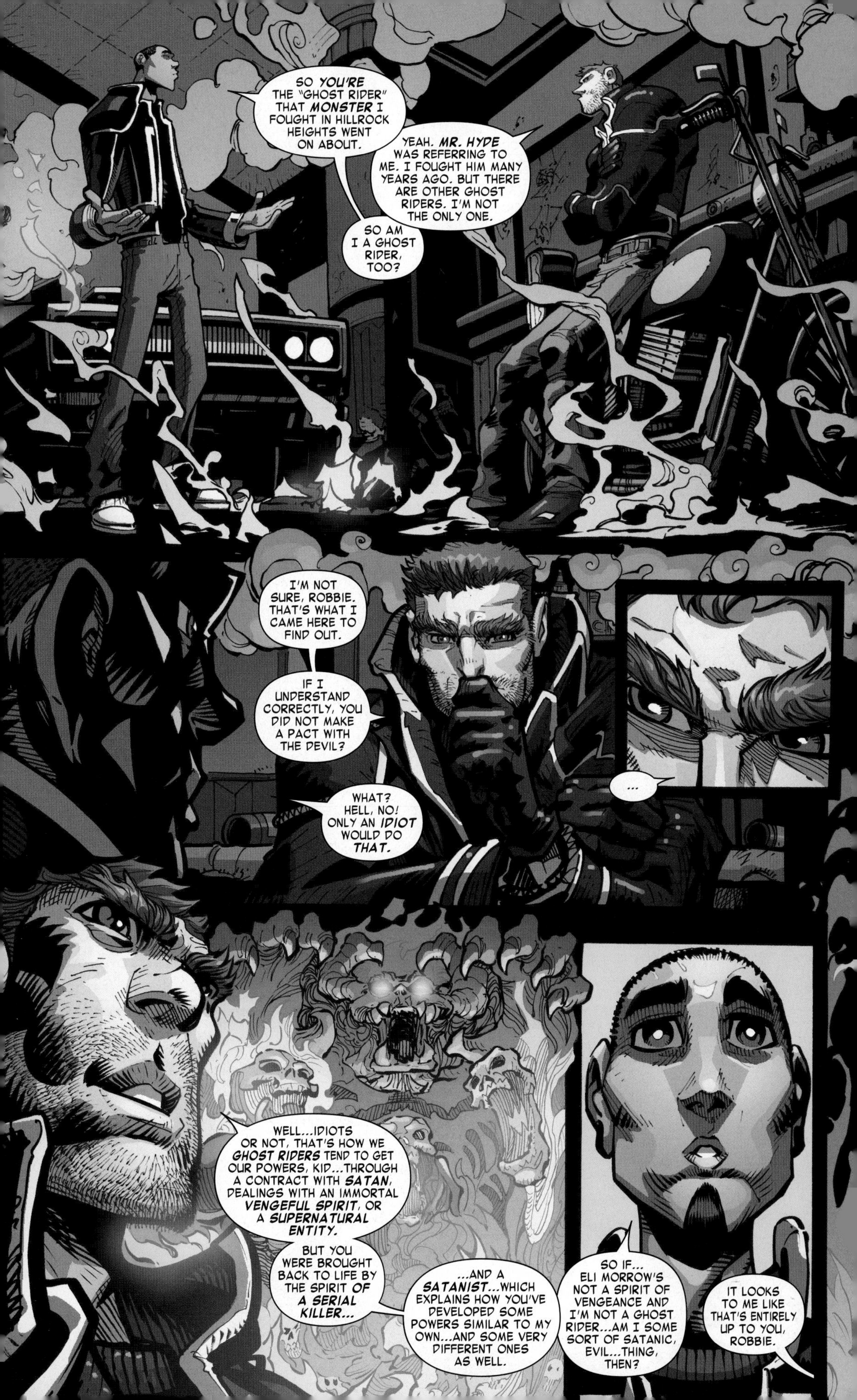
SO YOU'RE THE "GHOST RIDER" THAT MONSTER I FOUGHT IN HILLROCK HEIGHTS WENT ON ABOUT.
YEAH. MR. HYDE WAS REFERRING TO ME. I FOUGHT HIM MANY YEARS AGO. BUT THERE ARE OTHER GHOST RIDERS. I'M NOT THE ONLY ONE.
SO AM I A GHOST RIDER, TOO?
I'M NOT SURE, ROBBIE. THAT'S WHAT I CAME HERE TO FIND OUT.
IF I UNDERSTAND CORRECTLY, YOU DID NOT MAKE A PACT WITH THE DEVIL?
WHAT? HELL, NO! ONLY AN IDIOT WOULD DO THAT.
...
WELL...IDIOTS OR NOT, THAT'S HOW WE GHOST RIDERS TEND TO GET OUR POWERS, KID...THROUGH A CONTRACT WITH SATAN, DEALINGS WITH AN IMMORTAL VENGEFUL SPIRIT, OR A SUPERNATURAL ENTITY.
BUT YOU WERE BROUGHT BACK TO LIFE BY THE SPIRIT OF A SERIAL KILLER...
...AND A SATANIST...WHICH EXPLAINS HOW YOU'VE DEVELOPED SOME POWERS SIMILAR TO MY OWN...AND SOME VERY DIFFERENT ONES AS WELL.
SO IF... ELI MORROW'S NOT A SPIRIT OF VENGEANCE AND I'M NOT A GHOST RIDER...AM I SOME SORT OF SATANIC, EVIL...THING, THEN?
IT LOOKS TO ME LIKE THAT'S ENTIRELY UP TO YOU, ROBBIE.

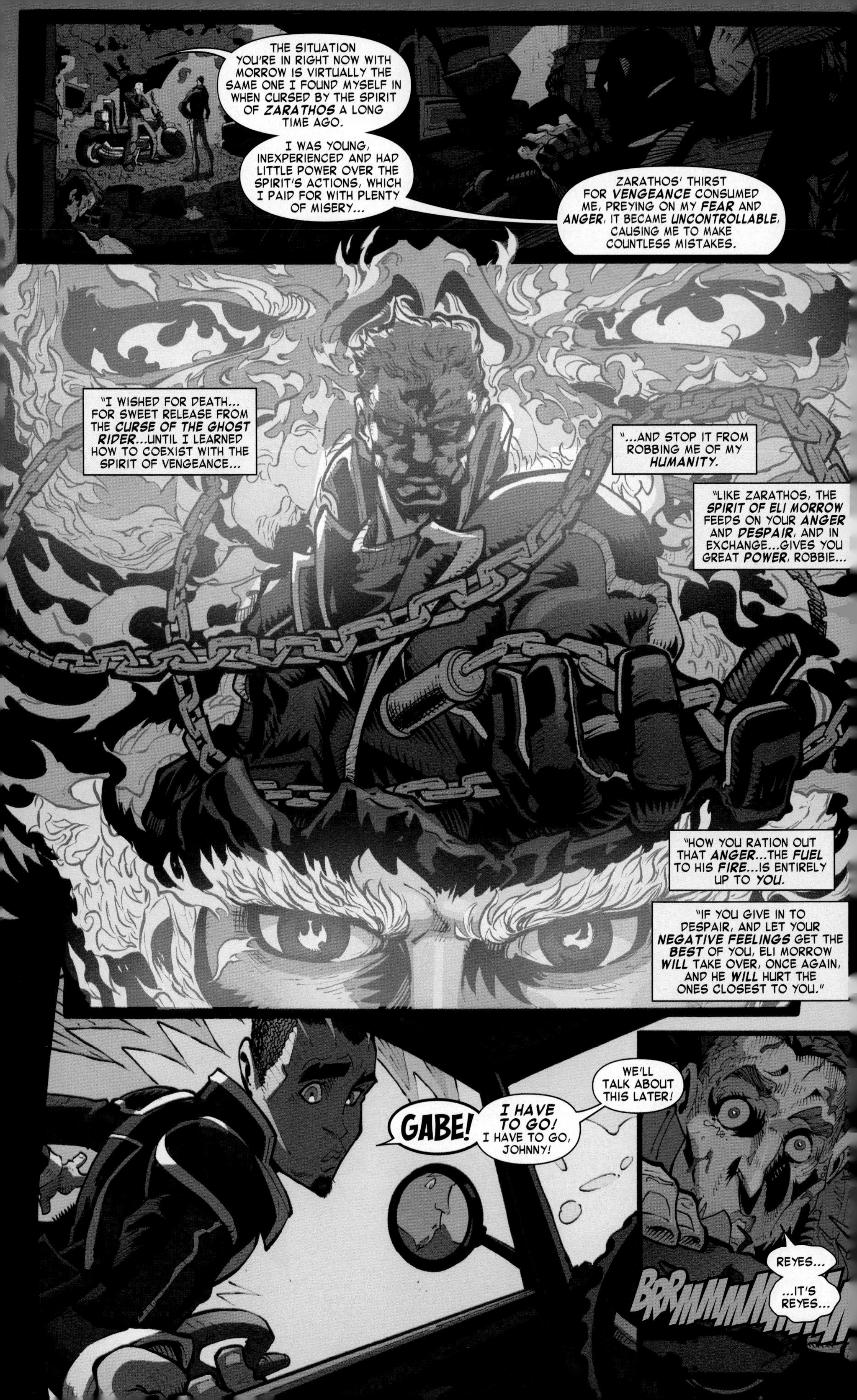
THE SITUATION YOU'RE IN RIGHT NOW WITH MORROW IS VIRTUALLY THE SAME ONE I FOUND MYSELF IN WHEN CURSED BY THE SPIRIT OF ZARATHOS A LONG TIME AGO.
I WAS YOUNG, INEXPERIENCED AND HAD LITTLE POWER OVER THE SPIRIT'S ACTIONS, WHICH I PAID FOR WITH PLENTY OF MISERY...
ZARATHOS' THIRST FOR VENGEANCE CONSUMED ME, PREYING ON MY FEAR AND ANGER, IT BECAME UNCONTROLLABLE, CAUSING ME TO MAKE COUNTLESS MISTAKES.
"I WISHED FOR DEATH... FOR SWEET RELEASE FROM THE CURSE OF THE GHOST RIDER...UNTIL I LEARNED HOW TO COEXIST WITH THE SPIRIT OF VENGEANCE...
"...AND STOP IT FROM ROBBING ME OF MY HUMANITY.
"LIKE ZARATHOS, THE SPIRIT OF ELI MORROW FEEDS ON YOUR ANGER AND DESPAIR, AND IN EXCHANGE...GIVES YOU GREAT POWER, ROBBIE...
"HOW YOU RATION OUT THAT ANGER...THE FUEL TO HIS FIRE...IS ENTIRELY UP TO YOU.
"IF YOU GIVE IN TO DESPAIR, AND LET YOUR NEGATIVE FEELINGS GET THE BEST OF YOU, ELI MORROW WILL TAKE OVER, ONCE AGAIN, AND HE WILL HURT THE ONES CLOSEST TO YOU."
GABE!
I HAVE TO GO! I HAVE TO GO, JOHNNY!
WE'LL TALK ABOUT THIS LATER!
REYES...
...IT'S REYES...
BRRMMMMM

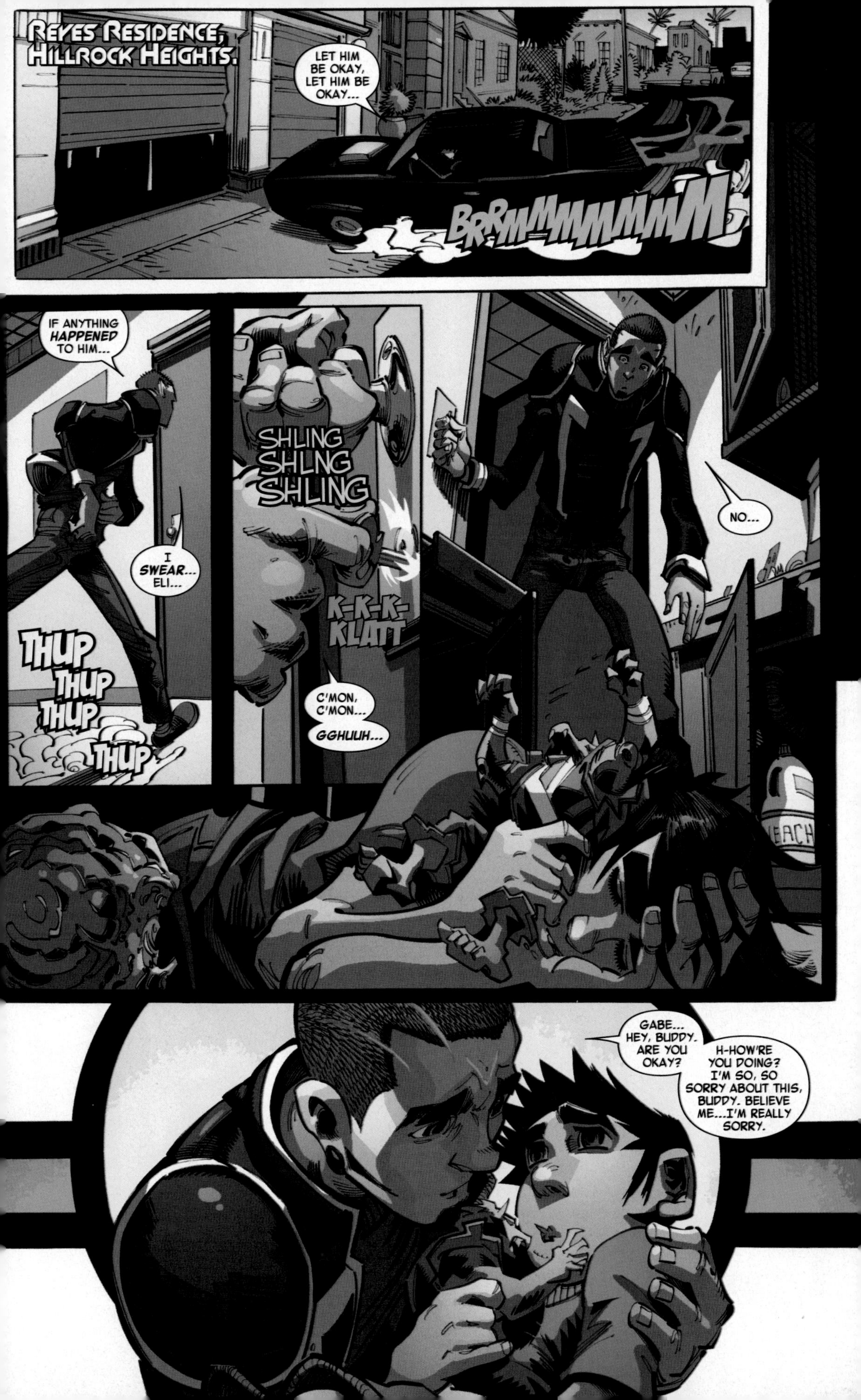

REYES RESIDENCE, HILLROCK HEIGHTS.
LET HIM BE OKAY, LET HIM BE OKAY...
BRRMMMMMMMMM
IF ANYTHING HAPPENED TO HIM...
I SWEAR... ELI...
THUP THUP THUP THUP
SHLING SHLNG SHLING
K-K-K-KLATT
C'MON, C'MON...
GGHUUH...
NO...
BLEACH
GABE... HEY, BUDDY. ARE YOU OKAY?
H-HOW'RE YOU DOING? I'M SO, SO SORRY ABOUT THIS, BUDDY. BELIEVE ME...I'M REALLY SORRY.

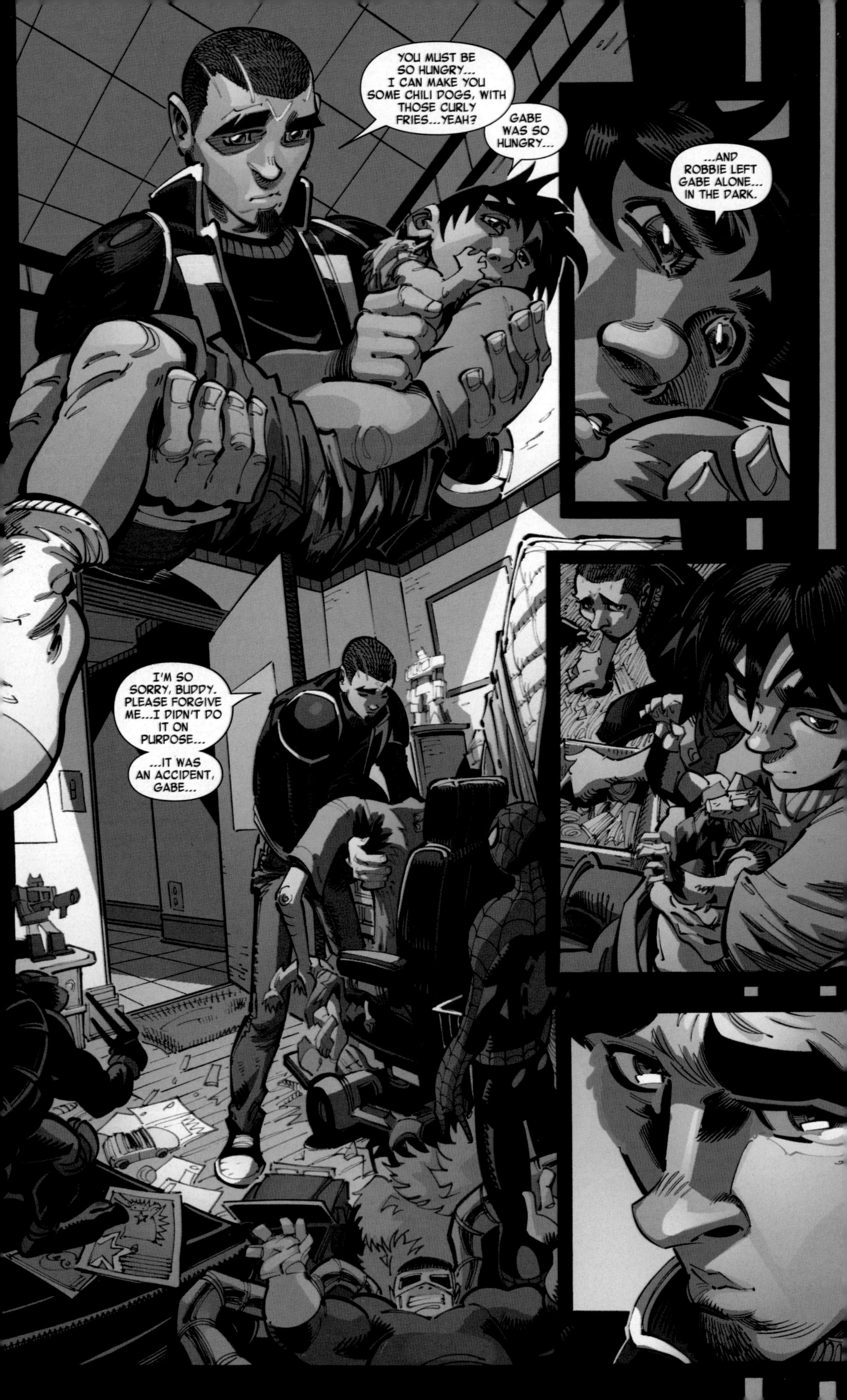
YOU MUST BE SO HUNGRY... I CAN MAKE YOU SOME CHILI DOGS, WITH THOSE CURLY FRIES...YEAH?
GABE WAS SO HUNGRY...
...AND ROBBIE LEFT GABE ALONE... IN THE DARK.
I'M SO SORRY, BUDDY. PLEASE FORGIVE ME...I DIDN'T DO IT ON PURPOSE...
...IT WAS AN ACCIDENT, GABE...

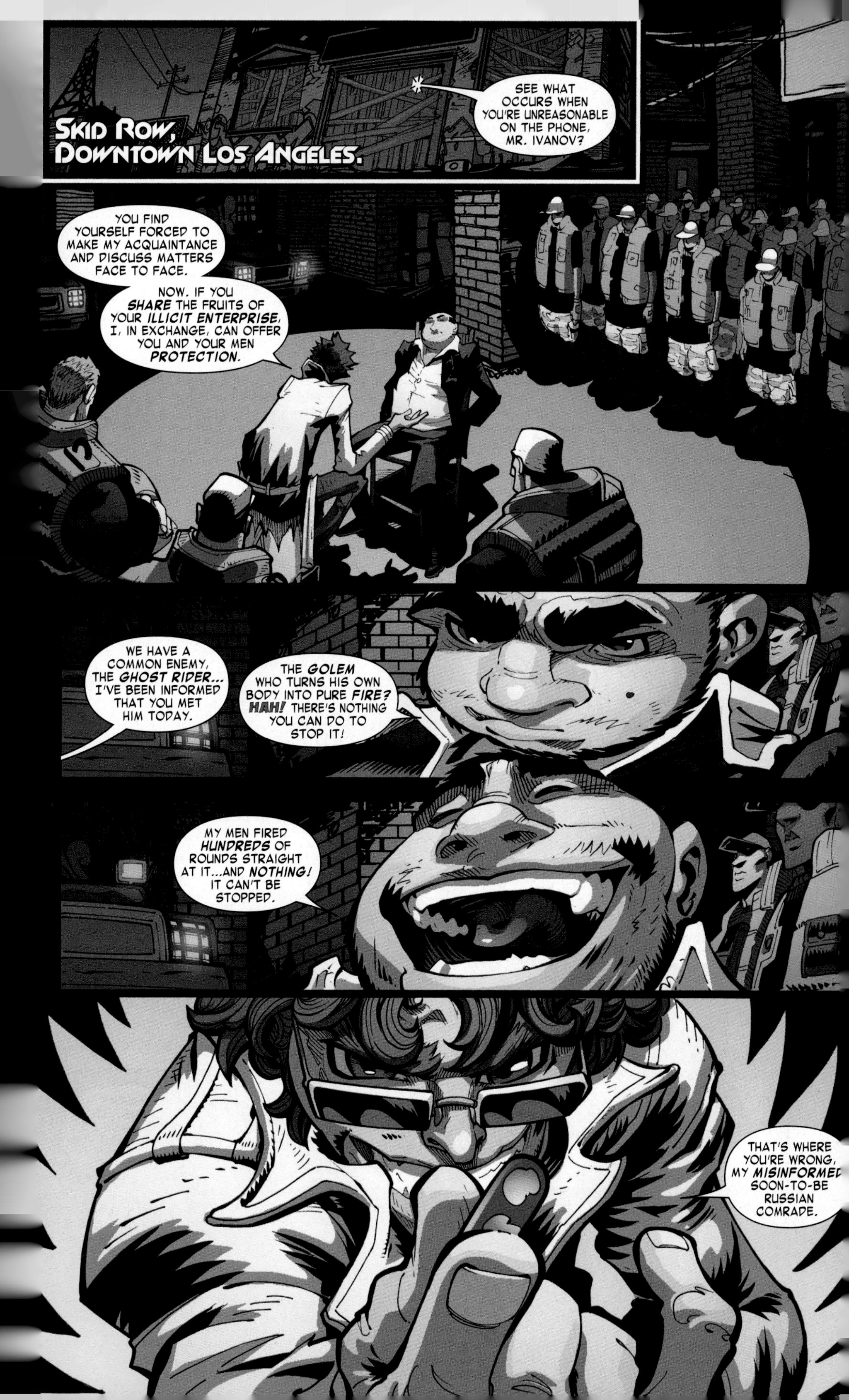
SKID ROW, DOWNTOWN LOS ANGELES.
SEE WHAT OCCURS WHEN YOU'RE UNREASONABLE ON THE PHONE, MR. IVANOV?
YOU FIND YOURSELF FORCED TO MAKE MY ACQUAINTANCE AND DISCUSS MATTERS FACE TO FACE.
NOW. IF YOU SHARE THE FRUITS OF YOUR ILLICIT ENTERPRISE, I, IN EXCHANGE, CAN OFFER YOU AND YOUR MEN PROTECTION.
WE HAVE A COMMON ENEMY, THE GHOST RIDER... I'VE BEEN INFORMED THAT YOU MET HIM TODAY.
THE GOLEM WHO TURNS HIS OWN BODY INTO PURE FIRE? HAH! THERE'S NOTHING YOU CAN DO TO STOP IT!
MY MEN FIRED HUNDREDS OF ROUNDS STRAIGHT AT IT...AND NOTHING! IT CAN'T BE STOPPED.
THAT'S WHERE YOU'RE WRONG, MY MISINFORMED SOON-TO-BE RUSSIAN COMRADE.

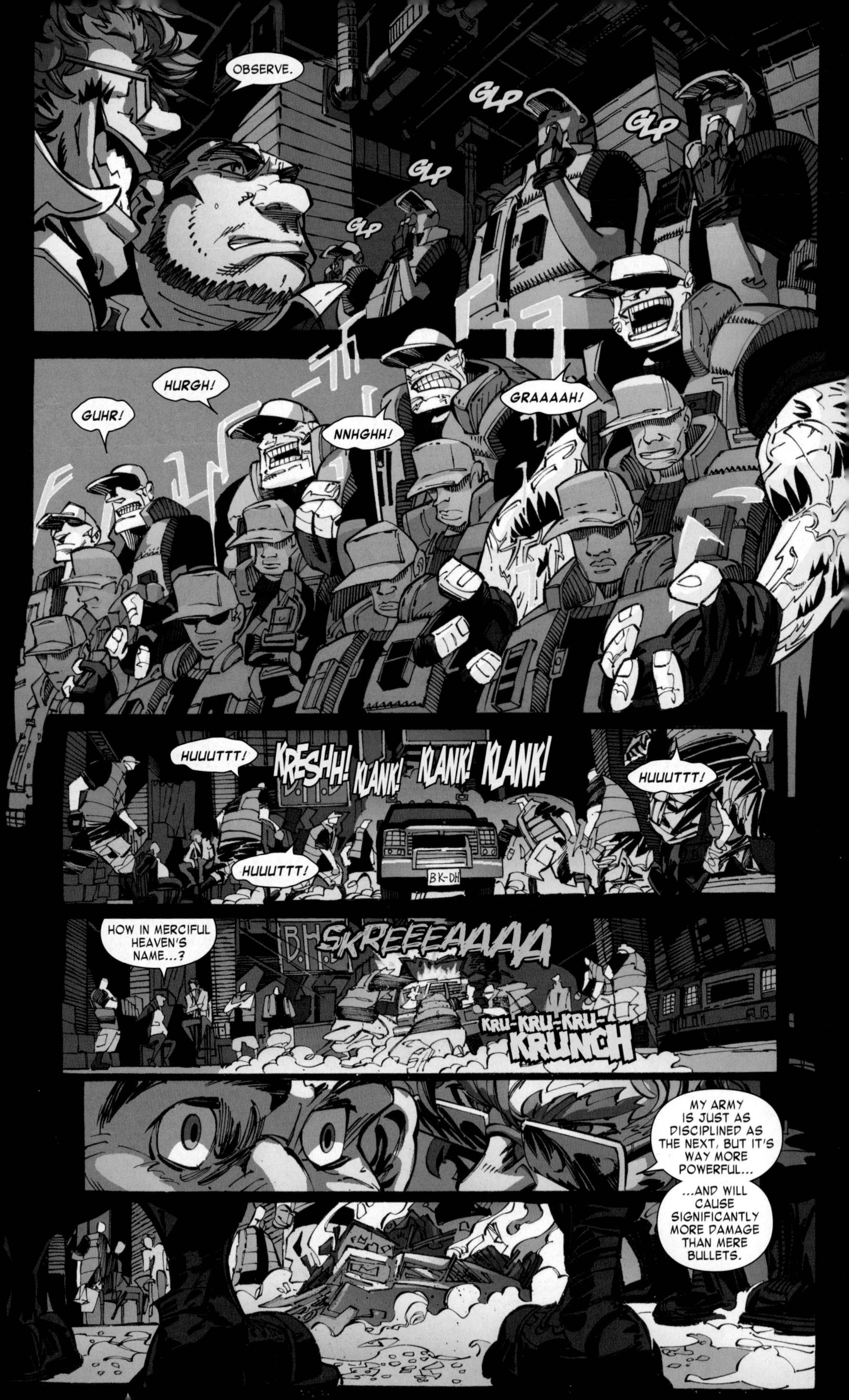
OBSERVE.
GLP
GLP
GLP
GLP
GUHR!
HURGH!
NNHGHH!
GRAAAAH!
HUUUTTT!
KRESHH! KLANK! KLANK! KLANK!
HUUUTTT!
HUUUTTT!
BK-DH
HOW IN MERCIFUL HEAVEN'S NAME...?
SKREEEAAAA
KRU-KRU-KRU-KRUNCH
MY ARMY IS JUST AS DISCIPLINED AS THE NEXT, BUT IT'S WAY MORE POWERFUL...
...AND WILL CAUSE SIGNIFICANTLY MORE DAMAGE THAN MERE BULLETS.

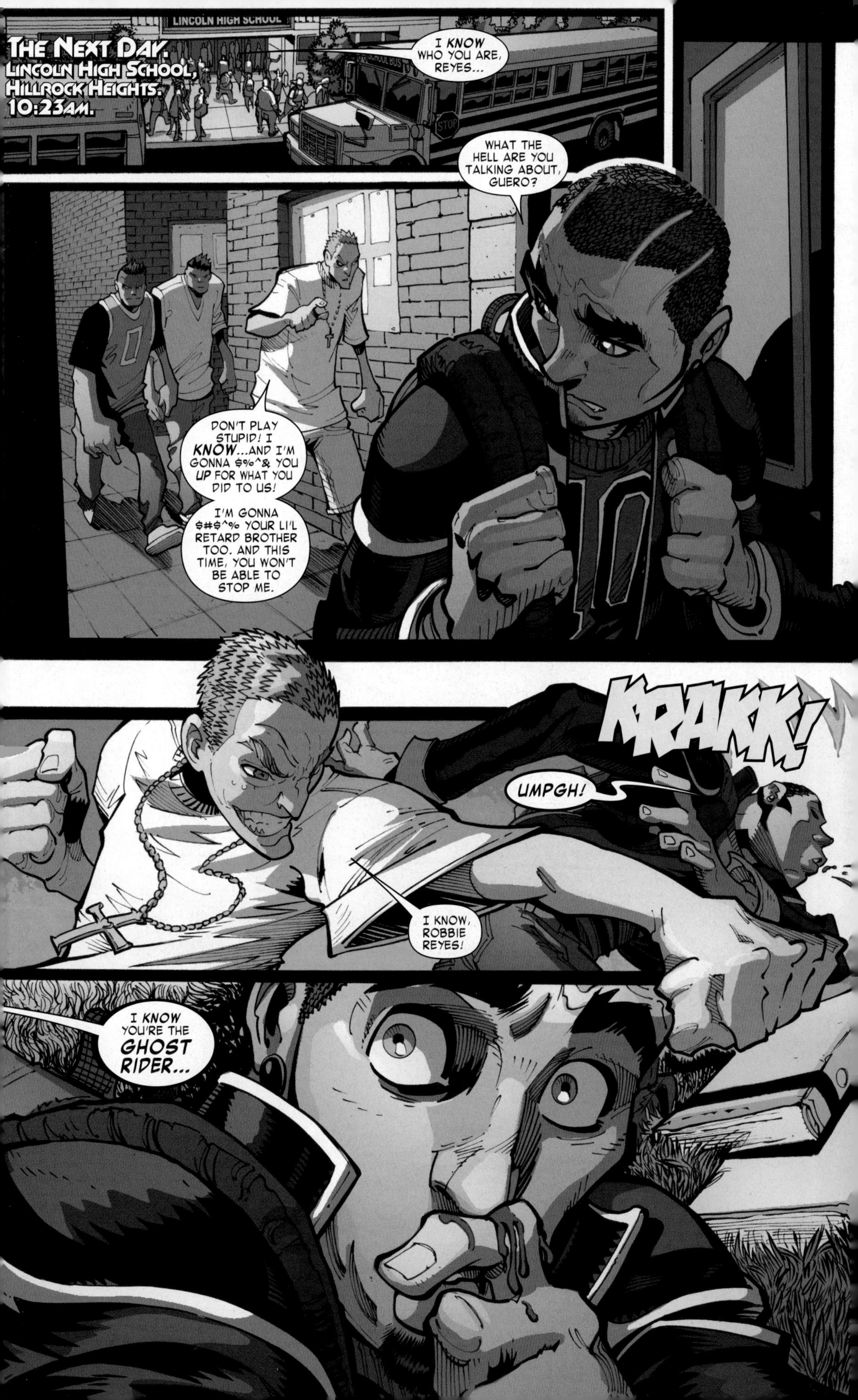
LINCOLN HIGH SCHOOL
THE NEXT DAY. LINCOLN HIGH SCHOOL, HILLROCK HEIGHTS. 10:23AM.
I KNOW WHO YOU ARE, REYES...
WHAT THE HELL ARE YOU TALKING ABOUT, GUERO?
DON'T PLAY STUPID! I KNOW...AND I'M GONNA $%^& YOU UP FOR WHAT YOU DID TO US!
I'M GONNA $#$^% YOUR LI'L RETARD BROTHER TOO. AND THIS TIME, YOU WON'T BE ABLE TO STOP ME.
KRAKK!
UMPGH!
I KNOW, ROBBIE REYES!
I KNOW YOU'RE THE GHOST RIDER...

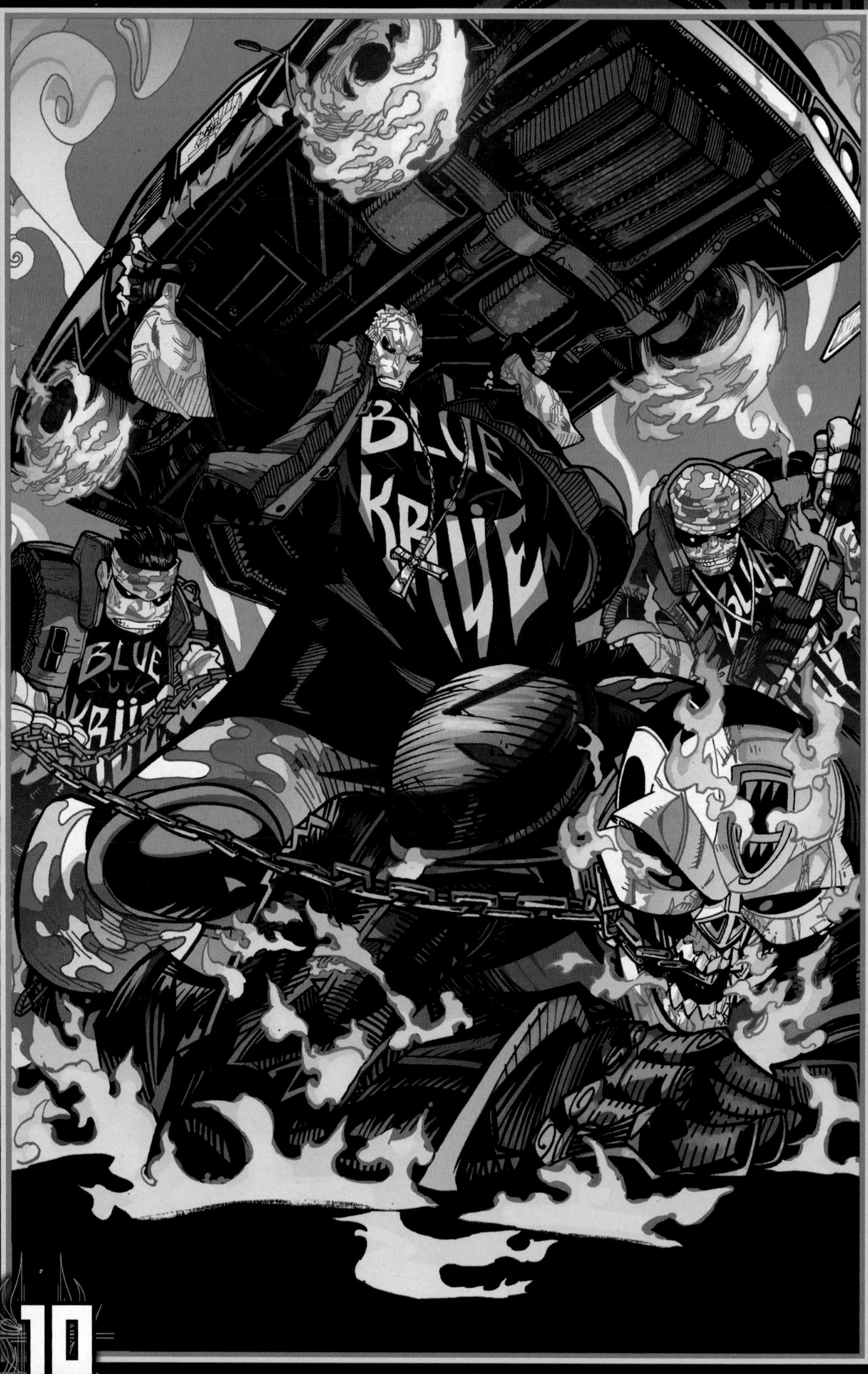
BLUE
KRUE
BLUE

10

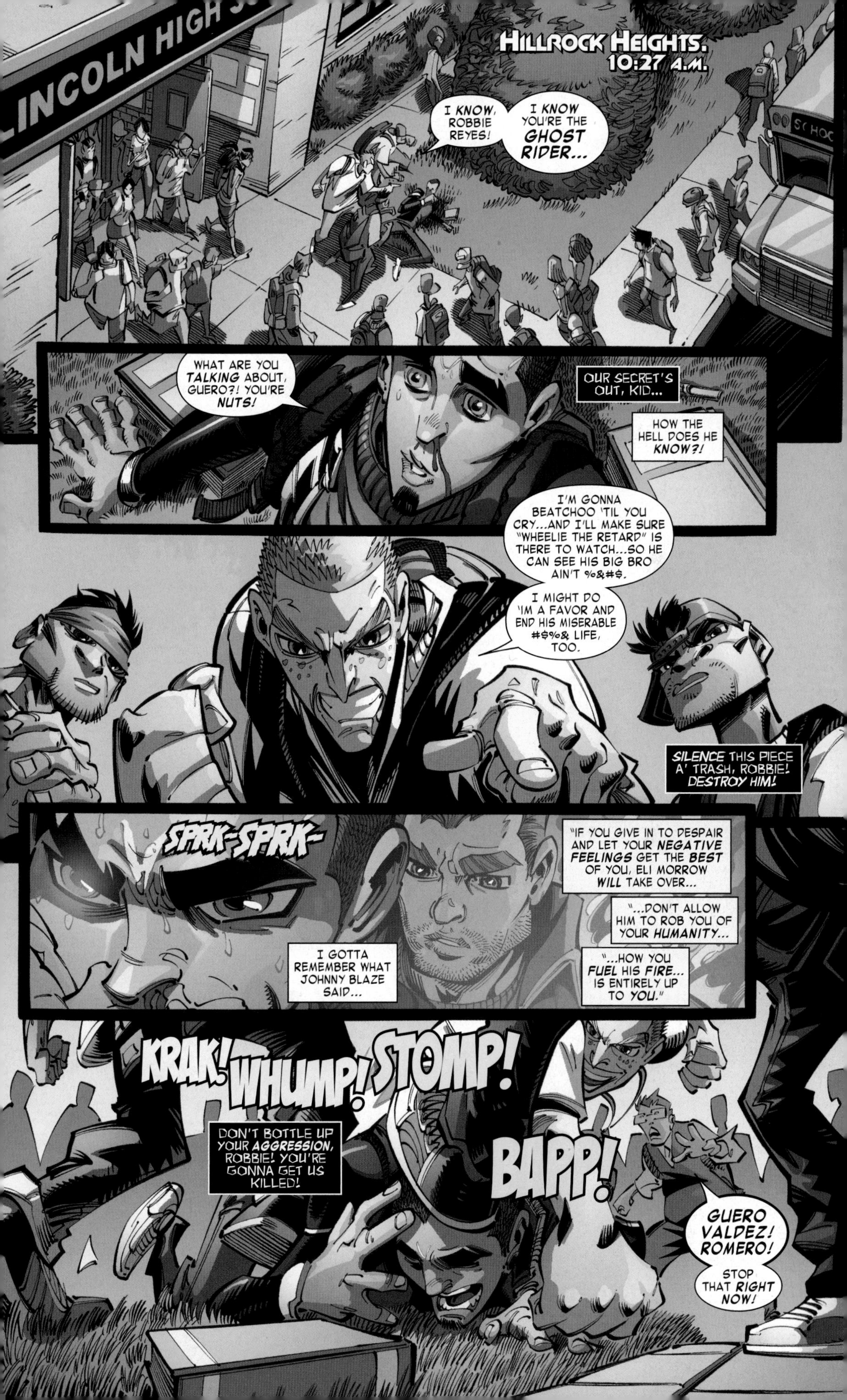
LINCOLN HIGH
HILLROCK HEIGHTS. 10:27 A.M.
I KNOW, ROBBIE REYES!
I KNOW YOU'RE THE GHOST RIDER...
WHAT ARE YOU TALKING ABOUT, GUERO?! YOU'RE NUTS!
OUR SECRET'S OUT, KID...
HOW THE HELL DOES HE KNOW?!
I'M GONNA BEATCHOO 'TIL YOU CRY...AND I'LL MAKE SURE "WHEELIE THE RETARD" IS THERE TO WATCH...SO HE CAN SEE HIS BIG BRO AIN'T %&#$.
I MIGHT DO 'IM A FAVOR AND END HIS MISERABLE #$%& LIFE, TOO.
SILENCE THIS PIECE A' TRASH, ROBBIE! DESTROY HIM!
SPRK-SPRK-
"IF YOU GIVE IN TO DESPAIR AND LET YOUR NEGATIVE FEELINGS GET THE BEST OF YOU, ELI MORROW WILL TAKE OVER...
"...DON'T ALLOW HIM TO ROB YOU OF YOUR HUMANITY...
I GOTTA REMEMBER WHAT JOHNNY BLAZE SAID...
"...HOW YOU FUEL HIS FIRE... IS ENTIRELY UP TO YOU."
KRAK! WHUMP! STOMP!
DON'T BOTTLE UP YOUR AGGRESSION, ROBBIE! YOU'RE GONNA GET US KILLED!
BAPP!
GUERO VALDEZ! ROMERO!
STOP THAT RIGHT NOW!

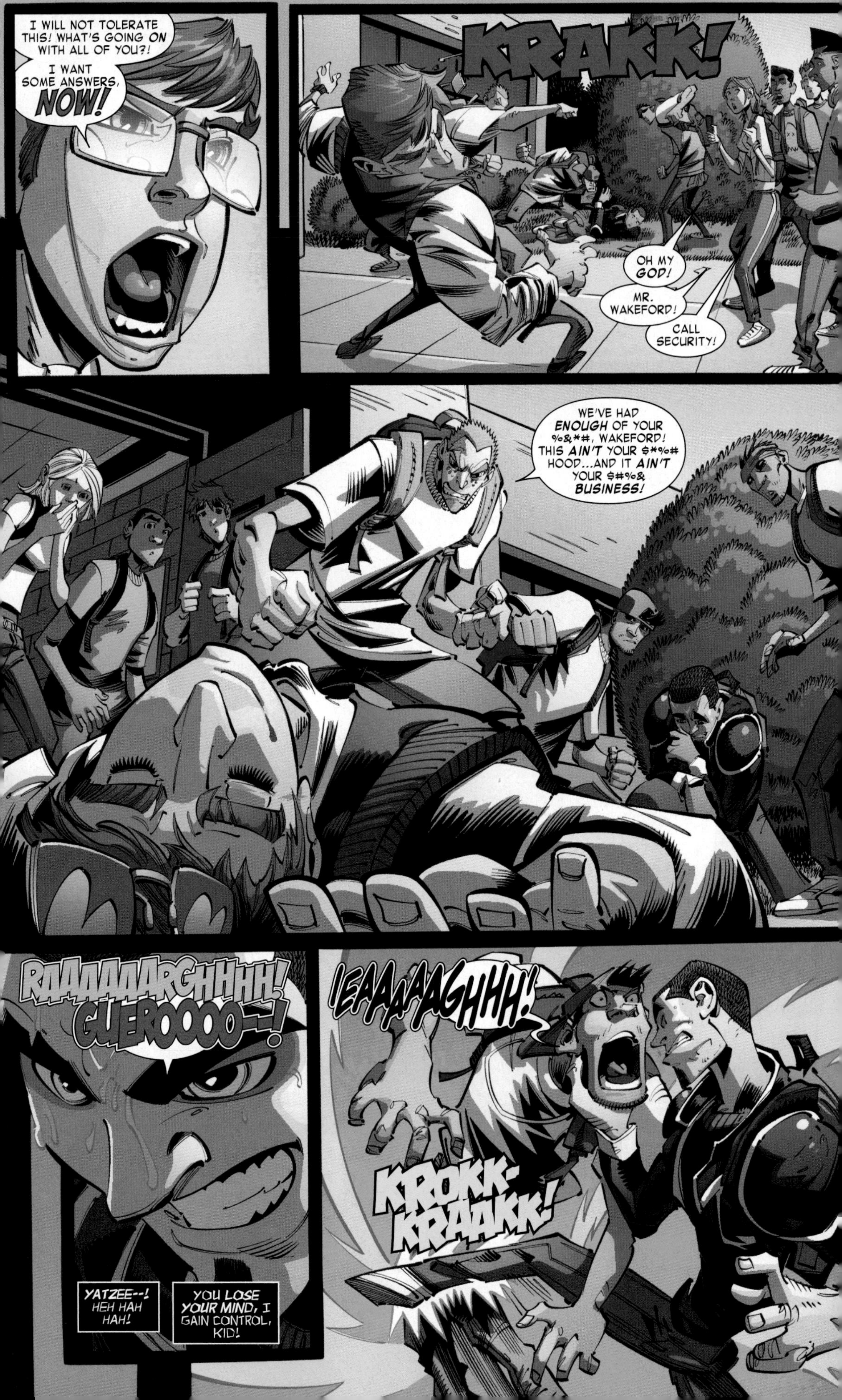
I WILL NOT TOLERATE THIS! WHAT'S GOING ON WITH ALL OF YOU?!
I WANT SOME ANSWERS, NOW!
KRAKK!
OH MY GOD!
MR. WAKEFORD!
CALL SECURITY!
WE'VE HAD ENOUGH OF YOUR %&*#, WAKEFORD! THIS AIN'T YOUR $*%# HOOD...AND IT AIN'T YOUR $#%& BUSINESS!
RAAAAAARGHHHH! GUEROOOO--!
IEAAAAAGHHH!
KROKK-KRAAKK!
YATZEE--! HEH HAH HAH!
YOU LOSE YOUR MIND, I GAIN CONTROL, KID!

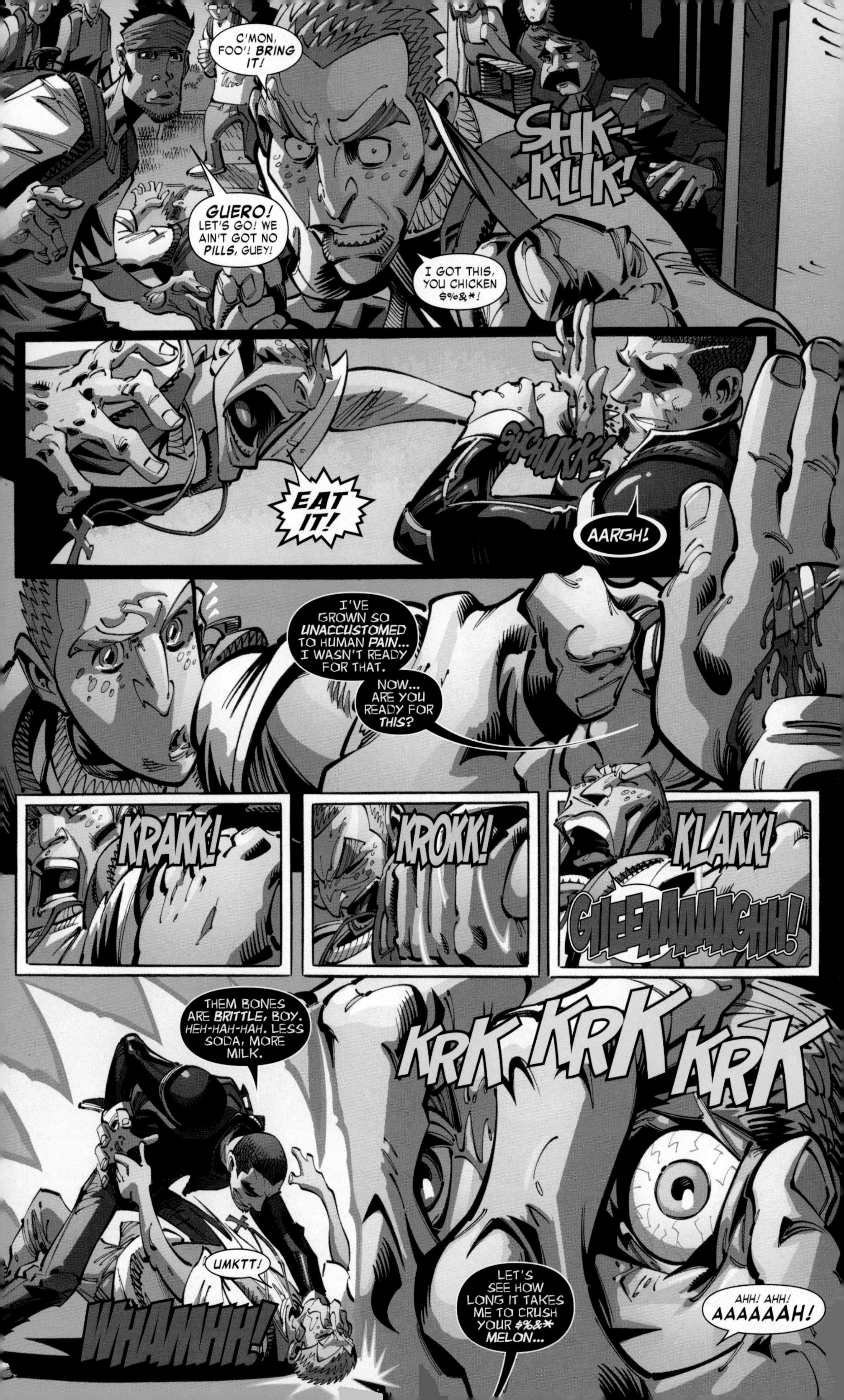
C'MON, FOO'! BRING IT!
GUERO! LET'S GO! WE AIN'T GOT NO PILLS, GUEY!
SHK-KLIK!
I GOT THIS, YOU CHICKEN $%&*!
SHCHUKK!
EAT IT!
AARGH!
I'VE GROWN SO UNACCUSTOMED TO HUMAN PAIN... I WASN'T READY FOR THAT.
NOW... ARE YOU READY FOR THIS?
KRAKK!
KROKK!
KLAKK!
GIEEAAAAAGHH!
THEM BONES ARE BRITTLE, BOY. HEH-HAH-HAH. LESS SODA, MORE MILK.
KRK KRK KRK
UMKTT!
WHAMHH!
LET'S SEE HOW LONG IT TAKES ME TO CRUSH YOUR $%&* MELON...
AHH! AHH! AAAAAAH!

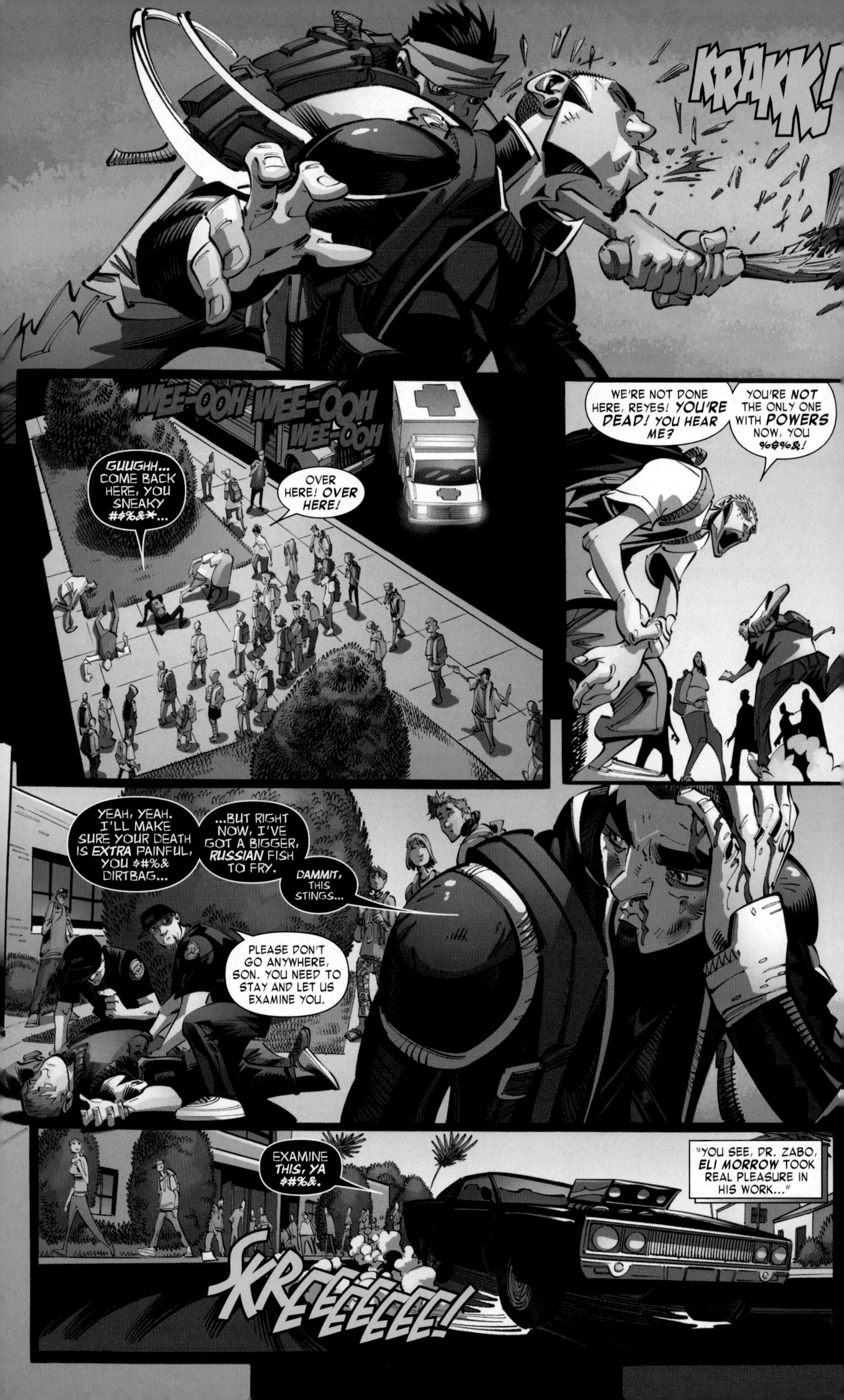
KRAKK!
WEE-OOH WEE-OOH WEE-OOH
GUUGHH... COME BACK HERE, YOU SNEAKY #$%&*...
OVER HERE! OVER HERE!
WE'RE NOT DONE HERE, REYES! YOU'RE DEAD! YOU HEAR ME?
YOU'RE NOT THE ONLY ONE WITH POWERS NOW, YOU %$%&!
YEAH, YEAH. I'LL MAKE SURE YOUR DEATH IS EXTRA PAINFUL, YOU $#%& DIRTBAG...
...BUT RIGHT NOW, I'VE GOT A BIGGER, RUSSIAN FISH TO FRY.
DAMMIT, THIS STINGS...
PLEASE DON'T GO ANYWHERE, SON. YOU NEED TO STAY AND LET US EXAMINE YOU.
EXAMINE THIS, YA $#%&.
"YOU SEE, DR. ZABO, ELI MORROW TOOK REAL PLEASURE IN HIS WORK..."
SKREEEEEEEE!

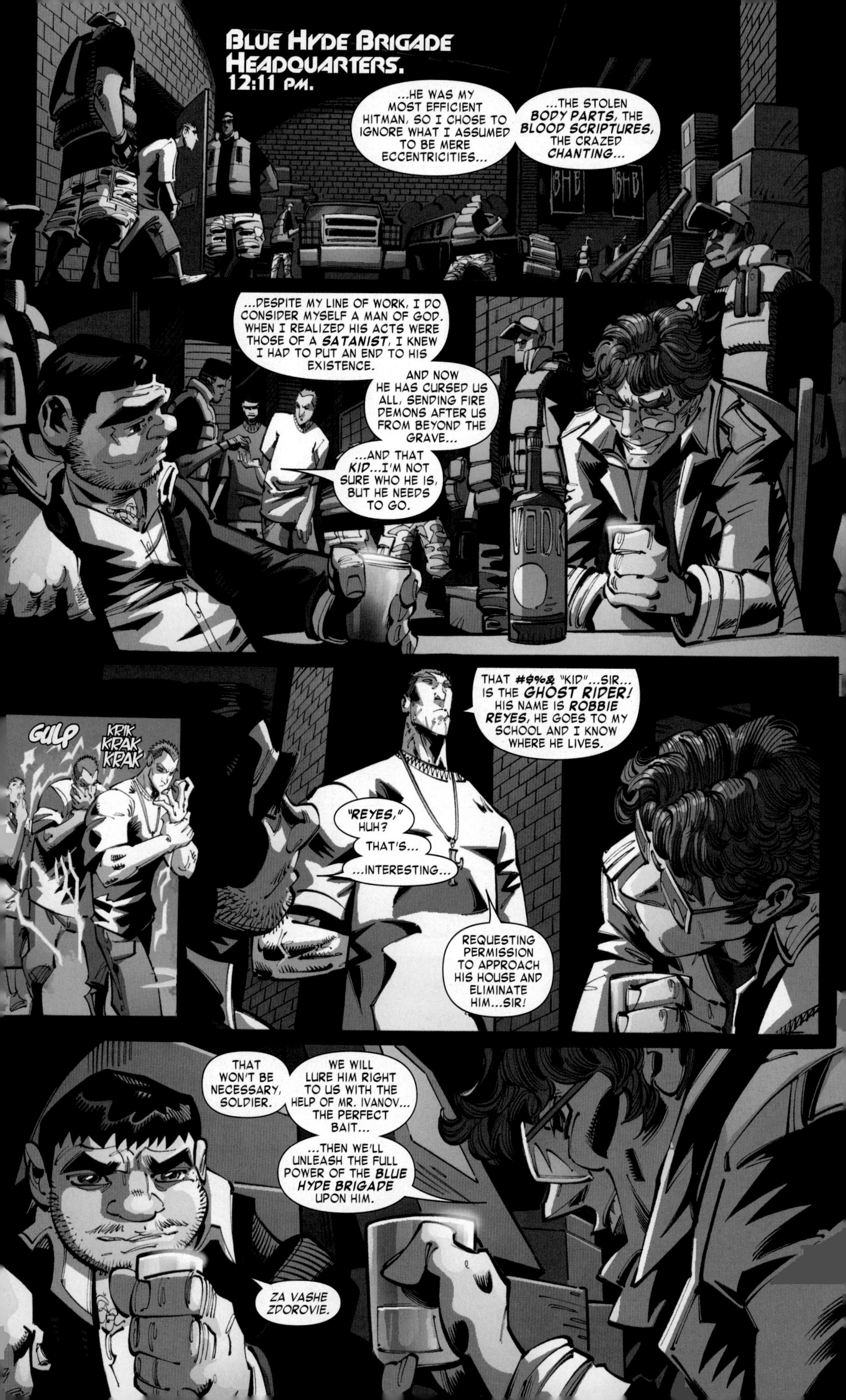
BLUE HYDE BRIGADE HEADQUARTERS. 12:11 PM.
...HE WAS MY MOST EFFICIENT HITMAN, SO I CHOSE TO IGNORE WHAT I ASSUMED TO BE MERE ECCENTRICITIES...
...THE STOLEN BODY PARTS, THE BLOOD SCRIPTURES, THE CRAZED CHANTING...
...DESPITE MY LINE OF WORK, I DO CONSIDER MYSELF A MAN OF GOD. WHEN I REALIZED HIS ACTS WERE THOSE OF A SATANIST, I KNEW I HAD TO PUT AN END TO HIS EXISTENCE.
AND NOW HE HAS CURSED US ALL, SENDING FIRE DEMONS AFTER US FROM BEYOND THE GRAVE...
...AND THAT KID...I'M NOT SURE WHO HE IS, BUT HE NEEDS TO GO.
GULP
KRIK KRAK KRAK
THAT #$%& "KID"...SIR... IS THE GHOST RIDER! HIS NAME IS ROBBIE REYES, HE GOES TO MY SCHOOL AND I KNOW WHERE HE LIVES.
"REYES," HUH?
THAT'S...
...INTERESTING...
REQUESTING PERMISSION TO APPROACH HIS HOUSE AND ELIMINATE HIM...SIR!
THAT WON'T BE NECESSARY, SOLDIER.
WE WILL LURE HIM RIGHT TO US WITH THE HELP OF MR. IVANOV... THE PERFECT BAIT...
...THEN WE'LL UNLEASH THE FULL POWER OF THE BLUE HYDE BRIGADE UPON HIM.
ZA VASHE ZDOROVIE.

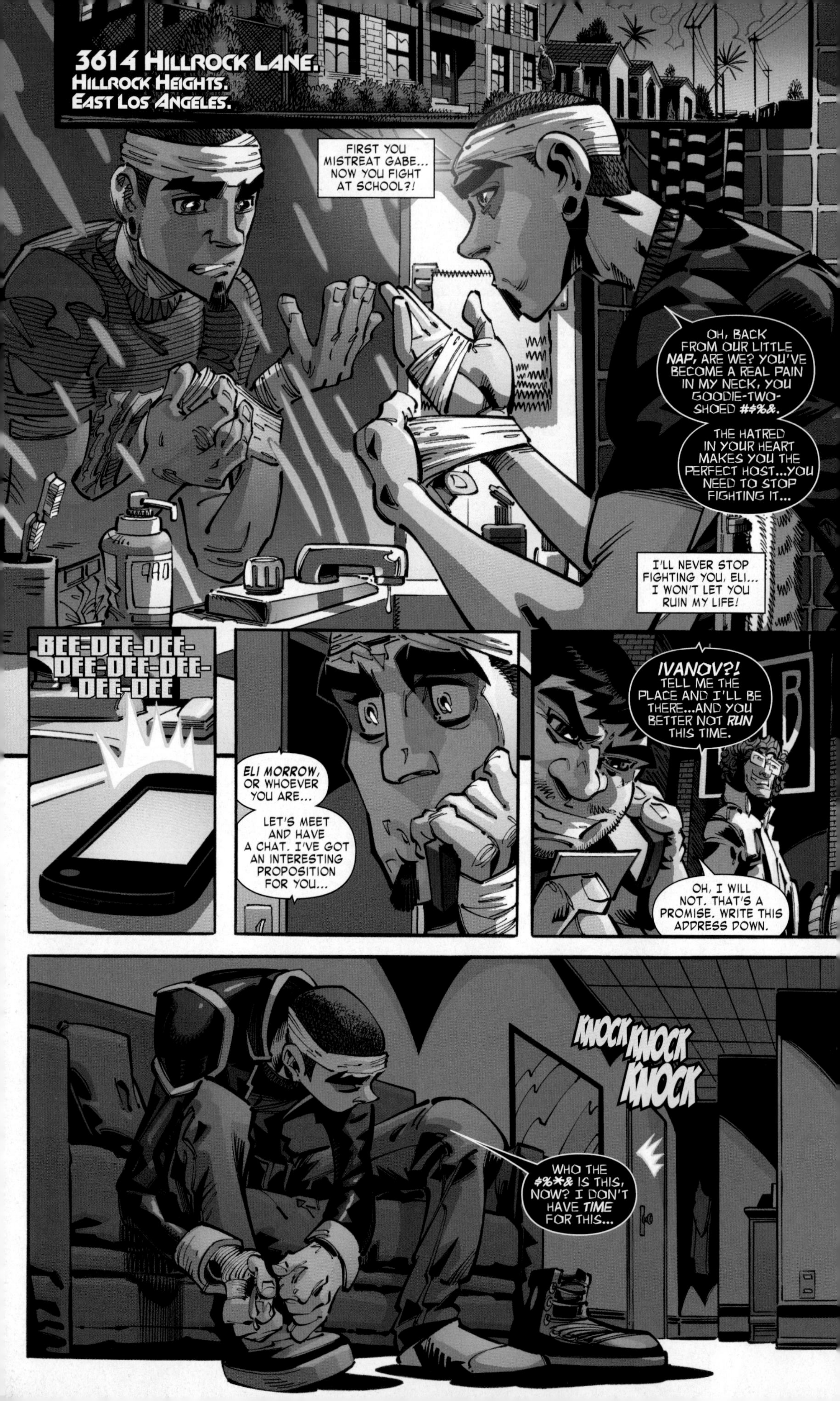

3614 Hillrock Lane.
Hillrock Heights.
East Los Angeles.
FIRST YOU MISTREAT GABE... NOW YOU FIGHT AT SCHOOL?!
OH, BACK FROM OUR LITTLE NAP, ARE WE? YOU'VE BECOME A REAL PAIN IN MY NECK, YOU GOODIE-TWO-SHOED #$%&.
THE HATRED IN YOUR HEART MAKES YOU THE PERFECT HOST...YOU NEED TO STOP FIGHTING IT...
I'LL NEVER STOP FIGHTING YOU, ELI... I WON'T LET YOU RUIN MY LIFE!
BEE-DEE-DEE-DEE-DEE-DEE-DEE-DEE
ELI MORROW, OR WHOEVER YOU ARE...
LET'S MEET AND HAVE A CHAT. I'VE GOT AN INTERESTING PROPOSITION FOR YOU...
IVANOV?! TELL ME THE PLACE AND I'LL BE THERE...AND YOU BETTER NOT RUN THIS TIME.
OH, I WILL NOT. THAT'S A PROMISE. WRITE THIS ADDRESS DOWN.
KNOCK KNOCK KNOCK
WHO THE $%*& IS THIS, NOW? I DON'T HAVE TIME FOR THIS...

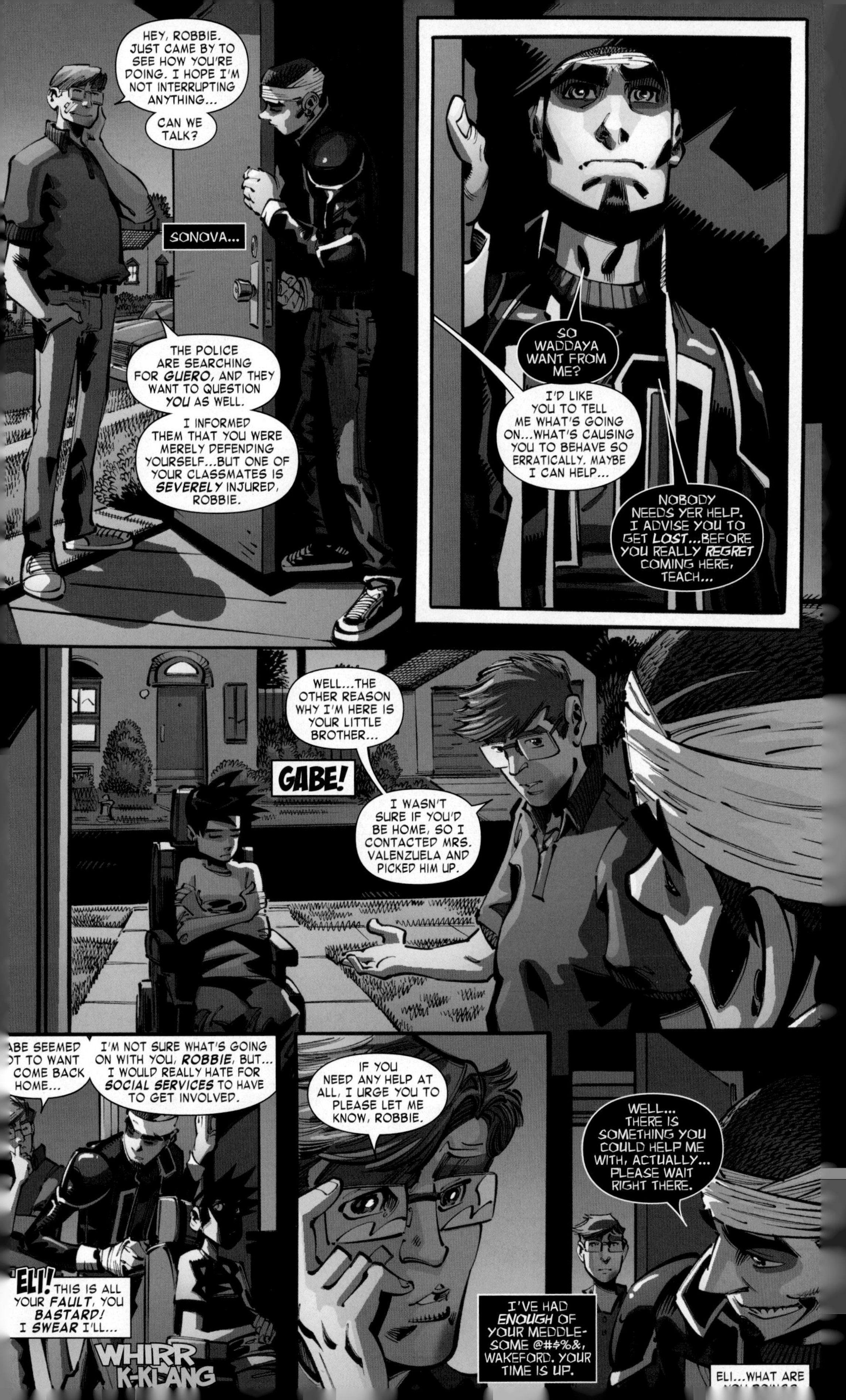
HEY, ROBBIE. JUST CAME BY TO SEE HOW YOU'RE DOING. I HOPE I'M NOT INTERRUPTING ANYTHING...
CAN WE TALK?
SONOVA...
THE POLICE ARE SEARCHING FOR GUERO, AND THEY WANT TO QUESTION YOU AS WELL.
I INFORMED THEM THAT YOU WERE MERELY DEFENDING YOURSELF...BUT ONE OF YOUR CLASSMATES IS SEVERELY INJURED, ROBBIE.
SO WADDAYA WANT FROM ME?
I'D LIKE YOU TO TELL ME WHAT'S GOING ON...WHAT'S CAUSING YOU TO BEHAVE SO ERRATICALLY. MAYBE I CAN HELP...
NOBODY NEEDS YER HELP. I ADVISE YOU TO GET LOST...BEFORE YOU REALLY REGRET COMING HERE, TEACH...
WELL...THE OTHER REASON WHY I'M HERE IS YOUR LITTLE BROTHER...
GABE!
I WASN'T SURE IF YOU'D BE HOME, SO I CONTACTED MRS. VALENZUELA AND PICKED HIM UP.
ABE SEEMED OT TO WANT COME BACK HOME...
I'M NOT SURE WHAT'S GOING ON WITH YOU, ROBBIE, BUT... I WOULD REALLY HATE FOR SOCIAL SERVICES TO HAVE TO GET INVOLVED.
ELI! THIS IS ALL YOUR FAULT, YOU BASTARD! I SWEAR I'LL...
WHIRR
K-KLANG
IF YOU NEED ANY HELP AT ALL, I URGE YOU TO PLEASE LET ME KNOW, ROBBIE.
I'VE HAD ENOUGH OF YOUR MEDDLE-SOME @#$%&, WAKEFORD. YOUR TIME IS UP.
WELL... THERE IS SOMETHING YOU COULD HELP ME WITH, ACTUALLY... PLEASE WAIT RIGHT THERE.
ELI...WHAT ARE

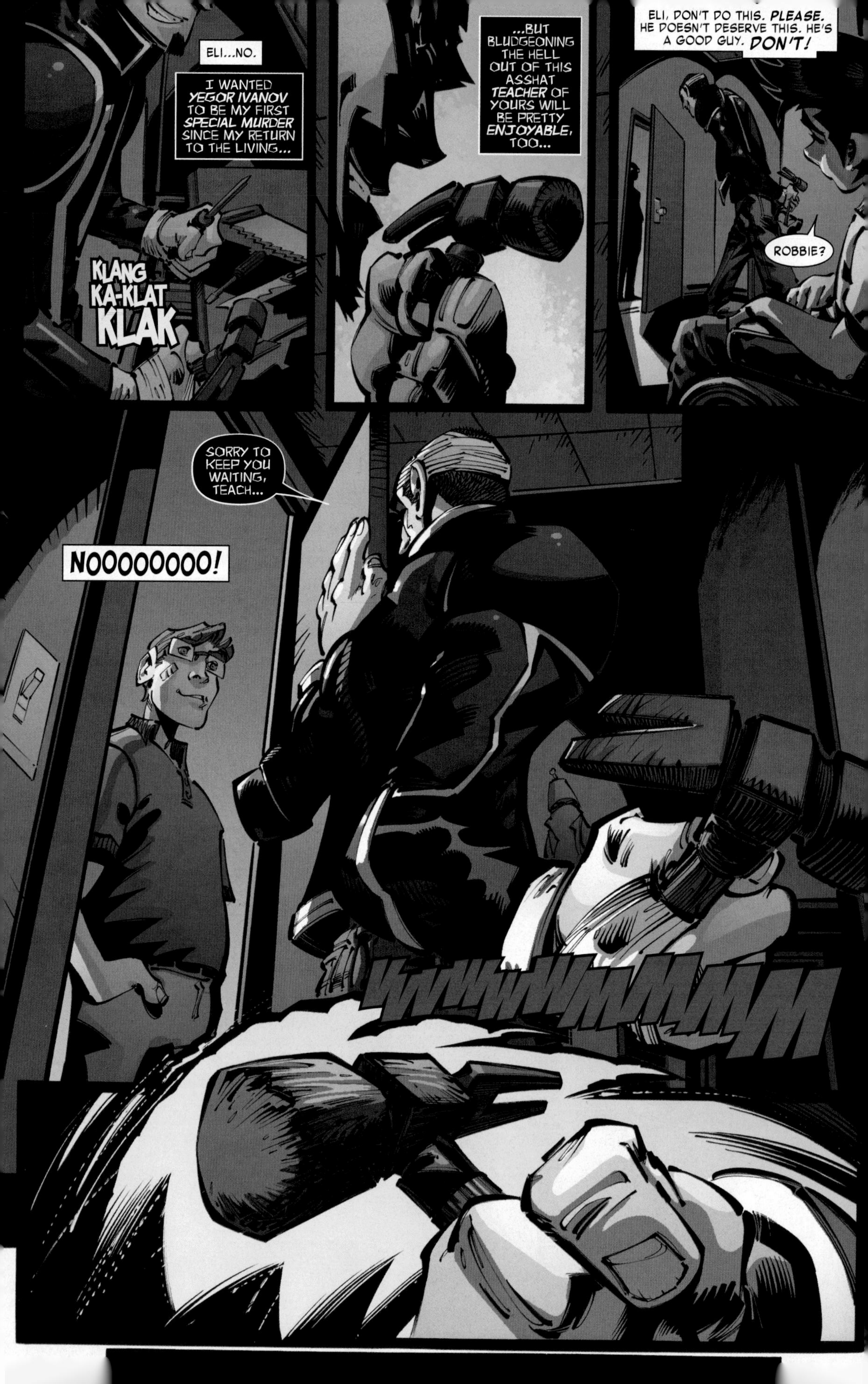

ELI...NO.
I WANTED YEGOR IVANOV TO BE MY FIRST SPECIAL MURDER SINCE MY RETURN TO THE LIVING...
KLANG KA-KLAT KLAK
...BUT BLUDGEONING THE HELL OUT OF THIS ASSHAT TEACHER OF YOURS WILL BE PRETTY ENJOYABLE, TOO...
ELI, DON'T DO THIS. PLEASE. HE DOESN'T DESERVE THIS. HE'S A GOOD GUY. DON'T!
ROBBIE?
SORRY TO KEEP YOU WAITING, TEACH...
NOOOOOOOO!

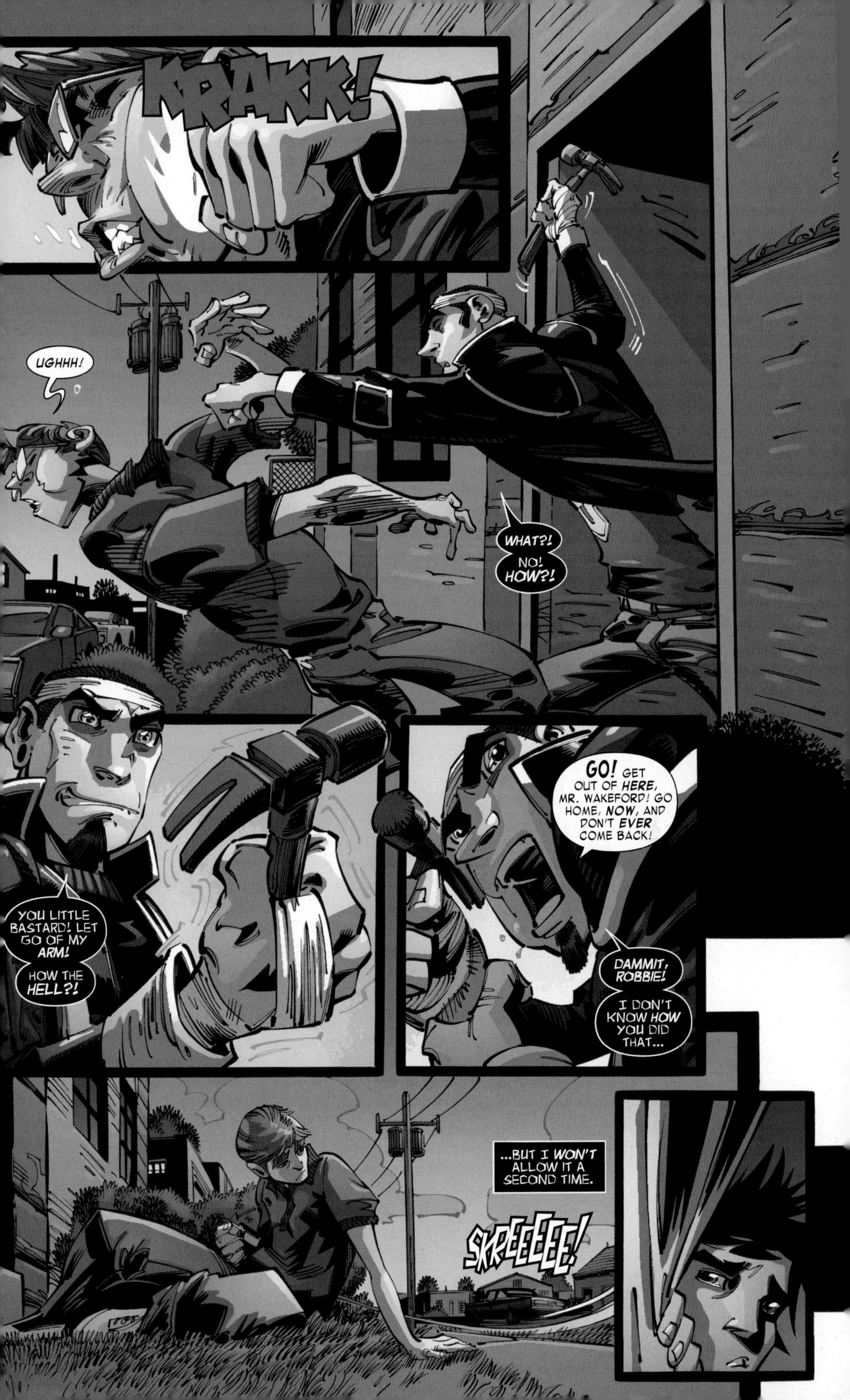
KRAKK!
UGHHH!
WHAT?! NO! HOW?!
YOU LITTLE BASTARD! LET GO OF MY ARM!
HOW THE HELL?!
GO! GET OUT OF HERE, MR. WAKEFORD! GO HOME, NOW, AND DON'T EVER COME BACK!
DAMMIT, ROBBIE!
I DON'T KNOW HOW YOU DID THAT...
...BUT I WON'T ALLOW IT A SECOND TIME.
SKREEEEEE!

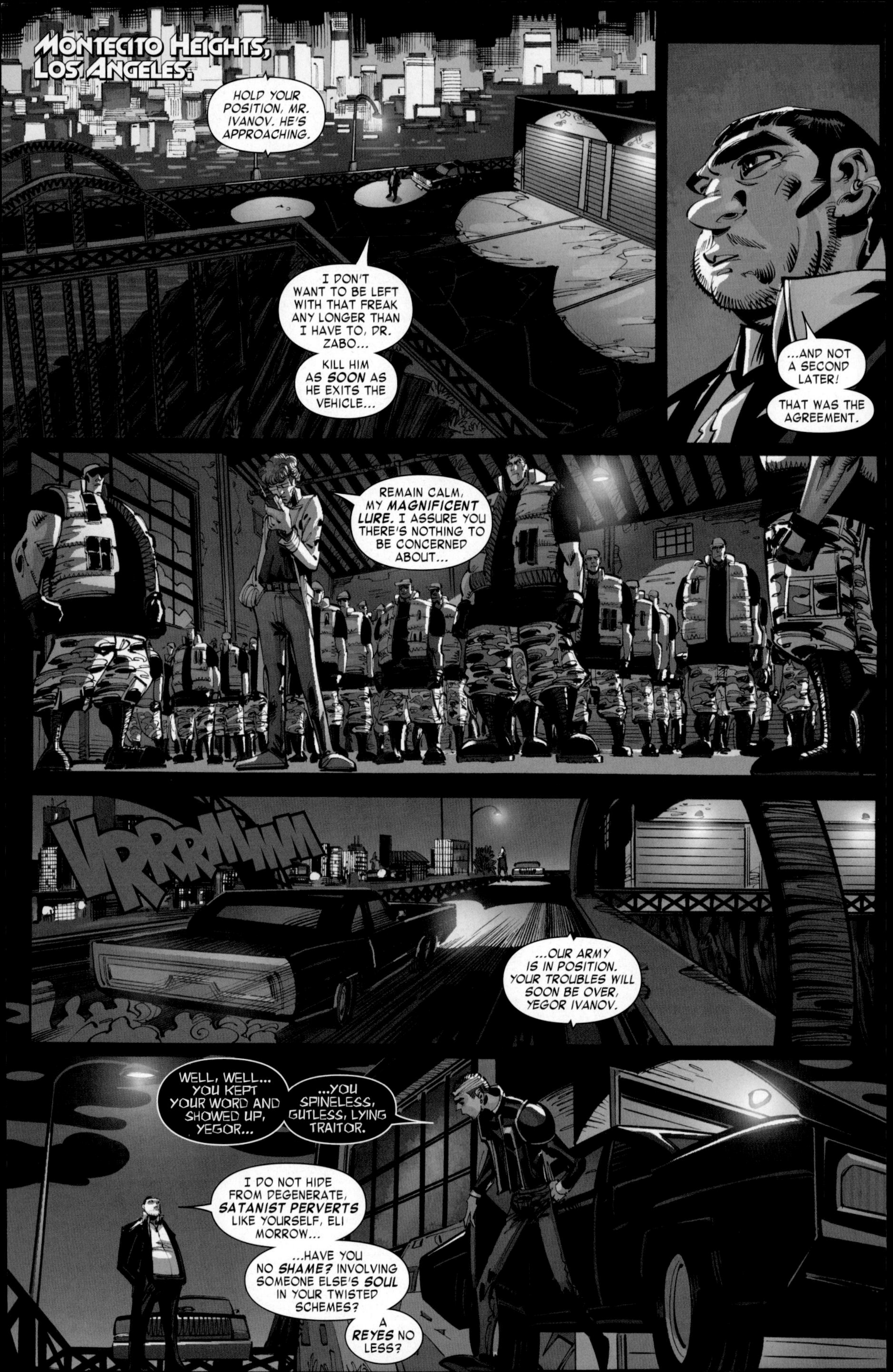

MONTECITO HEIGHTS, LOS ANGELES.
HOLD YOUR POSITION, MR. IVANOV. HE'S APPROACHING.
I DON'T WANT TO BE LEFT WITH THAT FREAK ANY LONGER THAN I HAVE TO, DR. ZABO...
KILL HIM AS SOON AS HE EXITS THE VEHICLE...
...AND NOT A SECOND LATER!
THAT WAS THE AGREEMENT.
REMAIN CALM, MY MAGNIFICENT LURE. I ASSURE YOU THERE'S NOTHING TO BE CONCERNED ABOUT...
VRRRMMM
...OUR ARMY IS IN POSITION. YOUR TROUBLES WILL SOON BE OVER, YEGOR IVANOV.
WELL, WELL... YOU KEPT YOUR WORD AND SHOWED UP, YEGOR...
...YOU SPINELESS, GUTLESS, LYING TRAITOR.
I DO NOT HIDE FROM DEGENERATE, SATANIST PERVERTS LIKE YOURSELF, ELI MORROW...
...HAVE YOU NO SHAME? INVOLVING SOMEONE ELSE'S SOUL IN YOUR TWISTED SCHEMES?
A REYES NO LESS?

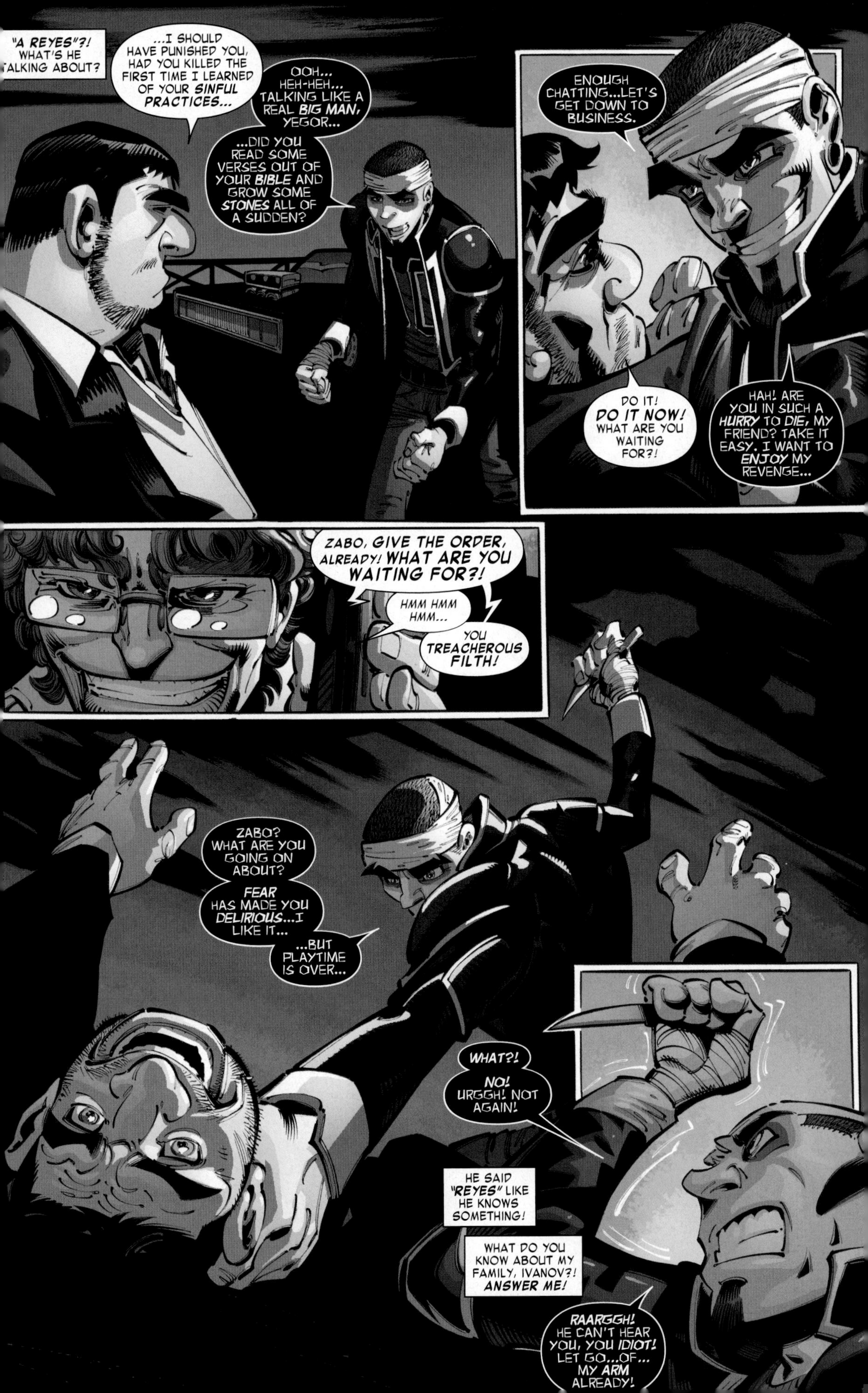
"A REYES"?! WHAT'S HE TALKING ABOUT?
...I SHOULD HAVE PUNISHED YOU, HAD YOU KILLED THE FIRST TIME I LEARNED OF YOUR SINFUL PRACTICES...
OOH... HEH-HEH... TALKING LIKE A REAL BIG MAN, YEGOR...
...DID YOU READ SOME VERSES OUT OF YOUR BIBLE AND GROW SOME STONES ALL OF A SUDDEN?
ENOUGH CHATTING...LET'S GET DOWN TO BUSINESS.
DO IT! DO IT NOW! WHAT ARE YOU WAITING FOR?!
HAH! ARE YOU IN SUCH A HURRY TO DIE, MY FRIEND? TAKE IT EASY. I WANT TO ENJOY MY REVENGE...
ZABO, GIVE THE ORDER, ALREADY! WHAT ARE YOU WAITING FOR?!
HMM HMM HMM...
YOU TREACHEROUS FILTH!
ZABO? WHAT ARE YOU GOING ON ABOUT?
FEAR HAS MADE YOU DELIRIOUS...I LIKE IT...
...BUT PLAYTIME IS OVER...
WHAT?!
NO! URGGH! NOT AGAIN!
HE SAID "REYES" LIKE HE KNOWS SOMETHING!
WHAT DO YOU KNOW ABOUT MY FAMILY, IVANOV?! ANSWER ME!
RAARGGH! HE CAN'T HEAR YOU, YOU IDIOT! LET GO...OF... MY ARM ALREADY!

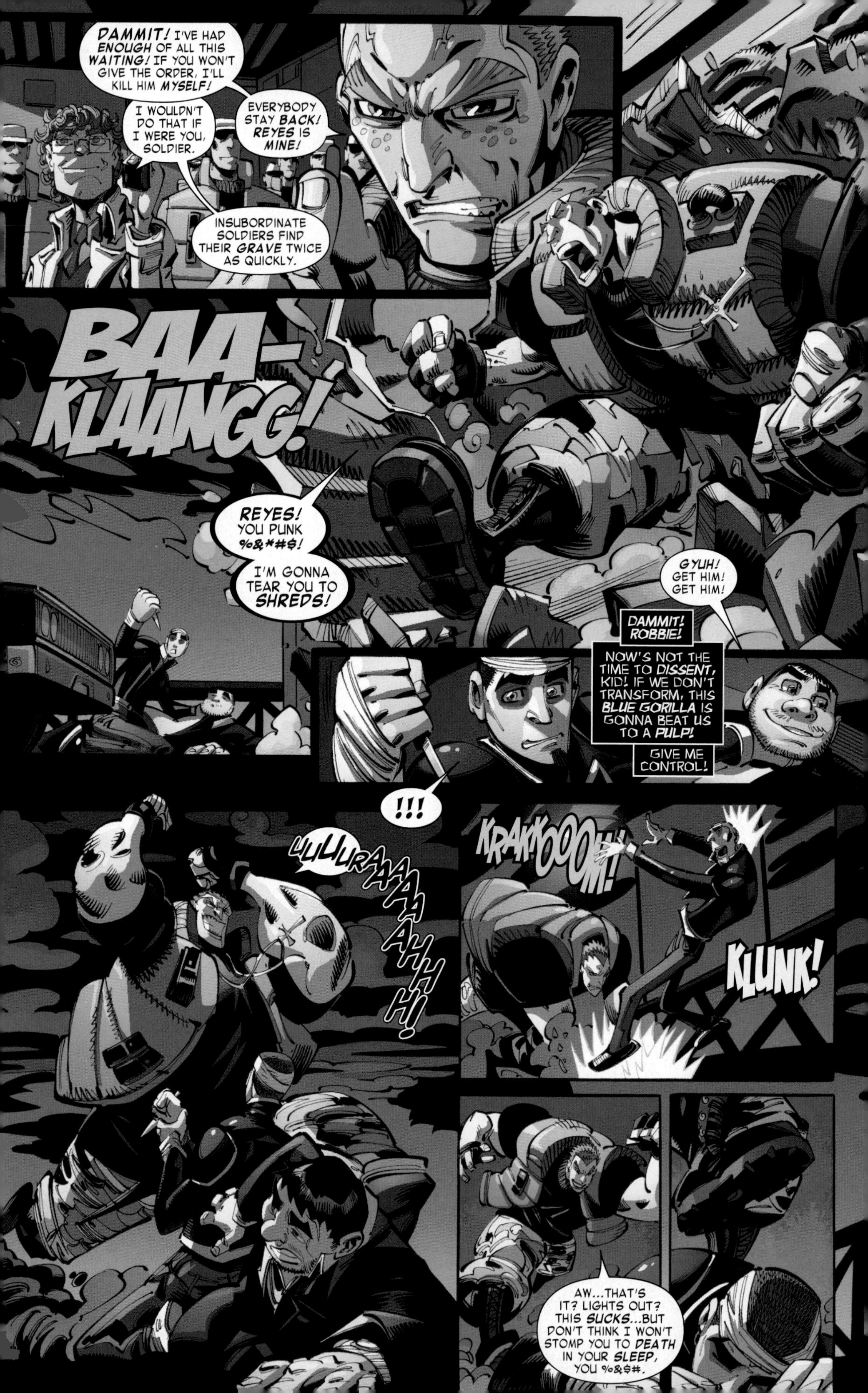
DAMMIT! I'VE HAD ENOUGH OF ALL THIS WAITING! IF YOU WON'T GIVE THE ORDER, I'LL KILL HIM MYSELF!
I WOULDN'T DO THAT IF I WERE YOU, SOLDIER.
EVERYBODY STAY BACK! REYES IS MINE!
INSUBORDINATE SOLDIERS FIND THEIR GRAVE TWICE AS QUICKLY.
BAAA-KLAANGG!
REYES! YOU PUNK %&*#$!
I'M GONNA TEAR YOU TO SHREDS!
GYUH! GET HIM! GET HIM!
DAMMIT! ROBBIE!
NOW'S NOT THE TIME TO DISSENT, KID! IF WE DON'T TRANSFORM, THIS BLUE GORILLA IS GONNA BEAT US TO A PULP!
GIVE ME CONTROL!
!!!
UUUURAAAAAAAHHHH!
KRAKKOOOM!
KLUNK!
AW...THAT'S IT? LIGHTS OUT? THIS SUCKS...BUT DON'T THINK I WON'T STOMP YOU TO DEATH IN YOUR SLEEP, YOU %&$#.

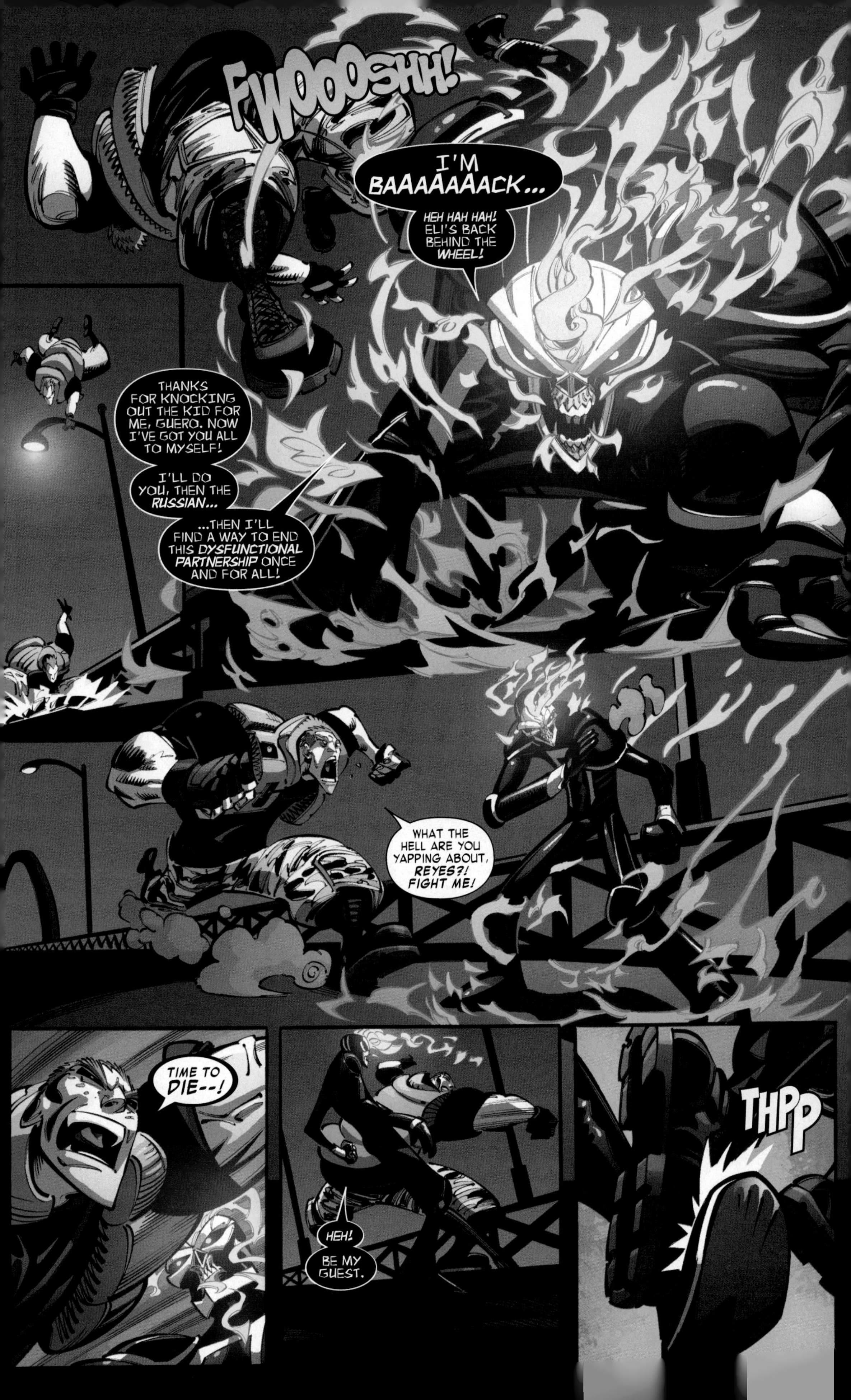
FWOOOSHH!
I'M BAAAAAAACK...
HEH HAH HAH! ELI'S BACK BEHIND THE WHEEL!
THANKS FOR KNOCKING OUT THE KID FOR ME, GUERO. NOW I'VE GOT YOU ALL TO MYSELF!
I'LL DO YOU, THEN THE RUSSIAN...
...THEN I'LL FIND A WAY TO END THIS DYSFUNCTIONAL PARTNERSHIP ONCE AND FOR ALL!
WHAT THE HELL ARE YOU YAPPING ABOUT, REYES?! FIGHT ME!
TIME TO DIE--!
HEH! BE MY GUEST.
THPP

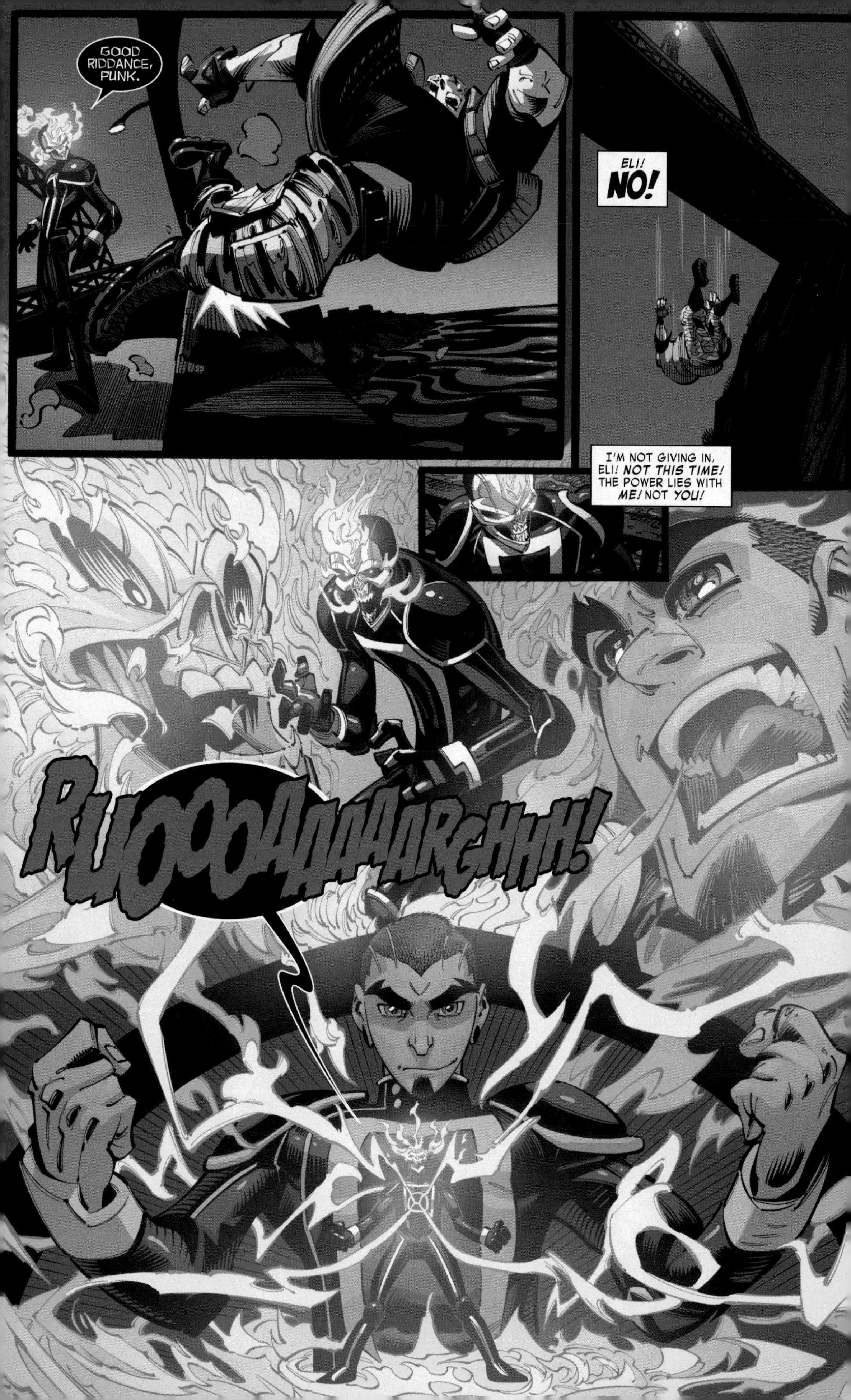
GOOD RIDDANCE, PUNK.
ELI! NO!
I'M NOT GIVING IN, ELI! NOT THIS TIME! THE POWER LIES WITH ME! NOT YOU!
RUOOOAAAAARGHHH!

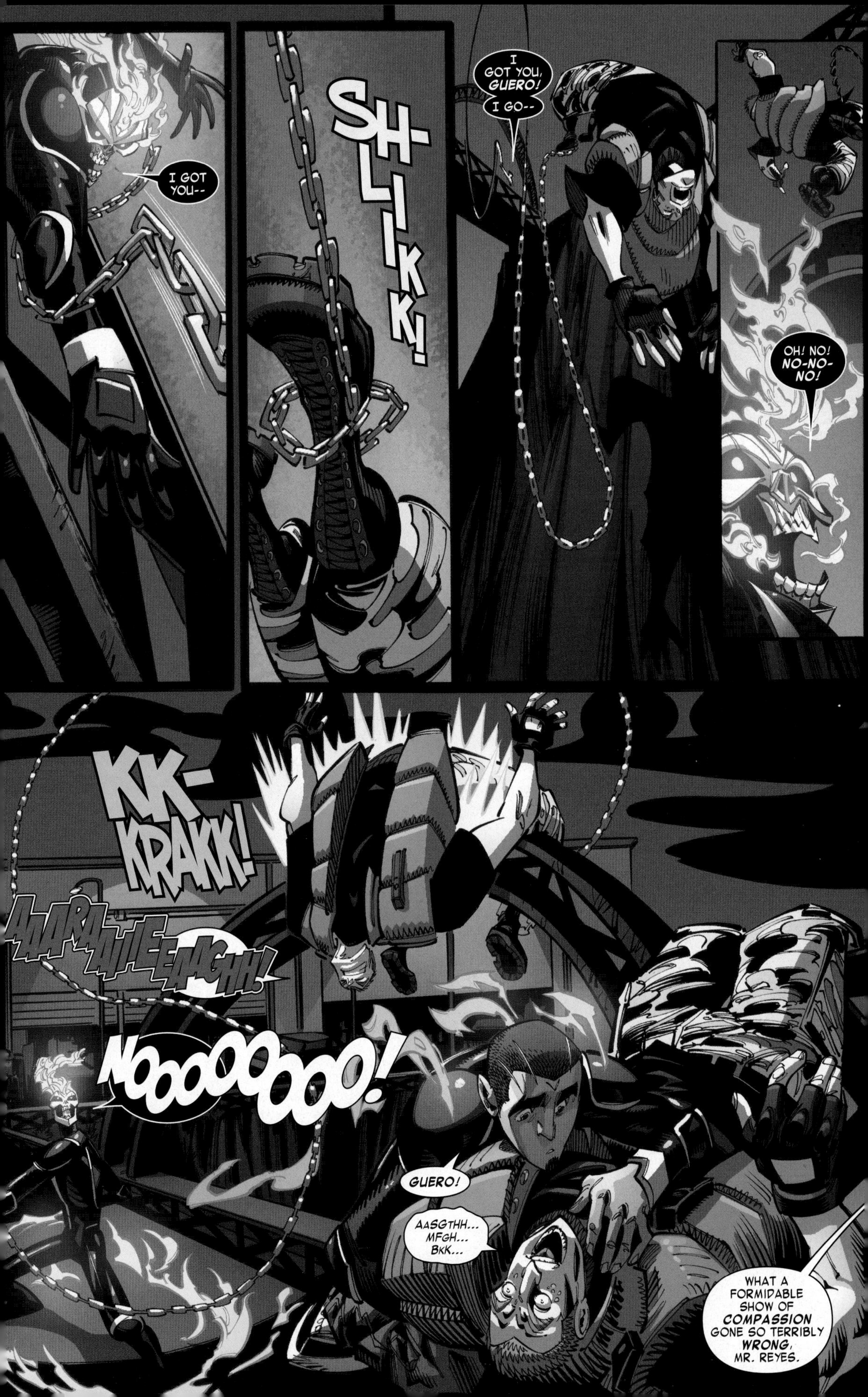
I GOT YOU--
SH-LIKK!
I GOT YOU, GUERO!
I GO--
OH! NO! NO-NO-NO!
KK-KRAKK!
NOOOOOOOO!
GUERO!
AASGTHH... MFGH... BKK...
WHAT A FORMIDABLE SHOW OF COMPASSION GONE SO TERRIBLY WRONG, MR. REYES.

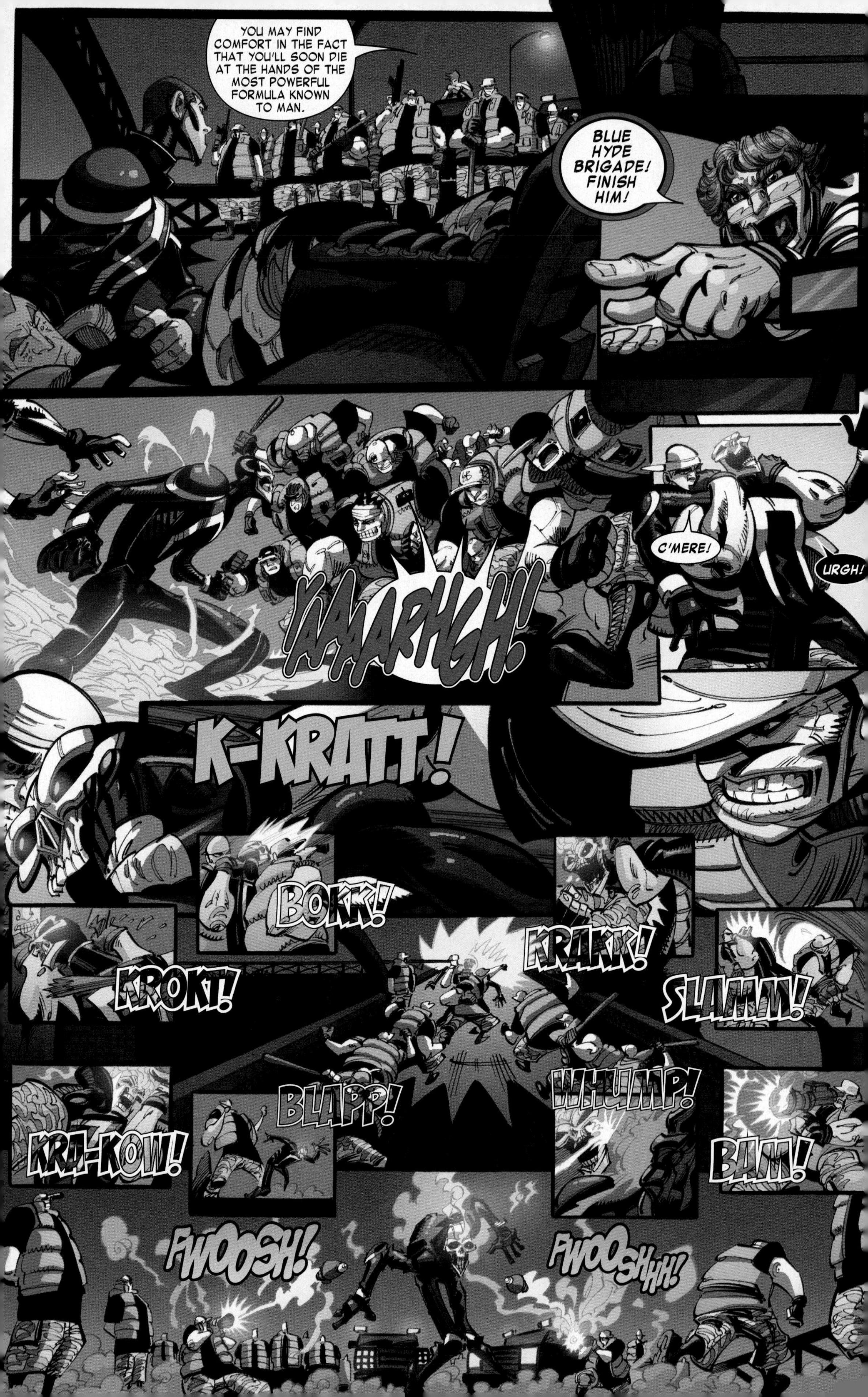
YOU MAY FIND COMFORT IN THE FACT THAT YOU'LL SOON DIE AT THE HANDS OF THE MOST POWERFUL FORMULA KNOWN TO MAN.
BLUE HYDE BRIGADE! FINISH HIM!
YAAARHGH!
C'MERE!
URGH!
K-KRATT!
BOKK!
KROKT!
KRAKK!
SLAMM!
KRA-KOW!
BLAPP!
WHUMP!
BAM!
FWOOSH!
FWOOSHHH!

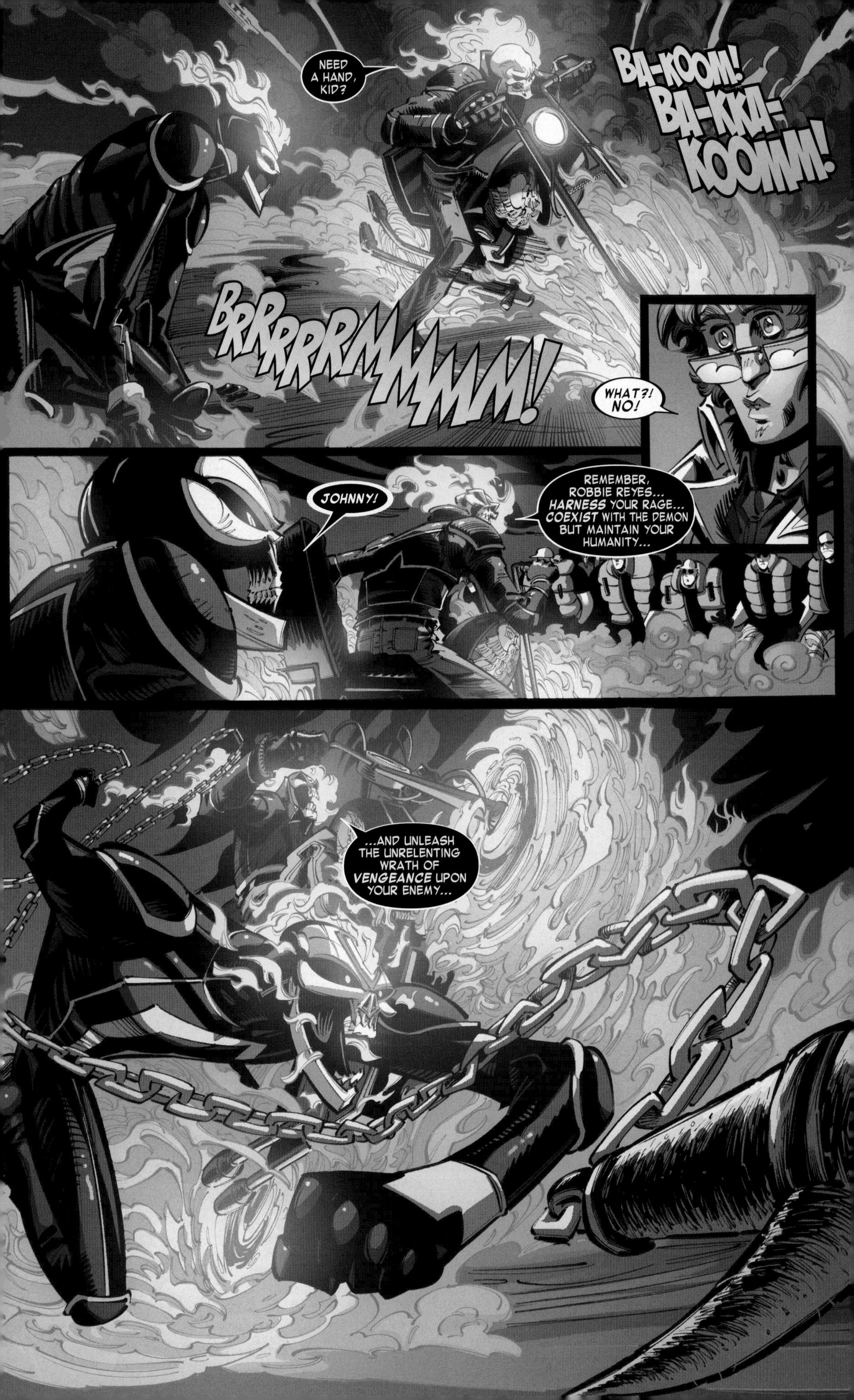
NEED A HAND, KID?
BA-KOOM! BA-KKA-KOOMM!
BRRRRRMMMMM!
WHAT?! NO!
JOHNNY!
REMEMBER, ROBBIE REYES... HARNESS YOUR RAGE... COEXIST WITH THE DEMON BUT MAINTAIN YOUR HUMANITY...
...AND UNLEASH THE UNRELENTING WRATH OF VENGEANCE UPON YOUR ENEMY...

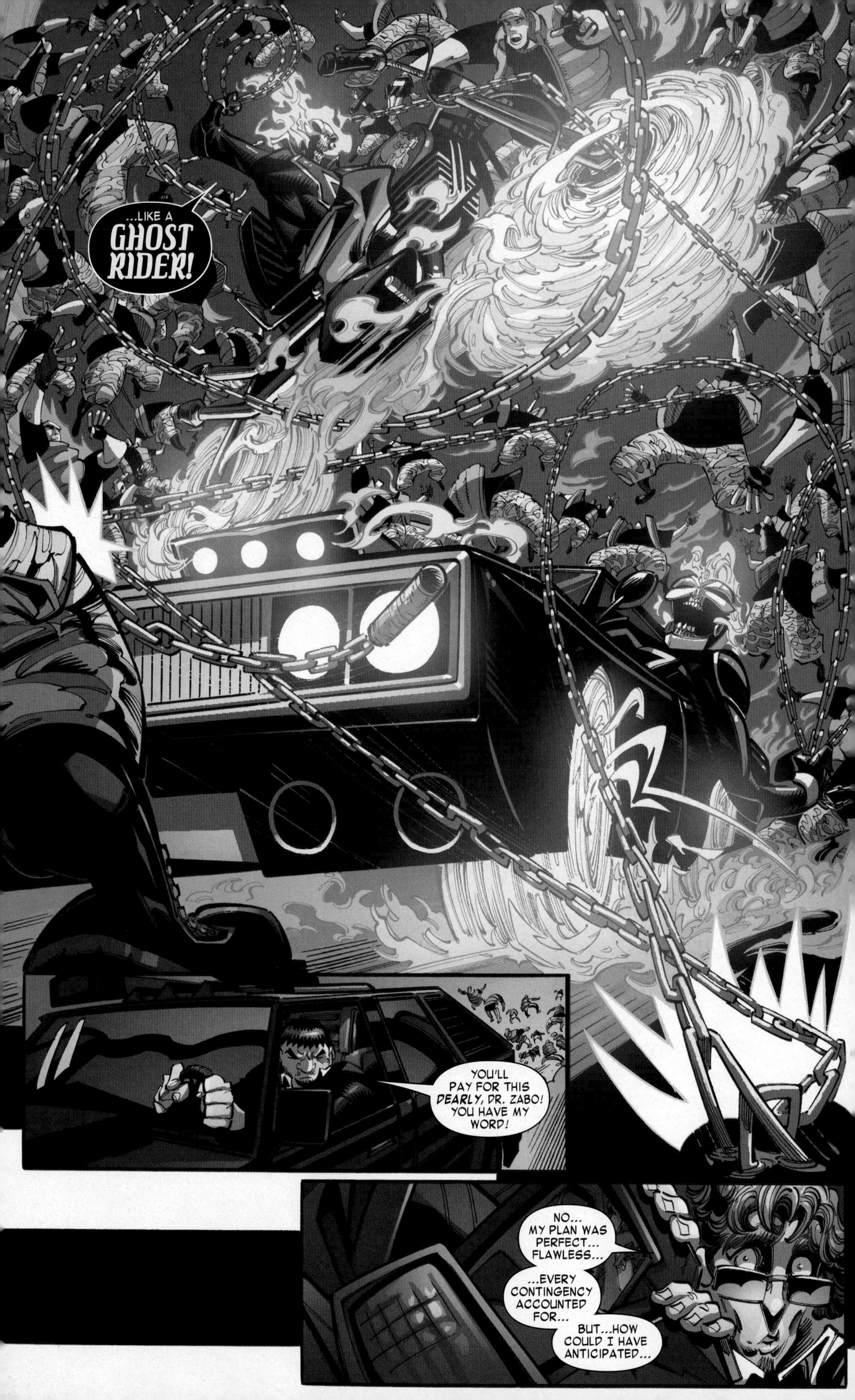
...LIKE A GHOST RIDER!
YOU'LL PAY FOR THIS DEARLY, DR. ZABO! YOU HAVE MY WORD!
NO... MY PLAN WAS PERFECT... FLAWLESS...
...EVERY CONTINGENCY ACCOUNTED FOR...
BUT...HOW COULD I HAVE ANTICIPATED...

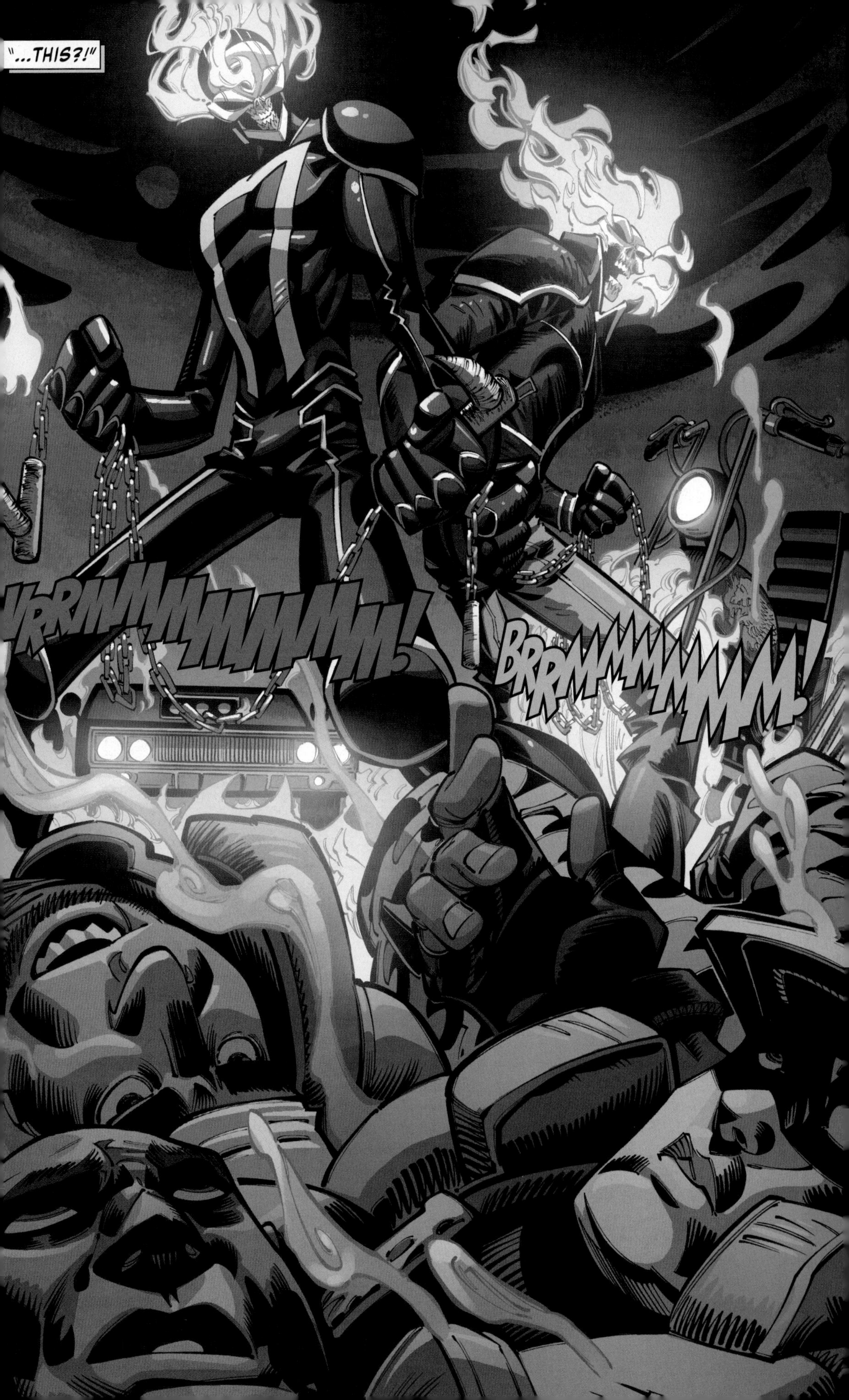
"...THIS?!"
VRRMMMMMMMMMMM!
BRRMMMMMMMM!

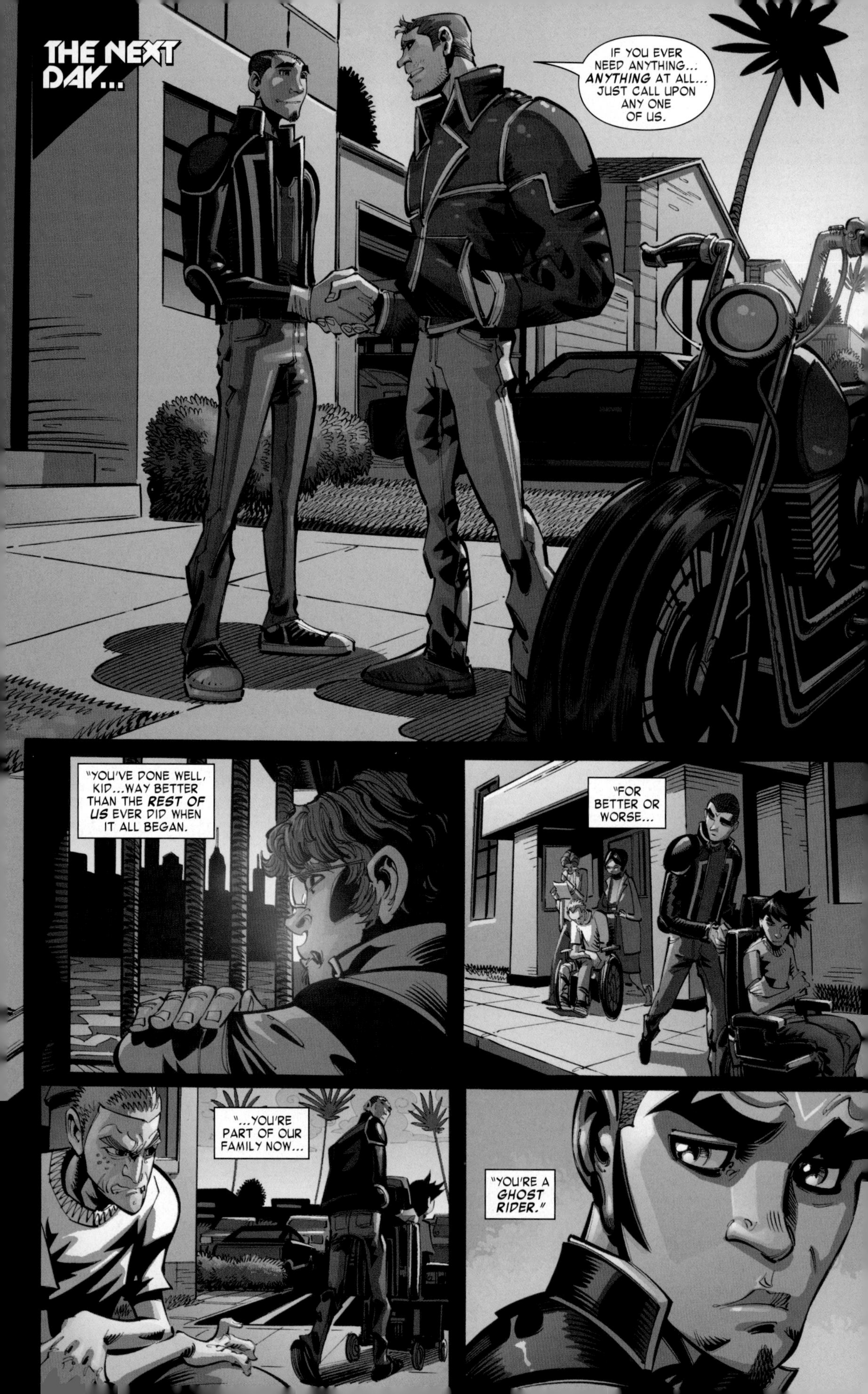
THE NEXT DAY...
IF YOU EVER NEED ANYTHING... ANYTHING AT ALL... JUST CALL UPON ANY ONE OF US.
"YOU'VE DONE WELL, KID...WAY BETTER THAN THE REST OF US EVER DID WHEN IT ALL BEGAN.
"FOR BETTER OR WORSE...
"...YOU'RE PART OF OUR FAMILY NOW...
"YOU'RE A GHOST RIDER."

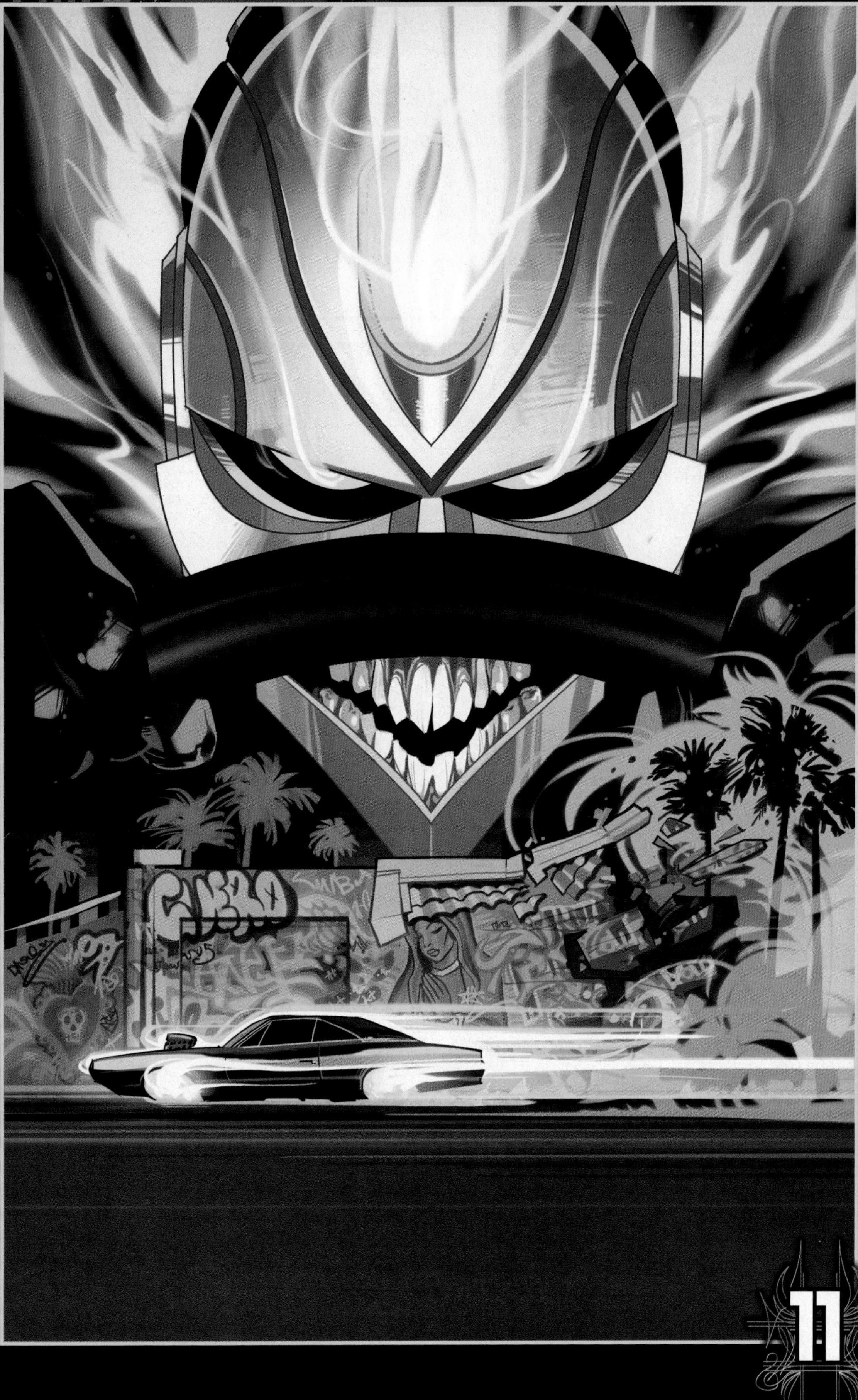

11

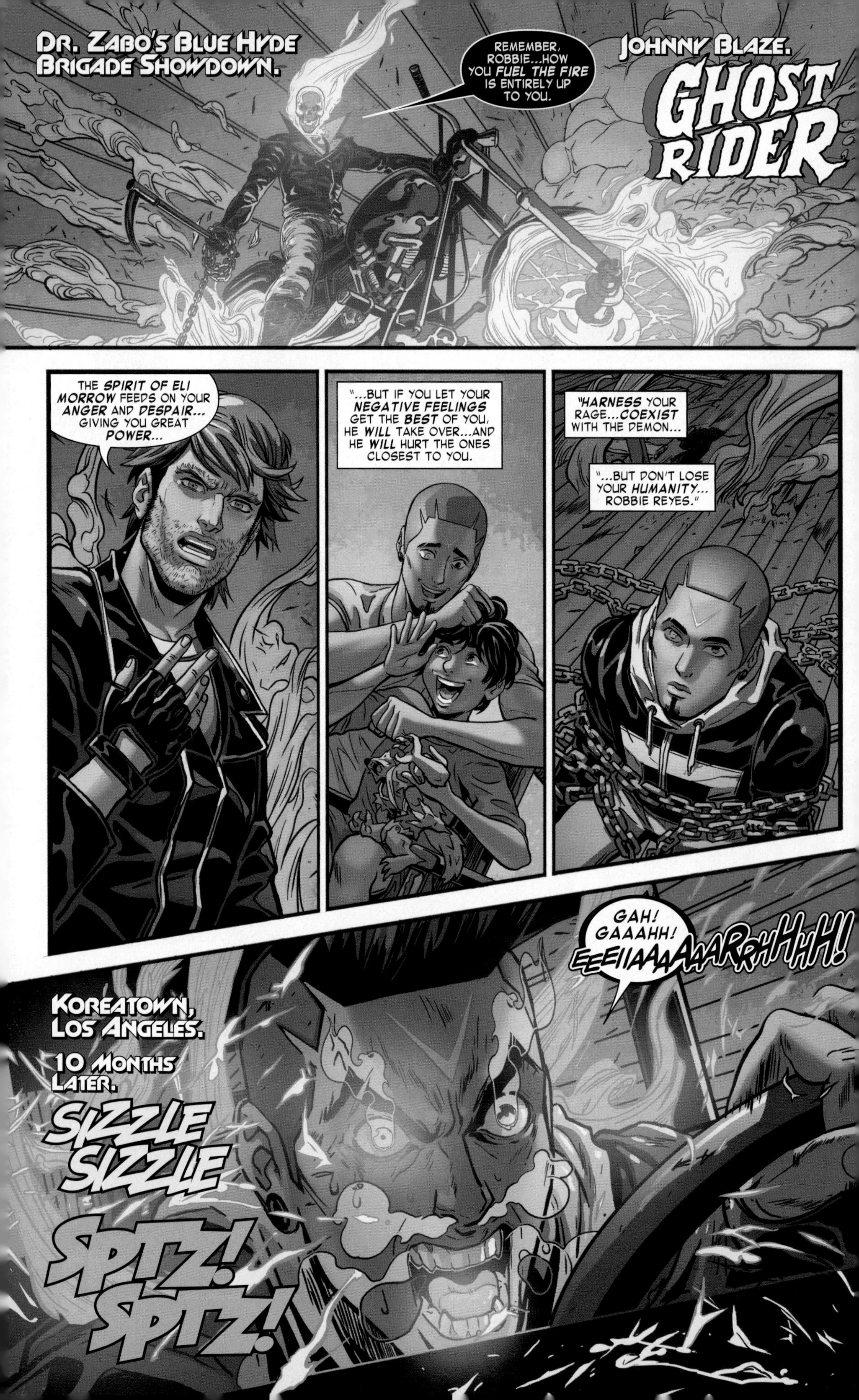
DR. ZABO'S BLUE HYDE BRIGADE SHOWDOWN.
REMEMBER, ROBBIE...HOW YOU FUEL THE FIRE IS ENTIRELY UP TO YOU.
JOHNNY BLAZE.
GHOST RIDER
THE SPIRIT OF ELI MORROW FEEDS ON YOUR ANGER AND DESPAIR... GIVING YOU GREAT POWER...
"...BUT IF YOU LET YOUR NEGATIVE FEELINGS GET THE BEST OF YOU, HE WILL TAKE OVER...AND HE WILL HURT THE ONES CLOSEST TO YOU.
"HARNESS YOUR RAGE...COEXIST WITH THE DEMON...
"...BUT DON'T LOSE YOUR HUMANITY... ROBBIE REYES."
GAH! GAAAHH! EEEIIAAAAAAARRHHHH!
KOREATOWN, LOS ANGELES.
10 MONTHS LATER.
SIZZLE SIZZLE
SPTZ! SPTZ!

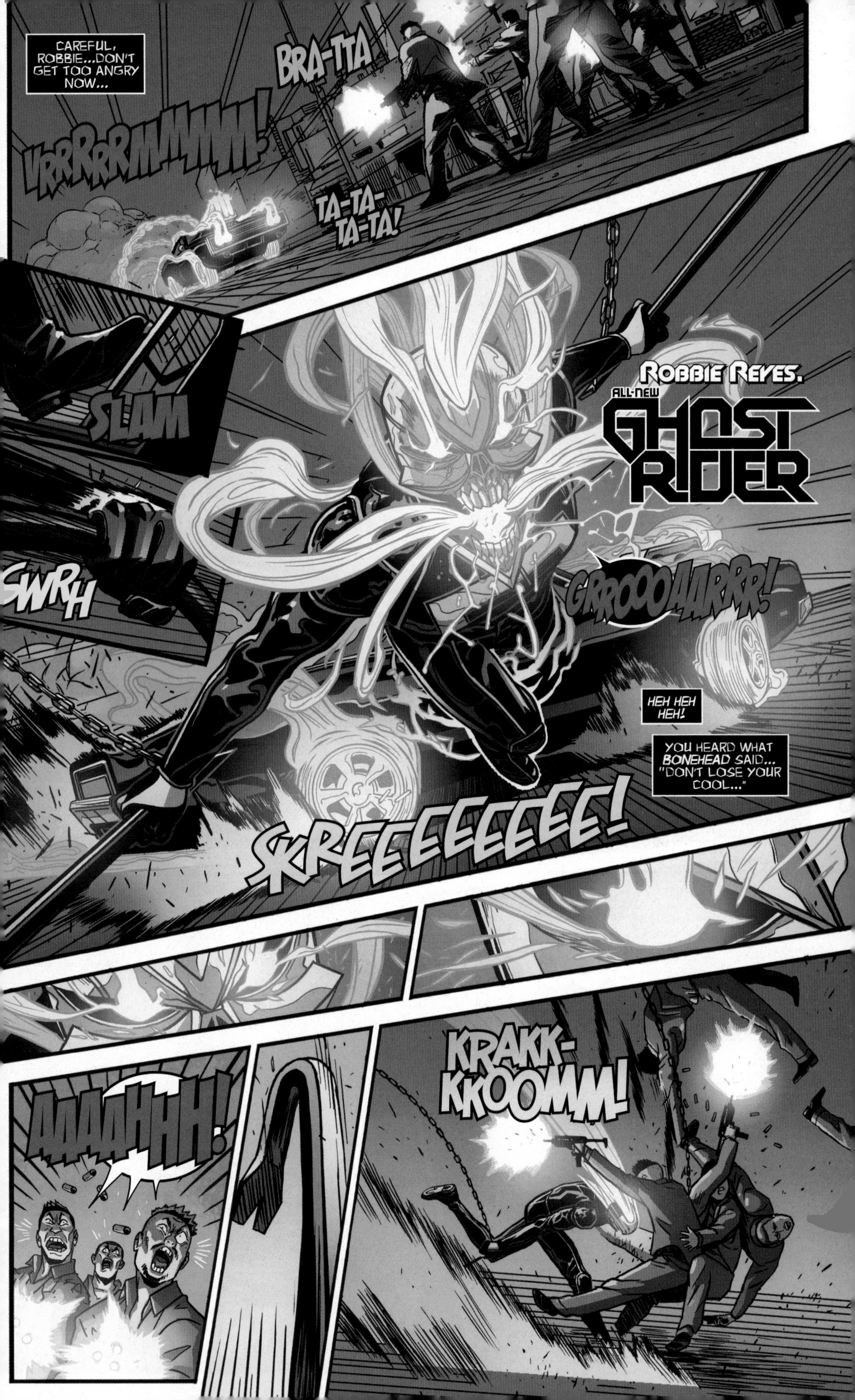
CAREFUL, ROBBIE...DON'T GET TOO ANGRY NOW...
BRA-TTA
VRRRRRMMMMM!
TA-TA-TA-TA!
ROBBIE REYES.
ALL-NEW GHOST RIDER
SLAM
SWRH
GRROOOAARRR!
HEH HEH HEH!
YOU HEARD WHAT BONEHEAD SAID... "DON'T LOSE YOUR COOL..."
SKREEEEEEEEC!
KRAKK-KKOOMM!
AAAAHHH!

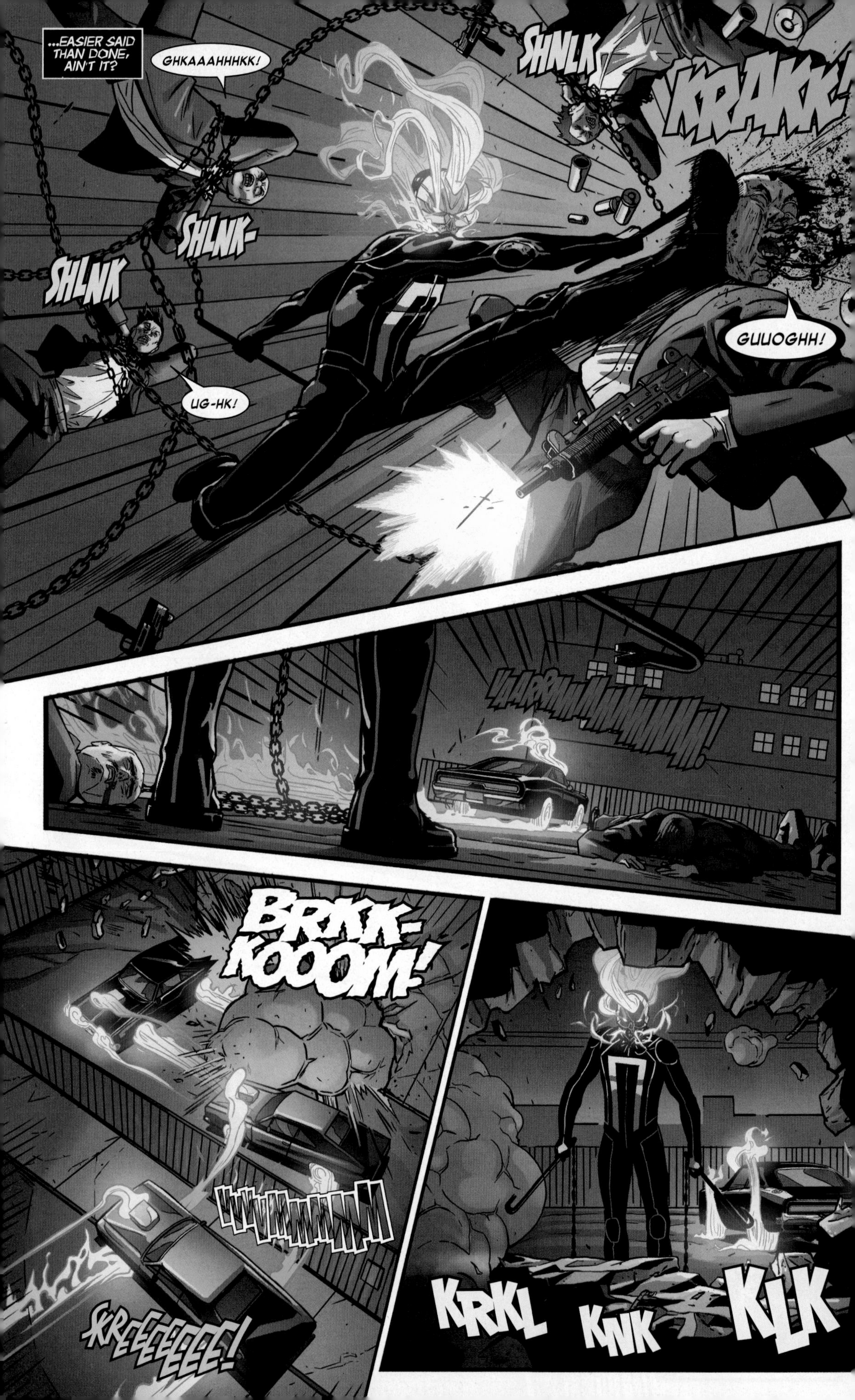
...EASIER SAID THAN DONE, AIN'T IT?
GHKAAAHHHKK!
SHNLK
KRAKK
SHLNK-
SHLNK
UG-HK!
GUUOGHH!
BRKK-KOOOM!
SKREEEEEEEE!
KRKL
KNK
KLK

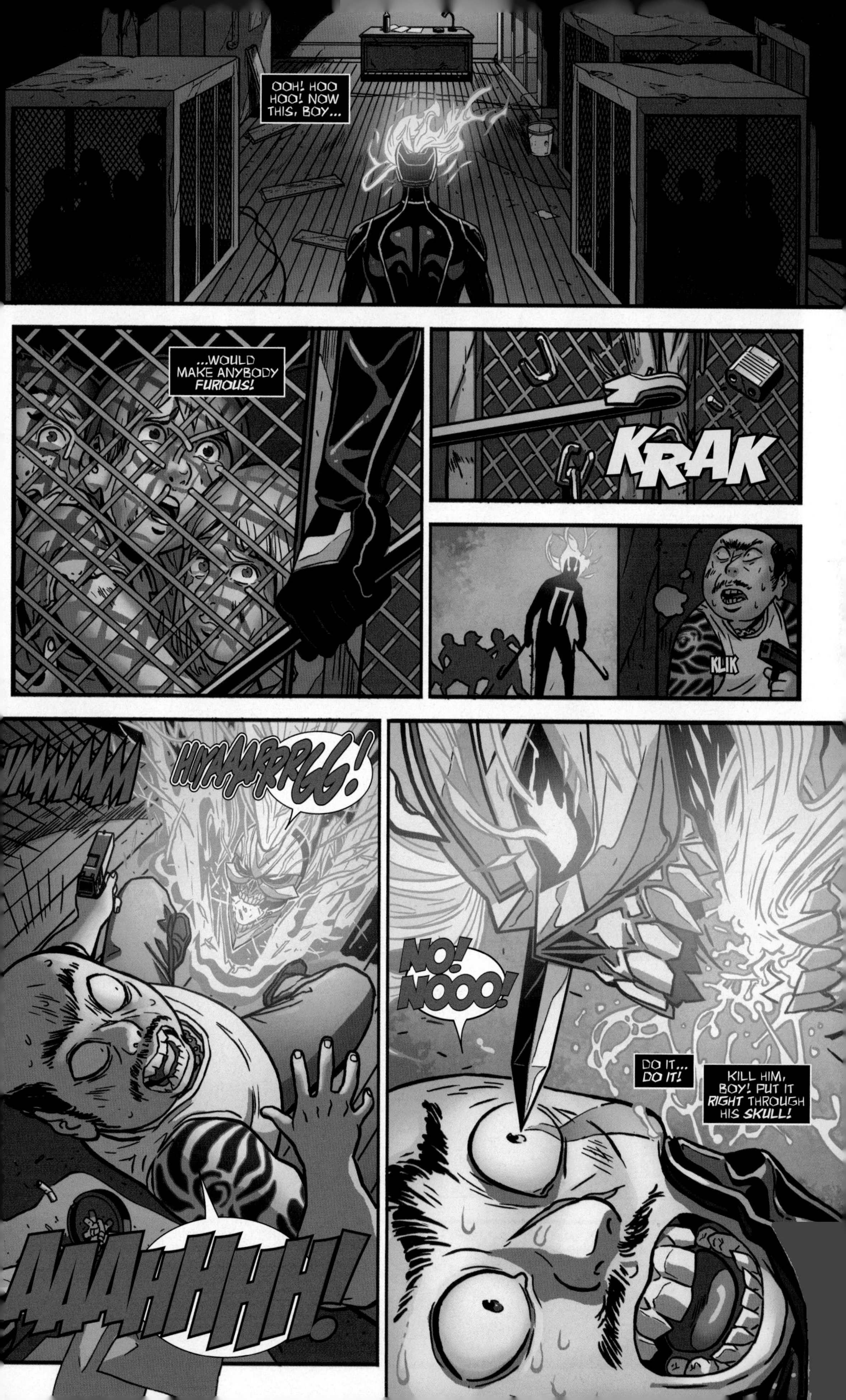
OOH! HOO HOO! NOW THIS, BOY...
...WOULD MAKE ANYBODY FURIOUS!
KRAK
KLIK
HIYAAARRRGG!
AAAHHHH!
NO! NOOO!
DO IT... DO IT!
KILL HIM, BOY! PUT IT RIGHT THROUGH HIS SKULL!

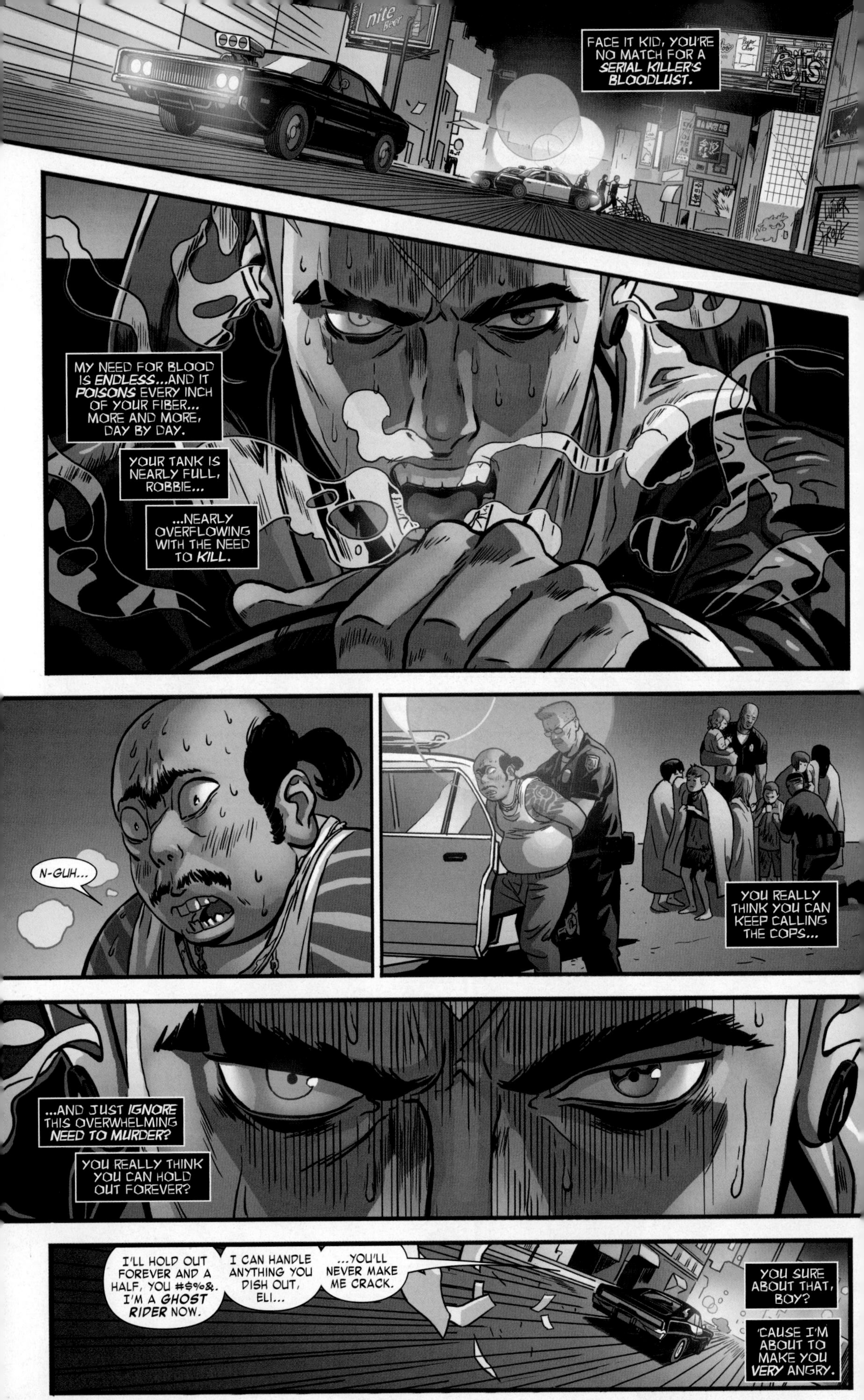
FACE IT KID, YOU'RE NO MATCH FOR A SERIAL KILLER'S BLOODLUST.
MY NEED FOR BLOOD IS ENDLESS...AND IT POISONS EVERY INCH OF YOUR FIBER... MORE AND MORE, DAY BY DAY.
YOUR TANK IS NEARLY FULL, ROBBIE...
...NEARLY OVERFLOWING WITH THE NEED TO KILL.
N-GUH...
YOU REALLY THINK YOU CAN KEEP CALLING THE COPS...
...AND JUST IGNORE THIS OVERWHELMING NEED TO MURDER?
YOU REALLY THINK YOU CAN HOLD OUT FOREVER?
I'LL HOLD OUT FOREVER AND A HALF, YOU #$%&. I'M A GHOST RIDER NOW.
I CAN HANDLE ANYTHING YOU DISH OUT, ELI...
...YOU'LL NEVER MAKE ME CRACK.
YOU SURE ABOUT THAT, BOY?
'CAUSE I'M ABOUT TO MAKE YOU VERY ANGRY.

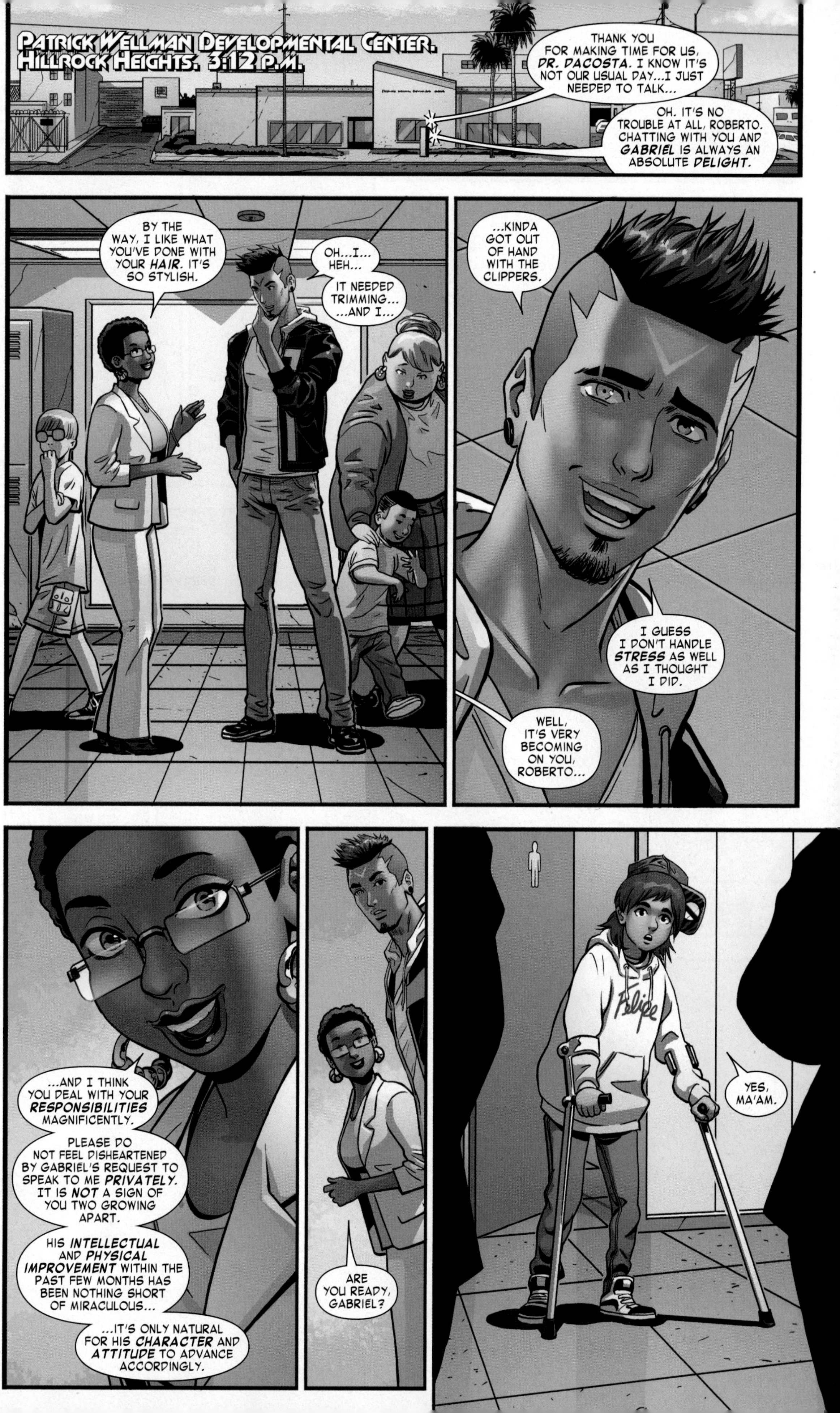
PATRICK WELLMAN DEVELOPMENTAL CENTER. HILLROCK HEIGHTS. 3:12 P.M.
THANK YOU FOR MAKING TIME FOR US, DR. DACOSTA. I KNOW IT'S NOT OUR USUAL DAY...I JUST NEEDED TO TALK...
OH. IT'S NO TROUBLE AT ALL, ROBERTO. CHATTING WITH YOU AND GABRIEL IS ALWAYS AN ABSOLUTE DELIGHT.
BY THE WAY, I LIKE WHAT YOU'VE DONE WITH YOUR HAIR. IT'S SO STYLISH.
OH...I... HEH...
IT NEEDED TRIMMING... ...AND I...
...KINDA GOT OUT OF HAND WITH THE CLIPPERS.
I GUESS I DON'T HANDLE STRESS AS WELL AS I THOUGHT I DID.
WELL, IT'S VERY BECOMING ON YOU, ROBERTO...
...AND I THINK YOU DEAL WITH YOUR RESPONSIBILITIES MAGNIFICENTLY.
PLEASE DO NOT FEEL DISHEARTENED BY GABRIEL'S REQUEST TO SPEAK TO ME PRIVATELY. IT IS NOT A SIGN OF YOU TWO GROWING APART.
HIS INTELLECTUAL AND PHYSICAL IMPROVEMENT WITHIN THE PAST FEW MONTHS HAS BEEN NOTHING SHORT OF MIRACULOUS...
...IT'S ONLY NATURAL FOR HIS CHARACTER AND ATTITUDE TO ADVANCE ACCORDINGLY.
ARE YOU READY, GABRIEL?
YES, MA'AM.
Felipe

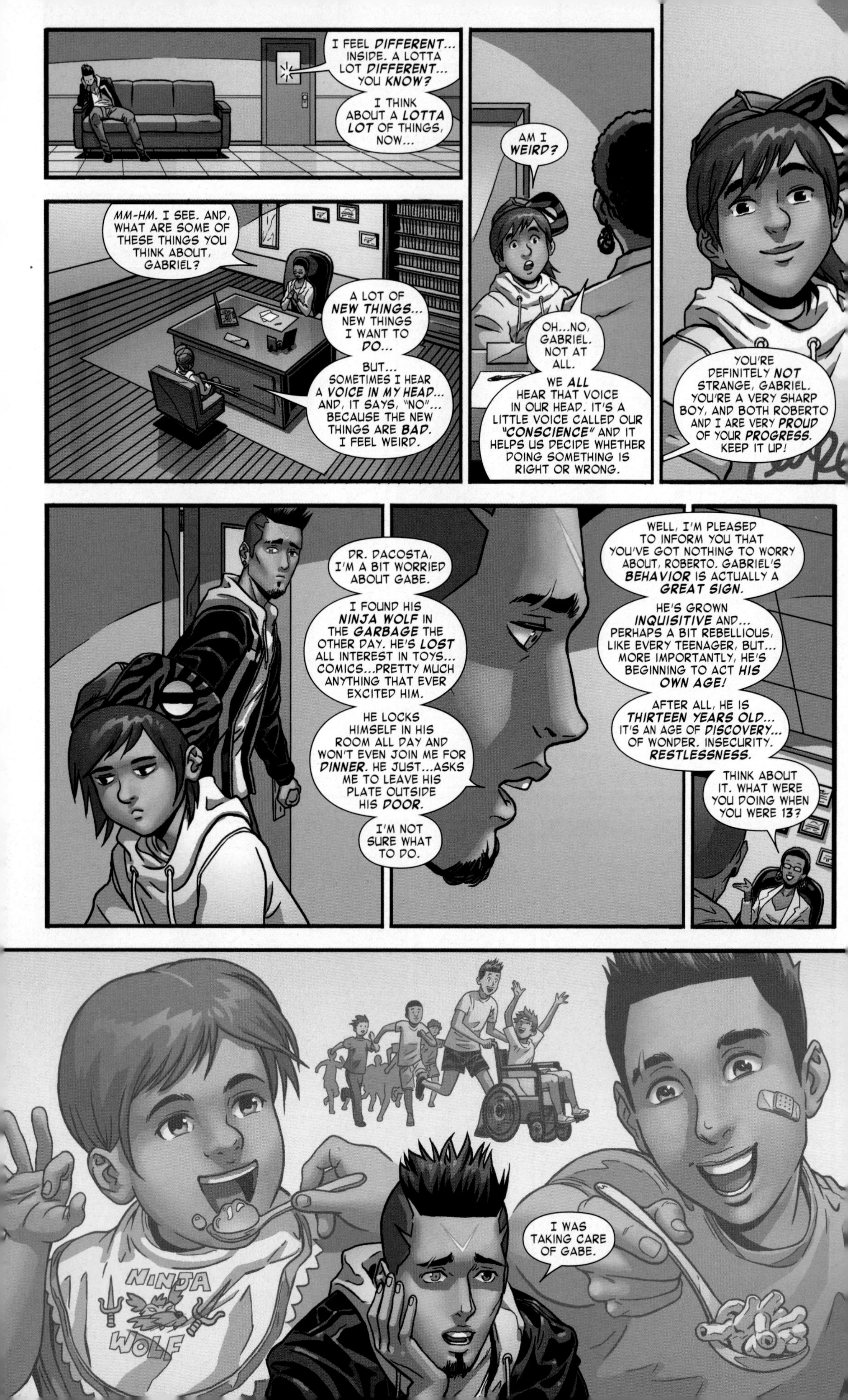
I FEEL DIFFERENT... INSIDE. A LOTTA LOT DIFFERENT... YOU KNOW?
I THINK ABOUT A LOTTA LOT OF THINGS, NOW...
MM-HM. I SEE. AND, WHAT ARE SOME OF THESE THINGS YOU THINK ABOUT, GABRIEL?
A LOT OF NEW THINGS... NEW THINGS I WANT TO DO...
BUT... SOMETIMES I HEAR A VOICE IN MY HEAD... AND, IT SAYS, "NO"... BECAUSE THE NEW THINGS ARE BAD. I FEEL WEIRD.
AM I WEIRD?
OH...NO, GABRIEL. NOT AT ALL.
WE ALL HEAR THAT VOICE IN OUR HEAD. IT'S A LITTLE VOICE CALLED OUR "CONSCIENCE" AND IT HELPS US DECIDE WHETHER DOING SOMETHING IS RIGHT OR WRONG.
YOU'RE DEFINITELY NOT STRANGE, GABRIEL. YOU'RE A VERY SHARP BOY, AND BOTH ROBERTO AND I ARE VERY PROUD OF YOUR PROGRESS. KEEP IT UP!
DR. DACOSTA, I'M A BIT WORRIED ABOUT GABE.
I FOUND HIS NINJA WOLF IN THE GARBAGE THE OTHER DAY. HE'S LOST ALL INTEREST IN TOYS... COMICS...PRETTY MUCH ANYTHING THAT EVER EXCITED HIM.
HE LOCKS HIMSELF IN HIS ROOM ALL DAY AND WON'T EVEN JOIN ME FOR DINNER. HE JUST...ASKS ME TO LEAVE HIS PLATE OUTSIDE HIS DOOR.
I'M NOT SURE WHAT TO DO.
WELL, I'M PLEASED TO INFORM YOU THAT YOU'VE GOT NOTHING TO WORRY ABOUT, ROBERTO. GABRIEL'S BEHAVIOR IS ACTUALLY A GREAT SIGN.
HE'S GROWN INQUISITIVE AND... PERHAPS A BIT REBELLIOUS, LIKE EVERY TEENAGER, BUT... MORE IMPORTANTLY, HE'S BEGINNING TO ACT HIS OWN AGE!
AFTER ALL, HE IS THIRTEEN YEARS OLD... IT'S AN AGE OF DISCOVERY... OF WONDER. INSECURITY. RESTLESSNESS.
THINK ABOUT IT. WHAT WERE YOU DOING WHEN YOU WERE 13?
NINJA WOLF
I WAS TAKING CARE OF GABE.

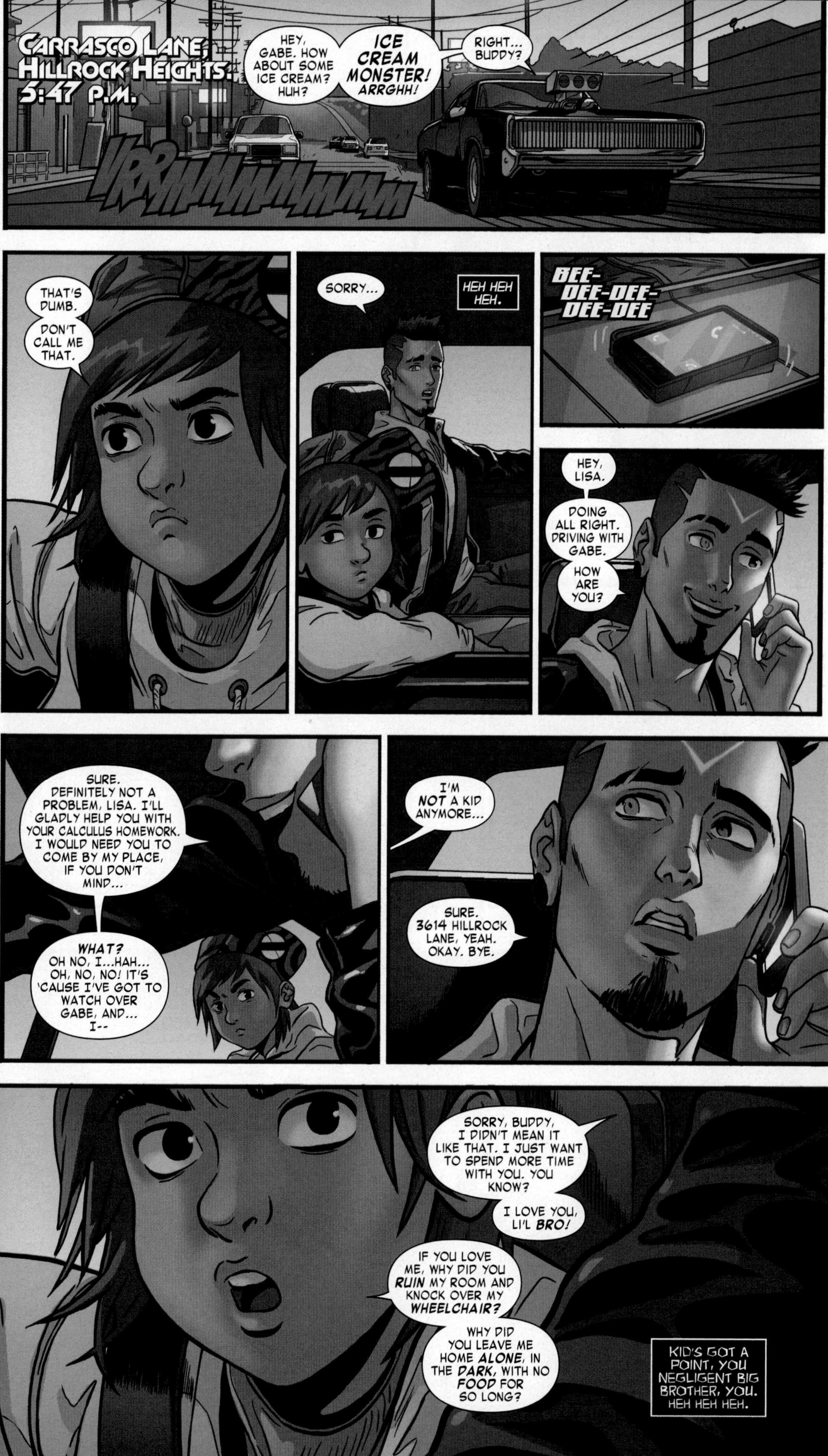

CARRASCO LANE, HILLROCK HEIGHTS. 5:47 P.M.
HEY, GABE. HOW ABOUT SOME ICE CREAM? HUH?
ICE CREAM MONSTER! ARRGHH!
RIGHT... BUDDY?
VRRMMMMMMMMM
THAT'S DUMB.
DON'T CALL ME THAT.
SORRY...
HEH HEH HEH.
BEE-DEE-DEE-DEE-DEE
HEY, LISA.
DOING ALL RIGHT. DRIVING WITH GABE.
HOW ARE YOU?
SURE. DEFINITELY NOT A PROBLEM, LISA. I'LL GLADLY HELP YOU WITH YOUR CALCULUS HOMEWORK. I WOULD NEED YOU TO COME BY MY PLACE, IF YOU DON'T MIND...
WHAT? OH NO, I...HAH... OH, NO, NO! IT'S 'CAUSE I'VE GOT TO WATCH OVER GABE, AND... I--
I'M NOT A KID ANYMORE...
SURE. 3614 HILLROCK LANE, YEAH. OKAY. BYE.
SORRY, BUDDY, I DIDN'T MEAN IT LIKE THAT. I JUST WANT TO SPEND MORE TIME WITH YOU. YOU KNOW?
I LOVE YOU, LI'L BRO!
IF YOU LOVE ME, WHY DID YOU RUIN MY ROOM AND KNOCK OVER MY WHEELCHAIR?
WHY DID YOU LEAVE ME HOME ALONE, IN THE DARK, WITH NO FOOD FOR SO LONG?
KID'S GOT A POINT, YOU NEGLIGENT BIG BROTHER, YOU. HEH HEH HEH.

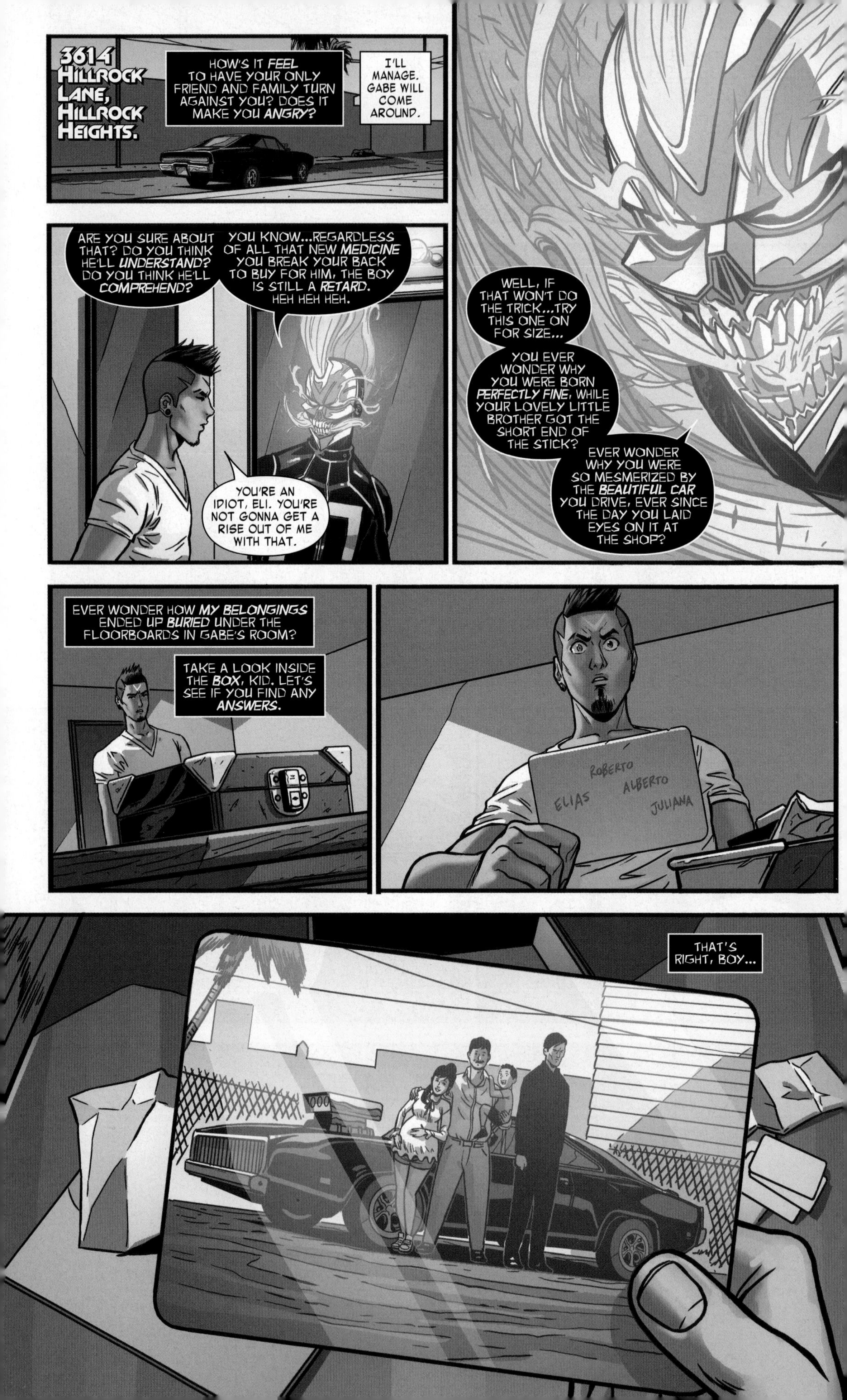
3614 Hillrock Lane, Hillrock Heights.
HOW'S IT FEEL TO HAVE YOUR ONLY FRIEND AND FAMILY TURN AGAINST YOU? DOES IT MAKE YOU ANGRY?
I'LL MANAGE. GABE WILL COME AROUND.
ARE YOU SURE ABOUT THAT? DO YOU THINK HE'LL UNDERSTAND? DO YOU THINK HE'LL COMPREHEND?
YOU KNOW...REGARDLESS OF ALL THAT NEW MEDICINE YOU BREAK YOUR BACK TO BUY FOR HIM, THE BOY IS STILL A RETARD. HEH HEH HEH.
YOU'RE AN IDIOT, ELI. YOU'RE NOT GONNA GET A RISE OUT OF ME WITH THAT.
WELL, IF THAT WON'T DO THE TRICK...TRY THIS ONE ON FOR SIZE...
YOU EVER WONDER WHY YOU WERE BORN PERFECTLY FINE, WHILE YOUR LOVELY LITTLE BROTHER GOT THE SHORT END OF THE STICK?
EVER WONDER WHY YOU WERE SO MESMERIZED BY THE BEAUTIFUL CAR YOU DRIVE, EVER SINCE THE DAY YOU LAID EYES ON IT AT THE SHOP?
EVER WONDER HOW MY BELONGINGS ENDED UP BURIED UNDER THE FLOORBOARDS IN GABE'S ROOM?
TAKE A LOOK INSIDE THE BOX, KID. LET'S SEE IF YOU FIND ANY ANSWERS.
ROBERTO
ELIAS
ALBERTO
JULIANA
THAT'S RIGHT, BOY...

...YOUR MOM AND POPS, YOUR FAVORITE MUSCLE CAR...AND ME...

...UNCLE ELI.

NO. YOU'RE NOT...MY...

YOU'RE ELIAS? YOU'RE "TIO MALDITO*"?!

HEH HEH.

MOM...SHE USED TO TELL ME... "STAY AWAY FROM TIO ELIAS...EL TIO MALDITO"...

I JUST THOUGHT SHE MEANT ANNOYING...BUT SHE KNEW?!

IN SPANISH, MALDITO CAN MEAN "ANNOYING" OR MORE LITERALLY, "CURSED." --MULTILINGUAL MARK.

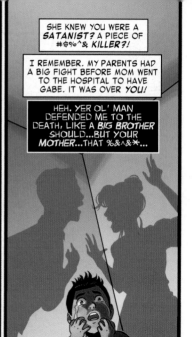

SHE KNEW YOU WERE A SATANIST? A PIECE OF #$%^& KILLER?!

I REMEMBER. MY PARENTS HAD A BIG FIGHT BEFORE MOM WENT TO THE HOSPITAL TO HAVE GABE. IT WAS OVER YOU!

HEH. YER OL' MAN DEFENDED ME TO THE DEATH, LIKE A BIG BROTHER SHOULD...BUT YOUR MOTHER...THAT %&^*...

...BOY DID YOUR DAD PICK AN ANNOYING WOMAN. HEH. BUT THEY WERE MADE FOR EACH OTHER...

...AND IN THE END, THEY GOT WHAT THEY DESERVED.

WHAT HAPPENED, ELI? WHY DID THEY LEAVE ME AND GABE? TELL ME!

DYING TO KNOW, AREN'T YOU? YOU PUSHED THOSE MEMORIES SO DEEP INSIDE, TRYING TO FORGET HOW THEY ABANDONED YOU...

...CHEATED YOU OUT OF YOUR CHILDHOOD...BURDENED YOU WITH SO MUCH RESPONSIBILITY...

...BURDENED YOU WITH GABE.

GABE'S NOT A BURDEN!

DING DONG

HEY, ROBBIE!

I, UM... I MADE YOU GUYS A CAKE!

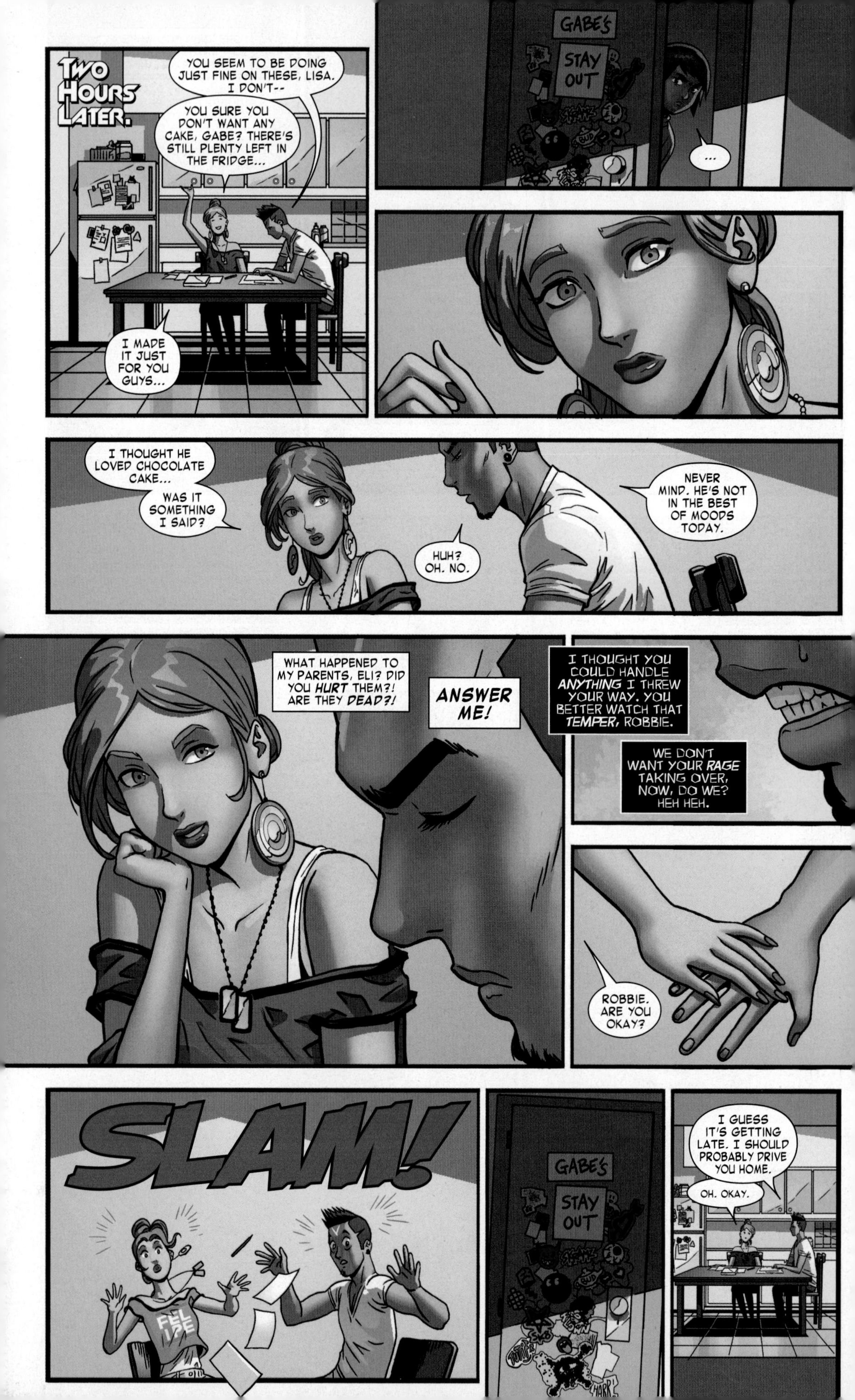
TWO HOURS LATER.
YOU SEEM TO BE DOING JUST FINE ON THESE, LISA. I DON'T--
YOU SURE YOU DON'T WANT ANY CAKE, GABE? THERE'S STILL PLENTY LEFT IN THE FRIDGE...
I MADE IT JUST FOR YOU GUYS...
GABE'S
STAY OUT
...
I THOUGHT HE LOVED CHOCOLATE CAKE...
WAS IT SOMETHING I SAID?
HUH? OH. NO.
NEVER MIND. HE'S NOT IN THE BEST OF MOODS TODAY.
WHAT HAPPENED TO MY PARENTS, ELI? DID YOU HURT THEM?! ARE THEY DEAD?!
ANSWER ME!
I THOUGHT YOU COULD HANDLE ANYTHING I THREW YOUR WAY. YOU BETTER WATCH THAT TEMPER, ROBBIE.
WE DON'T WANT YOUR RAGE TAKING OVER, NOW, DO WE? HEH HEH.
ROBBIE. ARE YOU OKAY?
SLAM!
GABE'S
STAY OUT
I GUESS IT'S GETTING LATE. I SHOULD PROBABLY DRIVE YOU HOME.
OH. OKAY.

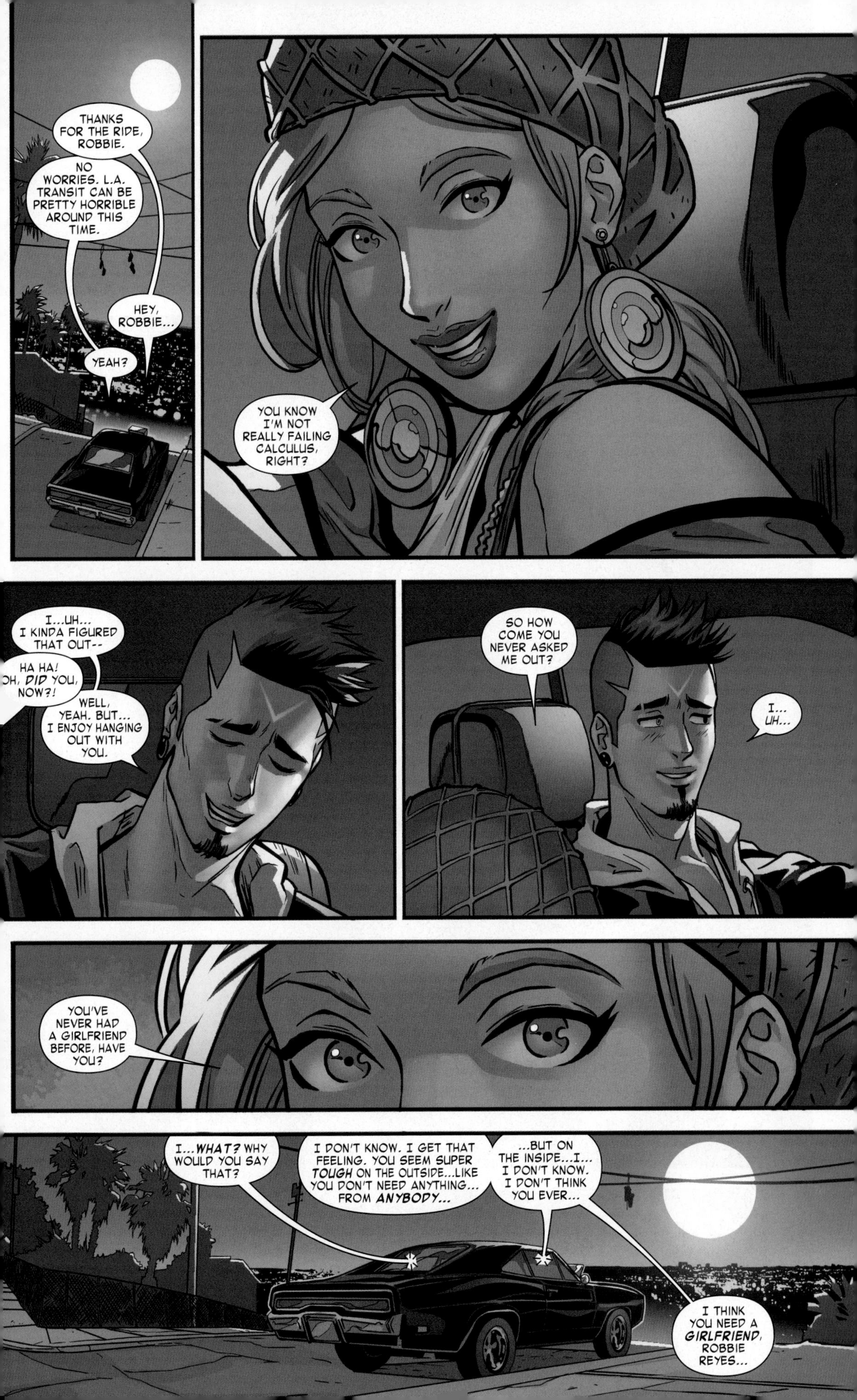

THANKS FOR THE RIDE, ROBBIE.
NO WORRIES. L.A. TRANSIT CAN BE PRETTY HORRIBLE AROUND THIS TIME.
HEY, ROBBIE...
YEAH?
YOU KNOW I'M NOT REALLY FAILING CALCULUS, RIGHT?
I...UH... I KINDA FIGURED THAT OUT--
HA HA! OH, DID YOU, NOW?!
WELL, YEAH. BUT... I ENJOY HANGING OUT WITH YOU.
SO HOW COME YOU NEVER ASKED ME OUT?
I... UH...
YOU'VE NEVER HAD A GIRLFRIEND BEFORE, HAVE YOU?
I...WHAT? WHY WOULD YOU SAY THAT?
I DON'T KNOW. I GET THAT FEELING. YOU SEEM SUPER TOUGH ON THE OUTSIDE...LIKE YOU DON'T NEED ANYTHING... FROM ANYBODY...
...BUT ON THE INSIDE...I... I DON'T KNOW. I DON'T THINK YOU EVER...
I THINK YOU NEED A GIRLFRIEND, ROBBIE REYES...

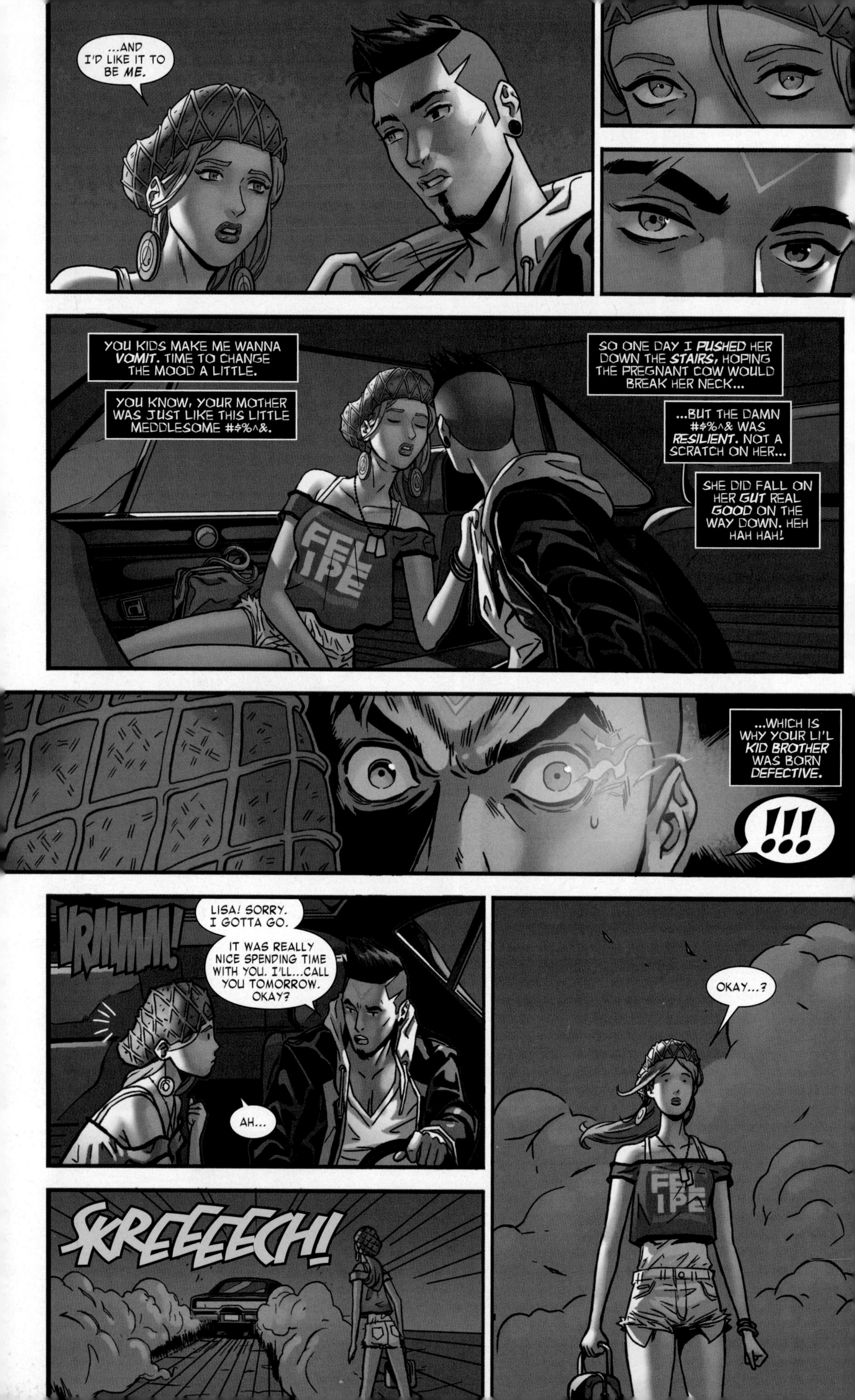
...AND I'D LIKE IT TO BE ME.
YOU KIDS MAKE ME WANNA VOMIT. TIME TO CHANGE THE MOOD A LITTLE.
YOU KNOW, YOUR MOTHER WAS JUST LIKE THIS LITTLE MEDDLESOME #$%^&.
SO ONE DAY I PUSHED HER DOWN THE STAIRS, HOPING THE PREGNANT COW WOULD BREAK HER NECK...
...BUT THE DAMN #$%^& WAS RESILIENT. NOT A SCRATCH ON HER...
SHE DID FALL ON HER GUT REAL GOOD ON THE WAY DOWN. HEH HAH HAH!
FELIPE
...WHICH IS WHY YOUR LI'L KID BROTHER WAS BORN DEFECTIVE.
!!!
VRMMMM!
LISA! SORRY. I GOTTA GO.
IT WAS REALLY NICE SPENDING TIME WITH YOU. I'LL...CALL YOU TOMORROW. OKAY?
AH...
SKREEEECH!
OKAY...?
FELIPE

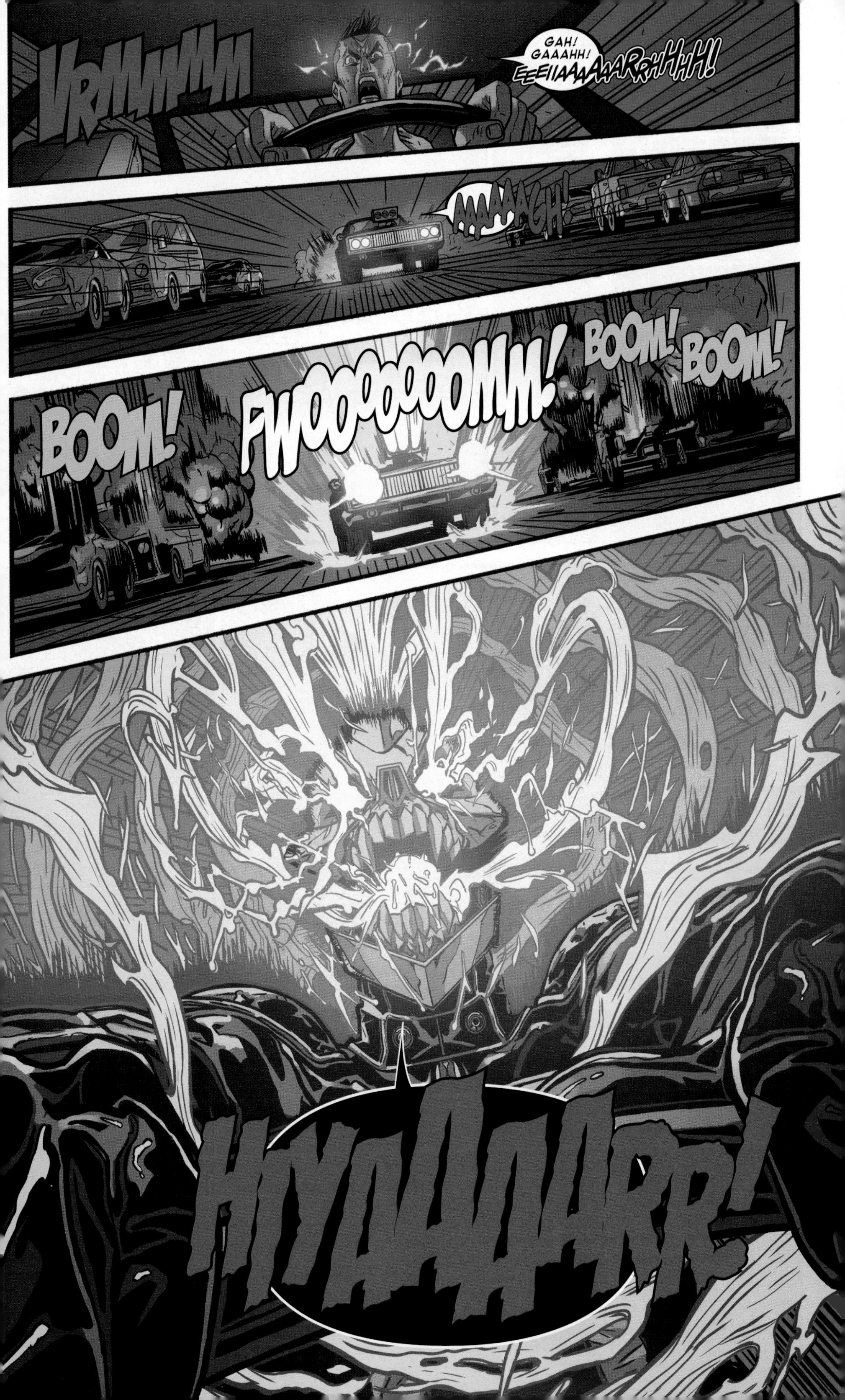
VRMMMMM
GAH! GAAAHH! EEEIIAAAAAARRHHHH!
AAAAAAGH!
BOOM!
FWOOOOOOOMM!
BOOM!
BOOM!
HYAAAARR!

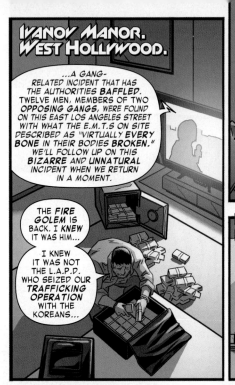

IVANOV MANOR. WEST HOLLYWOOD.

...A GANG-RELATED INCIDENT THAT HAS THE AUTHORITIES *BAFFLED.* TWELVE MEN, MEMBERS OF TWO *OPPOSING* GANGS, WERE FOUND ON THIS EAST LOS ANGELES STREET WITH WHAT THE E.M.T.S ON SITE DESCRIBED AS "VIRTUALLY *EVERY* BONE IN THEIR BODIES *BROKEN.*" WE'LL FOLLOW UP ON THIS *BIZARRE* AND *UNNATURAL* INCIDENT WHEN WE RETURN IN A MOMENT.

THE *FIRE GOLEM* IS BACK. I KNEW IT WAS HIM...

I KNEW IT WAS *NOT* THE L.A.P.D. WHO SEIZED OUR *TRAFFICKING OPERATION* WITH THE *KOREANS...*

...IT WAS *ELI MORROW'S* CURSED FIRE GOLEM...

...HE'S *BACK* TO GET ME.

REYES RESIDENCE. HILLROCK HEIGHTS, EAST LOS ANGELES.

...WHAT'S EVEN MORE *PERPLEXING...*AND TRULY *MIRACULOUS...*ALL GANG MEMBERS ARE EXPECTED TO *SURVIVE* AND FULLY *RECOVER* FROM THEIR TRULY SHOCKING INJURIES...

ONE MEDIC CLAIMED THAT "*WHOEVER* DID THIS PURPOSEFULLY *AVOIDED* INFLICTING *LETHAL* WOUNDS."

YOU *WANTED* TO *KILL* 'EM ALL...BUT YOU MANAGED NOT TO.

GOOD ON YOU, KID...

...BUT I'VE GOT ALL THE *TIME* IN THE WORLD... AND WAY MORE *TRICKS* UP MY SLEEVE. I'M GONNA *BREAK* YOU, ROBBIE...

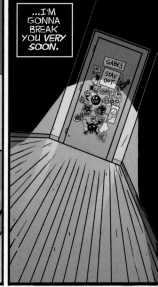

...I'M GONNA *BREAK* YOU *VERY* SOON.

GABE'S STAY OUT

YOU SAY STRANGE THINGS, *CONSCIENCE...*

I'M *NOT* YOUR *CONSCIENCE,* BOY... BUT I *AM* HERE TO *HELP* YOU...

WHAT *ARE* YOU, THEN?

I AM THE... *SPIRIT OF JUSTICE...* HEH, HEH...

...BUT YOU CAN CALL ME *ELI.*

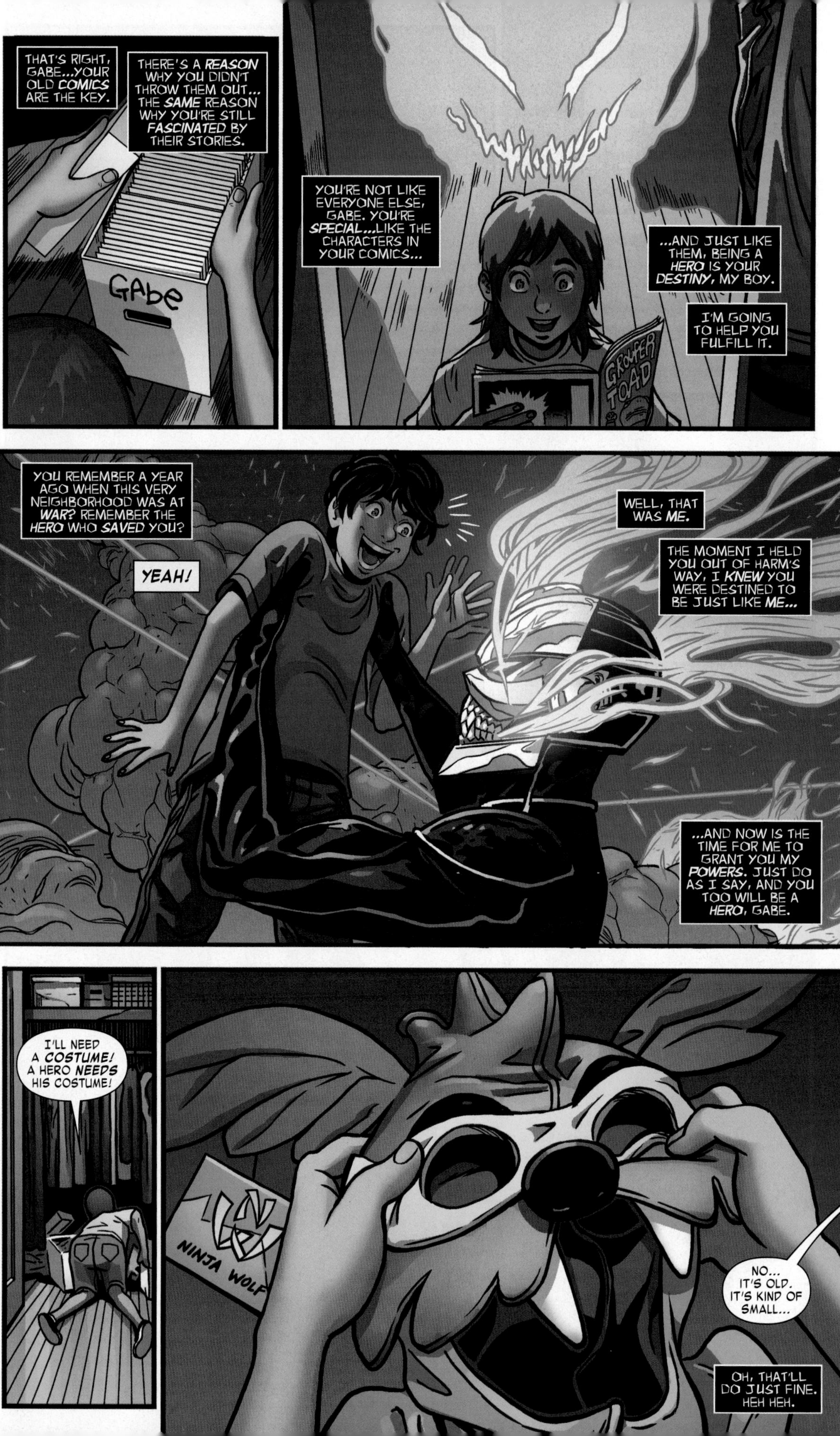
THAT'S RIGHT, GABE...YOUR OLD COMICS ARE THE KEY.
THERE'S A REASON WHY YOU DIDN'T THROW THEM OUT... THE SAME REASON WHY YOU'RE STILL FASCINATED BY THEIR STORIES.
GABE
YOU'RE NOT LIKE EVERYONE ELSE, GABE. YOU'RE SPECIAL...LIKE THE CHARACTERS IN YOUR COMICS...
...AND JUST LIKE THEM, BEING A HERO IS YOUR DESTINY, MY BOY.
I'M GOING TO HELP YOU FULFILL IT.
GROUPER TOAD
YOU REMEMBER A YEAR AGO WHEN THIS VERY NEIGHBORHOOD WAS AT WAR? REMEMBER THE HERO WHO SAVED YOU?
YEAH!
WELL, THAT WAS ME.
THE MOMENT I HELD YOU OUT OF HARM'S WAY, I KNEW YOU WERE DESTINED TO BE JUST LIKE ME...
...AND NOW IS THE TIME FOR ME TO GRANT YOU MY POWERS. JUST DO AS I SAY, AND YOU TOO WILL BE A HERO, GABE.
I'LL NEED A COSTUME! A HERO NEEDS HIS COSTUME!
NINJA WOLF
NO... IT'S OLD. IT'S KIND OF SMALL...
OH, THAT'LL DO JUST FINE. HEH HEH.

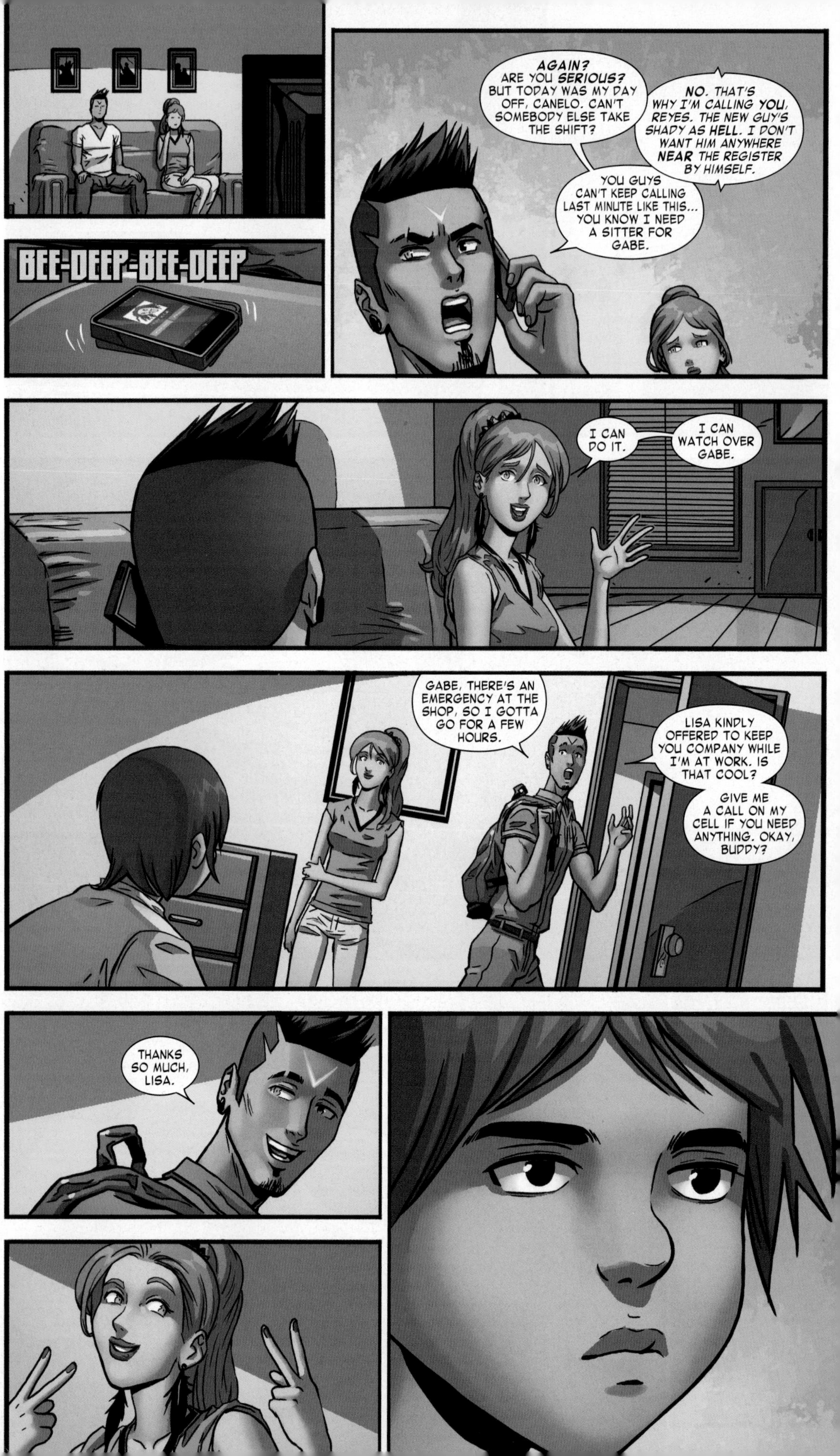
BEE-DEEP-BEE-DEEP
AGAIN? ARE YOU SERIOUS? BUT TODAY WAS MY DAY OFF, CANELO. CAN'T SOMEBODY ELSE TAKE THE SHIFT?
NO. THAT'S WHY I'M CALLING YOU, REYES. THE NEW GUY'S SHADY AS HELL. I DON'T WANT HIM ANYWHERE NEAR THE REGISTER BY HIMSELF.
YOU GUYS CAN'T KEEP CALLING LAST MINUTE LIKE THIS... YOU KNOW I NEED A SITTER FOR GABE.
I CAN DO IT.
I CAN WATCH OVER GABE.
GABE, THERE'S AN EMERGENCY AT THE SHOP, SO I GOTTA GO FOR A FEW HOURS.
LISA KINDLY OFFERED TO KEEP YOU COMPANY WHILE I'M AT WORK. IS THAT COOL?
GIVE ME A CALL ON MY CELL IF YOU NEED ANYTHING. OKAY, BUDDY?
THANKS SO MUCH, LISA.

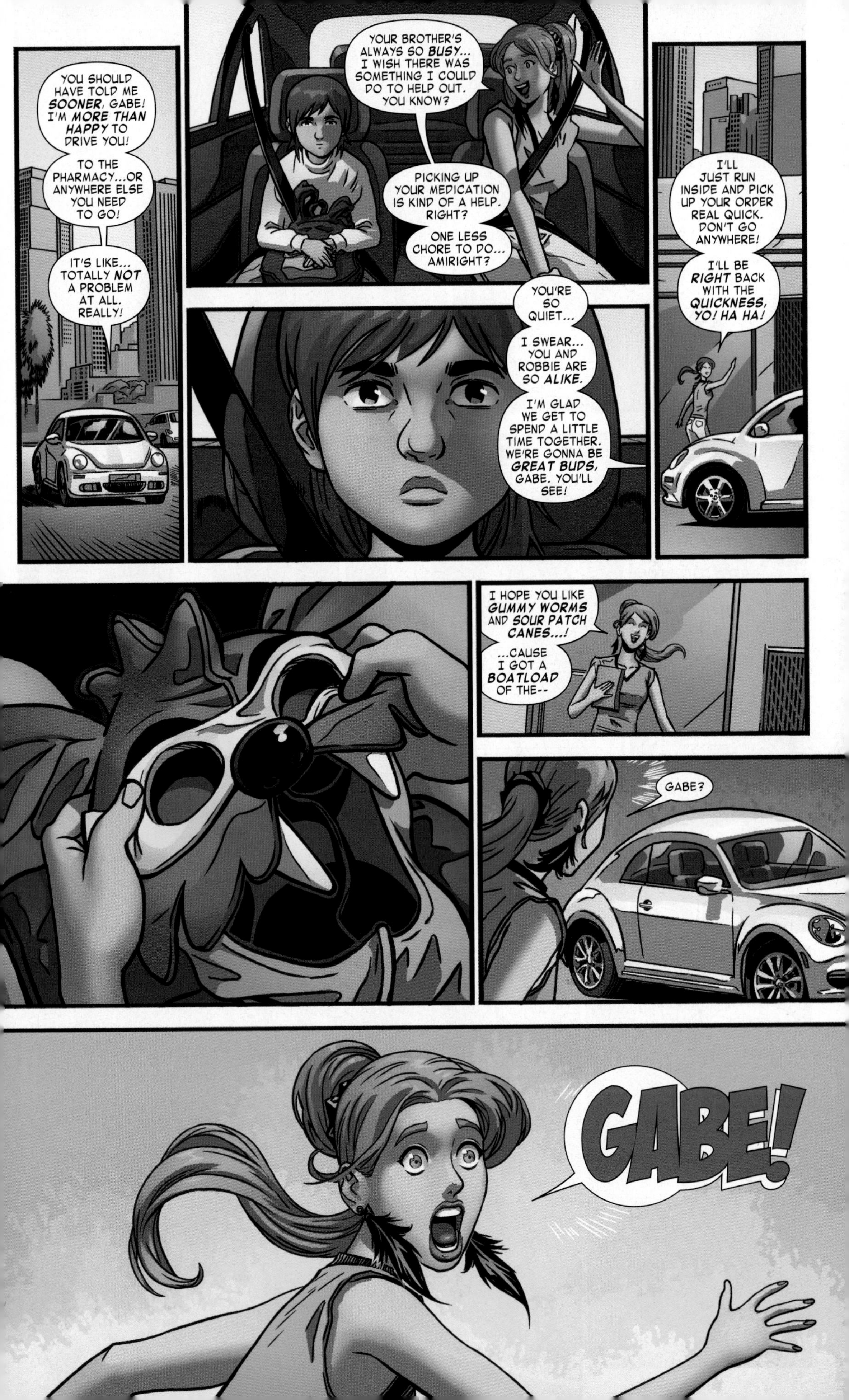
YOU SHOULD HAVE TOLD ME SOONER, GABE! I'M MORE THAN HAPPY TO DRIVE YOU!
TO THE PHARMACY...OR ANYWHERE ELSE YOU NEED TO GO!
IT'S LIKE... TOTALLY NOT A PROBLEM AT ALL. REALLY!
YOUR BROTHER'S ALWAYS SO BUSY... I WISH THERE WAS SOMETHING I COULD DO TO HELP OUT. YOU KNOW?
PICKING UP YOUR MEDICATION IS KIND OF A HELP. RIGHT?
ONE LESS CHORE TO DO... AMIRIGHT?
YOU'RE SO QUIET...
I SWEAR... YOU AND ROBBIE ARE SO ALIKE.
I'M GLAD WE GET TO SPEND A LITTLE TIME TOGETHER. WE'RE GONNA BE GREAT BUDS, GABE. YOU'LL SEE!
I'LL JUST RUN INSIDE AND PICK UP YOUR ORDER REAL QUICK. DON'T GO ANYWHERE!
I'LL BE RIGHT BACK WITH THE QUICKNESS, YO! HA HA!
I HOPE YOU LIKE GUMMY WORMS AND SOUR PATCH CANES...!
...CAUSE I GOT A BOATLOAD OF THE--
GABE?
GABE!

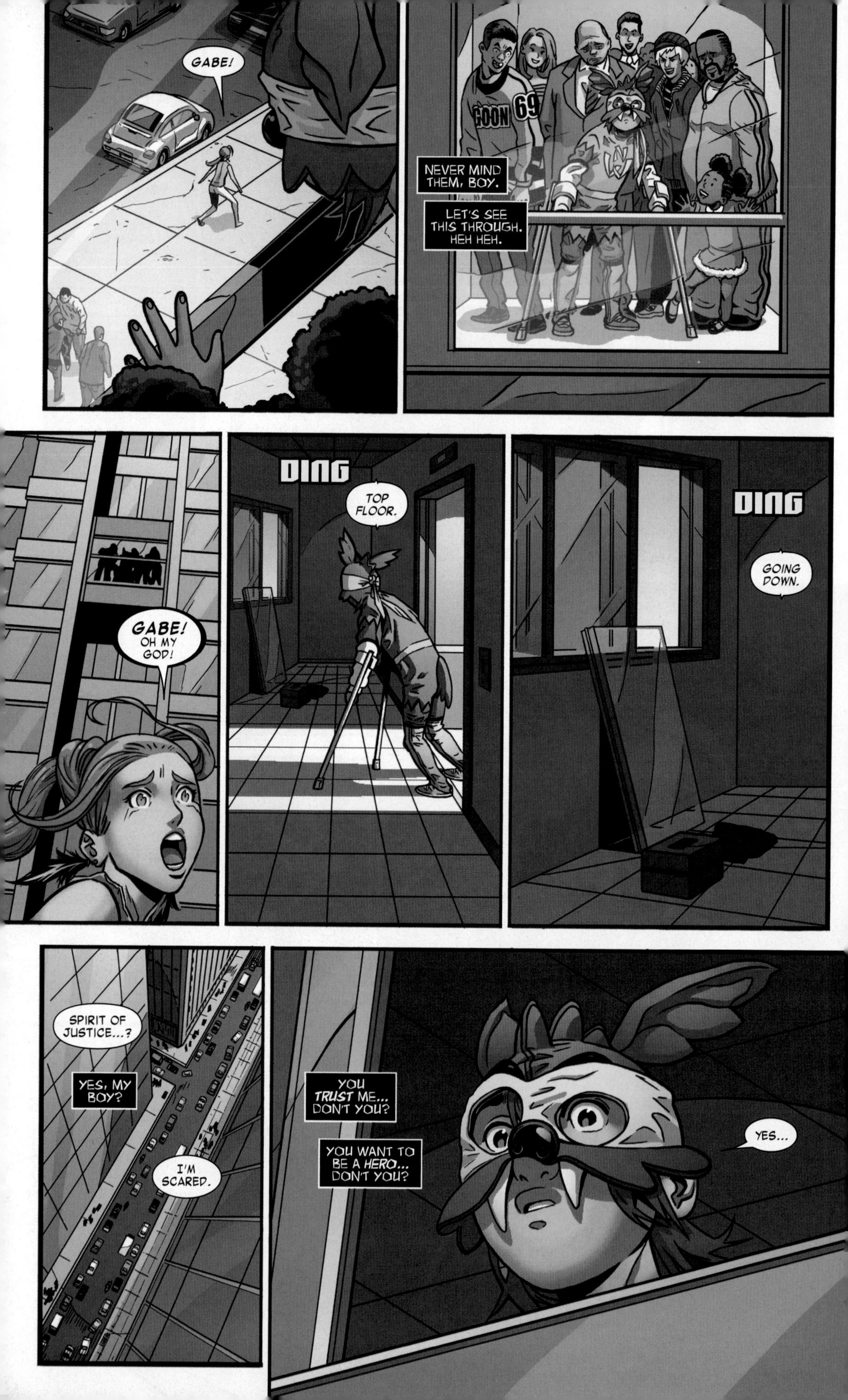
GABE!
NEVER MIND THEM, BOY.
LET'S SEE THIS THROUGH. HEH HEH.
GABE! OH MY GOD!
DING
TOP FLOOR.
DING
GOING DOWN.
SPIRIT OF JUSTICE...?
YES, MY BOY?
I'M SCARED.
YOU TRUST ME... DON'T YOU?
YOU WANT TO BE A HERO... DON'T YOU?
YES...

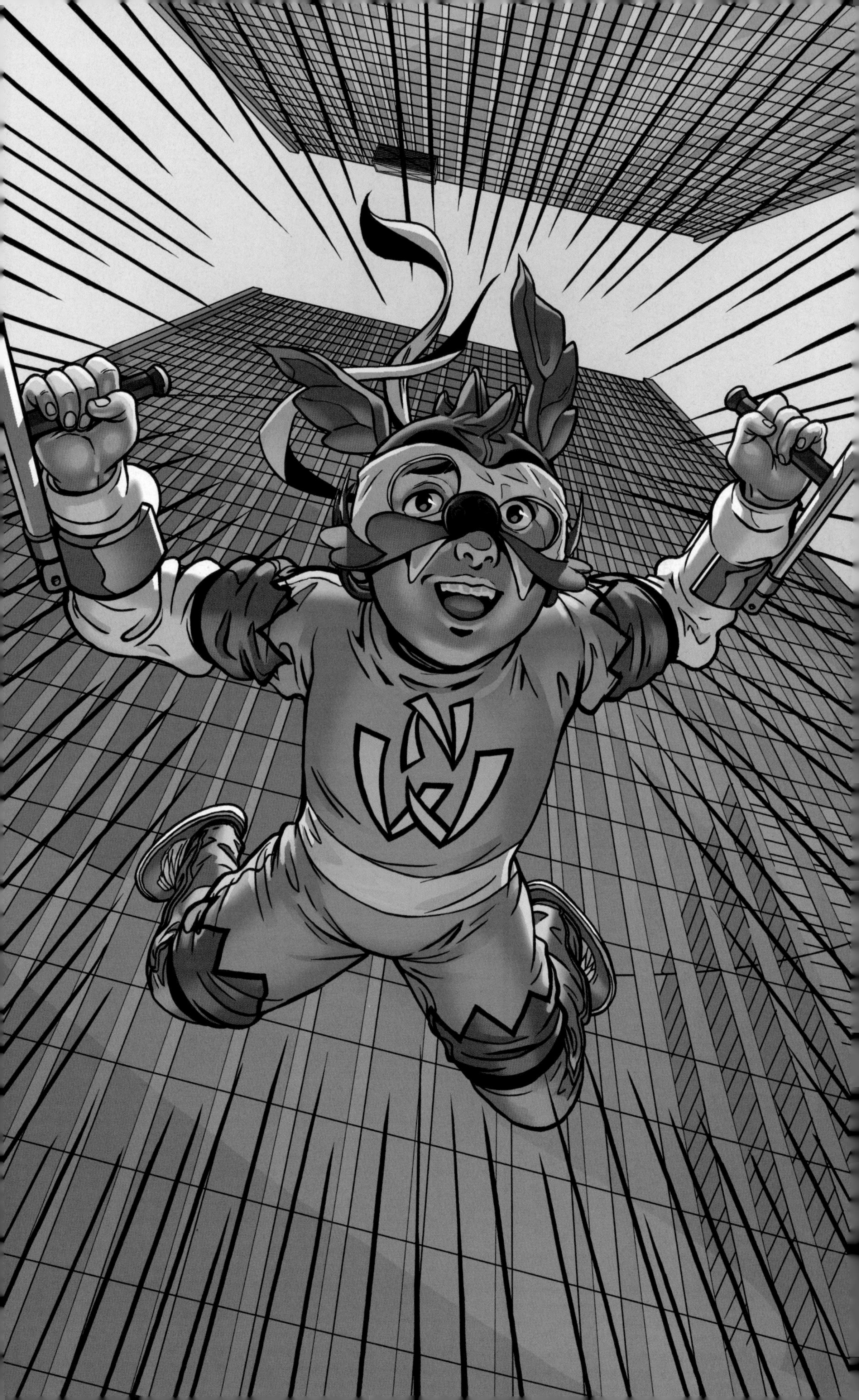

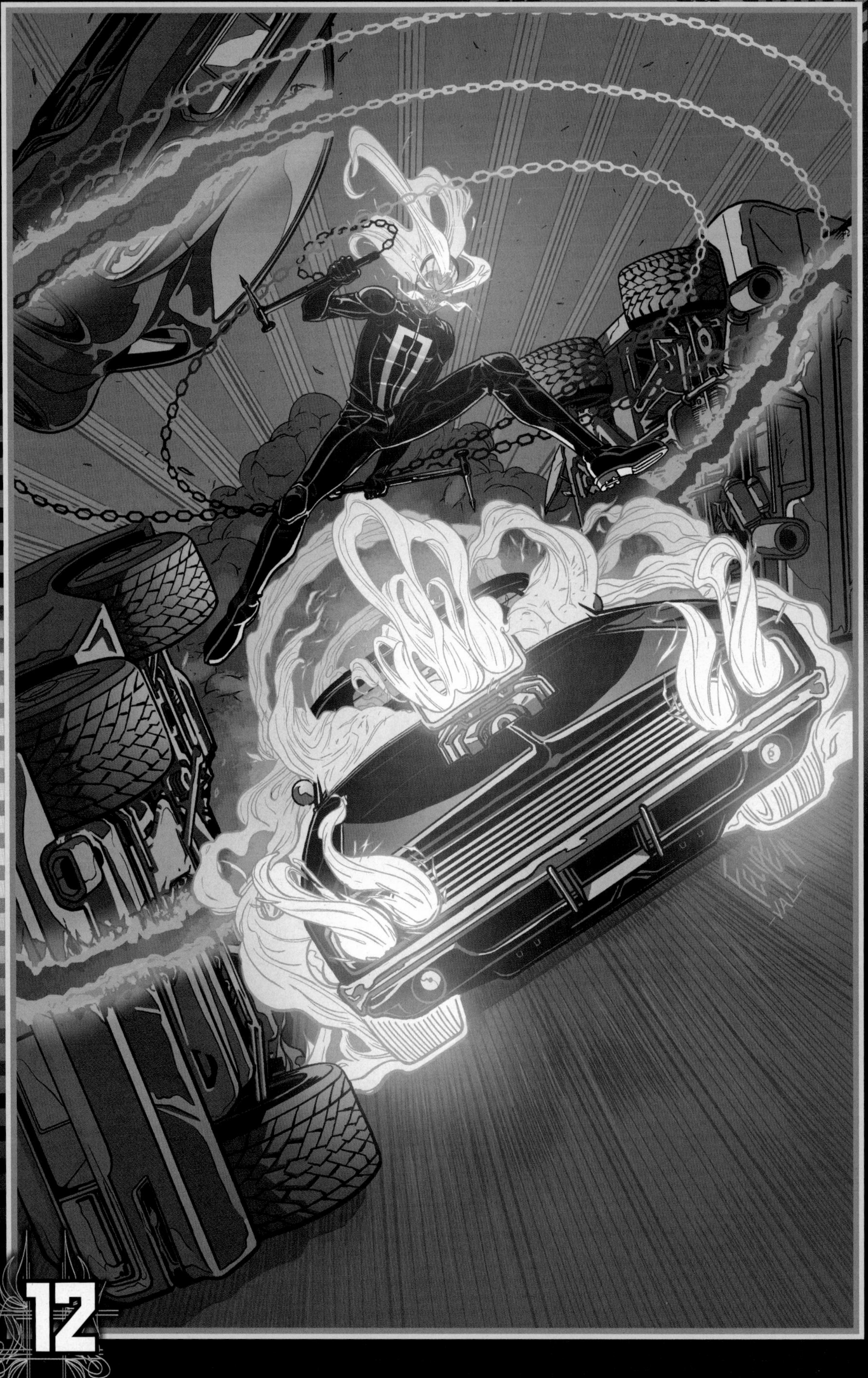

12

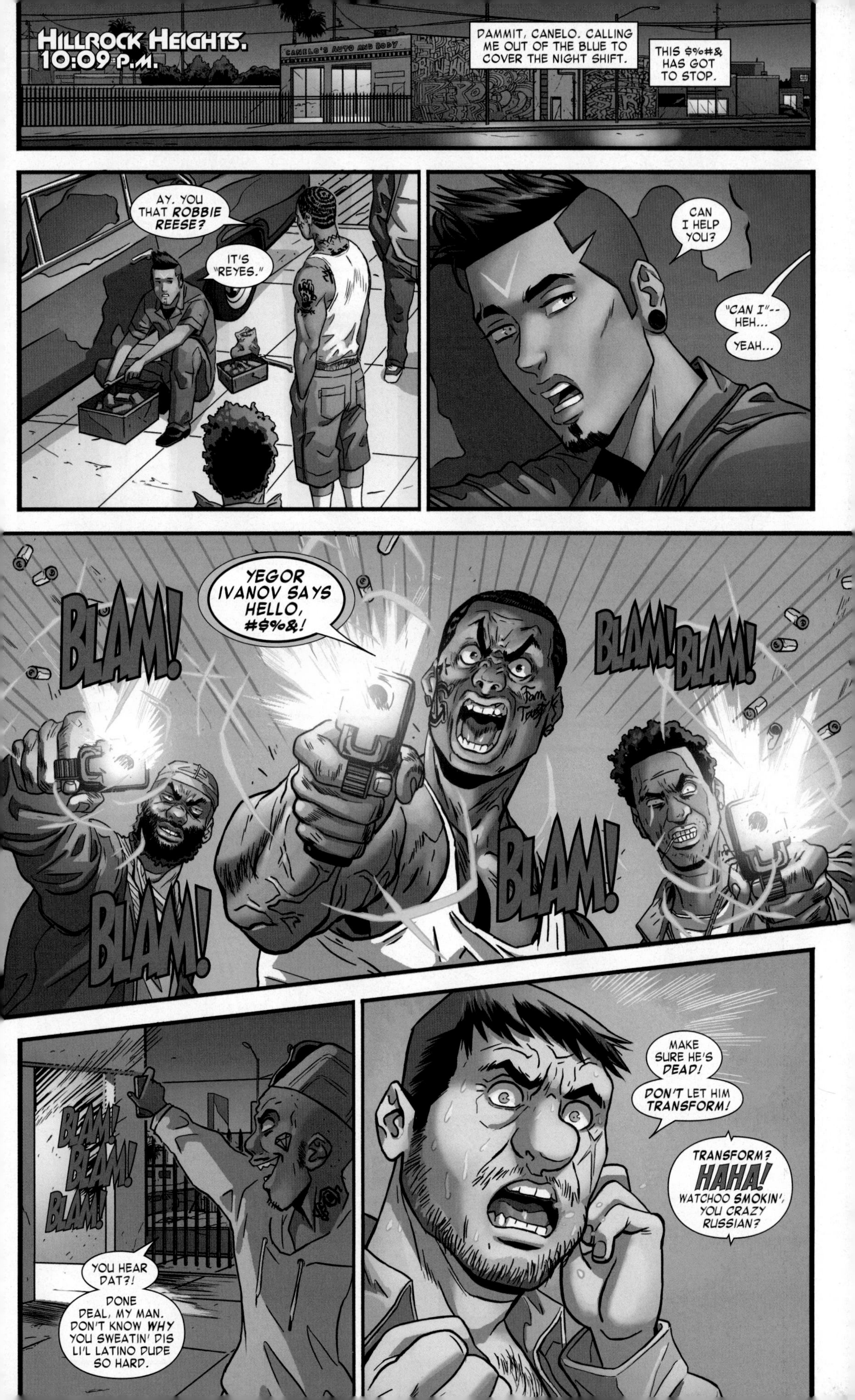
HILLROCK HEIGHTS.
10:09 P.M.
CANELO'S AUTO AND BODY
DAMMIT, CANELO. CALLING ME OUT OF THE BLUE TO COVER THE NIGHT SHIFT.
THIS $%#& HAS GOT TO STOP.
AY. YOU THAT ROBBIE REESE?
IT'S "REYES."
CAN I HELP YOU?
"CAN I"-- HEH...
YEAH...
BLAM!
YEGOR IVANOV SAYS HELLO, #$%&!
BLAM! BLAM!
BLAM!
BLAM!
BLAM! BLAM! BLAM!
YOU HEAR DAT?!
DONE DEAL, MY MAN. DON'T KNOW WHY YOU SWEATIN' DIS LI'L LATINO DUDE SO HARD.
MAKE SURE HE'S DEAD!
DON'T LET HIM TRANSFORM!
TRANSFORM? HAHA! WATCHOO SMOKIN', YOU CRAZY RUSSIAN?

FW
O
OOSHH

I'M TELLING YOU, KID...

AS LONG AS YEGOR IVANOV IS *ALIVE* AND I'M *UNAVENGED*...

HIYAAAARR!

KRAKK

...YOU'LL NEVER CATCH A BREAK.

YOU'LL BE UNDER CONSTANT ATTACK AT ALL TIMES.

SNAPP

KRATT

GHGK--!

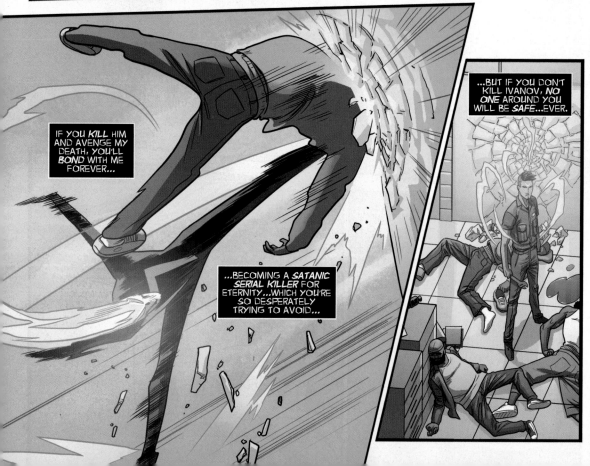

IF YOU *KILL* HIM AND AVENGE MY DEATH, YOU'LL *BOND* WITH ME FOREVER...

...BECOMING A *SATANIC SERIAL KILLER* FOR ETERNITY...WHICH YOU'RE SO DESPERATELY TRYING TO AVOID...

...BUT IF YOU DON'T KILL IVANOV, *NO ONE* AROUND YOU WILL BE *SAFE*...EVER.

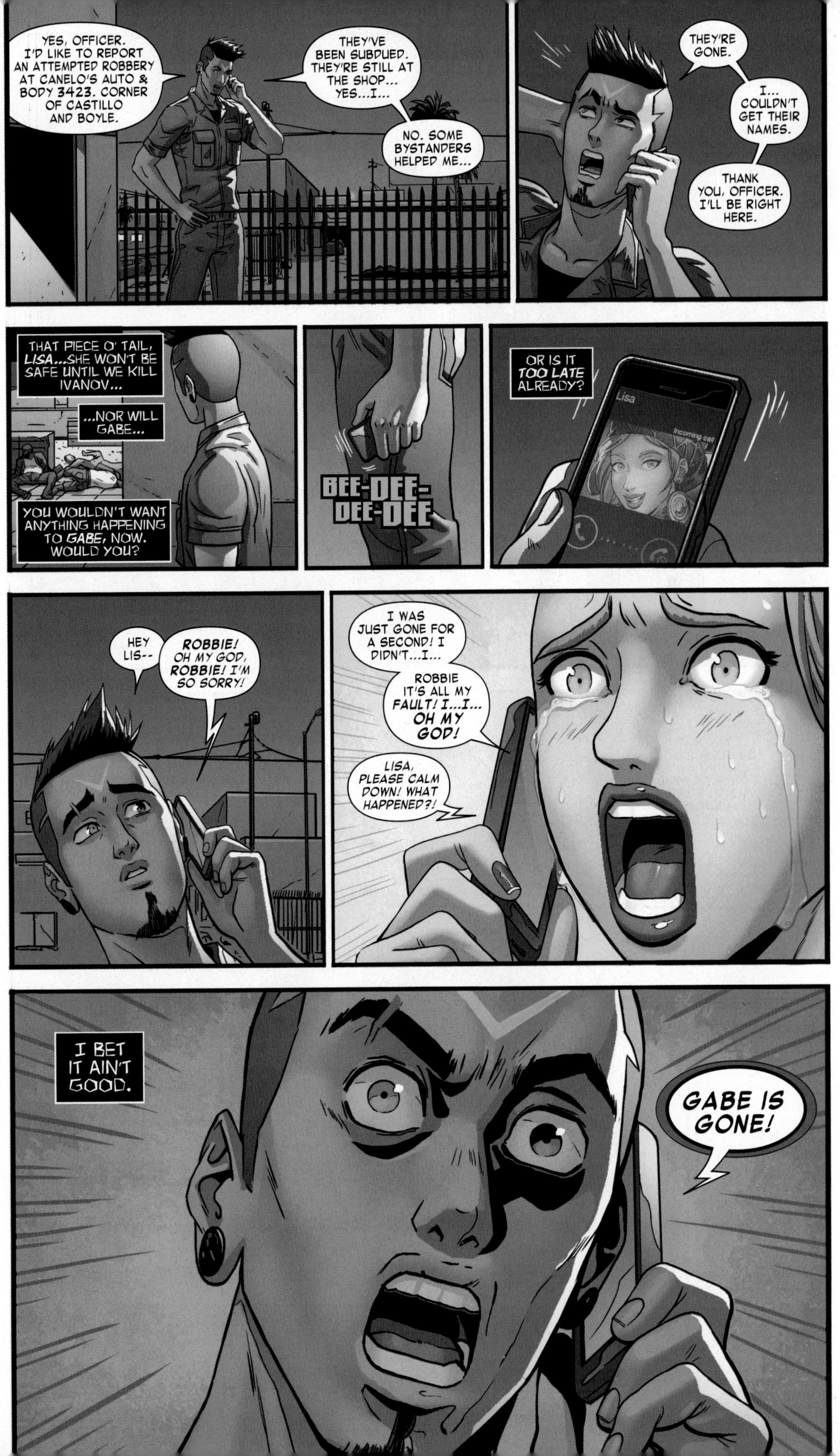

YES, OFFICER. I'D LIKE TO REPORT AN ATTEMPTED ROBBERY AT CANELO'S AUTO & BODY 3423. CORNER OF CASTILLO AND BOYLE.
THEY'VE BEEN SUBDUED. THEY'RE STILL AT THE SHOP... YES...I...
NO. SOME BYSTANDERS HELPED ME...
THEY'RE GONE.
I... COULDN'T GET THEIR NAMES.
THANK YOU, OFFICER. I'LL BE RIGHT HERE.
THAT PIECE O' TAIL, LISA...SHE WON'T BE SAFE UNTIL WE KILL IVANOV...
...NOR WILL GABE...
YOU WOULDN'T WANT ANYTHING HAPPENING TO GABE, NOW. WOULD YOU?
BEE-DEE-DEE-DEE
OR IS IT TOO LATE ALREADY?
Lisa
Incoming call
HEY LIS--
ROBBIE! OH MY GOD, ROBBIE! I'M SO SORRY!
I WAS JUST GONE FOR A SECOND! I DIDN'T...I...
ROBBIE IT'S ALL MY FAULT! I...I... OH MY GOD!
LISA, PLEASE CALM DOWN! WHAT HAPPENED?!
I BET IT AIN'T GOOD.
GABE IS GONE!

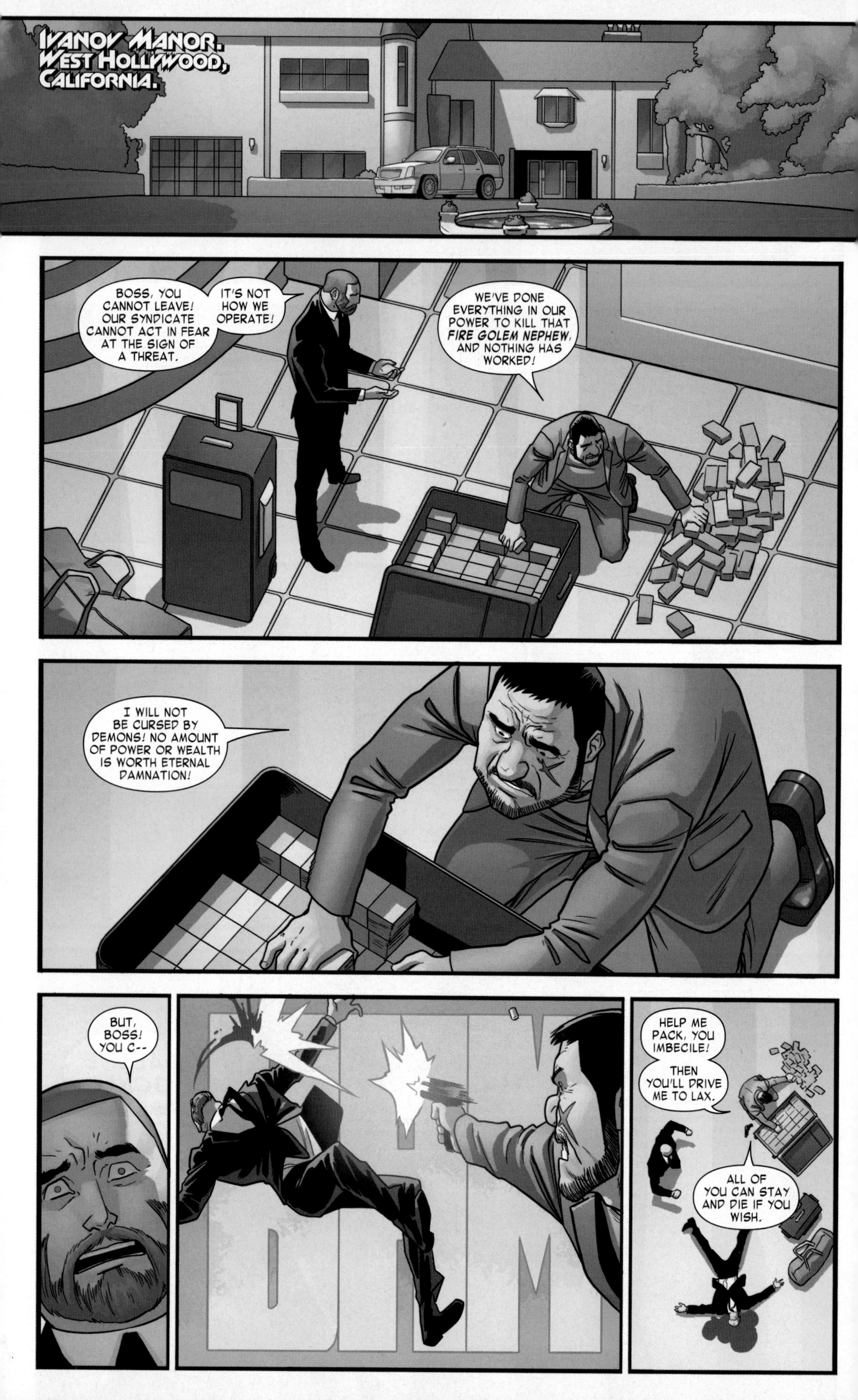
IVANOV MANOR. WEST HOLLYWOOD, CALIFORNIA.
BOSS, YOU CANNOT LEAVE! OUR SYNDICATE CANNOT ACT IN FEAR AT THE SIGN OF A THREAT.
IT'S NOT HOW WE OPERATE!
WE'VE DONE EVERYTHING IN OUR POWER TO KILL THAT FIRE GOLEM NEPHEW, AND NOTHING HAS WORKED!
I WILL NOT BE CURSED BY DEMONS! NO AMOUNT OF POWER OR WEALTH IS WORTH ETERNAL DAMNATION!
BUT, BOSS! YOU C--
BLAM
HELP ME PACK, YOU IMBECILE!
THEN YOU'LL DRIVE ME TO LAX.
ALL OF YOU CAN STAY AND DIE IF YOU WISH.

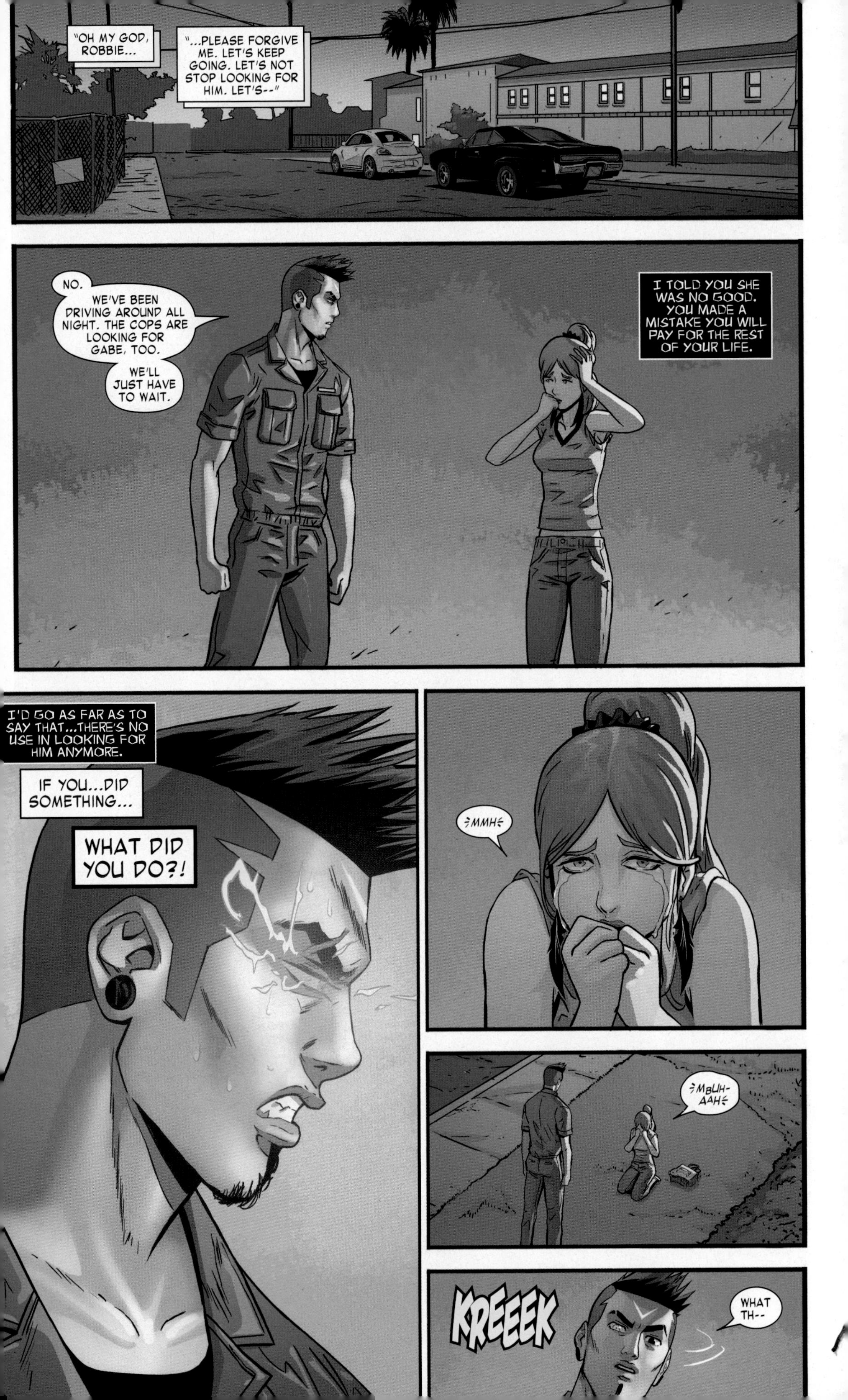
"OH MY GOD, ROBBIE...
"...PLEASE FORGIVE ME. LET'S KEEP GOING. LET'S NOT STOP LOOKING FOR HIM. LET'S--"
NO.
WE'VE BEEN DRIVING AROUND ALL NIGHT. THE COPS ARE LOOKING FOR GABE, TOO.
WE'LL JUST HAVE TO WAIT.
I TOLD YOU SHE WAS NO GOOD. YOU MADE A MISTAKE YOU WILL PAY FOR THE REST OF YOUR LIFE.
I'D GO AS FAR AS TO SAY THAT...THERE'S NO USE IN LOOKING FOR HIM ANYMORE.
IF YOU...DID SOMETHING...
WHAT DID YOU DO?!
MMH
MBUH-AAH
KREEEK
WHAT TH--

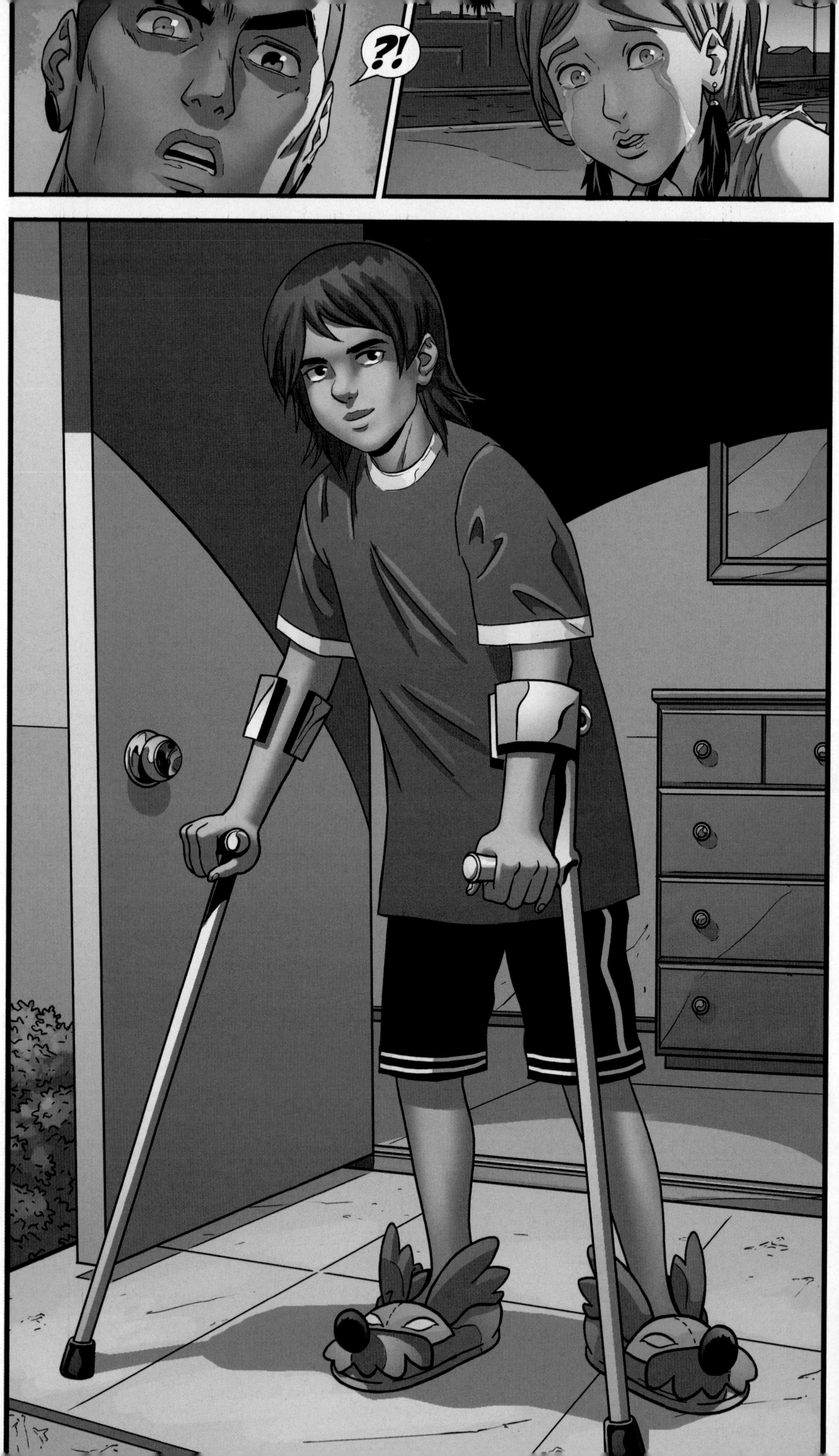
?!

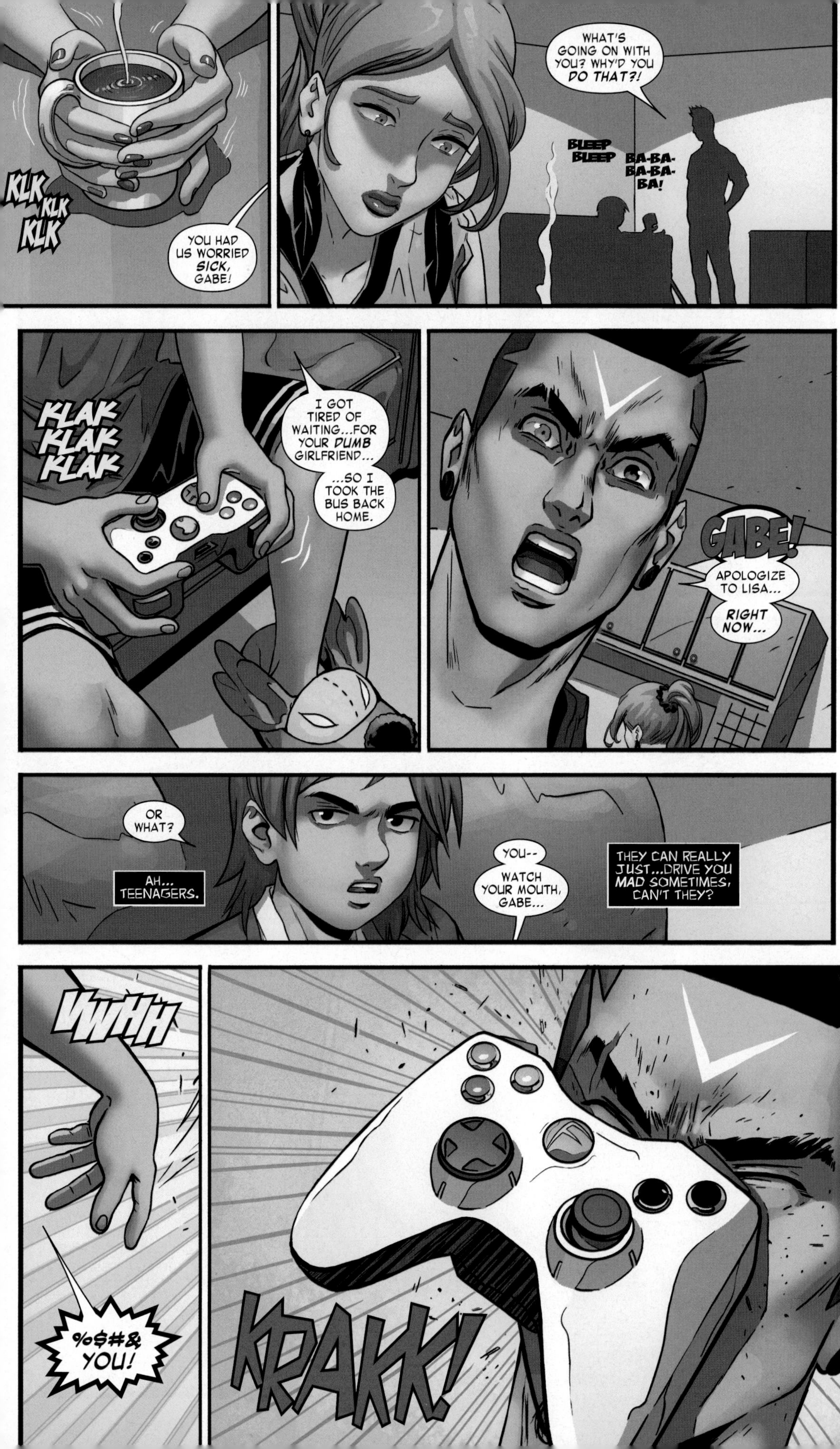
KLK KLK KLK
YOU HAD US WORRIED SICK, GABE!
WHAT'S GOING ON WITH YOU? WHY'D YOU DO THAT?!
BLEEP BLEEP
BA-BA-BA-BA-BA!
KLAK KLAK KLAK
I GOT TIRED OF WAITING...FOR YOUR DUMB GIRLFRIEND...
...SO I TOOK THE BUS BACK HOME.
GABE!
APOLOGIZE TO LISA...
RIGHT NOW...
OR WHAT?
AH... TEENAGERS.
YOU--
WATCH YOUR MOUTH, GABE...
THEY CAN REALLY JUST...DRIVE YOU MAD SOMETIMES, CAN'T THEY?
VWHH
%$#& YOU!
KRAKK!

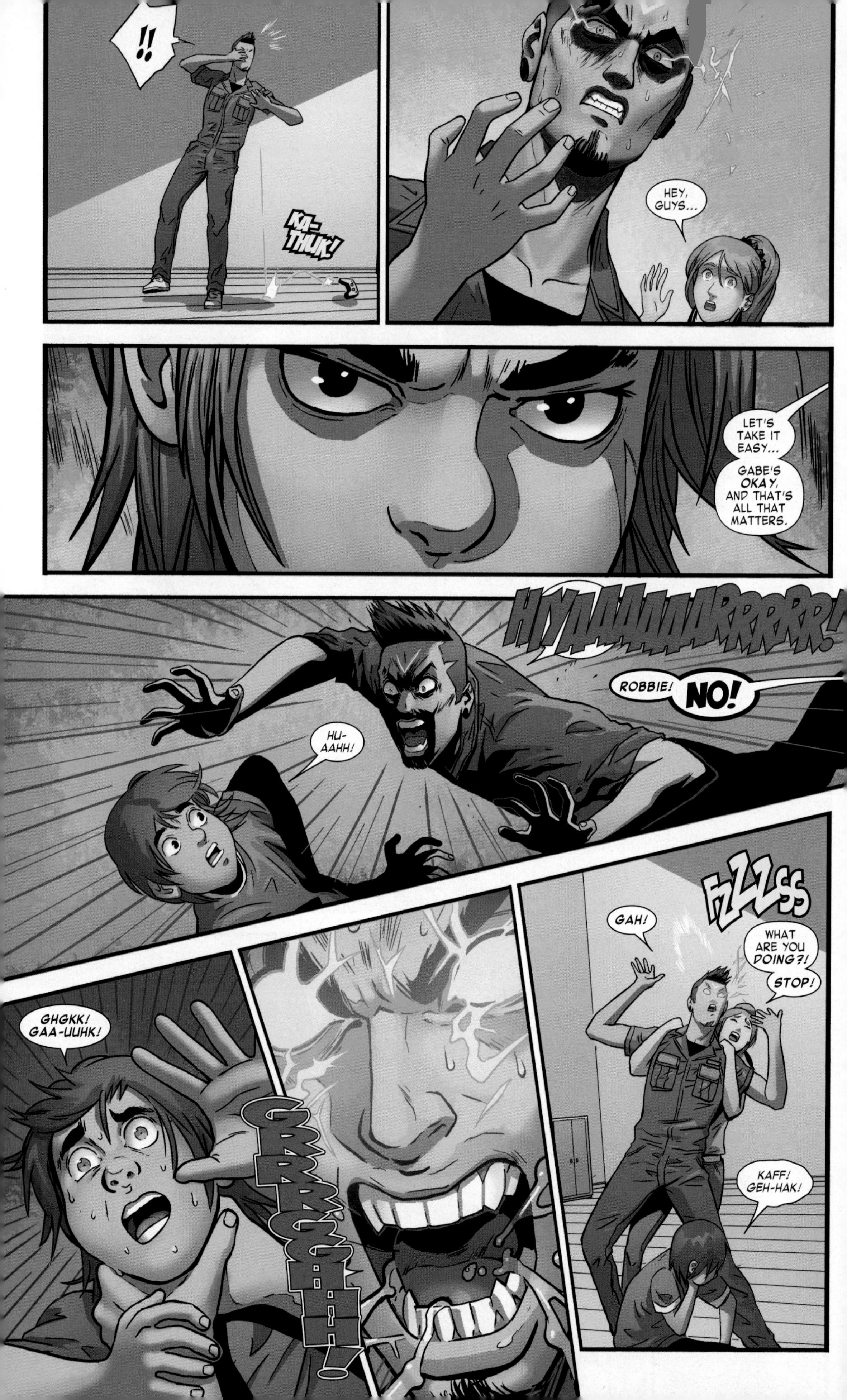
!!
KA-THUK!
HEY, GUYS...
LET'S TAKE IT EASY...
GABE'S OKAY, AND THAT'S ALL THAT MATTERS.
HIYAAAAAARRRRR!
ROBBIE! NO!
HU-AAHH!
GHGKK! GAA-UUHK!
GRAAAGHHH!
FZZZSS
GAH!
WHAT ARE YOU DOING?!
STOP!
KAFF! GEH-HAK!

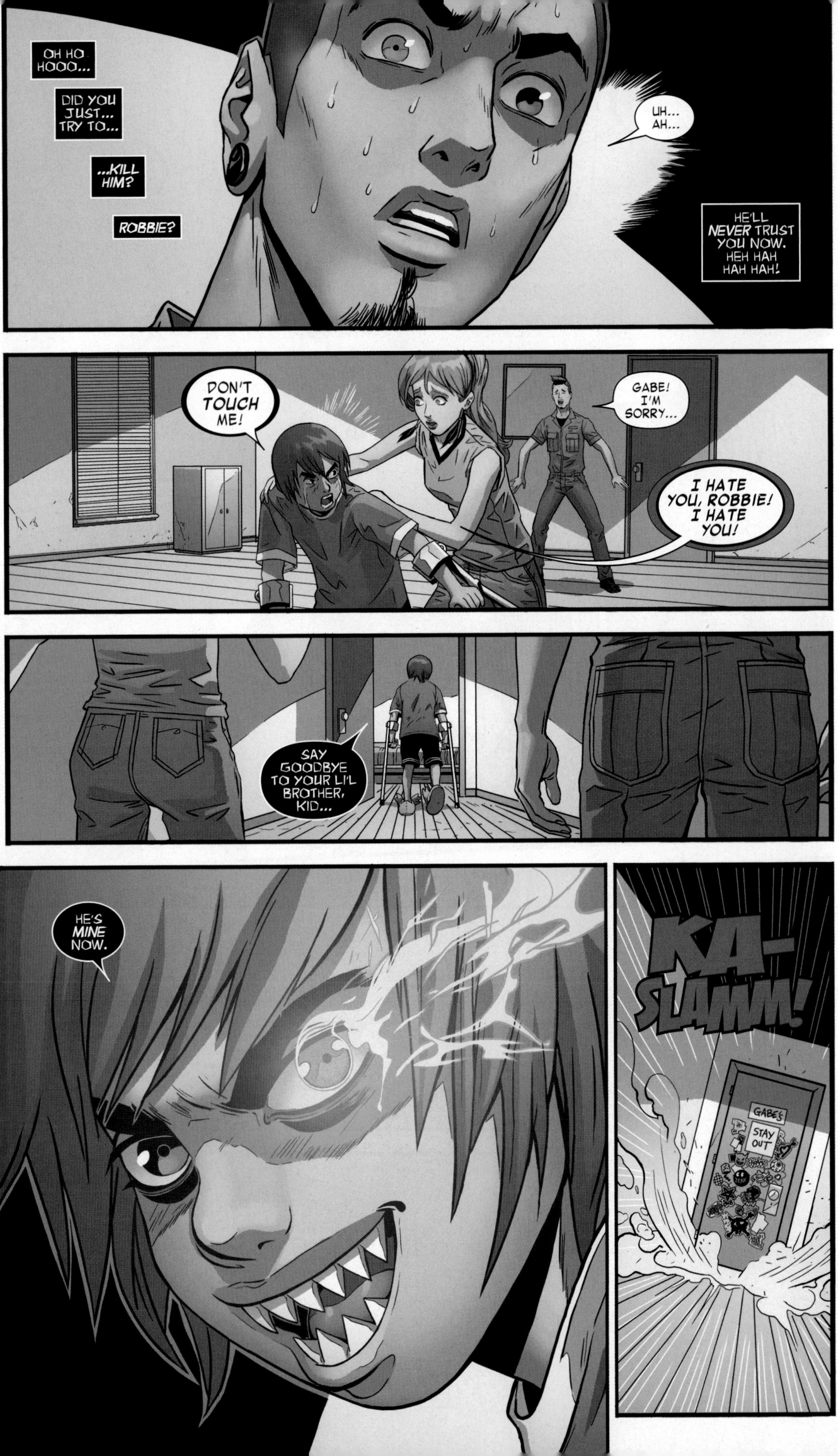
OH HO HOOO...
DID YOU JUST... TRY TO...
...KILL HIM?
ROBBIE?
UH... AH...
HE'LL NEVER TRUST YOU NOW. HEH HAH HAH HAH!
DON'T TOUCH ME!
GABE! I'M SORRY...
I HATE YOU, ROBBIE! I HATE YOU!
SAY GOODBYE TO YOUR LI'L BROTHER, KID...
HE'S MINE NOW.
KA-SLAMM!
GABE'S
STAY OUT

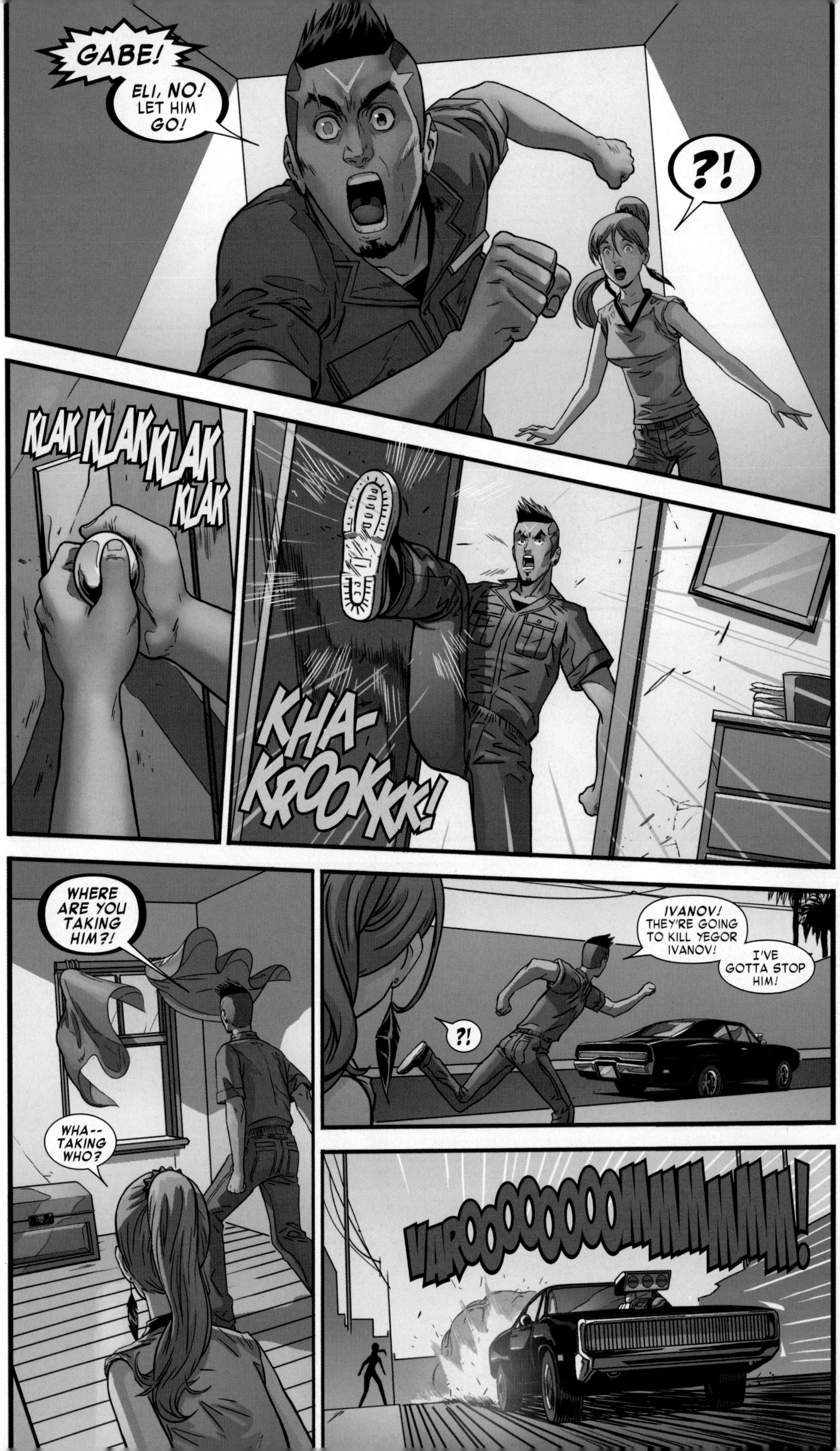
GABE!
ELI, NO! LET HIM GO!
?!
KLAK KLAK KLAK KLAK
KHA-KROOKKK!
WHERE ARE YOU TAKING HIM?!
WHA-- TAKING WHO?
IVANOV! THEY'RE GOING TO KILL YEGOR IVANOV!
I'VE GOTTA STOP HIM!
?!
VAROOOOOOOOMMMMMMM!

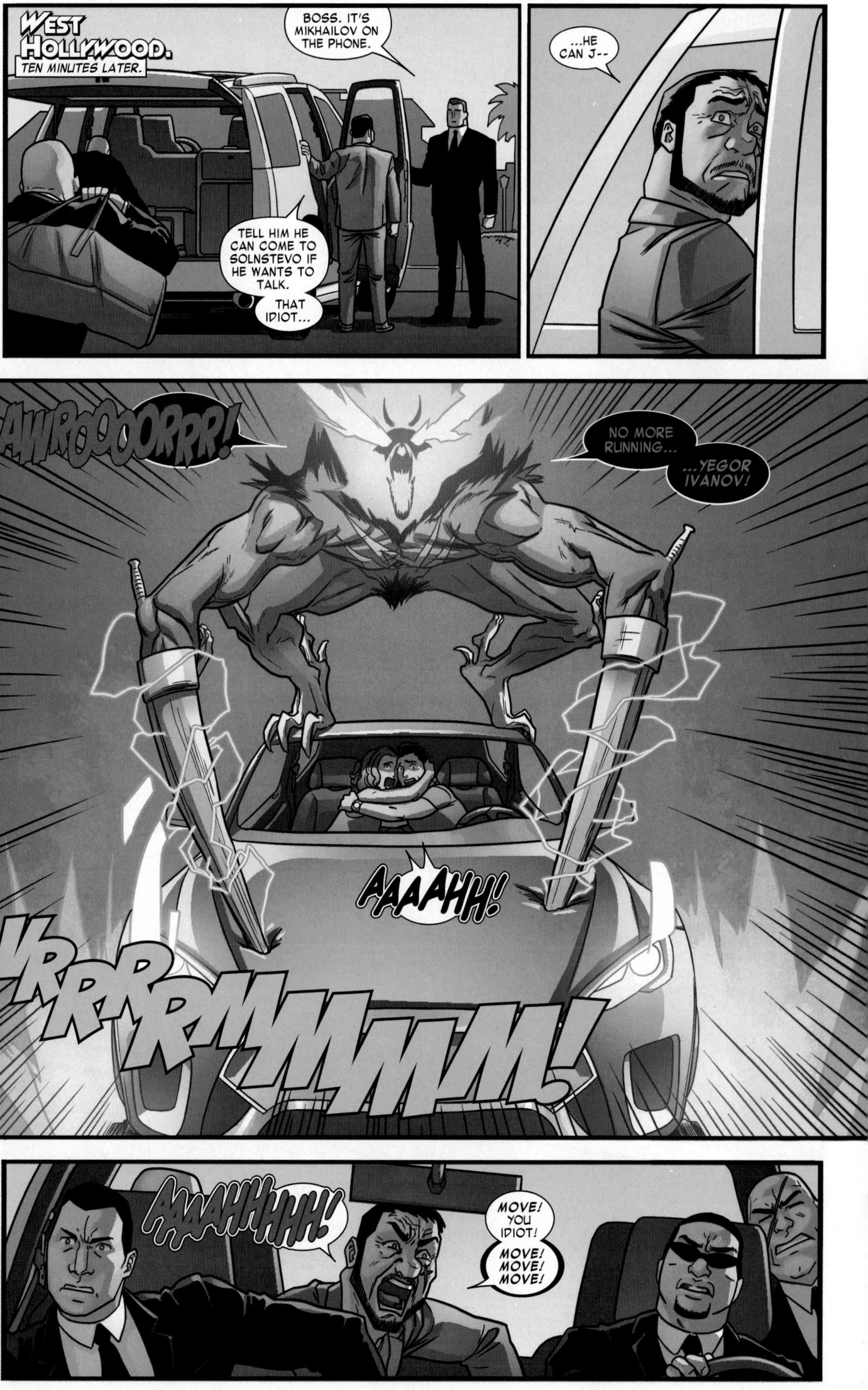
WEST HOLLYWOOD.
TEN MINUTES LATER.
BOSS. IT'S MIKHAILOV ON THE PHONE.
TELL HIM HE CAN COME TO SOLNSTEVO IF HE WANTS TO TALK.
THAT IDIOT...
...HE CAN J--
AWROOOORRR!
NO MORE RUNNING...
...YEGOR IVANOV!
AAAAHH!
VRRRRMMMMM!
AAAAHHHHH!
MOVE! YOU IDIOT!
MOVE! MOVE! MOVE!

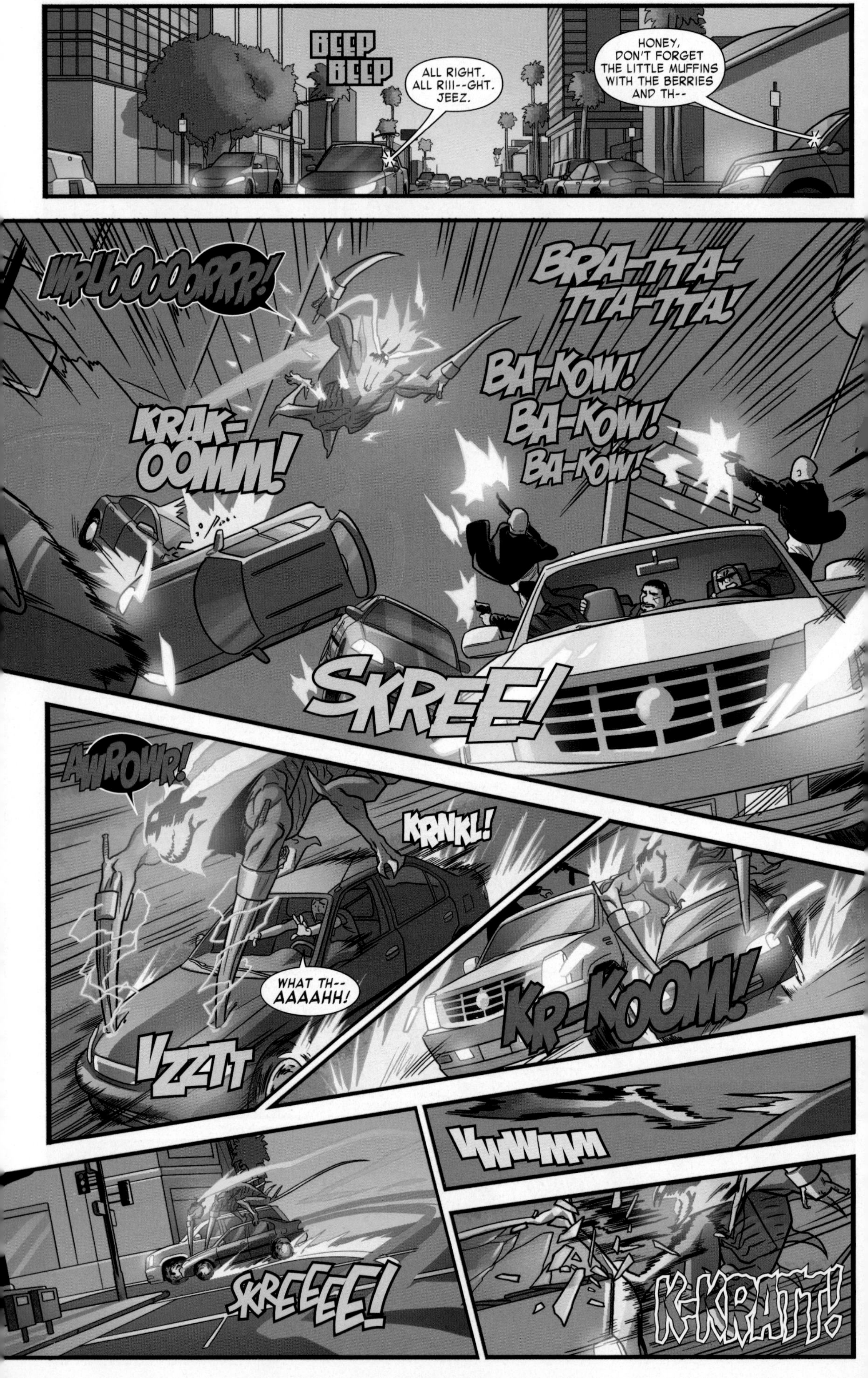
BEEP BEEP
ALL RIGHT. ALL RIII--GHT. JEEZ.
HONEY, DON'T FORGET THE LITTLE MUFFINS WITH THE BERRIES AND TH--
WRUOOOOORRRR!
BRA-TTA-TTA-TTA!
BA-KOW! BA-KOW! BA-KOW!
KRAK-OOMM!
SKREE!
AWROWR!
KRNKL!
WHAT TH-- AAAAHH!
VZZTT
KR-KOOM!
VWWMM
SKREEEE!
K-KRATT!

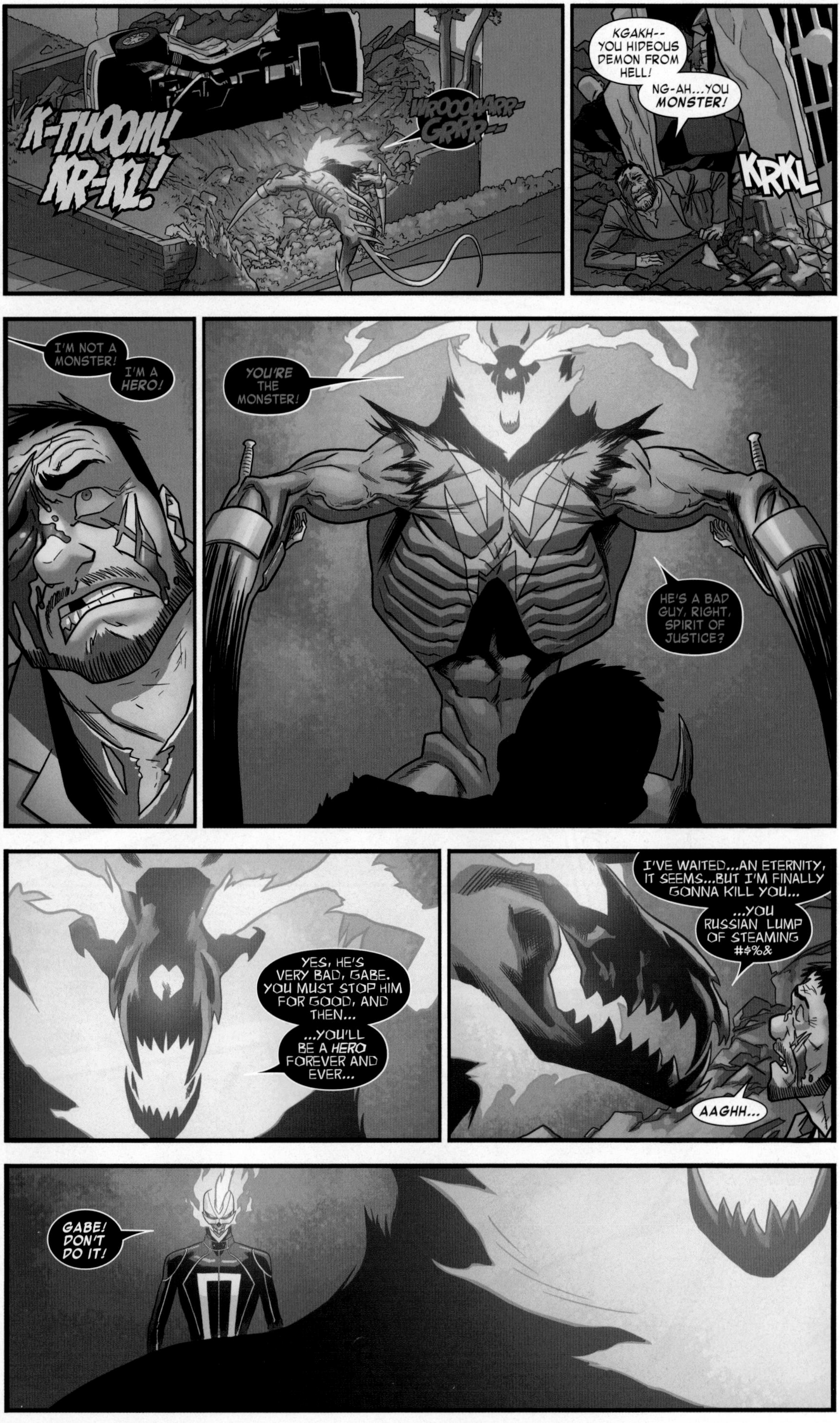
K-THOOM! KR-KL!
WROOOAARR-GRRR--
KGAKH-- YOU HIDEOUS DEMON FROM HELL!
NG-AH...YOU MONSTER!
KRKL
I'M NOT A MONSTER!
I'M A HERO!
YOU'RE THE MONSTER!
HE'S A BAD GUY, RIGHT, SPIRIT OF JUSTICE?
YES, HE'S VERY BAD, GABE. YOU MUST STOP HIM FOR GOOD, AND THEN...
...YOU'LL BE A HERO FOREVER AND EVER...
I'VE WAITED...AN ETERNITY, IT SEEMS...BUT I'M FINALLY GONNA KILL YOU...
...YOU RUSSIAN LUMP OF STEAMING #$%&
AAGHH...
GABE! DON'T DO IT!

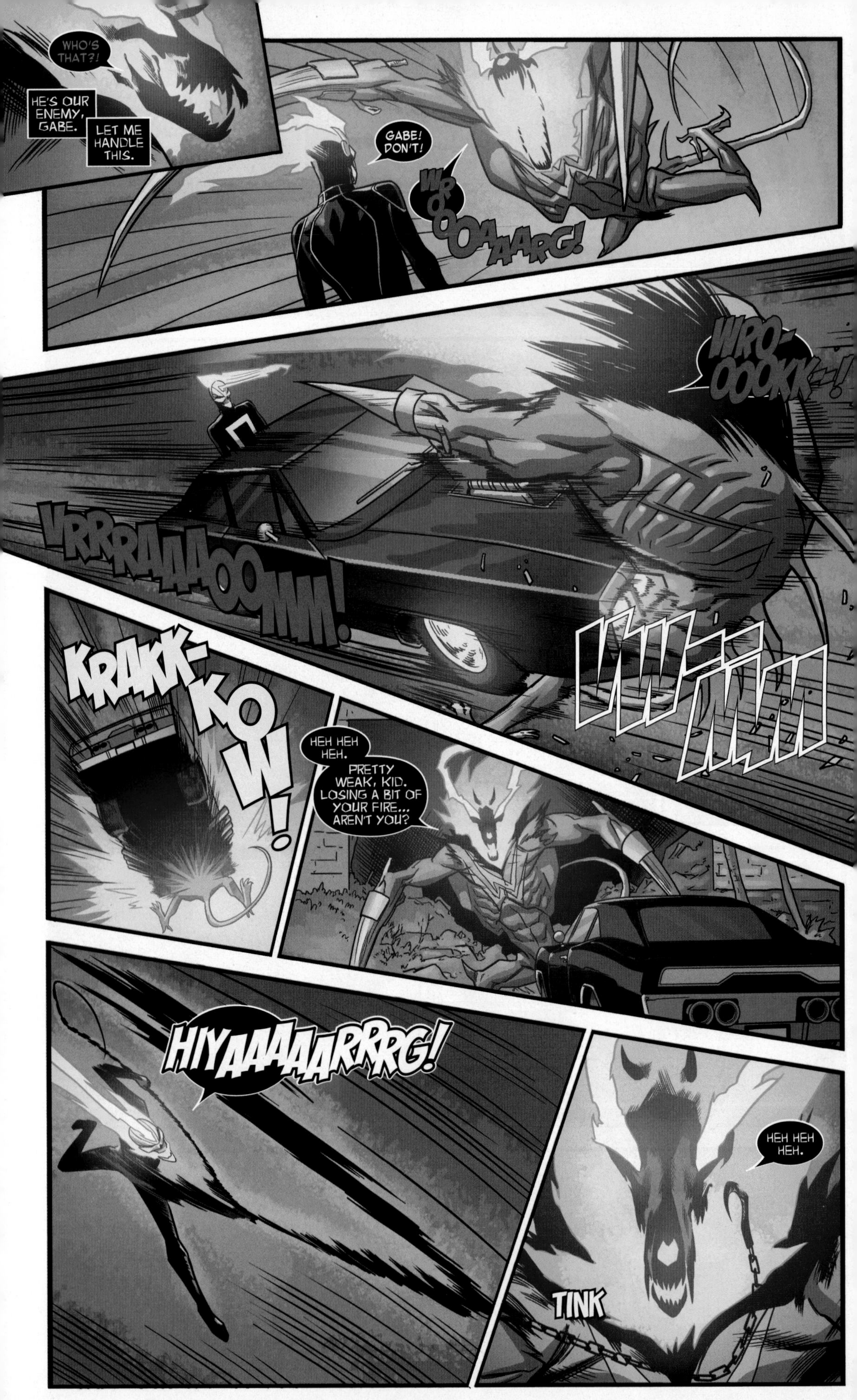

WHO'S THAT?!
HE'S OUR ENEMY, GABE.
LET ME HANDLE THIS.
GABE! DON'T!
WROOOAAARG!
WRO-OOOKK-!
VRRRAAAAOOMM!
KRAKK-KOW!
HEH HEH HEH.
PRETTY WEAK, KID. LOSING A BIT OF YOUR FIRE... AREN'T YOU?
HIYAAAAARRRG!
HEH HEH HEH.
TINK

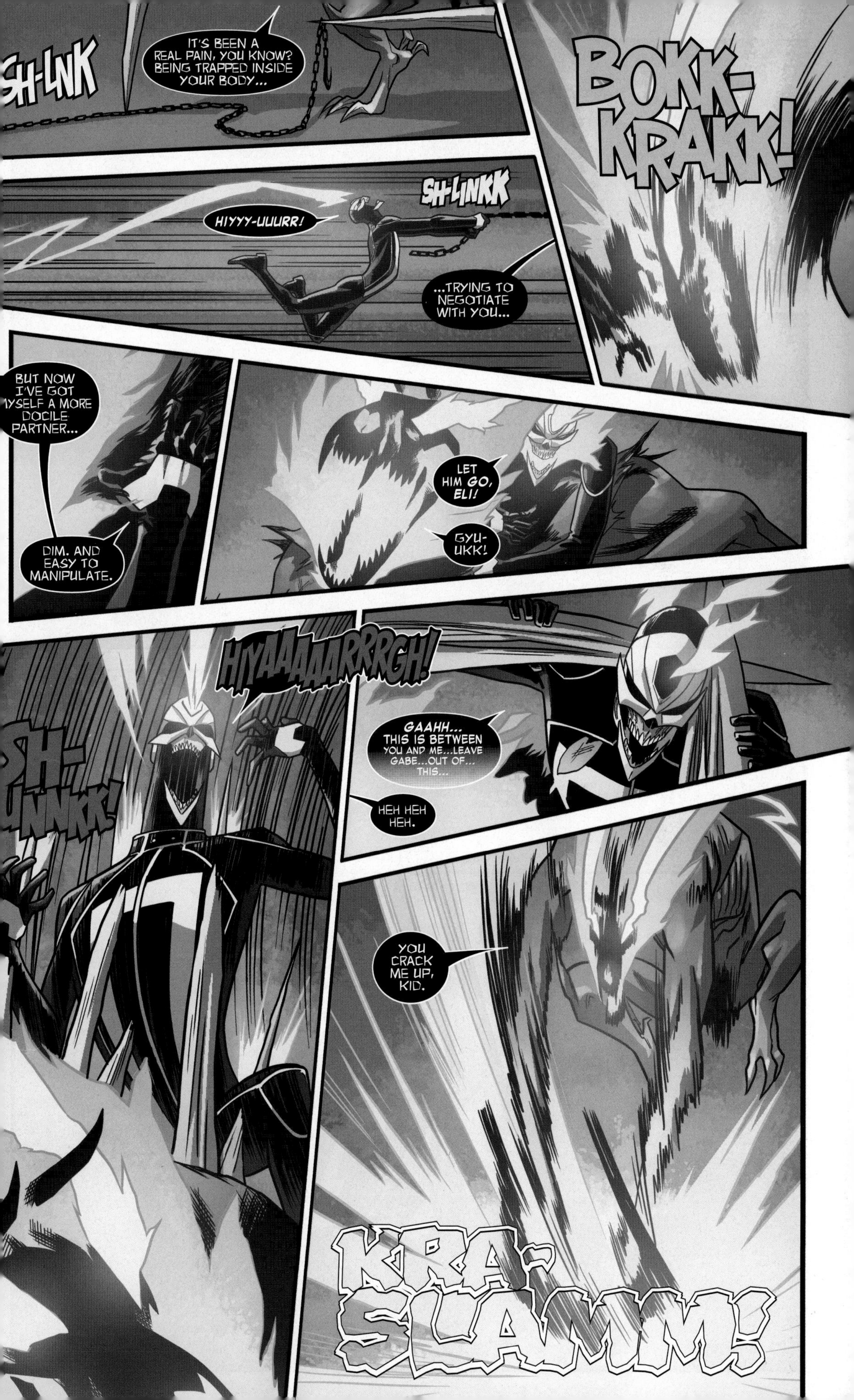
SH-LNK
IT'S BEEN A REAL PAIN, YOU KNOW? BEING TRAPPED INSIDE YOUR BODY...
BOKK-KRAKK!
SH-LINKK
HIYYY-UUURR!
...TRYING TO NEGOTIATE WITH YOU...
BUT NOW I'VE GOT MYSELF A MORE DOCILE PARTNER...
DIM. AND EASY TO MANIPULATE.
LET HIM GO, ELI!
GYU-UKK!
HIYAAAAARRRGH!
SH-UNNKK!
GAAHH... THIS IS BETWEEN YOU AND ME...LEAVE GABE...OUT OF... THIS...
HEH HEH HEH.
YOU CRACK ME UP, KID.
KRA-SLAMM!

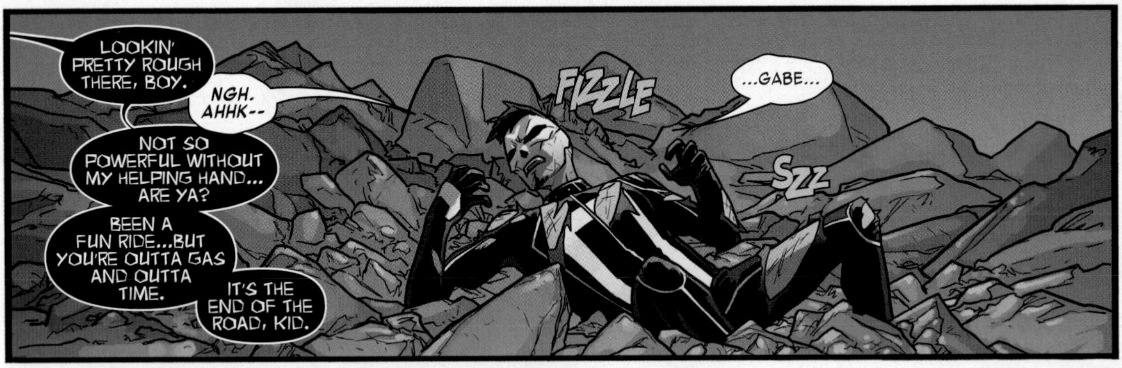
LOOKIN' PRETTY ROUGH THERE, BOY.
NGH. AHHK--
FIZZLE
...GABE...
NOT SO POWERFUL WITHOUT MY HELPING HAND... ARE YA?
SZZ
BEEN A FUN RIDE...BUT YOU'RE OUTTA GAS AND OUTTA TIME.
IT'S THE END OF THE ROAD, KID.

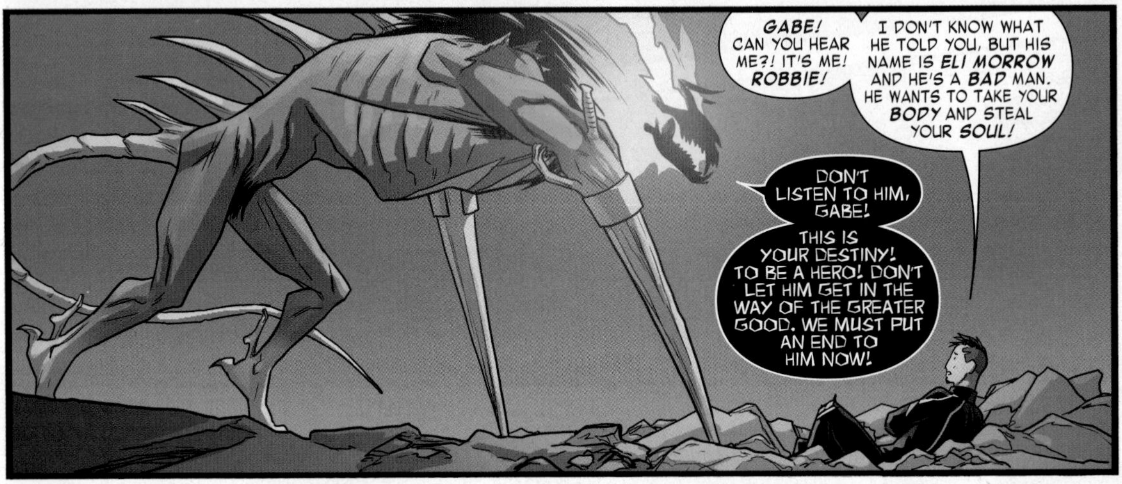
GABE! CAN YOU HEAR ME?! IT'S ME! ROBBIE!
I DON'T KNOW WHAT HE TOLD YOU, BUT HIS NAME IS ELI MORROW AND HE'S A BAD MAN. HE WANTS TO TAKE YOUR BODY AND STEAL YOUR SOUL!
DON'T LISTEN TO HIM, GABE!
THIS IS YOUR DESTINY! TO BE A HERO! DON'T LET HIM GET IN THE WAY OF THE GREATER GOOD. WE MUST PUT AN END TO HIM NOW!

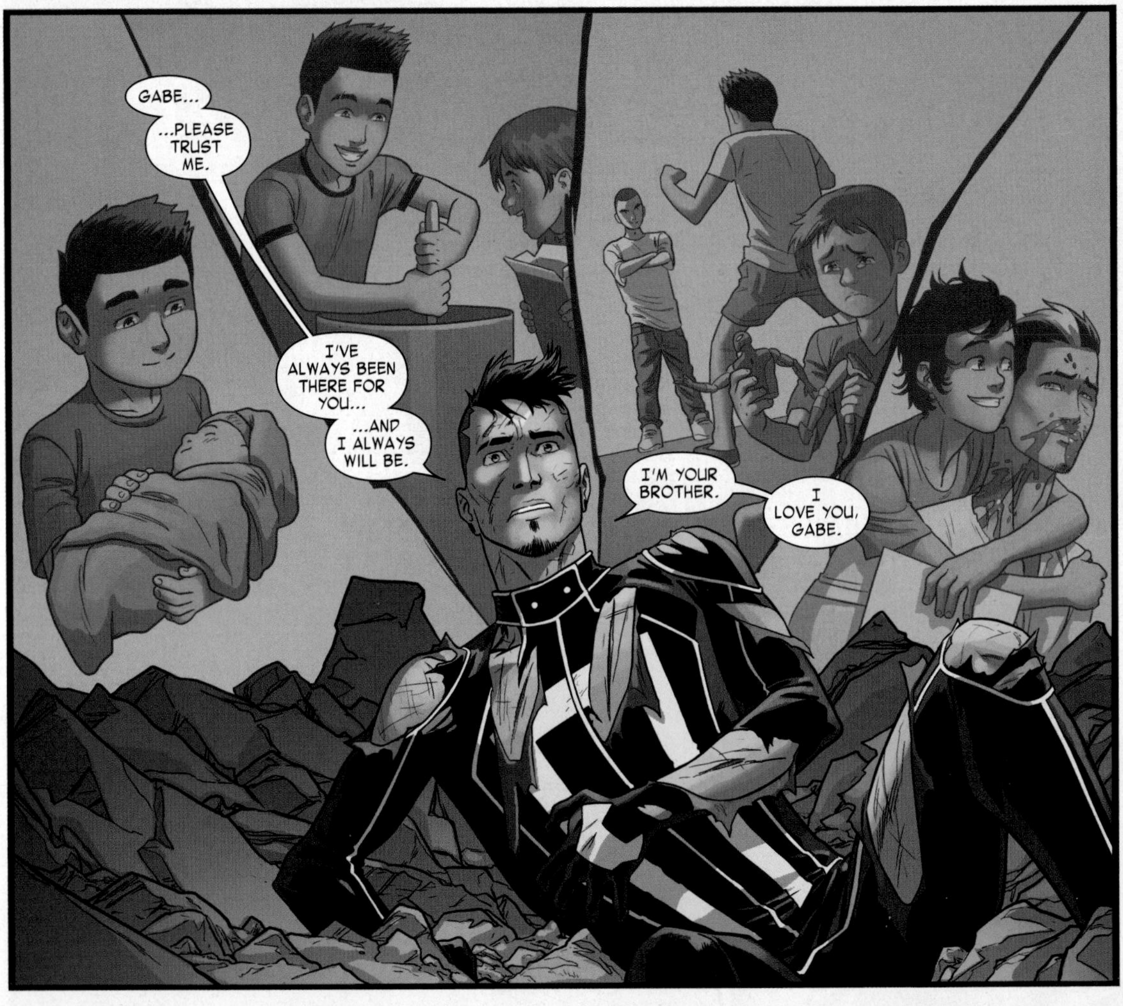
GABE...
...PLEASE TRUST ME.
I'VE ALWAYS BEEN THERE FOR YOU...
...AND I ALWAYS WILL BE.
I'M YOUR BROTHER.
I LOVE YOU, GABE.

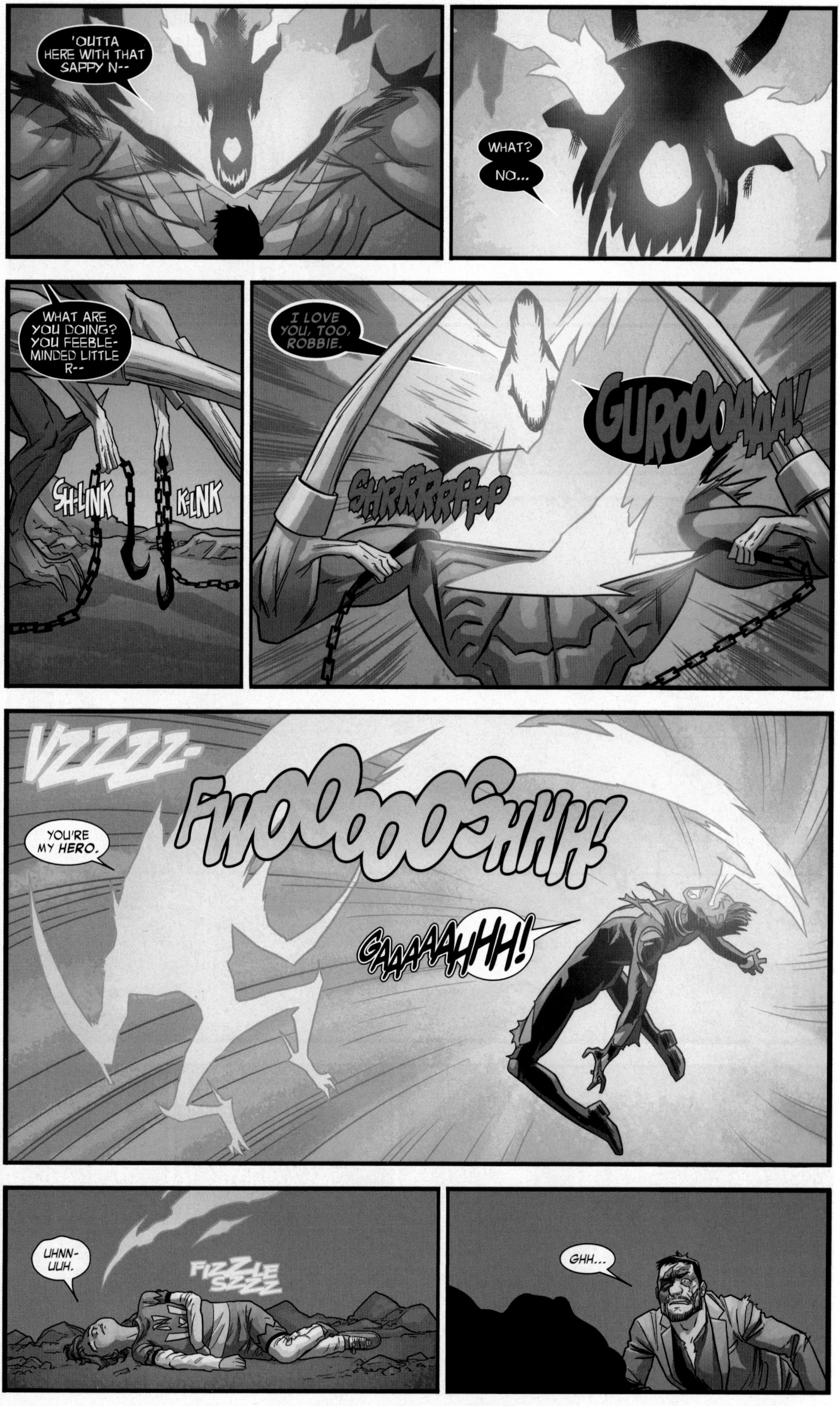
'OUTTA HERE WITH THAT SAPPY N--
WHAT?
NO...
WHAT ARE YOU DOING? YOU FEEBLE-MINDED LITTLE R--
SH-LINK
K-LNK
I LOVE YOU, TOO, ROBBIE.
GUROOOAAA!
SHRRRRAPP
VZZZZ-
FWOOOOOSHHH!
YOU'RE MY HERO.
GAAAAAHHH!
UHNN-UUH.
FIZZLE SZZZ
GHH...

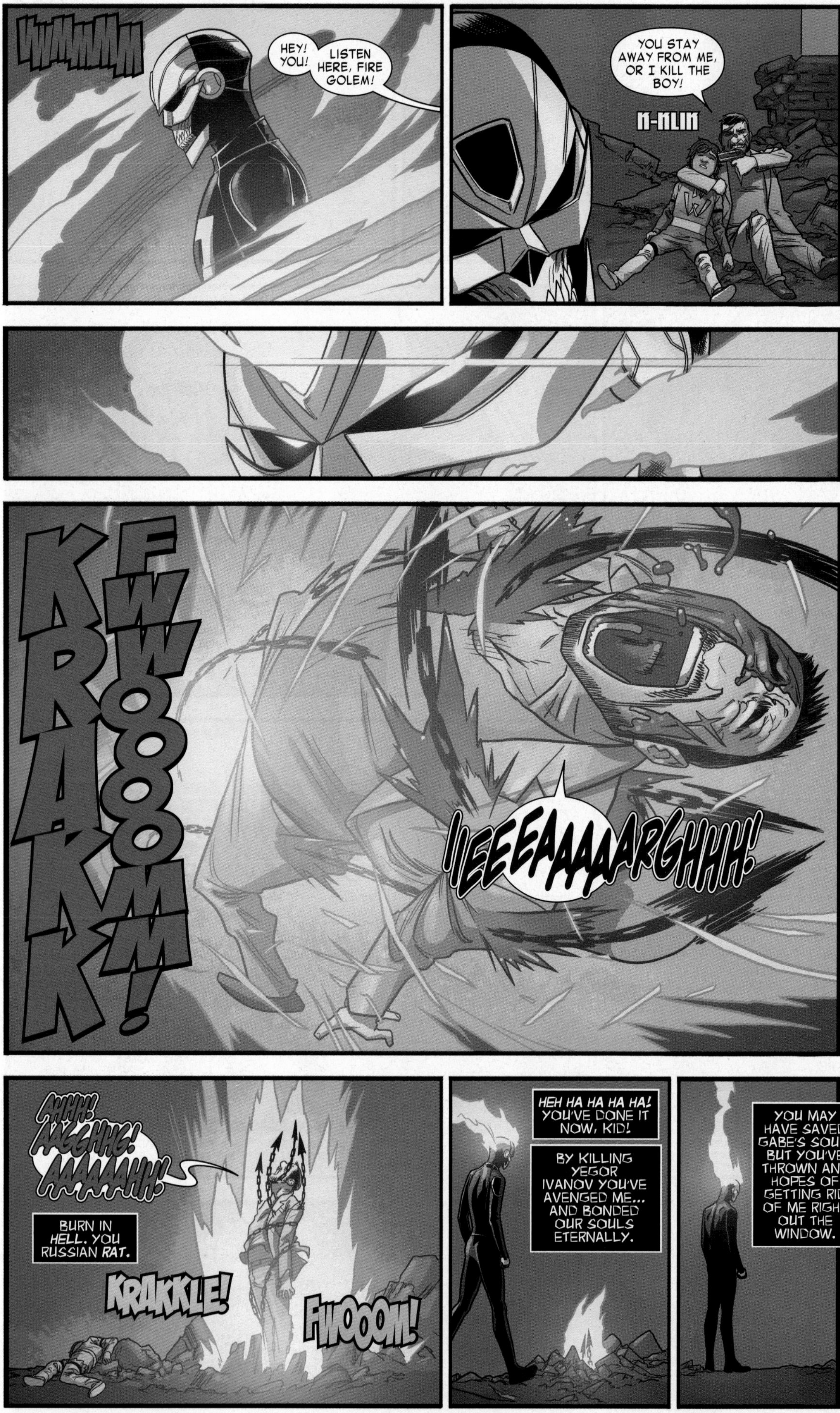
VWMMMMM
HEY! YOU!
LISTEN HERE, FIRE GOLEM!
YOU STAY AWAY FROM ME, OR I KILL THE BOY!
K-KLIK
KRAKK!
FWWOOOOMM!
IIEEEAAAAARGHHH!
AHHH! AAGHHG! AAAAAAHH!
BURN IN HELL. YOU RUSSIAN RAT.
KRAKKLE!
FWOOOM!
HEH HA HA HA HA! YOU'VE DONE IT NOW, KID!
BY KILLING YEGOR IVANOV YOU'VE AVENGED ME... AND BONDED OUR SOULS ETERNALLY.
YOU MAY HAVE SAVED GABE'S SOUL BUT YOU'VE THROWN ANY HOPES OF GETTING RID OF ME RIGHT OUT THE WINDOW.

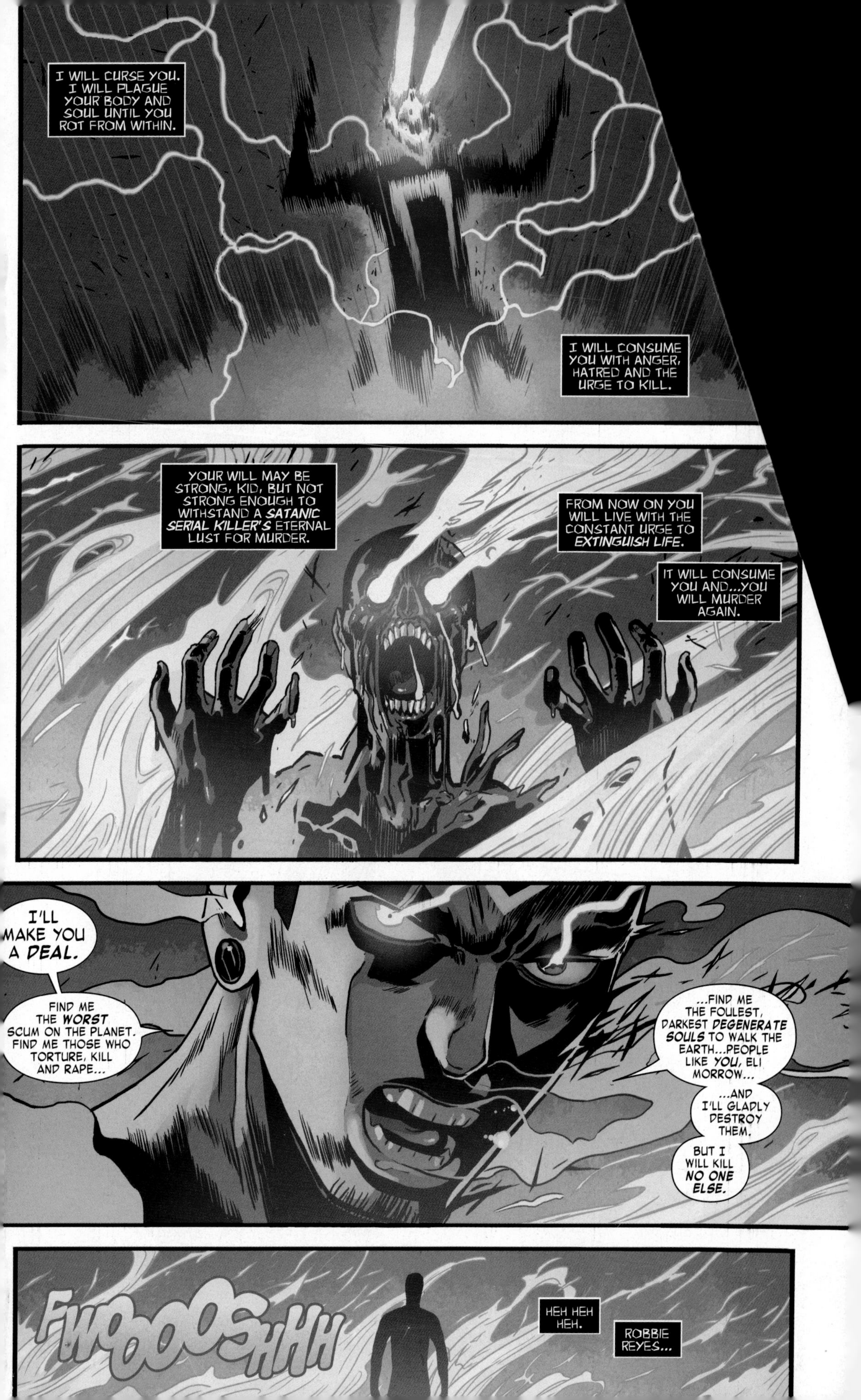
I WILL CURSE YOU. I WILL PLAGUE YOUR BODY AND SOUL UNTIL YOU ROT FROM WITHIN.
I WILL CONSUME YOU WITH ANGER, HATRED AND THE URGE TO KILL.
YOUR WILL MAY BE STRONG, KID, BUT NOT STRONG ENOUGH TO WITHSTAND A SATANIC SERIAL KILLER'S ETERNAL LUST FOR MURDER.
FROM NOW ON YOU WILL LIVE WITH THE CONSTANT URGE TO EXTINGUISH LIFE.
IT WILL CONSUME YOU AND...YOU WILL MURDER AGAIN.
I'LL MAKE YOU A DEAL.
FIND ME THE WORST SCUM ON THE PLANET. FIND ME THOSE WHO TORTURE, KILL AND RAPE...
...FIND ME THE FOULEST, DARKEST DEGENERATE SOULS TO WALK THE EARTH...PEOPLE LIKE YOU, ELI MORROW...
...AND I'LL GLADLY DESTROY THEM.
BUT I WILL KILL NO ONE ELSE.
FWOOOOSHHH
HEH HEH HEH.
ROBBIE REYES...

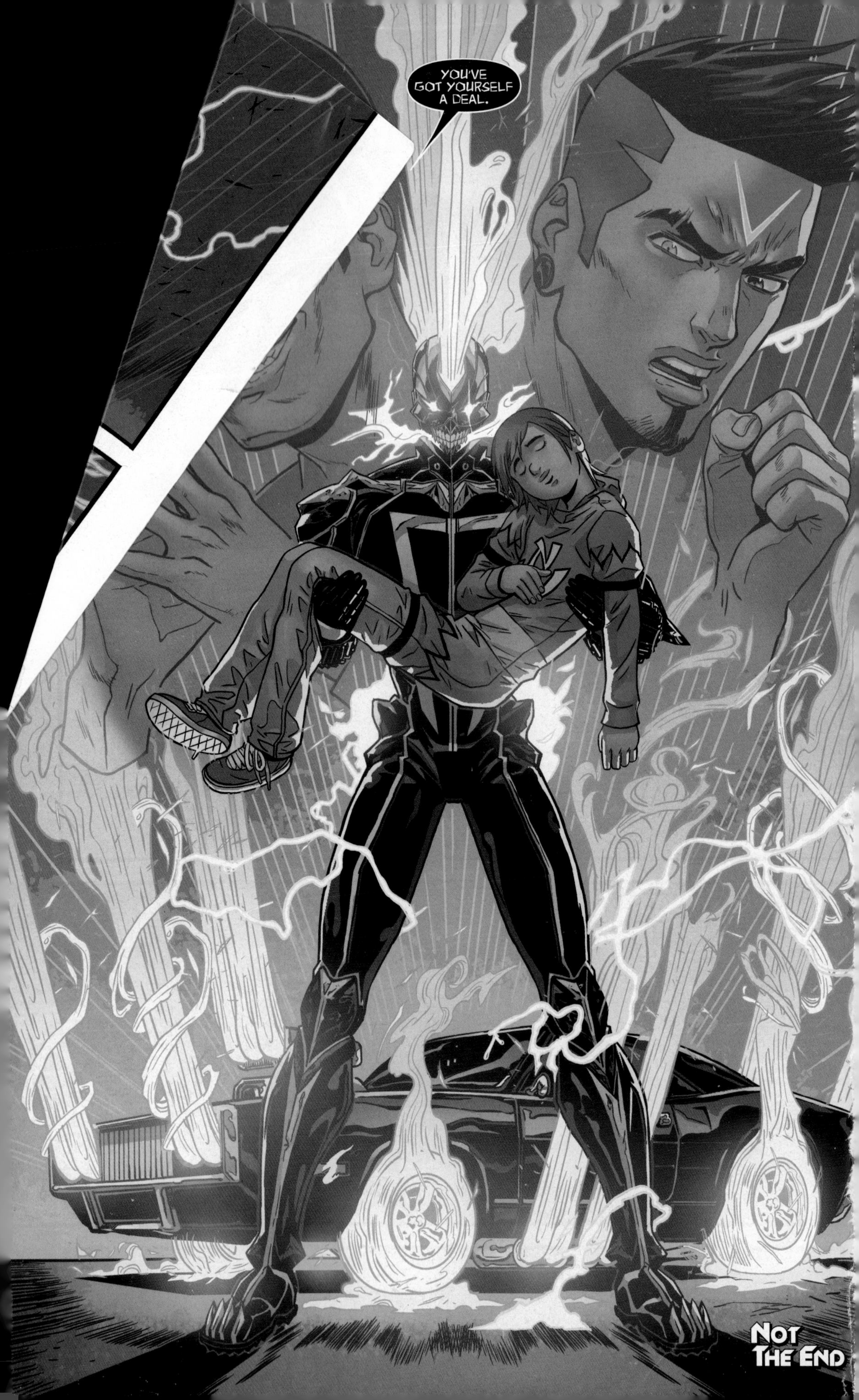
YOU'VE GOT YOURSELF A DEAL.
NOT THE END